HANS URS VON BALTHASAR

and the Critical Appropriation of Russian Religious Thought

HANS URS VON BALTHASAR

and the Critical Appropriation of Russian Religious Thought

JENNIFER NEWSOME MARTIN

University of Notre Dame Press
Notre Dame, Indiana

*The Press gratefully acknowledges the support of the Institute for Scholarship
in the Liberal Arts, University of Notre Dame, in the publication of this book.*

Library of Congress Cataloging-in-Publication Data

Martin, Jennifer Newsome.
Hans Urs von Balthasar and the critical appropriation of
Russian religious thought / Jennifer Newsome Martin.
pages   cm
Includes bibliographical references and index.
ISBN 978-0-268-03536-5 (pbk. : alk. paper)
ISBN 0-268-03536-9 (pbk. : alk. paper)
1. Balthasar, Hans Urs von, 1905–1988.
2. Philosophy, Russian—20th century.   I. Title.
BX4705.B163M37   2015
230'.2092—dc23
2015031758

To Jay, *sine qua non*,

and to the eternal memory of Douglas Michael Shippy
(1978–2002),
our dearest and most loyal friend.

CONTENTS

ACKNOWLEDGMENTS

I owe a great debt of gratitude first to my doctoral advisor and friend Cyril O'Regan, for demonstrating an extraordinary example of the elegance and artfulness of the theological craft, and for practicing it in good faith rigorously, responsibly, and without affectation. Thank you, Cyril, for reading drafts of this work with equal measures of swiftness, generosity, and practical wisdom, and for taking me as and holding me to my best self. Though he would certainly protest the characterization, his genius and saintliness are supreme manifestations of a life of faith, and proof that such a life is indeed possible.

I am also grateful to Lawrence Cunningham for being a consistently supportive and encouraging presence from the time I came to the University of Notre Dame in 2005. Your scholarship, teaching, and friendship model a rare balance of deep erudition, great generosity, and genuine humility. I am especially grateful for your assistance in submitting this manuscript for publication at the University of Notre Dame Press. Thank you as well to John Betz for kindly serving as a reader of this text in its nascent form as a dissertation, and especially for the searching questions about the status of Schelling's contribution, which I am still thinking about how best to answer.

I wish also to thank the many other kind and generous people associated with the theology department at the University of Notre Dame who have assisted and encouraged me throughout, especially

Mary Catherine Hilkert, who has mentored and advocated for me in many ways, and Robin Darling Young, who introduced me to Pavel Florensky over scotch in the summer of 2006 and started my long captivation with the Russians. A special thank you to my fellow classmates at Notre Dame, especially to Todd Walatka, whose willingness to read even the least-developed versions of my drafts improved the final work tremendously. Thanks also to Michael Altenburger for patiently checking the proofs.

To my colleagues in the Program of Liberal Studies, especially Gretchen Reydams-Schils, Julia Marvin, Pierpaolo Polzonetti, Joseph Rosenberg, Tom Stapleford, and Henry Weinfield: thank you for welcoming me enthusiastically into this rich and close-knit group of scholars and friends. Abundant thanks are also owed to the extended community of Balthasar scholars, especially Tony Sciglitano, whose excellent scholarship, remarkable personal graciousness, and generous friendship humble and hearten me.

At the University of Notre Dame Press, I am indebted to the editorial board as well as the readers of this manuscript, who provided enormously intelligent, detailed, and serious engagement with the text in their written reports. The book is much improved because of your careful attention and judicious suggestions. Thank you particularly to acquisitions editors Charles Van Hof and Stephen Little for your efforts in bringing this book to publication. I am grateful for the tireless work of Wendy McMillen, Susan Berger, and Rebecca DeBoer, and the many other supremely helpful people at the University of Notre Dame Press. I wish also to thank the Institute for Scholarship in the Liberal Arts for generously providing a grant for indexing. The book is also much improved due to the decisive and elegant work of copy editor Kellie Hultgren, to whom I remain grateful. Whatever infelicities, errors, or omissions that might inadvertently remain are my own.

I am thankful to my parents, stepparents, and parents-in-law, whose unfailing love is a testament to the unspeakable gratuity of the grace of God. Thanks especially to my beautiful children, James, John Moses, and Mary Frances Clare, whose ever-present affections and interruptions prevent me from ever taking myself too seriously. Above all, I am indebted to my friend and husband, Jay Martin, for reading,

editing, and offering extraordinarily profitable criticisms to this manuscript, and especially for first introducing me to Balthasar's theology
so many years ago. Far more, I am immensely grateful for your infinite patience, honesty, sense of humor, and profoundly self-giving—
even kenotic—love, in the rather unglamorous vicissitudes of the daily
life of two distracted academics with three small children. Thank you
for being a true partner in scholarship, parenthood, friendship, and
marriage.

CHAPTER 1

"DER SEELEN WUNDERLICHES BERGWERK"

On the Subterranean and the Speculative

Rainer Maria Rilke's great mythological poem "Orpheus. Eurydice. Hermes," from which this chapter's title is drawn, conjures a ghostly scene of the abortive attempt to lead Eurydice through the liminal space between the underworld and the world of the living. As the myth goes, Orpheus cannot contain himself and casts a forbidden backward glance at the two "light-footed" travelers tracking him, and his beloved Eurydice must return with Hermes to Hades.[1] The following conjugation of Swiss Catholic theologian Hans Urs von Balthasar (1905–1988) with several, far from homogenous figures of the nineteenth-century Orthodox Christian "Russian school," specifically Vladimir Soloviev (1853–1900), Nikolai Berdyaev (1874–1948), and Sergei Bulgakov (1871–1944), and their primary German Romantic interlocutor, F. W. J. Schelling (1775–1854), constitutes a subterranean excavation of its own, albeit with hopes of greater success.[2]

Resonant with Rilke's poetic rendering of the Orpheus myth, this book is likewise an excavation requiring not only a certain degree of coaxing in order to draw out Balthasar's un- or underacknowledged lines of pedigree from these theologians of the Russian diaspora, but also a delicacy in negotiating instances of the shadowy "in-between," whether between form and content, finite and infinite, body and spirit, time and eternity, life and death, heaven and hell, fidelity to Christian tradition and robust engagement with modernity, and so on. Nor is it irrelevant that the dense symbolic image of the *Bergwerk*, or mine, with which Rilke opens his poem has a long literary heritage in German Romanticism (not least in Novalis's *Heinrich von Ofterdingen*, Hugo von Hofmannsthal's play *Das Bergwerk zu Falun*, or again in the tenth of Rilke's *Duino Elegies*) invoking variously the darkness of the psychic unconscious, wisdom, sexuality, the knowledge of history, and the descent into the human soul.[3] Finally, construing Balthasar as we hope to do, especially with respect to his interest in rehabilitating a sense of the suppleness and fluidity of tradition, in no small part by his commitment to a dual engagement with the Fathers and the Zeitgeist, demands a declared embargo on nostalgic antiquarianism and its death-dealing backward glance.

Though content-rich with respect to the thinkers of the Russian school as well as Schelling, the gravamen of this book is a study of and apologia for Balthasar's own theological method, a task that perhaps ought to be held lightly in keeping with the Balthasarian ethos: "It is not our concern to get a secure place to stand, but rather to get sight of what cannot be securely grasped, and this must remain the event of Jesus Christ; woe to the Christian who would not stand daily speechless before this event! If this event truly is what the church believes, then it can be mastered through no methodology."[4] Acknowledging with Balthasar that theology ought to resist the mode of the "exact sciences" that could only feign to circumscribe its object, these chapters venture to characterize Balthasar's method as constitutively orthodox, but thoroughly probative, phenomenological, literary-critical, aesthetic-hermeneutic, and—despite his perhaps unjustly earned reputation as arch-*conservateur*—quintessentially non-nostalgic. Balthasar may indeed be operating in a mode of retrieval, but he is a visionary, innovative theologian who is far from retrograde. He is decidedly not a simple repristinator of the Fathers. Acknowledging that the distinction has been somewhat overplayed, it is nevertheless crucial to note here that Balthasar aligns himself first with the Russian school of Soloviev and Bulgakov, which self-consciously engaged modern Western philosophy, rather than the Neopatristic school of Vladimir Lossky and Georges Florovsky. The term *Russian school* traditionally designates one of the two major trends in Russian dogmatic theology prominent in the Paris émigré community after the Russian Revolution, a mode of theology that, while heartily affirming traditional sources, also sensed a need to go beyond the Fathers in a robust engagement with modern Western philosophy. The other trend, the so-called Neopatristic approach exemplified perhaps best by Florovsky and Lossky, was more straightforwardly a patristic retrieval.[5] It is thus the definitive burden of this exercise to demonstrate, as evidenced by critical excavation of the Schelling–Russian line, that Balthasar's theological method is, rather like Origen's, fundamentally daring and experimental, structurally hospitable to expressly nontheological categories, noncanonical sources, and modes of speculative thinking that probe but, under Balthasar's scrupulous watch and sense of moderation, do not exceed the elastic boundaries of tradition.

This book proceeds by analysis that is both descriptive and constructive. That is to say, it considers not only Balthasar's explicit mentions of Soloviev, Berdyaev, and Bulgakov (which are not on balance numerous), but also constructively analyzes "anonymous" or "subterranean" instances of thematic, theological, and philosophical affinities, filiations, or repetitions, and assesses the principles according to which Balthasar adjudicates, allows, or excludes elements in them. This investigation into what is, for Balthasar, live or dead in the Russians takes place at the following sites of inquiry: (1) beauty and aesthetics, (2) freedom, theogony, myth, and evil, (3) thanatology and traditional eschatology from an anthropological point of view, and (4) apocalyptic Trinitarianism, or what Balthasar calls the "theocentric eschatological horizon." While it might have been more straightforward to traverse seriatim the thought of each Russian thinker in relation to Balthasar, there are strong aesthetic and substantive grounds for this work's thematic organization. The thought of Soloviev, Berdyaev, and Bulgakov is intricately related one to the other: quite simply, the method of analysis used here provides the most elegant means not only of presenting a thick cross section of inquiry, but also of indicating at least a provisional genealogy. Comparative studies often swerve too nearly toward overemphasis, either of affinity or difference. This study aims not simply to catalogue one or the other, but rather comprises an examination of *how* these modes of intersection are modulated, received, changed, corrected, and so on. The working assumption is that, especially for the later Balthasar, Berdyaev almost certainly is postmortem, Soloviev possesses only a relative vitality, and Bulgakov—whose presence in Balthasar's theology is often undocumented but in some instances nearly isomorphic—remains fully viable.[6]

Despite the mining operations that may be required textually, the warrant to investigate the actual, cryptic, and potential dialogue between Balthasar and the thinkers of the Russian school is writ quite large. In a graceful little essay, "The Place of Theology," Balthasar speaks to his preferred method of theological reflection in a manner that seems to cast his lot with the Russian school religious philosophers rather than the Neopatristics: "What is required [in theology] is neither an enthusiastic revival of something or other (for example, the 'Fathers'), nor pure historical research, but rather a kind of Christian humanism that goes to the sources to find what is living and truly original (and not to a school of thought long since dried up) in a spirit of joy and freedom able to weigh the true value of things."[7] Indeed, Balthasar's impressive command of Western philosophical and cultural tradition, along with a deep retrieval of the classical theological sources, has a strong analogue in the Russian school, which resuscitated Romanticism as the premier instance of modern intellectualism.[8] Again, it is this shared broadmindedness in navigating between modern cultural and philosophical data and the ancient Christian tradition that brings Balthasar and the Russian school into natural dialogue, specifically with respect to their variously critical reception(s) of German Idealism and Romanticism.

RESISTING RATIONALISM: THE CONTEXT OF NEOSCHOLASTICISM

Balthasar's provocative theological methodology, hospitable to engagement with not only nontheological but also non-Catholic sources, ought to be considered with reference to Neoscholasticism, which, according to Balthasar and other proponents of *la nouvelle théologie*, was a distortion of the legitimate method of Thomas, characterized by brittleness, dry syllogisms, and a narrow intellectualism that employed an impoverished, reductive, "closed-circle" logic that diminished the glory and mystery of revelation to rationalistic categories.[9] His almost visceral reaction against this Neoscholastic conceptual rationalism decries the tendency to proceed theologically through an appeal to neutral, abstracted categories rather than the existing biblical, liturgical, mystical, and sacramental data of the living tradition. His intervention is far from shy: "In the end, [the hyperbolic rationalism of Neoscholasticism] leads to Hegel's God, who is without all mystery: behold the door to atheism."[10] The problem with Neoscholasticism was that it had lost the shining sense of glory and mystery, the "sensorium for the glory of Creation," that had enlivened the patristics and the theology of the early and high Middle Ages.[11]

In his early study of theology, Balthasar found traditional Neoscholasticism arid and stultifying, not only personally—he described his study at this time as "languishing in the desert"[12]—but also with regard to the ways in which the glory and the mystery of divine revelation were depicted so dispassionately. Partially in reaction to this perceived aridity, Balthasar attempted to open up theology by a two-pronged recovery: first—influenced deeply by Henri de Lubac—by the patristic and medieval retrieval of figures such as Maximus the Confessor, Evagrius of Pontus, Bonaventure, Pseudo-Dionysius, and other mystical literature, and second—no doubt influenced at least in part by his early interest and training in German literature—by an appeal to sources that were not properly "theological," namely art, literature, and theatrical drama. In fact, Balthasar considered certain novelists, playwrights, and poets to be valuable theological sources, equal in importance in their own right to the patristics and scholastics. Moreover, he considered the literature itself to be theological: for Balthasar, the transformative effects of the Incarnation enable the best of human culture to communicate a theological truth of being. In keeping with this twin recovery project, Balthasar completed monographs in patristics (on Origen, Gregory of Nyssa, and Maximus the Confessor) and literature (on Georges Bernanos, as well as translations of works by Charles Péguy, Paul Claudel, and Pedro Calderón de la Barca, among others). His lengthy theological trilogy of *The Glory of the Lord*, *Theo-Drama*, and *Theo-Logic* (*Herrlichkeit*, *Theodramatik*, and *Theologik*) corresponds respectively to the three transcendentals of beauty, goodness, and truth, making use of aesthetic categories and cultural sources of such integrative breadth that de Lubac referred to Balthasar as "perhaps the most cultivated [man] of his time."[13]

Balthasar should thus be broadly landscaped as a certain type of *nouvelle théologie* theologian, informed deeply not only by de Lubac, who provides an antidote to Neoscholasticism by rehabilitating the plurivision of a rediscovered patristic theology, but also by Erich Przywara, who deepens the concept of the *analogia entis*.[14] Balthasar's theological style, consonant with *nouvelle théologie* thinkers and the proponents of the Catholic Tübingen school who influenced them (Johann Adam Möhler's *Die Einheit in der Kirche* in particular), insists that theological speculation and the tradition must be organically integrated.

BALTHASAR AND HIS CRITICS

This judgment of the felicitousness of Balthasar's speculative theological method is by no means the universal opinion. Indeed, instances approaching hagiography notwithstanding, the general reception of Balthasar in the theological academy has been somewhat tepid, prompting Balthasar himself to lament, "So be it; if I have been cast aside as a hopeless conservative by the tribe of the left, then I now know what sort of dung-heap I have been dumped upon by the right."[15] Excavating the buried genealogy of Schelling and the Russians who read him helps to address a number of these issues in critical reception, and to pose and address questions of a more general and methodological nature. In this respect, then, this book functions in two ways: first, negatively, it intervenes in a number of common contemporary criticisms and (mis)interpretations of Balthasar, and second, it makes a number of positive claims about the nature of the Christian theological tradition and the tasks and methods of theology. Attention

to the neglected Schelling–Russian line in Balthasar thus helps to con-
textualize and make sense of some of the seemingly strange theological
claims that he makes—the passive descent into hell on Holy Saturday
rooted in the notion of Ur-kenosis, for example, which he imports
directly from Bulgakov—and also to construct an interpretation of
the dynamic, elastic nature of tradition that encourages a creative theological method.

Reading Balthasar through an excavation of this particular *Bergwerk*, which in its depths has the Russian thinkers and, at even lower
strata, Schelling and Jakob Böhme, suggests by what it unearths that
certain criticisms of Balthasar's work may be more superficial than not.
First, construing Balthasar as a particular sort of speculative theologian
certainly challenges the relatively common notion that Balthasar's
thought typifies a stodgy, backward-looking conservatism. The factors
behind Balthasar's reception in the Catholic theological academy as a
"conservative," "traditionalist," "restorationist," or "fideist" theologian
have been rehearsed elsewhere.[16] That reception is not surprising, given
not only Balthasar's stance on certain progressive causes, but also the
fact that—even as late as his death in 1988—most of his longer, complex theological works (including the majority of the trilogy) remained
untranslated while his shorter, controversial, sometimes patently acer-
bic pieces were available in English and thus more widely read. A close
examination of the particular way he sifts through the often-mixed
speculative contributions of these Russian thinkers, however, challenges the reading of Balthasar as simply regressive.

While Balthasar's theology is judged on the one hand to be "hopelessly conservative," evaluations made on the other hand tend to locate
aspects of his thought well beyond the Catholic pale. This category of
criticism might best be represented by Alyssa Lyra Pitstick's rather
prosecutorial *Light in Darkness: Hans Urs von Balthasar and the
Catholic Doctrine of Christ's Descent into Hell*, which finds his more
speculative contributions so eccentric to traditional Catholicism that
they enjoin "a *de facto* rejection of the Catholic Tradition and its authority."[17] Characterizing a theologian of Balthasar's sophistication and
subtlety as on either the "right" or the "left" is not a particularly constructive enterprise, and furthermore, projects that concern themselves

largely with such rigid classifications are perhaps both spent and mis-spent. These lines of criticism matter, however, even to theologians not particularly invested in the theological reception of Balthasar, because a broader view of tradition that governs the content of the critique is often latent in them. For instance, Pitstick's dismissal of Balthasar because of his minority speculative view of Christ's *descensus* into hell is connected with her particular construal of the nature of tradition. When considering the assessment of the descent into hell, she writes, "Hence, necessarily either we rely upon Tradition as an infallible guide to revealed truth and upon the ability of reason enlightened by faith to identify that Tradition under the magisterial guidance of the Church's hierarchy—or we *de facto* reject such Tradition in whole or in part. In the case of such rejection, theology becomes subjected to fallen reason's fancy, which inevitably leads to heresy, i.e., the picking and choosing of beliefs in which unaided reason cannot fail to err because the subject matter is beyond its capabilities."[18] For Balthasar and the Russians upon whom he relies, however, tradition is conceived of in far less mechanical, monochromatic terms.

Other forms of critique include those that assert Balthasar is over-determined by German Idealism, particularly the contribution of Ben Quash, which suggests in Balthasar a thoroughgoing Hegelianism and tendency toward the epical, especially given the formal similarities of their thought.[19] Karl Rahner has similarly registered hesitation with Balthasar's radically kenotic vision of Christology and Trinity, noting that it seems to evoke "a theology of absolute paradox, of Patripassian-ism, *perhaps even a Schelling-esque projection into God of division, conflict, godlessness and death.*"[20] In this book's thick description of Balthasar's adjudications at the various strata of influence vis-à-vis Schelling and the Russians, it will become clear(er) that, though some-times in close but always corrective proximity, Balthasar is not Hegel, nor is he Schelling.

Another related critique is levied in Karen Kilby's *Balthasar: A (Very) Critical Introduction* (2012), which registers anxieties that Bal-thasar's theology assumes a "God's eye view" in which everything fits together according to his own sense of fittingness, without giving suf-ficient attention to epistemological fallibility.[21] Her text, being introductory in nature, is deliberately less concerned with genealogy and questions of influence, but this particular criticism can still fall under the general ambit of a comprehensive rationalism (Hegelian or otherwise) that presumes to see and to know too much. According to Kilby, this "God's eye view" is not simply an unfortunate but occasional lapse, but rather "*the* characteristic mode of his theology."[22] She reads Balthasar's aesthetic analogy of "seeing the form" as requiring perception of the *totality* of revelation, objecting to any claim to an accomplished perspective of the whole. According to her analysis, the authorial posture Balthasar adopts "presupposes an impossible knowledge" such that even or especially when he indicates otherwise, he is always already "engaged in a performative contradiction."[23]

Because a near-obsession with wholeness is one of the most immediately apparent points of convergence between Schelling, Balthasar, and the Russian religious philosophers, it will be necessary to consider whether or not this posture actually necessitates a "God's eye view." The interest in the whole is particularly evident in the Russians after Soloviev, whose spirited advocacy of "all-unity" as the single, indivisible point of integration for all human knowledge and experience — which deeply influenced Berdyaev and Bulgakov and was affirmed heartily by Balthasar — is an appeal to the truth of the whole, or the unity of all things (*vseedinstvo* for the Russians; *Alleinheit* for Schelling).[24] This appeal, however, in Balthasar and the Russians is incentivized in no small measure by a shared and determined resistance to the deficiencies of an overly rationalistic and abstracted mode of thinking philosophy or theology. When the notion of *vseedinstvo* appears in Soloviev's doctoral dissertation, "A Critique of Abstract Principles" (1880), he argues that because abstract principles are, shall we say, "abstracted" from this whole, they have a false character and require an infusion of the unifying divine ground of all being.[25] Bulgakov likewise resists abstraction: "Our thought and knowledge always fragment their object, abstract from it its separate sides and thus inevitably take the part for the whole."[26] Berdyaev, though far from affirming Solovievian all-unity full stop, locates multiplicity and division in the (doomed) realm of objectified nature; personal (not monistic) wholeness and integration are the mark of the realm of the spirit. Likewise for Balthasar, apart from a consideration of the totality of the whole, analysis becomes only a forensic affair. As he puts it, rather colorfully, "We can never again recapture the living totality of form once it has been dissected and sawed into pieces, no matter how informative the conclusions which this anatomy may bring to light. Anatomy can be practiced only on a dead body, since it is opposed to the movement of life and seeks to pass from the whole to its parts and elements."[27] Similarly, Balthasar remarks that "there is simply no way to do theology except by repeatedly circling around what is, in fact, always the same totality looked at from different angles. To parcel up theology into isolated tracts is by definition to destroy it."[28]

Furthermore, the ascription of a status of arch-synthesizer to Balthasar is undercut by the very early expression of Balthasar's theological epistemology in his 1947 *Wahrheit*, which—significantly for establishing a continuity of thought—was reprinted without change in 1985 as volume 1 of *Theo-Logic* and ratified in *Theo-Logic* volumes 2 and 3. Even cursory attention to Balthasar's epistemology indicates a thorough and explicit resistance to any presumption of a "God's eye" view of wholeness. According to *Wahrheit*, the characteristic nature of truth is always the promise of more truth, even ad infinitum; thus it is for Balthasar a "scandal" to foreclose the alethic by making any finite perspective absolute, by "making the fragment self-sufficient to the detriment of the totality."[29] No single individual is privy to a view of total truth, which infinitely provides the horizon and background for what are always historically and situationally conditioned partial truths. For Balthasar, finite truth is thoroughly perspectival and symphonic. In his own words, "In no case . . . can a viewpoint afford a comprehensive grasp of the whole, a sort of bird's-eye view of the overall lay of the land."[30] Thus, an individual cannot assert any finite truth without acknowledging that it must be supplemented by other perspectives, and one individual's viewpoint can never be made identical with the absolute. Here we see intimations that the fragment is not a lamentable deficit; rather, its embrace has salutary effects. It is meant to disrupt, to unsettle totalizing theological discourse, since it requires the admission that all perspectives are finite and thus partial, even Balthasar's own.

The suggestion that Balthasar is interested in maintaining a vision of the whole, while true, does not necessarily countenance the critique that Balthasar operates according to a kind of naïve, totalizing impulse of systematization run amok. As demonstrated in the following pages, his notion of the whole does not necessarily exclude the notion of the fragment. His interest in an organic wholeness is not of a piece with a (Hegelian) rationalistic philosophy that attempts to fit every element of human experience into a logically necessary grand system. As is evident in his rejection of Neoscholasticism, Balthasar is motivated by his conviction that the "exact sciences" are not at all the appropriate mode of theological reflection. Rather, it is necessary to prescind from the specificity of exact discourse, "which can only pertain to one particular sector of reality, in order to bring the truth of the whole again into view — truth as a transcendental property of Being, truth which is no abstraction, rather *the living bond between God and world.*"[31] Indeed, Balthasar's nervousness about the overstepping rationalism of Hegel may even help to explain his somewhat ambiguous gravitation toward Schelling and those Russians influenced by his thought.

WHY SCHELLING?

Schelling — who, like Balthasar and the Russians, had much to say about art, time and eternity, nature, history, freedom and necessity, evil, myth, and eschatology — operates as something of a third premise for this project. Schelling constantly reinvented his philosophy throughout his career, and thus we may contend with many Schellings in subsequent pages. Nonetheless, for Balthasar it is Schelling rather than Hegel who represents the culmination of German Idealism.[32] He is not just a stepping-stone on the way from Johann Gottlieb Fichte to Hegel. Schelling functions, arguably, as the "bridge" between Idealism and Catholicism, as well as the "gateway from the Romantic view of art to the Catholic tradition of mysticism and symbol."[33] Balthasar's intricate negotiation with aspects of Schelling's thought, however, has not been treated to the same degree as his engagement with Hegel and Heidegger, and thus warrants particular scholarly attention.[34]

Balthasar's evaluation of Schelling is critical, but not tantamount to a straightforward and total denunciation. Though his critiques may seem to wound Schelling beyond any kind of theological serviceability, Balthasar's blows ought not to be taken as totally fatal for Schelling. Indeed, in his early *Apokalypse der deutschen Seele*, Balthasar characterizes Schelling tantalizingly as "an apocalyptic figure for whom all is arranged around revelation, around the disclosure of mystery, around breakthrough into the mysteries of God. From this magical and visionary style, so different from the ascetical Fichte and the cool Hegel, emerges the fact that he is a prophet and a poet."[35] The value of this philosophical discourse for Balthasar is not simply in its function as a foil for the proper mode of theologizing responsibly: German Idealism and Romanticism—though far from blameless—have value in themselves particularly as *religious* counterpoints to the predominating rationalism of the (post-)Enlightenment project. For instance, Balthasar lauds the "*religious* force" of a German Idealism that maintains the unity of the beautiful and the religious, a force weighted against Kierkegaard's rejection of aesthetics epitomized in *Either/Or*. Soloviev, with several others, is mentioned approvingly in this context as being representative of the same impulse:

> The spirituality of the Christian artists and esthetic philosophers of the last century (from 1860 to the present) is strongly brought out by their preserving a sense of the unity of beauty and religion, art and religion, when they had hardly any support from theology, and notwithstanding the breakdown of the old tradition and the prevalence of materialistic and psychological views incompatible with theirs. In this they were in accord with the original tradition of the West, as well as with the sentiment of the learned in various countries. For behind them lay, despite the solvent effect of Kierkegaard, the religious force of German idealism, of Goethe, Schelling and Novalis, and this exerted its influence on the England of Coleridge, Newman, Thompson and Hopkins, which in turn was connected by hidden but strong ties with the France of Péguy . . . Soloviev in Russia . . . maintain[s] the same general outlook.[36]

Schelling and Böhme are named right alongside Dante, Nicholas of Cusa, Erasmus, Luther, Pascal, Hamann, Kierkegaard, Péguy, Bloy, Bernanos, Soloviev, Hopkins, and Newman, among others, as belonging to the company of those who are representative of a valuable "opposition" movement that demands "an understanding of revelation in the context of the history of the world and the actual present."[37]

Further, the rehabilitation of Romanticism—and, more particularly, the Schellingian strand of concrete Idealism as an explicit alternative to Hegel—as a hugely influential philosophical source characterized by freedom, spirit, wholeness, subjectivity, organicity, process, imagination, and life, proved a natural fit for Slavic thinkers intent on opposing Western positivism and rationalism as well as their Catholic counterparts, particularly Johann Sebastian Drey (1777–1853) and his student Johann Adam Möhler (1796–1838) of the Tübingen school, who likewise engaged Romanticism with Catholic thinking in the early nineteenth century.[38] Indeed, an anecdote is reported about literary critic and Slavophile Ivan Kireevsky (1806–1856), who studied with Schelling in Munich, that upon his return to Russia, his wife related to him that the philosophical ideas of Schelling "had long been familiar to her from the works of the Church Fathers,"[39] actually prompting Kireevsky to rediscover Orthodoxy. To reiterate, Schelling's philosophical profile as visionary, dynamic, and organic is attractive to theological discourse not least because it contravenes the dryness of purely rationalistic systems.

It is perhaps precisely the fact that figures such as Drey and Möhler—as well as the Russians—articulated their theology against a backdrop of Romantic philosophy that funds and supports the notion of a living, dynamic tradition that can admit developments without loss of integrity. The crucial role of the language of the "positive" in Schelling[40] suggests not a reiteration from the archives of the past as a static deposit, but—consonant with the model of the Romantic Catholic Tübingen school—the ongoing and dynamic negotiation between old and new that motivates imaginative theological construction rather than reiterative representation alone. John Thiel suggests that the Romantic paradigm of doing theology is characterized precisely in these terms: that is, it is not mimetic, but a creative construction that, while faithful to the classical understanding of God as divine Author, relies in large part upon the individual theologian's talent, authority, and authorship.[41]

In the theological appropriation of Romanticism, this negotiation takes place between traditional religious ideas and the ongoing generative force that animates them: thus, religious data, given their peculiarly thick character in terms of both history and existential significance, resist exhaustive logical analysis.[42] As Paul Valliere rightly notes, the Schellingian philosophical tradition can veer too easily into "a mysticism which dissolves the multiplicity of positivities into a singular Positive [that] defeats the program of positive philosophy as surely as Hegelian rationalism,"[43] an ill that can be remedied only by "honoring the concrete idiom in which faith expresses itself, thereby limiting the degree to which dogma can be rationalized."[44] To translate this principle into analogous theological terms, we might turn to the notion—associated with John Henry Newman, but appearing earlier and significantly in the work of Drey—of the organic development of doctrine, which allows for the pneumatologically inspired and Christologically constrained evolution of new contributions to established theological concepts.

In Drey's articulation of the historicity of revelation and the development of doctrine, the authentically living tradition has a "fixed" aspect and a "mobile" aspect,[45] and both must be attended to with care: neglect of the former is a speculation unmoored and susceptible to heterodoxy, and neglect of the latter is by "hyperorthodoxy" to hazard the hypertrophy of tradition, the hardening of bedrock into slag.[46] It is clear that Balthasar, as well as Bulgakov, at least peripherally shares Drey's concerns with respect to the mummification or absolutizing of (particularly specific historical or cultural iterations of) the tradition.[47] Creative fidelity to tradition for Balthasar is precisely that: creative, even audaciously so. On his own telling,

> Being faithful to tradition most definitely does not consist . . . of a literal repetition and transmission of the philosophical and theological theses that one imagines lie hidden in time and in the contingencies of history. Rather, being faithful to tradition consists much

more of imitating our Fathers in the faith with respect to their attitude of intimate reflection and their effort of audacious creation,
which are the necessary preludes to true spiritual fidelity. If we
study the past, it is not in the hope of drawing from it formulas
doomed in advance to sterility or with the intention of readapting
out-of-date solutions. We are asking history to teach us the acts and
deeds of the Church, who presents her treasure of divine revelation,
ever new and ever unexpected, to every generation, and who knows
how, in the face of every new problem, to turn the fecundity of the
problem to good account with a rigor that never grows weary and
a spiritual agility that is never dulled.[48]

In another telling bon mot, Balthasar writes that traditional thought—
even that from which conciliar definitions have sprung—is "never a
pillow for future thought to rest on";[49] rather, the theologian must
actively engage it as with a living thing, renewing and moving it forward through diligent efforts to grapple with that which has been
handed down, not in cold storage, but as an organism that ought to be
tended well and carefully.

However, our interest in inviting Schelling to the theological table
and allowing his legacy, albeit greatly domesticated, to stay on (largely
under the hospitality of the Russians) requires qualification, as he—
both before and after his late-coming theological turn—can be something of an unruly guest. Schelling's thought contains unequivocally
and irremediably dark seeds that run counter to the mainline theological project, not least of which is a deeply rooted materialism and
the inheritance of Böhme's irrational, ungrounded abyss of an originary will.[50] Schelling's philosophical aesthetics cannot be thought
otherwise than a secular "aesthetic theology," which cannot be welcomed as it stands as an authentic (and thoroughly Balthasarian) theological aesthetics of "glory." Moreover, as Cyril O'Regan notes, German Idealism and Romanticism (genetically bound to Böhme) are
thoroughly implicated by Balthasar with respect to their latent Gnosticism in his *Apokalypse der deutschen Seele*.[51] Balthasar mines German
Idealism and Romanticism for possible precious stones (though the
rocks fall where they may), and yet he also mimes aspects of them: still,

his miming is far from an unsophisticated mimicry or borrowing. As demonstrated here, when Balthasar repeats or appears to repeat suspect elements of Schelling or Hegel, he self-consciously subverts them, ever dutifully maintaining a crucial corrective distance. Acknowledging the seductive appeal of these discourses, he allows them to contribute positively to his theological project while insisting that their content be thoroughly vetted.

Balthasar's recognition of the dangers both implicit and explicit in Schelling's thinking—considered in more detail in the following chapters—is clear. He resists absolutely the temptation of Romantic thought toward philosophical monism as well as pantheism.[52] He sharply criticizes Schelling's philosophy (along with Fichte's and Hegel's) as Promethean and Titanic, glorifying *human* being as the center of the philosophical absolute, claiming equality with the divine:[53]

> While Kant and Schiller stop short at the finiteness of the human spirit in a way that might be judged to be more "modern," the three Titans Fichte, Schelling and Hegel want to conceive of man within the wholeness of the Absolute, as its centre. This expressly demands that all philosophy, above all that of antiquity, should be fulfilled and transcended through the philosophical appropriation of the Christian revelation. . . . The "retreat to the man as the centre" is in no way retracted; for the first time it is "Titanically" pressed home, and is so with an appeal to Christianity as the point of the turning of the world to subjectivity. But this means that even when the idealist systems are at their closest to Plotinus (as the final figure of the classical age), the situation with regard to the open and Advent-like decision, which predominates in Plotinus, does not return; rather, everything is finally decided through the determination to conceive Christianity (in a post-Christian manner) as pure philosophy and ultimately as the potentiality of man, history and culture. . . . The die is cast. . . . Man is himself the manifest God.[54]

Berdyaev, Soloviev, and Bulgakov all engage with and assimilate Schellingian Idealism to varying degrees and with varying degrees of critical distance.[55] The presence of Schelling in Berdyaev, rather more than the others, is devastatingly qualified by a heavy inscription not only of Schelling but also of certain Böhmian elements that are transmitted genetically through Schelling. Soloviev's aesthetics in particular (enthusiastically received by Balthasar) relies heavily upon Schelling, although he does supply Schellingian philosophical concepts with a decidedly Christological specificity not present in the latter, even after the so-called theological turn of the later Schelling.[56] Indeed, although Soloviev may repeat in certain ways the vocabulary of the Idealists of the philosophical absolute, Soloviev's Absolute is accorded determinate theological content: it is, rather than a postulate, the *"living* God."[57] Finally, in his *Philosophy of Economy*, Bulgakov appeals to elements of Schelling's concrete Idealism—especially the identification of subject and object and the notion of nature as dynamic organism (which reappears in Soloviev)—as somewhat analogous to the Christian notion of the human being as incarnate spirit in the world: human beings are embodied in nature and enjoy a creative, dynamic, free, and mutually dependent relation with it.[58]

Ever mindful of the possible perils of engagement and assimilation of nontheological discourse, the Russian and Balthasarian reception of Schelling proves absolutely fundamental to this discussion in two important ways, in terms of justification for its selection of thematic content and an advocacy of a theological method both constrained by creative fidelity to the tradition and marked by inventiveness and development. These categories of aesthetics, myth, eschatology, and apocalyptic are not arbitrary, but rather are instances of potential and actual discourse between Schelling and the theologians: in effect, these categories function as synecdochic indices of the relation between infinite and finite. This triangulation of Schelling, the Russian school, and Balthasar can be parsed ultimately in terms of this (properly aesthetic) negotiation between the finite and infinite, which approximates but is not identical with the problem of the proper relation that obtains between God and world.[59] The early Schelling—far more philosopher than theologian—does not avail himself of this kind of terminology, although the major problematic that exercises him throughout his career is the negotiation between the real and ideal, the actual and the potential, language that Soloviev does employ. Schelling's system, though, is essentially monistic, and for Balthasar's quintessentially Christian theology, it is the case that God is wholly other than the world, not part of a mundane structure of real and ideal.

Russian religious history, too, has long been occupied with the problem of the finite and infinite. The doctrine of Divine Sophia, which will unfortunately remain undertreated here, is invoked in Russian religious philosophy at least in part as a mediating solution (though not a philosophical abstraction) for bridging the ontological frontier, the metaxic space between the divine world and the phenomenal world.[60] For certain of the thinkers considered here, this Sophia, or holy wisdom, is *bogochelovechestvo*, an abstract noun translated variously as the "humanity of God," "Divine-Humanity," or "Godmanhood," a concept that appears in Schelling's philosophy of mythology and revelation and is absolutely decisive for the religious philosophy of Soloviev's successors. The doctrine bears conceptual relation to the theological notion of deification and linguistic relation to the Greek *theandria*, and, as a derivation of *Bogochelovek*, or "God-human," is certainly evocative of Christological claims. As we shall see, Berdyaev and Bulgakov are both Solovievian heirs who proceed under the Sophianic mantle, though in disparate Christological metrics.

For Balthasar, this relationship between finite and infinite must be governed strictly by the *analogia entis*—"the ever great dissimilarity to God no matter how great the similarity to Him"[61] rather than the *identitas entis* that runs rampant in the German Idealist tradition.[62] Both the similarity to and dissimilarity from the being of God and the being of humans must be scrupulously maintained: on the one hand, if the *proportion* of finite to infinite is overemphasized, infinite and finite being are identified, and God is domesticated (the so-called human "I" in a loud voice); on the other hand, if the *disproportion* is overemphasized, there is no commerce at all between finite and infinite, and we edge toward Gnosticism. When identity rather than analogy provides the starting point for philosophical or theological reflection, conceptual pairs that are collated become purely dialectical, and God is absorbed or evacuated into the infinite I of a Fichte or a Schelling, or the mechanistic process of Spirit's gradual unfolding in

Hegel, and there is no longer any space for the operation of divine freedom, a curtailing that entails the contraction of the "advent-like openness of the coming of something greater."[63] The ever-greater dissimilarity is required not only to preserve the integrity of the infinite, but also, in its spacious act of letting-be, the finite is perfectly itself, as simultaneously poverty and fullness, in the image and likeness of the infinite. This ecstatic mode is for Balthasar the miracle of Being itself, as God is "the act of Being which is given out, which *as* gift delivers itself without defence . . . to the finite entities."[64]

The complex of relations of influence from German Idealism and Romanticism to Soloviev, Berdyaev, and Bulgakov supplies here the content for the investigation of a central methodological question: what is it precisely that occurs in the mechanics of both the Russian reduplication of Romantic philosophy and Balthasar's retelling of the respective thought of the Russian school that allows him to maintain simultaneously a general (and generally vociferous) opposition to certain aspects of Schelling's thought and a (tentatively qualified) affirmation of Soloviev and Bulgakov, who depend variously upon Schelling? Despite Schelling's influence, Balthasar appropriates Bulgakov in good conscience. He alibis Soloviev as "the watchman at the dawn and dusk of German Idealism,"[65] as one who stands vigil on the margins of Idealism but who does not fall victim to its excesses. As suggested above, however, Berdyaev's particular importation of Schelling and Böhme makes him a terminal case.[66] What, then, accounts for these variations on Balthasar's scale of affirmation?

In this comparative study, Schelling constellates a point of triangulation between Balthasar and the Russians, permitting not only the location of Balthasar's speculative method with relative nearness to or distance from each point, but also the demonstration of a secondary thesis that, for Balthasar, the Russians who rely upon Schelling's thought operate as successively successful antidotes—from Berdyaev to Soloviev to Bulgakov—and sites of the latter's sanitization. Thus, given the complex of relations of influence that obtain from Schelling to the Russians and the Russians to Balthasar (and even Schelling to Balthasar), Schelling serves current purposes as a catalyst for productive analysis of Balthasar's process of adjudicating the value and reliability of philosophical and theological sources. For example, in certain respects it could (and will) be argued that when Balthasar ratifies Soloviev, especially his thought on aesthetics and myth, it is a kind of ratification of Schelling by proxy. This impression of positive association between Soloviev and Schelling in Balthasar's mind is strengthened in particular by his designation in *The Moment of Christian Witness* of "the great and convincing" Soloviev as the "Christian Schelling."[67]

Balthasar, for whom the infinite and the finite, the divine and human, God and world must be continuous but separated by an absolute ontological gap, has a strong allergy to epical systems that collapse God and world, or that dissolve everything pantheistically or monistically into the All, mistakenly absolutizing one aspect at the expense of the other. For example, Balthasar's *Apokalypse der deutschen Seele*, which elaborates upon the three primary features of German literature as Promethean, Dionysian, and Götterdämmerung (twilight of the gods), indicates that all three constitute a denial of this analogous relation between God and world that leads either to the world's deification or to nihilism. For Balthasar, it is and must be Christ who capacitates the temporal for the eternal, the human for the divine, and so on. The solution to the reconciliation between God and world, then, must for Balthasar always be Christological, which is to say, always in an idiom that is historical, concrete, and particular. Christology must include more than an abstract or merely formal philosophical premise. In Idealism, according to Balthasar, "Christology becomes the inner form of the philosophical theory of 'creation' (and will necessarily remain so even with Schelling and Hegel.) Thus what began with Eckhart has become definitive: the assimilation of the God-man relation back into the inner-divine generation process, which as such is called upon to give formal expression to the God-world relation, or to the schematism of philosophy. Christ is only our elder brother, and we are all capable by virtue of our human nature of standing in his place."[68] The fundamental means of Balthasar's adjudication of the relative adequacy of the Russians is if the Idealistic forms borrowed from Schelling and Hegel are fleshed out (quite literally) with authentically Christian content. To recur again to the metaphor of the *Bergwerk*, and to borrow from another of Balthasar's preferred poets, to find Christ the WORD is to discover not rocks or even coal, but rather in a dark place to come upon "immortal diamond."[69]

(RE-)CONFIGURING THE PATRISTIC GENEALOGY: ORIGEN AS METHODOLOGICAL TYPE

In his monograph *The Systematic Thought of Hans Urs von Balthasar: An Irenaean Retrieval*, Kevin Mongrain indicates that Balthasar, in keeping with his privileging of Irenaeus of Lyons as theological archetype, "a quintessentially antispeculative theologian, who rigorously maintains that humans cannot form a concept of God because there is an ontological difference between God and creation,"[70] is himself also essentially antispeculative. While it may well be the case, as Mongrain has very elegantly demonstrated, that it is Irenaeus who serves as Balthasar's primary patristic source for his theological architectonics, it is, especially with respect to method, perhaps too univocal a claim. This excavation of the speculative Russian genealogy in Balthasar reveals that the appeal to the Irenaean principle cannot fully account for the trajectory of Balthasar's work, since Ireneaus tends to eschew the speculative.[71]

The present argument suggests that Mongrain's genealogy of Balthasar's thought ought to be broadened to include the decisive presence of Origen, who himself pioneers the cartography of speculative theological frontiers, as a more proximate *methodological* type than is Irenaeus. This claim can be corroborated not only in Balthasar's own strong assessment of Origen in his more scholarly work, but also in his own performance of the theological task. Tellingly, Balthasar once related in a 1976 interview that "Origen remains for me the most inspired, the most wide-ranging interpreter and lover of the Word of God. I never feel so at home elsewhere as I do with him."[72] With similar superlatives, in his posthumously published *My Work: In Retrospect*, Balthasar identifies Origen as "the most sovereign spirit of the first centuries" as he surprisingly describes *Geist und Feuer*, his own collection of Origen's works, as "even today the weightiest [book] of all

I have published."[73] He goes on to say that Origen possesses "the most logically consistent theology of the patristic age . . . purified from gnostic additions, an almost inexhaustible source of spiritual and theological stimulus for all later Christian thinking," especially, as he notes, in the speculative thought of Gregory of Nyssa and Maximus the Confessor.[74] Indeed, for Balthasar it was Origen rather than Irenaeus who provided "the key to the entire Greek patristics, the early Middle Ages, and, indeed, even to Hegel and Karl Barth"![75]

This association between Balthasar and Origen might well be affirmed as evidence for a problematic rather than a productive theological methodology by Pitstick, who registers anxiety that, with respect to method, Balthasar relies on "figures of questionable authority, often precisely with regard to positions of theirs not taken up or even rejected by the received tradition (e.g., Origen and Nicholas of Cusa)."[76] While a fully developed response either to Mongrain—which might make a strong claim for Origen against Irenaeus as *the* patristic father of Balthasar's thought—or to Pitstick—which would argue against the more specific points she enumerates that this method and the particular view of tradition it enjoins are salutary rather than deleterious—falls outside the parameters of this book, a few supplemental comments here and scattered throughout may suffice as a gesture toward Balthasar's own appreciative reception and even repetition of Origen in terms of a speculative method that includes an astounding theological creativity and interest in exploring open questions.

While Balthasar does acknowledge and temper some of Origen's more eccentric (of course, pre-Nicene and therefore underdeveloped) theological positions that were not preserved in the normative tradition, including a drift toward Trinitarian subordinationism, it is certainly arguable that he recapitulates Origen methodologically.[77] For instance, even when assessing Origen's own somewhat mixed contributions, he exemplifies a methodological posture that he will repeat consistently, especially in the test cases of how Schelling and the Russians fare. For Balthasar, it is not terribly productive to proceed, for instance, by simply subtracting from Origen's texts, in a purely mechanical way, that which is "heterodox," and leaving behind that which is "orthodox": the result would be a "flat, dull product which is full of nice, harmless things, but in which no one senses any longer the breath of genius."[78] When trying to get at an accurate portrayal of the dynamic spirit of Origen, the entire form or *Gestalt* of Origen as a theologian must be presented as a whole, even if some of his theological positions may be rather dubious. In this context Balthasar invokes that striking image from the dream-vision of King Nebuchadnezzar in the second chapter of Daniel, the vision of the great but hodgepodge colossus whose head was crafted of gold, its chest and arms of silver, its abdomen and thighs of bronze, its legs of iron, and its feet of mixed iron and clay. Although composed of mixed metals, the colossus in the dream was indubitably still a colossus.[79] Analogously, in his assessments of sources and resources in (and extraneous to) the tradition, Balthasar prefers to reserve judgment for as long as possible, eschewing hasty dismissals. He intends to represent first the greatness of Origen as a Christian thinker, and only then to identify those elements that may be theologically problematic. Analogously, the complex manner in which Balthasar receives (or does not receive) the Russians as mediated through Schelling provides concrete exemplification that he is a theologian friendly to speculative forms of theology, though this hospitality is constrained by certain parameters. He is generous in letting the wheat grow together with the weeds, so to speak, but there are points at which he declares, "Thus far and no farther will you come."

JOHANNINE "WORD-MYSTICISM" AND THE WHOLE IN/AS THE FRAGMENT

Balthasar's deeply Johannine disposition—especially with respect to the *missio* Christology of the Son's "coming-from-God" as *One Sent* by the Father—hardly needs documentation.[80] It is also the case, though, that Schelling, Hegel, and at least Soloviev and Bulgakov operate to some degree in a Johannine register, that is, according to a sensibility that is more mystical than not, Trinitarian, and concerned with the theme of love, the trope of light and darkness, the simultaneity of poverty and glory, a strong understanding of God as Spirit

(John 4:24), the kenotic self-sacrifice of the death of Christ that is linked to the advent of the Holy Spirit, the reconciliation of time and eternity, an eschatological orientation, and so on. Balthasar characterizes Schelling (and Hegel) as Johannine in the context of an analysis of Friedrich Hölderlin's successive drafts of "The Death of Empedocles." In the third draft, which accords "a social and eschatological dimension" to the death, there "is the Johannine Christianity emerging, as in the late Fichte, the old Schelling, and the young Hegel, as the alpha and omega of Idealistic thinking. The eternal Logos, in the world in the form of poverty and humility, glorifying himself through suffering and death, then to ascend back whence he came; declaring his mission and all-embracing love in great parting speeches, consoling even as he withdraws, promising the Spirit and a second coming—there is correspondence everywhere."[81] This specifically Johannine hermeneutic stands, but according to Balthasar, in Schelling (and Hegel) it is thoroughly deformed, insofar as it rejects the theophanous content of the Old Testament, "which is the site of emergent glory [in favor of] the Johannine final form of the New Testament, disassociated from Paul and the synoptics, in order to be able to reinterpret *agape* directly and freely in the direction of *gnosis*."[82] That is, for Schelling and Hegel, agape is no longer rendered in terms of Christ's likeness but placed in a wholly human manifold that redefines it as a salvific way of knowing.

In sharp contrast to his evaluation of the German Idealists, in his short preface to a selection of Origen's works including *An Exhortation to Martyrdom*, *Prayer*, and other excerpts,[83] Balthasar valorizes Origen for his profile as a decidedly Johannine theologian captivated with love for the Logos, and, relatedly, his connection of an authentically Christian gnosis that relates the *disciplina arcani* with personal and ecclesial holiness, where *pistis* and *gnosis* are reciprocal rather than antagonistic categories.[84] He rightly suggests not only that Origen is a thinker who happens to be interested in Logos theology, but that this bright love of the WORD is *the* principle of unity and intelligibility that is the "sustaining ground" of all his thought, the flame that imbues all of reality, cosmos, and sacred text with mysterious, hidden significance.[85]

For Origen, this Johannine Logos is incarnate at least triply: in the historical body of Jesus who was resurrected from the dead and is now broken in the Eucharist, in the body of the Church, and in the word-body of the Scriptures. The "word" of Christ is not just his teachings and deeds in the four Gospels, but also in Moses and the prophets, and the spiritual dynamism of the sacramentally present Logos pervades the whole text—Old Testament and New—enlivening the *littera*.[86] This absolutely sacramental view of Scripture, which insists on reading the Scriptures as a unity, even leads Origen to suggest that readings such as Marcion's, which deconstruct and dismember the text, do violence to the body of Christ, even prolonging his passion.[87] For Origen, the Scriptures ought to be held in the same esteem as the Eucharist.

Balthasar shares this Johannine word-mysticism with Origen, resolutely connecting reading and interpreting the Bible with Christology, making an analogy between the flesh of Jesus and the literal meaning of the Scriptures. For Balthasar, following Origen, the WORD took flesh in the human body of Jesus and in "a body consisting of syllables, scripture, ideas, images, verbal utterance and preaching, since otherwise men would not have understood either that the Word really was made *flesh*, or that the divine Person who was made flesh was really the *Word*."[88] Similarly, he invokes Origen to provide a Johannine, pneumatological excursus on the nature of the Scriptures as incarnate body of the Logos right alongside the corporeal form of the Eucharist, such that they are bursting with fullness and open to an infinite depth of interpretation.[89]

This Johannine idea of the Logos can be profitably connected to Balthasar's articulation of the Christologically governed, symbiotic relationship between the fragment and the whole in the slim and woefully understudied 1963 text *Das Ganze im Fragment*, which also serves in part to address Kilby's critique of Balthasar's theological epistemology.[90] In this text Balthasar suggests three basic options for thinking the relation between the fragmentary and the whole. The first might be called the way of Hegel or of Neoplatonism and ultimately elevates the whole at the expense of the fragment, whether by dialectics or ascent, respectively. Second is the "tragic" way of a Nietzsche or a

Heidegger, or of Greek and Germanic tragedy, which absolutizes the pain and the struggle of the fragmentary at the expense of the whole. Third is the Johannine way of Christ and of love, according to which the existence and truth-bearing character of the fragment is thoroughly dependent upon the existence of wholeness, though this wholeness comes from elsewhere and is neither the purview nor the privilege of human vision.

Balthasar begins the text with a close reading of Augustine's *Confessions*, attending in particular to book 10 on memory. For Augustine, who makes much of the etymological relation between *cogito* and *co-agito*, "what it is to learn and to think" is to gather up scattered, disparate, buried, and fragmentary things and bring them together.[91] For Augustine, and much later for Heidegger—who performs similar etymological work by connecting *logos* and *legein*, where "saying" is a kind of "gathering"—the essence of thought and of language is the practice of collecting fragments and laying them side by side. Unlike in Heidegger, though, where the "gathering Logos" is connected with the language of Heraclitus and the pre-Socratics, the "gathering Logos" in Balthasar is construed—as in Origen—only Christologically, and it is here that the possibility of gathering fragments up into some whole is fundamentally rooted.

The shattering into fragments of knowledge and the infinite "multiplicity of flesh" is divinely ordained, as Christ the Logos, in an essentially kenotic mode, takes up the flesh-body of Jesus, the word-body of the Scriptures, the sacramental body of the Eucharistic fragments: "Thus, the whole *in* the fragment only because the whole *as* the fragment."[92] Christ mysteriously embodies, in Balthasar's words, "the essentially irrefrangible wholeness within *the essentially uncompletable fragmentary*."[93] The whole is not apart from the fragment, nor is the fragment isolated from the whole, but wholeness and plenitude imbues and illuminates the fragmentary in a way that cannot be calculated, measured, or predicted. Taking from Bulgakov (here without acknowledgment) the idea that all of fragmentary existence operates in the wholeness of kenotic Trinitarian self-gift and is drawn toward Trinity and shaped by it, Balthasar intimates that the fragments are imbued and enlivened with the creative power of God. All manner of scattered and disparate things may "have the transparency of the whole," which exceeds the sum of the earthly fragments themselves.[94]

Balthasar continues this analysis of the fragment-whole relation in a Christological register by following the logic and chronology of Good Friday, Holy Saturday, Resurrection, and finally, Ascension and the turn toward the Spirit. Directly contrary to Kilby's critique that Balthasar's interest in wholeness constitutes a "God's eye view," these singular events in the life of Christ function as aporetic moments that disrupt theological reflection, making discourse impassible, impossible. On Good Friday, human beings are blind, grasping a shard of broken pottery in an effort to intimate from it the unforeseeable and unseeable whole, where it is impossible to claim perfection, totality, or wholeness in advance. The fragment is the cross of Christ, where mysteriously "innumerable lines of significance intersect . . . disentangle, and then entangle themselves again,"[95] so that no syntheses can be simply beheld "at a glance," or aestheticized into a coherent whole. The God-ordained multiplicity of the Word, the scattering into finitude (a human body, the syllables and genres of Scripture, into broken body and broken bread) reaches its peak at the cry of Jesus from the cross, and "it is as if here, where all the elements are shattered and all light is darkened, even the alphabet of the eternal word is so fractured that no saving word can be formed out of it."[96]

The resounding cry of Jesus is the shattering of the indicative and the evocation of the laments of a Jeremiah, the discursively unanswered questions of a Job. Here at the cross, theological "statements are possible only in the interrogative,"[97] and the word is not a sayable word but a "sub-word" that always invisibly undergirds the cogent and the understandable and capacitates Christian mysticism. Following Bulgakov, at Holy Saturday, the inarticulate cry of Jesus falls to the silence of death, absence, and abandonment, where theological talk devolves to "a mere clatter of formal logic [and] empty syllogisms."[98] It is the logic of Resurrection that shatters all the more, a resurrection "whose nature is to burst open the graves of our ideas, to surpass our conceptions of time and space, to pass through in sovereign manner the closed doors of our minds."[99] Finally, it is at Christ's Ascension, in which the Word—made unsayable on Good Friday, silenced in death and the

passive descent into hell on Holy Saturday, and then powerfully renewed and ratified at the Resurrection—inaugurates the sending of the
Holy Spirit, calling into question any suggestion that the theological
project might be circumscribed, for, "in God there is no end, only a
breakup of what appeared to be final and finite, showing that it is really
infinite."[100] This logic of the Ascension resonates with Balthasar's early
epistemology, where truth is ever-greater, nonexhaustible, and infinitely open.

A theological discourse that emerges from a Christological and
pneumatological vision with the slain Lamb of the Apocalypse as its
governing symbol seems to require an attitude of joyful acceptance of
human finitude and imperfectability.[101] According to the *Wahrheit*, and
again recalling Heidegger, the *only* immediate knowledge that any person can have is the knowledge of his or her own fragmentary and
contingent existence.[102] The fact that human beings can only glimpse
"minute fragments" of the whole suggests the need to withhold ultimate judgment and evaluation;[103] generous dialogue is imperative, but
it is always both unfinished and governed by a generous love that
"gives the other's truth credit for being able to reveal itself as truth."[104]

The shattering pneumatological turn suggests a humble awareness
that "a whole . . . never emerges from worldly and human pieces."[105]
Because the "whole in the fragment" is a Christological singularity
alone, it cannot be an achieved perspective: it is all gift. If the whole
might sometimes be glimpsed, it is only as a grace and not as a due, and
it cannot be controlled or manipulated. Formulaic efforts to round off
the fragment's sharp edges and shape it into a whole will be unsuccessful, and Balthasar suggests that this lack of success is shared across
ideological divides, since the eternal mystery of the slain Lamb cannot
be harnessed or economized or functionalized into programs, whether
social or ecclesial, "right" or "left."[106] Moreover, because the precise
image of wholeness is the wounded Christ, the Lamb slain from the
foundations of the world, the theologian ought also to adopt a paradoxical posture that, instead of striving for a harmoniously comprehensive picture, is closer to genuine wholeness the more it abandons
all efforts to that end. This renunciation of the possibility of seeing the

whole is for Balthasar the practice of wholeness, since "God is nowhere nearer than in the humility and poverty of indifference, in the
openness to death, in the renunciation of every hold on or attempt to
make certain of God."[107] At the fundament—determined by Bulgakov
and resonant of Origen—we find only a Johannine *Gelassenheit*, the
self-surrender of the Lamb slain from the foundation of the world, and
for Balthasar, this posture is for the theologian simultaneously *ascesis*
and license.

THE SPECTER OF "SPECULATION": ILLEGITIMATE
AND LEGITIMATE MODES

This license, however capacious, is not unchecked. In his *Senses of
Tradition: Continuity and Development in Catholic Faith*, John Thiel
notes that the coincidence in Balthasar's work of a "valorization of
tradition's literal sense even as it engages in mystical speculation" constitutes his "particularly Catholic genius."[108] In keeping with the sense
of balance required to maintain simultaneously the "fixed" and "mobile" aspects of a living Church tradition, it ought to be recognized
that Balthasar does guard vigorously against *illicit* modes of speculative theologizing. First, like Origen, Balthasar's theology is scrupulously grounded in biblical exegesis, a commitment that is prior—both
dispositionally and structurally in his treatment of particular issues—
to the examination of the more speculative questions.[109] Balthasar's
speculative theological moves begin with and are constrained by what
is given in sacred revelation.[110] For instance, to justify his Trinitarian
reflections he notes that "it is only on the basis of Jesus Christ's own
behavior and attitude that we can distinguish . . . plurality in God.
Only in him is the Trinity opened up and made accessible. . . . We
know about the Father, Son and Spirit as divine 'Persons' only through
the figure and disposition of Jesus Christ. Thus we can agree with the
principle, often enunciated today, that it is only on the basis of the
economic Trinity that we can have knowledge of the immanent Trinity
and dare to make statements about it."[111] Received theological truths
cannot be denatured by forcing them to lie upon the Procrustean bed

of ahistorical, abstracted human constructions of, say, natural religion or philosophies of history: with no apologies to Hegel, "neither Good Friday nor Easter nor Pentecost can be turned into a speculative principle."[112] For Balthasar, the givenness of Christianity ought not to be circumvented or manipulated.

Secondly, as discussed above, Balthasar objects to those formal philosophical discourses that concern what he terms (technically) the *"speculative doctrine of God,"*[113] marked by making coincident God and creation and thus contributing in no small part to the tragic waning of the sensibility of glory in the modern world.[114] When the philosophical system of speculative German Idealism is taken to its logical end, the collateral damage to both the cosmos and the human being is serious indeed. Balthasar observes, for instance, that when human autonomy and freedom are inflated at the expense of the divine, and the cosmos is considered only to be the unfolding or self-mediation of the freedom of the absolute, the world and the people in it can become raw material for the exercise of power, for experiment and manipulation. He uses the image of a great tree whose roots are planted in speculation, but whose trunk and branches lift into the rarefied air of "exact science," such that "what began as an attempt at a speculative supposition was later corroborated on an empirical basis, with the consequence that can now be manipulated with impunity in a purely experimental way."[115] This describes a gnosis void of love, and cannot stand.

Finally, mystery as a positive good must be preserved: "And in what concerns the knowledge of the heart of God's mysteries here too Christianity offers the only approach. Whoever violently breaks through the doors, finds the treasuries bare."[116] This rationalistic overreaching represents the degeneration of the speculative into the specular and the spectatorial and, with its presumption to know too much, does violence to mystery. Both Balthasar and Bulgakov object to Böhme's metaphysics on precisely this point, among many others: though he is ostensibly a mystic, an inexorable rationalism actually dominates Böhme's thought. Bulgakov in particular minces no words with this line of criticism, though, like Balthasar, he leaves some room for the possibility of finding in his thought even a handful of valuable stones:

In the Böhmian God from his first movement towards revelation to the remote little corner of the universe, from the angel to the last bug, *everything is comprehensible*, everything is explained, everything is rationalized. Here there is no place for antinomy with its logical interruption, or for Mystery. Unalloyed rationalism—here is the other side of that global knowledge or "gnosis" which Hegel thought he possessed on certain grounds, and Böhme on others. . . . This is why his separate insights are dazzling, astounding, and precious—in part but not entirely so; it is necessary to break open the shell in order to get the nut. . . . [H]is system is like a mine in which precious metals are hidden under coarse rocks.[117]

It is particularly ironic that though it was Schelling who aptly noted this strain of rationalism in Böhme, in Balthasar's and Bulgakov's estimation Schelling also falls on the same sword of "mystical rationalism." Balthasar's Johannine word-mysticism, borrowed from Origen, fundamentally resists this "unalloyed rationalism," insofar as the divine content, whether in the Scriptures or the inexpressible nature of God, exceeds and surpasses its own expression. For Balthasar, perceiving or knowing the hidden truth of the divinity of Jesus in his humanity, or the spirit in the letter of the Scriptures, "can only be grasped in the setting of faith, that is to say, in a mode of hearing that never issues in final vision, but in a progression without end, a progression ultimately dependent, in its scope, on the Holy Spirit."[118] This is why, for Balthasar, it is the saint rather than the theologian or the philosopher who is closest to understanding God.

THE RECIPROCAL CORRELATIVES OF *PISTIS* AND *GNOSIS*

According to Mongrain, on the Irenaean model, "true gnosis is to know the limits of theory, abstraction, and speculation in theology; for Irenaeus, to know less is to know more."[119] Mongrain's privileging of the Irenaean model of gnosis, however, can here be supplemented with deeper attention to Balthasar's turn to Alexandrian Christianity, especially Origen, to sketch a profile of the "Christian gnostic." Here Balthasar makes a finer categorical distinction between true or "biblical" gnosis and false gnosis, which is to say, between legitimate and illegitimate modes of speculation. This connection between *pistis* and gnosis, while certainly not absent in Paul or in the synoptics, is for Balthasar most explicit in the Gospel of John: "We *believe and know* that you are the holy one of God! (John 6:69)."[120] In this most unambiguously Trinitarian gospel, where to see the Son is to see the Father, "the circumincession of *pistis* and *gnosis* becomes fully manifest, because it is only through faith in Christ's divinity that one can gain access to this sphere of truth within the Godhead, in which one learns to see and understand the very essence of truth."[121] For the Alexandrians, and particularly for such a Johannine thinker as Origen, it is decisive that the relationship between knowledge and faith is a mutual rather than competitive one, so much so that Origen can identify this biblical gnosis with "perfect faith."[122] This is a genuine circumincession, too; gnosis is for Origen neither a preliminary nor a subsequence to faith. Indeed, to separate faith and knowledge from one another such that there is an inverse relation between them, in which as knowledge increases, faith decreases, and vice versa, is the unacceptable tendency of Gnostic*ism*. According to Balthasar, though, it was the particular contribution of Alexandrian theology to restore a robust concept of biblical gnosis "by which *pistis* is perfected to its place of honour."[123]

Thus, on this model, it is a perfection rather than a betrayal of Christian identity to be a "gnostic," though what is meant by this appellation is something quite other than its perhaps more familiar and intellectually elitist iteration. The Christian Gnostic, enlightened by the Johannine *Logos*, is one who enters into a visionary, interior, authentic understanding of the faith in contemplative *theoria*, which allows "the essential content of faith [to] unfold before his [or her] vision."[124] This vision is not the purview of intellectuals; it is the illumined capacity of the ordinary baptized believer to see, when reading the Scriptures, the Spirit in the letter, the New Testament in the Old Testament, the divinity in Christ's humanity, and, through the Holy Spirit, the Father in the Son. Origen is particularly attuned to these mysterious depths: Balthasar earlier rhapsodizes that Origen is among the true contemplatives, able to see "the Spirit blazing through the letter."[125] Furthermore, it is salutary that this Alexandrian way of seeing and of reading the hidden depths of the Scriptures resists relying only upon the "exact sciences" (though these are valuable for establishing the *littera*). Balthasar also cites this connection of the Logos to *theoria* and the infinitude of interpretation in the theological aesthetics as concretely infusing and shaping the theological imagination:

> If this is the Logos that comes to us from God, in which and for which we have been created, then its contemplation in us can only be infinite. Now, it is always *this* unity which is revealed to us in every intellectual act of opening and "breaking the bread" of the Logos (Origen)—not a purely divine or a purely human unity, but always a human-and-divine unity. Thus, Christian contemplation becomes an ever deeper and richer living from Christ and into Christ, and progressively both the living triune God and the whole of creation as recapitulated in Christ enter into this life, not, however, in the rarefied space where ideal contents are beheld in abstract purity, but within the shaping (*Einbildung*) of the image (*Bild*) of Christ in the contemplative subject. For the theological imagination (*Einbildungskraft* = "power to shape an image") lies with Christ, who is at once the image (*Bild*) and the power (*Kraft*) of God.[126]

Methodologically, when Balthasar conceives of the nature of genuine theology, it emerges when the strictly academic or scientific "passes over into the science of faith proper—a 'science' which presupposes the act of faith as its locus of understanding"[127] and thus can and should exceed the discursive, conceptual, dogmatic, and propositional to include also prayers, homilies, spiritual commentaries, mystical literature, confessions, "rhapsodies," and so on.[128] It is not surprising, then, to note that Balthasar privileges Origen's biblical commentaries as a more genuine representation of Origen than the text of *On First Principles*. To be capacitated by the Logos to see the inward depths of spiritual meaning is, for Origen, to be on holy ground, to enter into a great mystery for which rationalism is inadequate. Balthasar puts an even sharper point on it, no doubt motivated by his chafing against the propositionalism of Neoscholasticism: "When weighed on the scales, the rich substance—the inner sanctum of theology, so to speak—lies rather on the side of rhapsody than on the form of discourse which externalizes itself in distinctions and definitions."[129] Christianity is therefore much richer than a merely extrinsicist assent to a set of abstract propositions unclear to and disconnected from the simple believer but accepted out of sheer force of will in deference to ecclesial authority.[130]

What Balthasar takes from Origen here is that the *theoria* or contemplation that marks the Christian gnostic enlightened by grace means that a purely extrinsic relation to faith is surpassed. Knowing God is therefore neither a function of rationalism nor a mysticism available merely to a select few, but instead is a reciprocal act of *pistis* and this contemplative, Spirit-filled gnosis situated squarely in the sacramental life of the Church. It is the response of the whole person to the free and glorious gift and presence of God's Self in revelation.[131] Thus, Origen's Christian gnosis—which permits the vision of the hidden mysteries of the faith in the Scriptures and in the cosmos—is a total human act requiring not only an engaged and attentive intellect but, more fundamentally, personal holiness and prayer.[132] Origen and Balthasar likewise insist, then, upon a *kniende Theologie* ("kneeling theology").

In his 1938 introduction to *Origenes: Geist und Feuer*, Balthasar draws further attention to this connection between the theologian's contribution and the deeply Christian shape of his life, forged in love for and devotion to the Logos. The latter is not incidental or accidental to the former, but actually is the condition of the possibility for the unity and intelligibility of his theological thought, so here too, form and content are of a piece. Rowan Williams offers a similar characterization of Origen, noting also the correlation between his allegiance to the Johannine Logos made flesh in the *verba Christi*—as simultaneously incarnate physical body, Eucharistic body, ecclesial body, and the sacramentalized word-body of the Scriptures—and Origen's own practice of spiritual exegesis, a process of reading that requires a convergence of mental acuity and, most importantly, spiritual health, where the "safeguards for the unity and coherence of Christian speech [are] bound up with the life and example of the spiritual exegete."[133] Williams goes on to point out that in Origen's commentary on the Gospel of John, it is manifest that "the task of [spiritual] exegesis is *to erect a structure within which contemplation or speculation can safely occur.*[134] Because the unity of truth capacitated by the Logos is not restricted to the discursive or the rational, but extends to the theological imagination and the total lived existence of the Spirit-led Christian practitioner, this speculation is connected to, rather than disconnected from, forms and practices of the contemplative spiritual life.

In sum, our suggestion that Balthasar has a significant speculative *Tendenz* that recalls Origen's own has to do with the relation of excess between the theological subject of inquiry—nothing less than the "absolute Trinitarian love of God, which discloses itself and offers itself in Jesus Christ"[135]—and the method employed for its study. Again, Balthasar strenuously resists "exact science," in which the method is *exactly* correlative to its object, as inadequate to the mysterious task of theology, insofar as it only counterfeits scientific precision and the full comprehensive competence of a closed system.[136] On Balthasar's own telling, authentic speculation takes into account the fact that "while it is in God that the perfect reality and therefore exactness, precision (*praecisio*) consist, the derivatory thought can only be inexact, approximate, supposition, parabolic, and in the true sense of the word, 'reflective,' speculative."[137] That the penetrating love of the Word, personal piety, and bold speculative methodology exist together in Origen's ardent desire to remain within the bounds of the Church is instructive here.[138] Balthasar agrees that the truly speculative, contemplative, and often quite daring method of theologizing is performed always in reference to and within the bounds of the faith of the Church, with reference to the personal faith commitments of theologians themselves, and, most importantly, accompanied by prayer.[139] Theological speculation is a necessary good, but prayer must be its context, its true home and port, insofar as the intimacy of the one who prays with the Holy Spirit annuls the tendency for authentic speculation to devolve into the spectatorial, characterized as it is with an "external, critical attitude to the truth."[140]

LOOKING FORWARD

The remaining chapters of this work provide a substantial enactment of what is here only an introductory sketch, examining by turns the aesthetic, mythic, eschatological, and apocalyptic confluences and departures that obtain between the three thinkers of the Russian school and Balthasar, with Schelling playing the *tertium quid*. Again, by way of excavating subterranean instances of homologous content and analyzing how Balthasar judges the relative adequacy of the Russian thinkers on these issues, the primary aim is to provide a reasonable *Gestalt* of Balthasar as a theologian who engages cultural data and modes of speculative thought but does not permit these to run roughshod over tradition. Chapter 2, "'Denn da ist keine Stelle, die dich nicht sieht': Theological and Quasi-Theological Aesthetics," examines the way in which the aesthetic discourse of Schelling, the Russians, and Balthasar can be plotted along the axes of the dialectical pairs of the real and the ideal, finite and infinite, with particular attention to the decisively Schellingian function of art or the beautiful as the necessary mediating principle between the "two realms." Soloviev's eschatological aesthetics of the concrete actualization of the ideal, which is formally similar to Schelling's own aesthetic theory, Berdyaev's fundamentally destructive meaning of the creative act, and Bulgakov's pneumatologically inflected understanding of beauty are weighed in turn against the balance of a thoroughly Christological, Balthasarian theological aesthetics of glory that is regulated by the concepts of form and splendor.

Chapter 3, "'Du Dunkelheit, aus der ich stamme': Ontology, Evil, and Myth at the Root," begins with an excavation of the assimilations of theogonic speculative ontology of Jakob Böhme in Schelling, Berdyaev, and Soloviev, particularly as it informs their respective theologies or philosophies of freedom, evil, and the relation of myth to history. Though Balthasar's evaluation recognizes the worth of these discourses insofar as they rehabilitate myth, value freedom, and take evil seriously in the face of a conceptual rationalism that does no such thing, he finds their Böhmian heritage extremely problematic. Berdyaev is indicted far more severely than Soloviev, who with his Christological commitments filtered through Maximus the Confessor manages for the most part to escape the gravitational pull of the Böhme–Schelling–Berdyaev line.

Chapter 4, "'Grün wirklicher Grüne, wirklicher Sonnenschein, wirklicher Wald': Anthropological *Eschata* and the Logic of Resurrection," and chapter 5, "'Denn Armut ist ein großer Glanz aus Innen': The Theocentric Horizon," are a diptych, in that both consider the last things. Following the trajectory of German Idealism, the Russians each locate the discourse of *ta eschata* at the forefront of their respective theological reflections. These two chapters follow Balthasar's distinction of "anthropocentric" and "theocentric" eschatology, with chapter 4 considering that which falls under the ambit of more traditional eschatology: death, judgment, hell, and salvation. It undertakes an investigation of each thinker's theology of human death, which entails some reflection on questions proper to theological anthropology: the nature of hell, particularly as an auto-contraction of human being; and the prospect of universal salvation. Again, Berdyaev is overdetermined by Schelling's philosophy and its dependence on Böhme; the ambivalence of Schelling on human finitude reasserts itself fatally in Berdyaev, engendering an otherworldliness that Balthasar simply cannot abide, despite certain critiques of Balthasar to the contrary. With respect to the question of universal salvation, Balthasar's experimental theologizing remains in the optative, while Bulgakov's Origenist indicative regarding the Alexandrian theorem of *apokatastasis* is thought to be overly assertive. Chapter 5, "The Theocentric Horizon," attends to the broader, Trinitarian context of Balthasar's eschatology, including further reflections on the shared Johannine register between Schelling, the Russians, and Balthasar, figurations of the Antichrist particularly as the instance of religious counterfeiting or imposture, and finally, paschal Trinitarianism, the site of the most explicit and fecund of Balthasar's borrowing from Bulgakov on Ur-kenosis.

The final remarks provide a more methodological manifesto, distilling principles for theological method based upon this analysis of how Balthasar receives or rebuffs elements from the functional test cases of Soloviev, Berdyaev, and Bulgakov through Schelling. First, there is a direct rather than inverse relation between fidelity to tradition and the capacity for creative, speculative thought. It is Christ the Logos who provides the necessary ballast from which liminal theological "play" might take place and the Holy Spirit who capacitates that play. Second, theologians ought to exercise a lack of neurosis and scrupulosity with respect to contamination by "impure" sources and desist from condemning thinkers with guilt by simple association:

engagement is not, after all, tantamount to uncritical approval. Indeed, there is much to be gained theologically from entertaining noncanonical sources, though the wheat must be carefully sifted from the chaff.

This principle of undecidability and resistance to full closure is often salutary, insofar as withholding judgment can be more theologically fruitful than immediate classification and dismissal of the heterodox. Third, and quite related, is Balthasar's insistence that the theological project be thoroughly culturally engaged, not at all shy about entertaining the contributions not only of philosophy, but also of art, music, and literature, whose forms of expression gesture toward the symbolic excesses of divine plentitude that cannot be conveyed in discursive language alone. Here, perhaps, is where the epigraphs of the chapter titles—all lines drawn from poems of Rilke,[141] who, though certainly not unambiguously "on the side of the angels," was the subject of much rich, if usually critical, Balthasarian theological reflection—operate. They are not simply ornamental, but act as symbolic reminders of two things: first, that the theologian can, without fear, weigh "the value of things" and appropriate with confidence all that is good from a good world, and second, that there is far, far more in theology than can be expressed discursively. For Balthasar, theological method must always be appropriate to the "object," or in this case, the subject of inquiry, which in the case of theology, means excess, plurality, mystery, even auspicious vision.

CHAPTER 2

"DENN DA IST KEINE STELLE, DIE DICH NICHT SIEHT"
Theological and Quasi-Theological Aesthetics

Hans Urs von Balthasar's name can be said to be nearly synonymous with Roman Catholic theological aesthetics in the twentieth century. The current task, however, is not to present a systematic introduction to his thinking on the matter, which has been done at length elsewhere.[1] Nor is it simply to catalogue seriatim the deeply aesthetic proclivities of the religious philosophers who set in motion a new stage of Russian religious aesthetics—beginning with Soloviev, continuing in Berdyaev, and cresting in Bulgakov—and who maintain and develop the Solovievian aesthetic legacy.[2] Neither is it an exhaustive survey of philosophical aesthetics, even that which has been through the centuries theologically inflected. The convergence of art and religion has a long pedigree among the ancients, the medievals, the moderns, and the postmoderns, but here we shall focus primarily on Balthasarian and Russian engagement with, responses to, reliance upon, and departures from modern articulations of aesthetics, with particular attention to Schelling.

Generally, then, this chapter is an examination of affinities, parallels, or repetitions between Balthasar and the Russians—again, not so much a vocabulary that catalogues the *what* as a grammar that indexes the *how* (that is, the mechanics of use)—with an eye toward advancing the thesis that Balthasar's mode of theologizing is constrained by tradition and at the same time fundamentally experimental. This thesis will be tested by an analysis and assessment of the principles according to which Balthasar adjudicates, allows, or excludes certain aesthetic elements in Russian thought—mainly in Soloviev—particularly as they have been inspired by or mediated through Schelling. How do these thinkers either duplicate or correctively reduplicate Schellingian aesthetics? In particular, this chapter will demonstrate that Balthasar soundly ratifies the aesthetics of Soloviev, despite the fact that the latter is deeply, but apparently for Balthasar not fatally, determined by Schelling.[3] The interesting point here is not that Balthasar makes use of Romantic and Idealist aesthetics, either full-stop or through Soloviev, but rather the means by which Balthasar attempts to salvage this secularized aesthetics for theology. Ultimately, Balthasar's debts to Schelling's aesthetics, whatever they may be, are "purified" through the Russian Soloviev. Comparing the thought of Soloviev, who passes, and Schelling, who is rendered a more complicated verdict but ultimately does not, on matters aesthetic will serve as concrete exemplification of Balthasar's process of adjudication.

This treatment is inclusive of several complex and disparate thinkers; thus, analyzing repetitions and departures within its constructed triangulation of Schelling, the Russian theologians, and Balthasar on the question of overlapping aesthetic commitments is a complicated endeavor that does not pretend in the least to be comprehensive. As suggested in chapter 1, each of the categories investigated—aesthetics, speculative ontology and myth, the problem of evil and freedom, and eschatology—provides an index of thinking "the dialectic between God and world, between the One and what is Other (the Many)."[4] This dialectical characterization sets the stage and provides the framework for managing our analysis of the aesthetics of Schelling, the Russians (particularly Soloviev), and Balthasar. The investigation proceeds with a presentation and analysis of these thinkers' respective understandings of the relation of aesthetics to the broadly construed, purportedly dialectical, and variously named pairs of real/ideal, finite/infinite, matter/spirit, with special attention to both the function of art or aesthetics as such for negotiating between the two realms, and the degree to which each (quasi- or actually theological) system of aesthetics can be said to be authentically revelatory. Addressed throughout are several other, more narrowly aesthetic elements that put Schelling, the Russians, and Balthasar in dialogue, including the potential ambiguity of beauty (that is, the phenomena of ugliness, evil, and the nonideal), the strong correlation in our thinkers between aesthetics and *ta eschata*, and thinking aesthetics "theurgically," what is here called the Rilkean Clause, from the last line of Rilke's poem "The Archaic Torso of Apollo," from which this chapter's title is drawn.[5]

Even leaving aside the sheer bulk of material that must be taken into account and the even larger bulk that must regrettably be left to the side, this approach is not without its share of difficulties. First, though unavoidable, it is somewhat alien to the spirit of Balthasar's own intentions to set off aesthetics as a discrete chapter, which might suggest a determinate beginning and end of his aesthetic allegiances, as aesthetic categories and analogies both motivate and saturate Balthasar's systematic theology throughout. Beauty is, for Balthasar, not at all ornamental, but the very "blazing forth of the primal, protological and eschatological splendour of creation . . . in which redeemed man is admitted to participation in God's act of praising himself in his creation."[6]

Secondly, especially in an attempt to do justice to a wide cross section of thinkers in a field that can invoke not only the study of the beautiful (in art or nature), but also notions of fittingness (which may be inflected morally) and various other modes of expression, signification, valuation, or judgment, there is an implicit vagueness of naming our category—what, indeed, do we intend to suggest by "aesthetic"?— which must be addressed outright. The modern discipline of aesthetics (Alexander Baumgarten and Immanuel Kant forward) is much more narrowly circumscribed than the premodern, indicating quite literally that which has got to do with sense perception.[7] This meaning of the term will at least loosely govern our analysis, though with the recognition that Balthasar mourned the rationalism and the divorce from metaphysics that these modern thinkers engender. Such a narrowing of the field is justified textually, insofar as in the thinkers of the Russian school and in Balthasar, the "aesthetic" indicates the diptych of form and matter, and the concrete, actual expression of the former in the latter. For instance, in the foreword to his introductory volume of *Herrlichkeit*, Balthasar invokes both Thomas Aquinas and Kant, suggesting that the category of sensible perception, or "beholding and perceiving"[8] governs his view of the aesthetic as marked by an immediate vision.

Balthasar's commitment to a direct "seeing" that reveals the transcendent invisible locates his aesthetics within the purview of the essentially modern, having a strong family resemblance—if somewhat disinherited—to the aesthetic project of German Idealism. The genetics are complex, though, given that Balthasar locates the origins of German Idealism in Christian theology, as "reason cannot catch up with the deepest layer of [the human], be it act or will or drive; what is ultimate in [human being] is so absolute that it cannot be mastered by the categories of reason."[9] Though for Balthasar expressive form is theologically conditioned in a way that departs ultimately from German Idealism and Romanticism, the way these discourses actually operate in his thought reveals, at least implicitly, that they admit of degrees of theological serviceability and influence.

More particularly, Balthasar's position toward Schelling is, though on balance negative, actually fairly ambivalent: although he remains relentlessly critical, Balthasar finds parts of Schelling's aesthetic theory compelling and able to inform—even in excess of his own telling—his project of theological aesthetics.[10] It may well be the case for both Balthasar and the Russians who make use of Schelling that they are reading his early aesthetics through the late Schelling of the *Philosophy of Mythology* and *Philosophy of Revelation*. It is certainly worth asking whether Balthasar is indebted to this Schelling rather more than he admits, particularly given his commendation of myth as disclosive of being which finds its true realization in Christian revelation, which will be treated in the next chapter.

While Balthasar ultimately determines Schelling's thought to be insufficient for a full-bodied theological aesthetics, he is far more amenable to Schelling than he is to Hegel, especially when Schelling's philosophy of mythology and revelation is read retroactively into his early aesthetics. Certainly Balthasar's preference is for a Schellingian

form of Idealism, which is in a register that is not primarily epistemological and that is more easily appropriated critically by theology
than the rationalistic Hegelian form. All the caveats hence and forth
stand—yes, Schelling and Hegel are often lumped together in Balthasar
as illicitly speculative thinkers who introduce process in the self-
becoming of God, and whose failures are generally spectacular—but
Balthasar's fundamental priority to ontological disclosure finds some
resonances with Schellingian aesthetics, which, at least in the early *System of Transcendental Idealism* of 1800, considered art to be the "revelation" of divinity. As chapter 1 indicated, the Russians likewise prefer
Schelling over either Kant or Hegel, largely because the trajectory of
his career prioritizes categories other than the strictly rational and
epistemological. We will stipulate Balthasar's complex reception of
Schelling and complicate it even further by introducing and examining
the way he is able to offer a resounding affirmation of the one he names
the "Christian Schelling," that is, Vladimir Soloviev. Berdyaev and Bulgakov receive far less attention in this chapter than Soloviev, but the
former appears briefly as an example of a form of theological aesthetics
that is for Balthasar beyond the pale in its denigration of the finite, and
the latter comes under discussion because of his valuable associations
of beauty with pneumatology.

DIALECTICAL PAIRS IN SCHELLING'S AESTHETICS

In order to draw out profitable comparisons with Soloviev's aesthetics
vis-à-vis Schelling, it is necessary first to provide a brief account of
Schelling's own.[11] Acknowledging that Schelling's specific aesthetic
commitments are parsed somewhat differently through his career, and
that the status of art in his philosophy was, after 1807, knocked from
its high perch of the *System of Transcendental Idealism* (though art
does enjoy unique privilege throughout his career), we shall proceed
to characterize the general contours of a Schellingian aesthetic, providing an impressionistic sketch somewhat in the manner of Balthasar
himself, without overmuch concern for successive shades of development. The works in Schelling's oeuvre most material to his mainly

theoretical philosophical aesthetics are the *System of Transcendental Idealism*, especially the concluding section, "Deduction of a Universal Organ of Philosophy, or: Essentials of the Philosophy of Art according to the Principles of Transcendental Idealism,"[12] the dialogue *Bruno, or, On the Natural and the Divine Principle of Things* (1802), and *The Philosophy of Art* (1859), a text based upon lectures given at the University of Jena from 1802 to 1803. As noted, there are internal developments in his aesthetic system involving, for instance, the mechanics of artistic production, but they cannot be catalogued in full here.[13] In *nuce*, following Kant, Schelling's aesthetics is a *dialectical* project, emerging from the negotiation between finite and infinite, subject and object, human consciousness and unconsciousness, the real and the ideal, and the visible and the invisible as he attempts to locate in his *System* a principle that can fund his transcendental philosophy, address the Kantian distinction between nature and spirit, and make sense of the whole of cognitive processes.[14] Unlike Kant, who assumes an inaccessible transcendent realm in addition to the phenomenal, Schelling's talk of "two realms" as a philosophical monist is essentially artifice. Any separation between real and ideal does not comprise an actual problem that would require transcendental mediation, but this fact can be bracketed for the sake of argument: it is enough that phenomenologically, the aesthetic experience of human beings is felt to be revelatory of a "deeper" reality.[15]

Both Kantian and Schellingian aesthetics have a theoretical, epistemological inflection, rather than an interest in critically analyzing particular works of art, and both are intent on seeking (what turn out to be aesthetic) solutions that negotiate between the "two realms" of real and ideal. Though Schelling's primary interests evolved from his early critiques of the ego philosophy of Fichte, through philosophies of nature, identity, art, freedom, and finally mythology and revelation, the unifying theme that resounds throughout is the relationship between real and ideal, between the finite and the infinite.[16] It is precisely in the negotiation of the aporia between these positions that Balthasar judges the mechanics of Schelling's philosophy as a whole to be aesthetic: "Thus within absolute identity distinction is nevertheless postulated and, being transcended (*aufgehoben*) in its very postulation, if 'transfigured': the Infinite appears in the 'form', while the latter is interpreted and understood with reference to the Infinite. But that is the form of the beautiful. *More so than any other modern philosophy, the philosophy of Schelling, as a philosophy of the balance between the Infinite and the finite, is an aesthetic one.*"[17]

The problem that Schelling calls on aesthetics to solve (echoing Schiller's *Lectures on the Aesthetic Education of Humanity*) is mediation between theoretical philosophy (the rule of knowledge/objectivity/nature) and practical philosophy (the rule of human choice/subjectivity/freedom). Schelling's early appeal to "intellectual intuition" is important in this context, understood in general terms as "the capacity to see the universal in the particular, the infinite in the finite, and indeed to unite both in a living unity."[18] This "seeing" is not a mechanical conceptualization, but rather is an immediate (though nonmystical) insight into the whole of things, into the fundamental unity of the universal and the particular, an insight that firmly resists conceptual explanation.

In his *System of Transcendental Idealism*, Schelling suggests that there are two convictions regarding human knowing that lead to contradiction: first, there is a world "out there" that is independent of human beings but nonetheless allows "that our presentations are so far coincident with it that there is *nothing* else in things save what we attribute to them";[19] in short, that there is a reliable coincidence between appearance and reality, which suggests an unalterability or (over-)determination of things in reality and as they are perceived and known by human beings. According to Schelling, the second conviction appears to contravene the first particularly with respect to this question of determination: namely, that "presentations, arising *freely and without necessity* in us, pass over from the world of thought into the real world, and can attain objective reality."[20]

To put it another way, the first conviction indicates "a dominance of thought (the ideal) over the world of sense; but how is this conceivable [when according to the first conviction] the presentation is in origin already the mere slave of the objective?"[21] This is the central problematic and the "highest task" of Schelling's transcendental philosophy. He argues that the only way that commerce between the objective world and the subjective human experience and presentation of it is intelligible is to posit a "predetermined harmony" between real and ideal, a notion possible only if there is an identity relationship between that which is produced and that which is expressed volitionally. He writes, "Now it is certainly a *productive* activity that finds expression in willing; all free action is productive, albeit *consciously* productive. If we now suppose, since the two activities have only to be one in principle, that the same activity which is *consciously* productive in free action, is productive *without consciousness* in bringing about the world then our predetermined harmony is real, and the contradiction resolved."[22]

This resolution is effected not by means moral or philosophical, but rather by means aesthetic: the "producing" activity is *artistic* production. He needs to appeal to an activity in the self that is both conscious and nonconscious, and, for him, the only possibility is the aesthetic: "The ideal world of art and the real world of objects are therefore products of one and the same activity; the concurrence of the two (the conscious and the nonconscious) *without* consciousness yields the real and *with* consciousness the aesthetic world."[23] Thus, in the *System of Transcendental Idealism*, the appeal to art is not as a subsidiary or simply decorative element of his transcendental philosophy, but as the fundamental, undergirding principle of it: no less than "the universal organon of philosophy—and the keystone of its entire arch."[24] It is the express function of the work of art (and, at this stage of his thinking, *only* the work of art) to disclose the ideal in the real, the infinite in the finite, and thus to indicate the ultimate union of spirit and nature. It is in this sense, perhaps, that despite its fundamental monism, Schellingian aesthetics can be said to be revelatory, that is, it functions to alert the Self to some originary unity between real and ideal to which its attention would otherwise not be drawn.[25]

Schelling's *Bruno* and *The Philosophy of Art* both speak directly to beauty's mediating function as the intersection of the real and the ideal, and to the necessity of both sensible/phenomenal/particular and intelligible/noumenal/universal elements for beauty to exist. Again, art alone has the capacity to combine real and ideal, sensible and intelligible (although in these later works philosophy ultimately displaces art from its premier place in the *System.*) Even though art manifests philosophy in the real realm, it is not philosophy because it has phenomenal form. In his interpretive summation of *Bruno's* concluding pages, John Hendrix notes that

> Beauty is the synthesis of the dialectic, the combination of the two extremes, which are codependent. The task of art is not just to conceive the union of the ideal and real, but then to re-conceive the ideal and real out of that union, to separate them out and differentiate them, to represent eternal beauty and sensible beauty in relation to their union. To do this the artist must represent the infinite and the finite, the eternal and temporal, the actual and possible, and then "we shall grasp how that simple ray of light that shines forth from the absolute and which is the absolute itself appears divided into difference and indifference, into the finite and the infinite."[26]

The Philosophy of Art details the mechanisms of the negotiation of real and ideal according to three *potences* in the real: (1) matter (in the main, the real, being; neither universal nor particular), (2) light (the ideal, activity), and (3) the essence of the real, organism, or "natural form," which "contains the indifference of the real and ideal."[27] For Schelling, these three *potences* of matter, light, and organism have their analogues in the transcendentals of *veritas*, *bonitas*, and *pulchritudo*, respectively.[28] In Schelling's own words, "matter, viewed according to its corporeal appearance rather than in itself, is not substance but rather merely *accidens* (form) with which the essence or the universal within light is juxtaposed."[29] Beautiful forms in art (and, derivatively, in nature) are the result of "the same informing of infinite ideality into the real,"[30] an *Einbildungskraft*.

Moreover, according to Schelling, the artist produces art products that are in excess of what he or she knows consciously, and again it is this product—the work of art itself—that is of premier importance to Schelling, more important even than the artist as creator of it. In the art product is reflected the identity of conscious and unconscious, a "synthesis of nature and freedom";[31] although the artist may begin with a conscious idea, there is always some mysterious element in artistic production that cannot be predicted or even explained by the artist after the fact. Thus (and here we may anticipate Balthasar), fine or high art is the product of the coincidence of freedom and necessity.[32] This aesthetic coincidence of freedom and necessity in the real reappears in *The Philosophy of Art* (§16ff). Artistic or natural forms are beautiful at the meeting of greatest maximals of subjective freedom (creativity, imagination, and so on) and objective necessity (order, custom), "when the dialectic is visible but the ideal predominates over the real."[33] In Schelling's own words, "since only in the ideal world does the antithesis of the universal and the particular, the ideal and the real manifest itself specifically as that between necessity and freedom, the organic product represents that same antithesis still unresolved (because it is not yet developed) that the work of art represents as suspended (in both the same identity)."[34]

The artistic excess of meaning evident in art products—which is indicative of the fact that art presents the infinite in finite form—is discovered through the phenomenon of infinitely or indefinitely multivalent interpretations of (true, nonderivative) works of art (he uses enduring Greek mythology as his example). A work of this caliber is "capable of being expounded *ad infinitum*, as though it contained an infinity of purposes, while yet one is never able to say whether this infinity has lain within the artist himself, or resides only in the work of art."[35] Art, which proceeds from characteristics of both nature and freedom, is a phenomenal (finite) symbol and expression of the infinite Absolute, the means of human coming-to-awareness of the underlying totality and identity of all things, a function that opens up "the holy of holies, where burns in eternal and original unity, as if in a single flame, that which in nature and history is rent asunder."[36] This sort of religious, virtually evangelical language from Schelling appears in an earlier passage in the same text, and in the same context of the realization of the coincidence of freedom and necessity:

> The intelligence will therefore end with a complete recognition of the identity expressed in the product as an identity whose principle lies in the intelligence itself; it will end, that is, in a complete intuiting of itself. Now since it was the free tendency to self-intuition in

that identity which originally divided the intelligence from itself, the feeling accompanying this intuition will be that of infinite tranquility. With the completion of the product, all urge to produce is halted, all contradictions are eliminated, all riddles resolved. Since production set out from freedom, that is, from an unceasing opposition of the two activities, the intelligence will be unable to attribute this absolute union of the two, in which production ends, to *freedom*; so as soon as the product is completed, all appearance of freedom is removed. *The intelligence will feel itself astonished and blessed by this union, will regard it, that is, in the light of a bounty freely granted by a higher nature, by whose aid the impossible has been made possible.*[37]

DIALECTICAL PAIRS IN BERDYAEV'S AESTHETICS

Berdyaev's aesthetics, though somewhat similar to Schelling's insofar as the creative or aesthetic act is a means by which the relation between real and ideal can be negotiated, functions here as an example of what absolutely cannot pass muster for Balthasar, in large part because finitude is not simply denigrated, but is even vilified. The dialectical pairs of real/ideal, finite/infinite, matter/spirit, and freedom/necessity are radicalized drastically in Berdyaev's oppositional relation between the realm of matter and the realm of spirit, which is based on the Kantian distinction between phenomenal and noumenal. Indeed, in *The Beginning and the End*, Berdyaev even rhapsodizes Kant's dualism as "the greatest merit of his philosophy."[38] Unlike Kant, however, Berdyaev understands both realms to be both ontologically real and accessible. For Berdyaev, the realm of spirit is marked by love, creativity, dynamism, personality, freedom, and experience, whereas the realm of nature is characterized by object-ness, necessity, passivity, determination, immobility, disintegration into temporal and spatial divisions, and a decisive separation from the divine. It is the realm of spirit that is *concretely* real, nonabstract.[39] For Berdyaev, the primary impediment to the human being's return to God is this "thingification" of the spirit that occurs on the fallen (that is, phenomenal) world, in which "the living spirit and its living creative cognition must be 'chilled down'—congealed—*coagulated*, for the purposes of day-to-day commerce and administration according to established custom."[40] In keeping with his existentialist commitments and the strong Kantian distinction he maintains between phenomenal and noumenal, Berdyaev actually praises German ego philosophy—in a move that would likely make Balthasar apoplectic—as an essentially *Christian* phenomenon, harshly critiquing systems that suggest any "dependence of man upon the object and upon the world."[41]

In Berdyaev, the means by which commerce can take place between the two realms is, similar to Schelling's aesthetic theory, through an artistic or creative act, an act that "signifies an *ek-stasis*, a breaking through to eternity."[42] The creative act itself is not specifically Christian, though, but is for Berdyaev "beyond Christianity."[43] Though the creative act itself belongs to the noumenal realm, the art product in its finite, circumscribed form belongs to the phenomenal and is therefore a failure.[44] Here, unlike in Schelling, it is the act of ecstatic creativity and not the artwork itself that matters for Berdyaev. Likewise departing from Schelling, he sets these two realms in an antagonistic relationship: "Art is always a victory over the heaviness of 'the world,'" a world that is "deformed, it is not cosmic, beauty is not in it."[45] The world is of a constricting, deadening materiality in which Berdyaev feels ever enslaved.

The creative act is a profoundly eschatological one for Berdyaev, although, in keeping with his strict dualism between spirit and nature, his eschatological reflections seem less about transfiguration of the material world and more about its destruction. For him, the "crowning point of world creation is the end of this world . . . [which] must be dissolved in creative ecstasy."[46] Analogously, as Berdyaev does not seem to recognize a synthetic or balanced relationship between finite and infinite, spirit and nature, and so on, he asserts (showing a debt perhaps to Joachim de Fiore) that "ontology should be *replaced* by pneumatology."[47] This triadic philosophical history culminates in the Age of the Spirit and represents a line of thought that Balthasar absolutely will not countenance. This reserve will be addressed at greater length in the next chapter.

DIALECTICAL PAIRS IN SOLOVIEV'S AESTHETICS

Though Soloviev's work did not include the completion of a robust aesthetic, the conclusion of his doctoral dissertation at St. Petersburg University ("A Critique of Abstract Principles," 1880) does indicate a provisional outline for a proposed treatment of a full aesthetic program. Despite this early turn toward aesthetics, most of his more properly aesthetic essays—"Three Addresses in Memory of Dostoevsky" (published together for the first time in 1884, though composed a bit earlier), "Beauty in Nature" (1889), "The Universal Meaning of Art" (1890), "The Meaning of Love" (1892–1894), and "A First Step toward a Positive Aesthetic" (1894)—were written in approximately the last decade of his life. Despite the thinness, provisionality, and scattered nature of material that speaks directly to Soloviev's aesthetic theory, Balthasar suggests rightly that "everything" in Soloviev's system is oriented toward and supplements his aesthetics.[48]

Again, what matters here is that Solovievian aesthetics is formally quite similar to Schelling's, but is received by Balthasar while Schelling's is not. The first point of resonance with Schelling is that Soloviev's aesthetics is motivated and underwritten by broader philosophical concerns regarding the organic unity of all reality, which is borne only in the whole. The dynamic principle of his aesthetic theory is the notion of *vseedinstvo*, variously translated as "pan-unity," "total-unity," "all-unity," "unity of everything," and the like, a theory that unifies all universal forces, both spiritual and material. It is actualized in three spheres: (1) the material (technical, applied art), (2) the formal (fine arts), and (3) the absolute (mysticism), which unite theurgically in a "single, mystical creative process."[49]

Second, this *vseedinstvo* provides the express content for his understanding of *Idea*/ideality, which in turn funds the quite "formal and specific" meaning of beauty, nonreducible to either the material phenomenon or subjective evaluation.[50] Beauty is the *"embodiment of Idea,"*[51] where "Idea" restricts the content to "that which in itself is worthy of existence."[52] Idea, formally defined as *"the absolute freedom of constituent parts in a perfected unified whole,"*[53] thus has three conditions that must be met for ideality to be realized: "(1) the free-dom or autonomy of existence; (2) the plenitude of content, or mean-ing; and (3) the perfection of expression, or form,"[54] which, like in Schelling, map roughly upon the transcendentals of the true, the good, and the beautiful. The Idea is neither abstract-universal nor incidental-particular, but the expression of both together; relatedly, it is the result of the mutual action and mutual penetration of ideal and material prin-ciples. The consistent concrete example that Soloviev supplies to illus-trate this fundamental aesthetic principle is that of the diamond, which, as a crystallized carbon, materially has the same constitution as ordi-nary coal.[55] The difference for him, as in Schelling, is lucidity, light, in this case "a supra-material, ideal agent,"[56] which interacts with the carbon in such a way that "the ideal principle takes possession of the material fact and is embodied in it; and for its part, the material ele-ment, embodying in itself ideal content, is transformed and becomes resplendent."[57] Light is an important aesthetic principle for Soloviev (again invoking Schelling), insofar as it is the first principle of beauty in nature and the signifier of universal pan-unity. Beauty is located in neither the chemical composition of the diamond nor the light re-fracted through it, but rather is the product of their interaction: it is *"the transformation of matter through the embodiment in it of another, supra-material principle."*[58]

For Soloviev, "an abstract embodiment of spirit incapable of cre-ation and a spiritless matter incapable of animation are both incom-patible with ideal or worthy existence, and both carry upon themselves the manifest sign of their unworthiness in the fact that neither one nor the other can be beautiful."[59] A "plentitude" of beauty requires first that the spiritual essence be directly materialized, second that the material element is completely animated, and third that, in the abso-lutely mutual penetration of matter and spirit, the material phe-nomenon authentically "become[s] beautiful, that is, really having embodied in itself Idea, it should become in the very same way as abiding and immortal as Idea itself."[60] In this way the finite must truly—not only transitorily—have a share in the infinite, and both can retain integrity. The ultimate aim is the aesthetic transfiguration and not (as in Berdyaev) the conflagration of the material world—an interest that safeguards *against* the denigration of matter and sense perception, a charge that has been leveled against him.[61]

Furthermore, in Soloviev, beginning with the natural (even the inorganic), Idea/spirit generates a hierarchy of forms that gain in complexity and ideality through kingdoms Plantae through Animalia, culminating in the form of human being. Soloviev, in his essay "Beauty in Nature,"—revealing his Darwinian influence—addresses the beauty of the sky (solar, lunar, and astral, as well as clouds and rainbows), the water of the sea, the soil, noble metals, precious stones, thunderstorms, plants (including flowers and the algae and mosses of *cryptogamae*), invertebrates (with extended commentary on the lowly worm and the "monstrous phenomenon" of the nematode), fish, birds, and mammals, and finally the human being, who, unlike the animals, can realize the goal of beauty or the embodiment of Idea self-consciously and, "consequently, [labor] over its achievement freely and intelligently."[62] The purpose of the reduplication of beautiful natural forms in art is, according to Soloviev, not a repetition of nature, but rather an extension of the gradual embodiment of spirit begun in the natural world, but unable to be completed in biological forms.[63]

For Soloviev, the teleological (anthropological) end of these natural processes is that the human being as a conscious agent of this universal process can achieve an "ideal goal—a complete, mutual permeation and liberated solidarity of the spiritual and the material, the ideal and the real, the subjective and the objective."[64] Note here that Soloviev recognizes beauty in nature and even considers it to be a precursor to a philosophy of art; this recognition constitutes a departure from Schelling, who considers the forms of nature to be only derivative.[65] The unfulfilled task must be taken up deliberately in the creative, artistic work of human beings, who are participating in the highest task of art: the spiritualization of matter, the "perfected incarnation of . . . spiritual fullness in our reality, a realization in it of absolute beauty."[66]

This perfection, however, can be realized only eschatologically, a feature of Soloviev's thinking redolent of Schelling, which Balthasar affirms enthusiastically.[67] Indeed, Balthasar characterizes Schelling's early philosophy of art eschatologically: "art as the inner fulfillment of science and philosophy, beauty as the eschatological ideal of the history of the world and of [human]kind."[68] Similarly, in the realm of the beautiful, the interaction of matter and idea is fulfilled by the creator of works of art, who participates as the mediator in what is for Soloviev a divine–human cooperation toward the perfection of the world. In Balthasar's estimation, *the* fundamental theme of Solovievian aesthetic theory is "the progressive eschatological embodiment of the Divine Idea in worldly reality; or (since the Divine Spirit is indeed in and for itself the highest reality, while the material being of the world is in itself no more than indeterminacy, an eternal pressure toward and yearning after form) the impress of the limitless fullness and determinacy of God upon the abyss of cosmic potentiality."[69] This, too, is Balthasar's own view of truly great art: it is fundamentally eschatological and anticipatory, the "proleptic appearance of what is ideal, in reality, of 'heaven' on 'earth,' of the fulfillment in the promise,"[70] which facilitates a sense of yearning for that which is coming and becoming. Art, then, functions prophetically, nondidactically: it is a sign of contradiction in the world, a grasping after the infinite and a prophetic anticipation of the life that is to come.[71] According to Soloviev, the essential definition of art is thus as follows: *"every tangible representation of any object and phenomenon from the point of view of its final, definitive status, or in light of the world to come, is artistic work."*[72]

Finally, Soloviev also values preserving the transcendentals in a balanced relationship with Being; like Balthasar, he rehabilitates the common Christian Neoplatonic inheritance of East and West and has an aesthetic commitment to the ontology of symbol—even an entire symbolic economy—while taking into account German Idealist philosophy.[73] Soloviev, also like Balthasar, rejects "l'art pour l'art," or the "pure art" movement, as a "playful game"[74] devoid of objective significance, which radicalizes the claim of aesthetics as autonomous, breeding a destructive, insular "aesthetic separatism" in which the following poor conclusion is reached: "Let the artist be only an artist, think only about excellence aesthetically, about the beauty of form, and let nothing consequential exist for him in the world besides this form."[75] Soloviev lauds Fyodor Dostoevsky's artistic and religious conviction that the transcendentals of truth, goodness, and beauty must be preserved as "three inseparable forms of one absolute Idea,"[76] a commitment that funds Dostoevsky's famous line that beauty will save the world. The self-evaluation of the work of many Russian artists, from icon writer Andrei Rublev to Wassily Kandinsky, as possessing a religious sensibility, or *dukhovnost'*, "meaning that this art was 'lofty,' 'elevated,' having to do with higher rungs of reality,"[77] is pertinent here not only in resistance to "art for art's sake" as unspiritual or *bezdukhovnoe*, but also as this quality provides in its transcendentality a living link between art and religion.[78]

SEEING THE FORM: BALTHASAR'S THEOLOGICAL AESTHETICS

Balthasar shares with Soloviev this interest in recovering the status of beauty as a transcendental with objective, even revelatory significance. The seven-volume *Herrlichkeit*, Balthasar's magisterial theological aesthetics, is a complex tale of mourning for metaphysical aesthetics that makes widespread indictments. This lament elegizes beauty and, more importantly for Balthasar, its theological analogue of glory as steadily declining entities,[79] and calls for the rehabilitation of theology to beauty, an intervention purposed to restore theology to the "main artery which it has abandoned."[80] For Balthasar, the classical and early medieval experience of understanding the world as potentially expressive of the divine and, with that, an interpretation of salvation history within a larger, cosmic context permitted the antique conception of beauty to function as the language in which the revelation of God could be expressed.

The sense in which aesthetics can be revelatory, possessing what Balthasar calls a "theological *a priori*,"[81] is not restricted to the explicitly Christian data of revelation, but extended to antiquity. For Balthasar, in keeping with his strong Logos theology, "all the mythical, philosophical and religious knowledge that Antiquity had of God was always itself theological," insofar as God "was always truly revealed in the cosmos, and the fundamental resolution of human existence was to be found in its transcendence in God as the ground, form and goal of human existence."[82] In short, the antique world got the relation between God and world, transcendence and immanence at least formally right and, in an (or perhaps even *the*) instance of *spolia Aegyptiorum*, provided the conceptual framework for Christianity's own articulation of faith.[83]

According to Balthasar, Aquinas, as one instance of the larger medieval aesthetic of form and splendor, was the last to achieve that fragile balance in which the relation between infinite and finite, God and world, is properly construed and the transcendentals of the true, the good, and the beautiful are maintained in their proper relation to being.[84] This situation, however, rapidly destabilized, first with Scotus's ontotheological articulation of b/Being as univocal and thus open to purely rationalistic constructions or interpretations that would exclude transcendental beauty (extending from Ockham through Suarez to twentieth-century rationalism and scientism), and then again (differently, but no less devastatingly) with Eckhart's identification of Being with God (inverting Aquinas's formula), which not only forecloses the possibility of any "remaining space in which and through which [the Absolute] can become manifest,"[85] but also, especially when a posture of religious devotion is exchanged for one of illicit speculation, enjoins the declining of glory.[86]

The disconnection of the transcendentals from being opens the way for an understanding of aesthetics as being nothing more than pure sensory epiphenomenalism, and the tensions in the dialectical process collapse into identity, as in Mark C. Taylor's *Hiding*: "In the end, it all comes down to a question of skin. And bones. The question of skin and bones is the question of hiding and seeking. And the question of hiding and seeking is the question of detection. Is detection any longer possible? Who is the detective? What is detected? Is there anything left to hide? Is there any longer a place to hide? Can anyone continue to hide? Does skin hide anything or is everything nothing but skin? "Skin rubbing at skin, skin, skin, skin, skin."[87] The rupture of the transcendentals from being initiates the immanentization and consequent ghettoization of modern aesthetics to a separate, rationalistic discipline, "a science confined to a particular area of knowledge"[88] rather than being expressive of the whole, which becomes aestheticism. This bereavement of a metaphysics that had once maintained a dynamic and organic unity between the immanent sciences and the transcendence of Christian revelation leads to an unbalanced state of affairs in which the sciences gain an exclusive superiority and absolutely replace the metaphysical.[89]

Balthasar, the Russians, and the Romantics share this distaste for a formal, scientific "exact aesthetics," unable to account for what exceeds that which is observable empirically and thus gives an incomplete picture, seeing "only a fragment and an aspect of the total object for which worldly beauty is only a 'part', and can thus necessarily offer only 'fragments' and 'aspects' that cannot become a whole."[90] Following after Baumgarten's *Aesthetica* (1750–1758), Balthasar flags Kantian aesthetics as guilty of restricting aesthetics to the finite and immanent, disconnecting it from its proper ontological depth, a philosophy according to which

> reason, taken in its purity, *hovers indeterminately* in its finitude (as interrelationship of finite perception and finite concept) and loses every anchorage in in-finite *esse*. Therefore beauty, whose essence is the pure interrelationship of the powers of the subject (an interrelationship which prescinds from the true and the good), possesses exactly the same indefinite character of the finite in itself which, when the rigour of the ethical imperative wanes and is no longer seen, can at some point lead to the pure play of finite existence in nothingness with itself, a play which is not only disinterested and without purpose (*l'art pour l'art*) but also ultimately lacking in meaning.[91]

There is a native ambiguity of beauty when it is disconnected from the true and the good, when it is not weighted symbolically to the finite, the material; beauty which is either only natural or else disincarnate can be an awful, devilish thing. Balthasar knows this ("no *transcendentale* is more demonic than the *kalon*")[92] as did Soloviev, Dostoevsky, and Bulgakov.[93] In *The Idiot* (1868), for instance, Dostoevsky puts Prince Myshkin in the awkward position of deciding between two beautiful women, and the Prince replies, "It is difficult to pass judgment on beauty. I'm afraid I am not ready yet. Beauty is a riddle." Balthasar glosses this passage by suggesting that "beauty is in no way a straightforward transparency for the divine: it can just as easily be a mask and sacrament of the devil,"[94] echoing Dmitri Kara-mazov's judgment on the terrible, mysterious nature of beauty, the very site on which God fights with the devil, in which the human heart is the battlefield.

According to Balthasar, Christianity should dialogue with revela-tory transcendental aesthetics but eschew a "partial aesthetics" that is restricted only to the mundane.[95] The double threat of the Renaissance, which challenged the element of a specifically Christian glory, and the Reformation, which by a focus on the particularity of biblical glory alone threatened the munificent sense of all-cosmic beauty, induced a crisis for the organicity of the relation between beauty and divine glory. According to Balthasar's narrative, this interest in reconciling or even identifying (a by now deeply self-conscious) aesthetic theory and Christian revelation reemerges in German Idealism and Romanticism and at the very least instigates a *krisis*, which poses the question of "whether the aesthetic element, which in Idealism and Romanticism appears as wholly secularized, could not be purified and salvaged by a consideration of its historical origins, or: whether now the only alter-native left is to abandon the aesthetic totally, a way which we have investigated in the previous sections on the elimination of aesthetics from theology. That a theology deprived of aesthetics is far from sat-isfactory should have become obvious by now."[96] Needless to say, Bal-thasar does not abandon aesthetics. The theological a priori (though much less determinate) is for Balthasar evident in antiquity (steeped in the epiphanous) but also to the "speculative aesthetics from Kant, through Schiller, Goethe, and Hölderlin to Schelling, to Romanticism and to Hegel and the variety of post-Hegelian hangers-on."[97] It will, however, prove necessary to acknowledge the important distinction between *revelatory* (of an unspecified transcendent) and, say, *Revela-tory* (of, for instance, Christ or the Trinity) and to ask with Balthasar whether or not, with respect to "speculative aesthetics,"

> such philosophical aesthetics [can] be justified in the face of the theological *a priori* of Antiquity, to which it still for the most part appeals (in part against Christianity)? Further: can this aesthetics

recover the fundamental presupposition, common to Antiquity and Christianity, that reality as such, being itself, is *kalon*, radiant goodness, glory endlessly to be affirmed? And if it no longer has the power, what can such an aesthetics have to say? If the transcendental *kalon* is to be removed from being, why then is being any better than non-being? If we have come to a period which no longer has any answer to this question, then the beauty that we meet with within the world will sooner or later be stripped of its radiance and worth; and even where it is still perceived it will simply be classified pleasant, as a mere quality of nature, to which one has no sooner succumbed, than in that very moment on has seen through it. Aesthetics then becomes an epiphenomenon of psychology and relinquishes any claim to being a philosophical discipline.[98]

In Balthasar's case, theological aesthetics must be supremely content-rich: it is, in fact, the perception of the revealed form of Christ, who is the primary object of vision, and not necessarily artistic production as such: thus, Balthasar's system of aesthetics is in the theological sense decisively revelatory.[99] The Balthasarian concept of *Gestalt*, which also derives in part from the particular sort of Romanticism of Goethe, functions as a signpost of the numinous; it has an ontological, pointing function. Beauty for Balthasar is "the inexplicable active irradiation of the center of being into the expressive surface of the image, an irradiation that reflects itself in the image and confers upon it a unity, fullness, and depth surpassing what the image as such contains."[100] Indeed, the appearance of form only has currency as a beautiful thing because it is the reflection of that which *is*, an expression of reality itself, and "this manifestation and bestowal reveal themselves to us as being something infinitely and inexhaustibility valuable and fascinating."[101] The form, as Balthasar describes it, is a participation in the totality of being, in infinitude itself.

In his foreword to the first volume of *The Glory of the Lord*, Balthasar indicates, following medieval Neoplatonism, that beauty is objectively located at the complementary junction of *species* and *lumen*, or "form" and "splendor," and that this happy meeting is characterized by the simultaneous moments of beholding and being enraptured, each of which is a condition of the possibility for the other.[102] This form-and-splendor aesthetic, recurring in some sense in Goethe's elaboration of the *Urphänomen*, has great precedence in medieval aesthetics rooted in Christian Neoplatonism, and particularly in Bonaventure's notion of "expression."[103] For Balthasar, the complementary relationship between form and splendor, or interior luminosity, is evident insofar as in the perception of beauty the perceiver encounters coincidently the *Gestalt/Gebilde* and "that which shines forth from the figure, making it into a worthy, a love-worthy thing."[104] It is precisely the fact that this luminosity is expressed organically from *within* the interior of the form, and not from without or from above, that mediates against dualism between *species* and *lumen*.

Unlike in Berdyaev, for Balthasar there is no dualism or competitive relation between form and splendor, matter and spirit. The originary "primal phenomenon" of beauty is exhibited neither in "a disembodied spirit which looks about for a field of expression and, finding one, adjusts it to its own purposes as one would set up a typewriter and begin typing, afterwards to abandon it."[105] Nor is beauty simply a collection or collocation of material forces without spirit. Much as in the case with the Idealists and Romantics, to whom Balthasar (and the Russians) owe no small debt, "spirit" in Balthasar's aesthetics ever seeks expression in the material. Preserving the typewriter analogy, Balthasar continues,

> The freedom of the spirit that is at home in itself, therefore, is simultaneous with the "keyboard," which it has appropriated and which allows the spirit self-expression. Such simultaneity is possible because *it is the spirit's native condition always to have gone outside itself in order to be with another*. This ability can only exist in a tension between deliberate choice and spontaneity between a firm rootedness in its own particular field of expression and despite this the spontaneous ability to emerge from the inner depths and to appear in the windows of the specific, individual response. As we proceed from plant to animal to man, we witness a deepening of this interiority, and, at the same time, along with the continuing organic bonds to a body, a deepening in the freedom of the expressive play of forms.[106]

The simultaneous commitment to spirit and matter, and the gradual, teleological embodiment of spirit/Idea in progressively advanced finite forms evident in this passage sound both Schellingian and Solovievian.[107]

Moreover, the form of revelation in salvation history is the presentation of the depths of God; it could not have been invented or predicted, nor could the tiniest element be altered. Indeed, "the weights have been poised in such a way that their balance extends to infinity, and they resist any displacement."[108] Like the particular necessity that obtains in a classic work of art, God's free movement in human history could not have been otherwise:

> In the last analysis, this is not a vague "appropriateness" which would also leave room for other diametrically opposed solutions; rather, it is the recognition that in the apparently non-necessary elements of revelation's historical data there is also revealed the rightness of the divine dispositions and decisions as the expression of the divine Being itself. Leaving open other possibilities, which are always God's prerogative *de potentia absoluta*, is in this context but faith's act of homage to the divine freedom, which is manifested together with the divine necessity; but such openness is in no way a calling into question of the theological necessity. This state of things is best explained by analogy with aesthetic judgment which registers with admiration the aesthetic necessity in the free creations of art: that they must be just so and not otherwise.[109]

Here it is instructive to compare the mechanics of the construal of the unity of necessity and freedom in Balthasar, who owes far more to Irenaeus and Anselm, to that in Schelling, for whom the coincidence is within a thoroughly aesthetic register.[110] Balthasar, like Schelling, has commented extensively upon the aesthetic phenomenon of the coincidence of freedom and necessity, insofar as the best fine art products express both maximal necessity in the finest details and a deep artistic freedom that the work itself need not have existed at all. Classic works of art are by definition irreproachable, utterly unique, appearing "like inexplicable miracles and spontaneous irruptions on the stage of history."[111] As a whole and in the composition of its parts they are marked by "strict givenness":

With a certain contrast to the forms of expression of the beauty of nature, the element of freedom holds sway in human expression, and therefore in all beauty of art. Certainly the forms of nature in their inscrutable emergence from the ground of life are never simply released by a mechanical necessity; they too are "freedom manifesting itself" (*erscheinende Freiheit*—Schiller). *In human self-expression, in its highest form in the work of art, the will to express itself not only freely creates suitable form; it incarnates in this very form its freedom.* It is only that which gives to the form the radiance from the depths. . . . *The true artist is not so subject to the necessity of creating that he does not preserve sovereign freedom in the choice of form.* Goethe could write his *Iphigenie* both in prose and in verse, and no-one can know whether he could not have made of his *Werther* just as good a play, or whether the fashioning of *Hyperion* in verse would not have produced a wholly effective work. What a sovereign freedom in the use of individual themes, individual harmonies, even of complete pieces there is in Bach and Mozart. . . . In the case of the beautiful it is not primarily the immanent harmony of number and proportion that is enjoyed, but the considered freedom which is manifested in it and is "necessitated."[112]

Structurally speaking (if we may bracket his faith commitments to a theologically rich content from Scripture and tradition), Balthasar's aesthetic theory—the infinite mediated through the finite in a manner that not only elicits wonder, but is likewise characterized by the synthesis of freedom and necessity—is not terribly far from the German Romantic articulation of the processes by which the aesthetic is experienced.[113] Indeed, the glory of God (*Herrlichkeit*) is described precisely as "the divinity of the Invisible, which radiates in the visibleness of Being of the world."[114] For Balthasar, the aesthetic as the concrete expression of spirit in the world is that which mediates between infinite and finite, immanent and transcendent.

A fundamental Balthasarian *desideratum* for the success of a theological aesthetics of glory, however, is a commitment to the *analogia entis* (Przywara being the great influence here), in language that both reflects his Ignatian principle of *Deus semper maior* and borrows from the fourth Lateran council of 1215, "the ever great dissimilarity to God no matter how great the similarity to Him."[115] A proper understanding of the *analogia entis*—and translated to our analysis, the "dialectical" pairs—requires as a general hermeneutical principle a simultaneous obligation to sameness and difference, and to a sense of dynamic proportion between the similar and the dissimilar in order to preserve with integrity the infinite and finite, God and world, immanence and transcendence, and so on.[116] According to Balthasar, the identity thinking characteristic of German Idealism (for instance, Fichte's *Ich*, Schelling's *Identitätsphilosophie*, or Hegel's *Geist*) proceeds from the *identitas entis* rather than the *analogia entis*. It appropriates all things— God, the human subject, creation—to a formula of the absolute, divine "I," and *Herrlichkeit* denigrates to *Selbstherrlichkeit*.[117] Note here that Balthasar's generous account of the pervasiveness of the light of God's self-manifestation, which falls upon all human beings, certainly does not exclude that the moment of genuinely free artistic creation that Schelling so rhapsodically described might indeed be suffused with a kind of grace. It is even possible that this sort of exalted artistic production "more or less explicitly indicate[s] an attitude of obedience toward the light of the self-revealing God."[118] This hidden truth, however, does not ultimately militate against the constitutive Titanism of Schelling's aesthetics, for at the very moment of what ought to be a self-abandonment to God, "the place of redemption by God is taken by a titanic kind of self-redemption."[119] There is no longer space for the manifestation of divine glory and thus for an authentic maximally Christian aesthetics: only the possibility of an ever-immanent philosophy of beauty, "aesthetics as science" remains.[120]

So, despite apparent structural similarities (along with the elements in Schelling's thought to which Balthasar would be sympathetic, namely, understanding the beautiful in light of the totality of things, a coincidence of the transcendentals, a sense of wonder elicited from the experience of the Absolute, and so on), Balthasar is absolutely uncompromising in his judgment that the monistic thought of Schelling operates from first to last according to the *identitas entis*;[121] the gap closes between infinite/Absolute "I" and human being, and "the world and man can in the end be nothing more than the goal of its Odyssean voyage of self-discovery."[122] Furthermore, unlike Schelling, Balthasar translates the phenomenon of the aesthetic synthesis of the maximally free and the maximally necessary into decisively theological terms: in short, to revelation. As suggested above, Balthasar's account owes much to the traditional theological idea of aesthetic verisimilitude articulated, for instance, in the Anselmian notion of concordance, proportionality, and fittingness.[123] The givenness of revelation, with an elegance that far exceeds the mundane instances of high art or mathematical principles, is the personal self-disclosure of the Trinitarian being of God, expressions of inexhaustible divine freedom that could not have been predicted but must, by their perfect harmony, simply be so. The vision of divine revelation is such that "what it can perceive of necessity within it is only a fragment which nevertheless clearly contains within itself a guarantee of the meaning of the whole."[124] The quality of the whole, however, cannot be reconstituted simply by adding the parts together; contemplating the mystery of Christ "traces a course back into the very mystery of God, who manifests his 'mystery, more dazzling than the light' by this stroke of 'christological genius.'"[125]

In sum, Balthasar is hardly demure when it comes to distancing his project of a decidedly *theological* aesthetics from secular philosophical aesthetics. For him, it is a dangerous and ill-advised game to qualify or quantify revelation in terms of preexisting philosophical categories: theological aesthetics is governed by God's sovereign freedom, not philosophical abstraction; it never "descend[s] to the level of an inner-worldly aesthetics."[126] For Balthasar, theological aesthetics, in *nuce*, is a theology that does not avail itself of "extra-theological categories of a worldly philosophical aesthetics (above all poetry), but which develops its theory of beauty from the data of revelation itself with genuinely theological methods."[127] The emphasis on Schelling here is not, then, to suggest that Balthasar is actually—despite his own explicit protestations to the contrary—participating in the same kind of project as secular philosophical aesthetics, or that he is only adding on the Christological proviso to strengthen a wobbly philosophical foundation. It must be perfectly clear at the outset that Balthasar's theological aesthetics begins and ends with "the transfigured, blood-stained features of Jesus Christ where the glory of God streams forth as the beauty of the love that will save the world."[128] Thus, it is precisely *glory*—the properly theological analogue of beauty—that is for Balthasar the premier concern. Though Balthasar certainly avails himself of more subsidiary forms (the beauty of nature, human culture, human institutions [marriage, primarily], the saints), he is concerned most particularly with Jesus Christ as the *Ur-form*.

A COMPLEX RECEPTION

Given Balthasar's strong allergy to secular aesthetic theology, it is interesting that though Schelling's aesthetic theory—as monist, Promethean, and complicit in the "eclipse of glory"—is ultimately unsatisfactory (though not absolutely uninformative) for Balthasar, Soloviev's purification of him in his articulation of a "universal theological aesthetics—a vision of God's coming to be in the world"[129]—is fairly decisively affirmed. Indeed, Balthasar proposes, rather hyperbolically, that "Soloviev's skill in the technique of integrating all partial truths in one vision makes him *perhaps second only to Thomas Aquinas* as the greatest artist of order and organization in the history of thought. There is no system [including, presumably, Schelling's] that fails to furnish him with substantial building material, once he has stripped and emptied it of the poison of its negative aspects."[130] Moreover, for Balthasar, Schelling's influence on Soloviev is actually beneficial *rather than detrimental* insofar as his version of Idealism expanded the latter's universal vision beyond narrowly specified forms exclusive to Eastern Christianity.[131] Balthasar characterizes Soloviev as a religious thinker "of universal genius" who is capable of bringing valuable concepts from Idealist philosophy into the Christian fold as he engages sources from the Eastern patristic tradition through to Dostoevsky, Tolstoy, and Leontiev.[132]

Importantly, Balthasar puts Soloviev directly in the genealogical line (preceded, it must be noted, by Origen) of the cosmic liturgy of Maximus the Confessor, who, according to Balthasar, permits simultaneously speculation and a mooring to traditional resources. For Balthasar, it is Maximus rather than Schelling who is Soloviev's "true starting point," especially insofar as the Chalcedonian dogma of the hypostatic union of divine and human in Christ (Soloviev's *bogoche-lovechestvo*, Godmanhood, or "Divine-Humanity") provides "the foundation upon which the entire structure of natural and supernatural reality in the world is erected"[133] to which the (here, again, salutary) dynamism of German Idealism is added.[134] The Maximian influence on Soloviev is textually supported by Soloviev's article on Maximus in the Russian *Brockhaus-Efron* encyclopedia (published between 1890 and 1907) in which Soloviev suggests that Maximus is "the most significant philosophical spirit in the Christian East after Origen, the only significant philosopher of that era in the whole Christian world, the link between Hellenic Christian theosophy and the mediaeval philosophy of the West."[135] It is likewise important that Balthasar suggests in his *Cosmic Liturgy* that Maximus anachronistically is the Christian antidote to Hegel, a point Soloviev speaks to as well in his article.[136] As Balthasar notes, the entirely theological starting point of Maximus, even as he engages with philosophical thought, is "luminously open," insofar as his ontological and cosmological speculations extend directly from his Christology "in that the synthesis of Christ's concrete person is not only God's final thought for the world but also his original plan."[137] According to Balthasar, Soloviev's antidote takes effect in remedies Christological, Chalcedonian, and Maximian. Indeed, the agreement between Balthasar and the Russians is facilitated in no small part by this common acceptance of Maximus.[138]

What separates Soloviev decisively from Schelling for Balthasar is the central position of the Incarnation of Christ for aesthetics, particularly as controlled by Chalcedonian dogma.[139] Christ is the *hen-kai-pan* and the "opening up . . . of the limited, finite spirit to . . . total plenitude."[140] According to Balthasar, this syzygy between real and ideal in Christ, "the encounter between a divine reality, understood in its maximal, most concrete fullness, and a human and worldly reality, taken equally in its maximal concrete fullness,"[141] is what both motivates and constrains Soloviev's aesthetics, a theological obligation with which Balthasar has much sympathy.[142] This commitment to the fact that the ideal "is always [God's] own reality, and it is this reality that draws the still imperfect creation, existing for itself alone, home to himself,"[143] exempts Soloviev from solving the aporia of whether the beautiful is located in the ideal realm or whether "ideality eternally include[s] reality in itself."[144] Balthasar further exempts Soloviev's theosophical religious philosophy from the destructive elements of German Idealism, due in no small part to the way in which he parses the relation between freedom and necessity with respect to Christian revelation. Because for Soloviev the interventions of God in human history are supremely free and comprise "a revelation of the highest kind of rationality surpassed by nothing else," the witness of revelation—naturally, historically, and even protologically—is fully intelligible and "must" be exactly as it is, in a repetition of the Anselmian version of *necessitates*.[145] In Balthasar's theological aesthetics, too, it is necessary that the coincidence of real and ideal be concretized in the archetype of the perfectly free Christ.

Schelling's deep identification of subject and object can thus only be resolved in the person of Christ, who is for Balthasar the concrete *analogia entis*, the "bridge between infinite and finite, between absolute glory and absolute adoration, the mediator of the religious act. Ontologically and psychologically, He is the full reality of analogy."[146] Here again, analogy rather than identity must govern, as the latter perspective would render Christ, as coincident with "the philosophical relationship between God and man, indeed between the Infinite and the finite,"[147] transposable with, as Balthasar wryly notes, Schiller's *Deutsche Größe*. Christ is for Balthasar not only the "unique, hypostatic union between archetype and image,"[148] but also (in Bonaventurean turn of phrase) "*God as expression*, that is, as truth, and therefore he is the principle of the fact that the things in creation have been expressed and of the fact that they express themselves as created essences."[149] The genuine union of finite and infinite that exceeds a self-abolishing dialectical process is possible only when God (impossibly!) reveals God's Self as Trinity in the visible form of Christ the Logos. In the light of faith, Schelling's attempt to synthesize real and ideal, finite and infinite with rationalistic, simply logical speculation is therefore insufficient.[150] For Soloviev (as well as Dostoevsky), Christ as incarnate beauty is the absolutely foundational premise.[151] Because Christ is "God's greatest work of art,"[152] the full expression of both divinity and perfect humanity, the finite, immanent forms of beauty in the created world can be welcomed in all their diversity. Indeed, this very diversity and richness of beautiful forms in the good world is testimony to "the transcendental origin of the beautiful."[153] Finally, as we shall see in a subsequent chapter, it is the Christian doctrine of bodily resurrection of the dead that preserves and protects the finite from a totalizing absorption into the infinite.[154]

A "MOCK-BATTLE" AND THE HOLY FOOL

In his judgment that the classical aesthetics of antiquity and of the eighteenth and nineteenth centuries are concerned with beauty and are in some degree revelatory of the divine (but both deficient vis-à-vis authentically Christian revelation), Balthasar appeals to forms of the antique world and those of the nineteenth century, the latter of which, in an image borrowed from Goethe, has retained "the fleeing garments of beauty, which are the contours of the ancient world as it dissolves,"[155] in order to revitalize a robust conception of beauty and restore it to its rightful, original place at the creative center of theological reflection. It is certainly true—as Mongrain suggests—that Balthasar prioritizes classical aesthetics as the more natural companion to theology, since, insofar as it is cosmocentric and other-centered (that is, on the gods) rather than anthropocentric and self-centered (that is, on the human being *as* god, or as god-maker), it is more amenable to Christian thinking.[156]

Certainly, the failures of Romanticism in general and Schelling in particular are well documented in Balthasar's relentless analysis of the disastrous waning of the category of glory in the twentieth century. In the context of analyzing Johann Gottfried Herder's works, Balthasar speaks of "the great amphiboly between pantheism and Christianity that pervades the whole age, from Fichte and Schelling to Hegel: the fluid identification of the natural and the supernatural which both 'humanized' Christianity and failed to hear its true message."[157] Further, in his critique of Catholic Romantic Alois Gügler's *Die heilige Kunst*, Balthasar identifies two hazards—monistic identity thinking and the mistaken equation of nature and spirit with nature and grace—that are

Gügler's own and also belong pervasively to his age (1782–1827), especially to Fichte and to Schelling.[158] Further, though Gügler's theological reflections on art ought to be counted among "the most significant achievements of Catholic Romanticism,"[159] he failed to communicate adequately the *analogous* nature of his reflections. This muddying of the distinction between creation and revelation constitutes for Balthasar "a deep theological inadequacy" and the fundamental failure of Romantic theology, however well-meaning.[160]

The assertion that classical aesthetics is Balthasar's "primary dialogue partner,"[161] however, may need further texture. Indeed, as we have seen, German Idealist and Romantic aesthetics—in part undiluted and in part filtered through the Russians—is operative in Balthasar's own formulation and performance of his theological aesthetics, though never does Balthasar capitulate to the Titanism of the Romantics. Further, Balthasar elaborates a more receptive version of Romanticism illustrated especially by the figure of Goethe, who is capable of mediating between antiquity and modernity, and—partially, but not totally— contravening the Promethean hubris of someone such as Schelling. Ultimately, however, both Classical forms and Romantic forms fail.

A strong dichotomy between Classicism and Romanticism that suggests a privileging of one at the expense of the other is overstated, as they are for Balthasar far from competing sources. Berdyaev likewise considers the distinction between Classicism and Romanticism to be "a wrongly-stated and, indeed, an imaginary problem."[162] Balthasar's simultaneous commitment to (and simultaneous ambivalence toward) Classical forms and Romantic forms indicates that strong claims regarding valuations of their respective divergences are misguided.[163] Balthasar simply does not decide between them. He writes, "In different periods of intellectual history . . . one or the other . . . aspects may be emphasized: on the one hand, classical perfection (*Vollendung*: the form which contains the depths), on the other, Romantic boundlessness, infinity (*Unendlichkeith*: the form that transcends itself by pointing beyond to the depths). Be this as it may, however, *both aspects are inseparable from one another, and together they constitute the fundamental configuration of Being.*"[164] As is evident from this passage, Balthasar explicitly connects the inseparability of these features of

Classicism and Romanticism to the (similarly noncompetitive) fundamental concepts of form and splendor, a dual commitment that ensures both approaches and forms are kept in play.

For instance, Balthasar's serious reservations regarding the Promethean humanism of Romanticism do not preclude him from emphasizing the triumphs of Goethe (among others, Hölderlin included). Goethe's singular version of Romantic aesthetics, itself uncomfortable with the excesses of Idealism, certainly informed Balthasar's own project decisively.[165] According to Balthasar, Goethe offers a "double front" against Kant and Schiller on the one hand and Schelling on the other, tempering (though not totally absolving) the Titanism that generally characterizes Romanticism by limiting the power of human being with respect to nature.[166] His elaboration of the *Urphänomen*— the luminous, originary, primordial phenomenon of being evident in finite forms—is amenable to Balthasar's recuperation of the medieval form–splendor aesthetic. Balthasar's affirmation of Goethe provides another instance of the easy freedom he employs vis-à-vis cultural sources. He will not affirm Goethe's ultimately humanist allegiances against Christianity, but there is much in Goethe's ontology that recommends itself, including a high valuation of concrete phenomena, the sense that finite beings exist ec-statically, and an openness to mystery and being, and Balthasar is not embarrassed to say so.

All this notwithstanding, Balthasar finds both Classicism and Romanticism fundamentally wanting with respect to his own theological project, in which the moment of the beautiful ought to function first as a reference to the Christ-event, and for Balthasar, "there can be no simple recipe for getting this right. Neither distortion nor elegance, neither Romanticism nor Classicism . . . can claim a fundamental preeminence."[167] Again,

> the "battle between the ancients and the moderns" is a mock-battle, which obscures the real intellectual and historical points of engagement. The decision falls uniquely—and the history of the modern period has no clearer result—for or against the Glory of Being, and history has fashioned the Either-Or so simply that it has become a decision between Christianity and nihilism. The "gods," the "di-

vine" hold sway still only where God's personal love in the Son of God is recognized and acknowledged, and the storming-ahead of metaphysical speculation is bridled only where thought—in the same epiphany—confronts the not-to-be-mastered majestic freedom of the God of love.[168]

Classicism gives undue pride of place to the cosmos; Romanticism to the human being. Thus, neither Classicism nor Romanticism is more or less adequate to the theological task.

Our thesis of compatibility and resonance between Balthasar and the Russians is strengthened at least obliquely by the fact that Balthasar's tertium quid—and the culmination of his theological aesthetics—offered beyond Classicism and Romanticism, those two "great attempts in the modern age to reduce glory to beauty,"[169] is the phenomenon of the holy fool, which arguably reached its apogee in Russian literature and religious culture, and is found according to Balthasar in its most perfect elaboration in Dostoevsky's *The Idiot*. Neither Classicism nor Romanticism has the natural advantage, but it is preeminently the Russian Dostoevsky who gestures toward and even achieves literarily a (partial) corrective, though even the "thrown-ness of the fool" is not enough to "claim to conquer as a whole the world and existence therein."[170] In the post-sacred world, Balthasar suggests that the metaphysics of the saints in their often radical self-abandonment to God (*Gelassenheit*) cannot be communicated adequately (in art or literature) as the "canonical image" of human being because "the heart of sanctity, abandonment in transcendence to the open will of God, cannot be put into epic or dramatic form."[171] It is rather, those foolish, preposterous tropes of buffoonery in art and literature, such as Wolfram von Eschenbach's *Parzival*, Erasmus's *The Praise of Folly*, Cervantes's *Don Quixote*, Hans Jakob Christoffel von Grimmelshausen's *Simplicissimus*, the clown-Christ paintings of Georges Rouault, and, climactically and vitally, Dostoevsky's Prince Myshkin, who capture more adequately the Christian experience.[172] Even if it is unconscious, Balthasar sees in the fool some degree of sanctity, because the fool is vulnerable and open to God in a way that the clever or even the scrupulously moral are not. The holy fool is in his vulnerability for

Balthasar "*the unprotected man*, essentially transcendent, open to what is above him. . . . Since he is never quite 'in his right mind,' never quite 'all there,' he lacks the ponderousness that would tie him down to earth. He stands nearest to the saint, often nearer than the morally successful man preoccupied with his perfection. The Russians knew that the fool belongs to God, has his own guardian angel, and is worthy of veneration."[173] In particular, these figurations of the holy fool point definitively to Jesus Christ, to "the night of God's Wisdom broken in folly on the cross."[174]

This cruciform love, as the form of Trinitarian existence, is absolutely central to Balthasar's theological aesthetics, a feature that departs decisively especially from the aesthetic theology of Idealism and Romanticism. As Georges de Schrijver comments, with respect to the aesthetics of Kant, Fichte, Schelling, and Nietzsche, Balthasar assesses their understanding of beauty as both "too tragic, and also too artificial, to be the revelation of the moving beauty of the God who is Love who, under the deformed traits of his Suffering Servant, comes to share human misery. Neither the high and mighty status of Prometheus the ravisher nor the tragic personality of Dionysius broken by his rapture, bears comparison with the divine-human figure in whom the unnamed God speaks his name, by way of the radiance of his grace and glory of his kenosis."[175]

Balthasar's theological aesthetics has been criticized for "an unacceptable exalted character since it pays no attention to ugliness,"[176] but this judgment is simply not accurate. How else could it be, for an aesthetic with the dark kernel of the cross of Christ at its center, which becomes for Balthasar not the exception to but the very model for aesthetics? The Christian aesthetic of glory is certainly not identical to cultural beauty, but is instead counterintuitive, capable of embracing "the most abysmal ugliness of sin and hell by virtue of the condescension of divine love, which has brought even sin and hell into that divine art for which there is no human analogue."[177] The nocturnal elements of suffering and cross are transfigured to become "precisely the critical touchstones of love and glory."[178] To ignore the tragic and nocturnal elements of life is to operate according to a principle of "aestheticism," which attempts to systematize and explain away that which is patently unsystematic and inexplicable.[179] According to Balthasar, it is the trope of the holy fool, particularly Dostoevsky's Prince Myshkin, which best anticipates but is far superseded by Jesus, the "gentle divine Idiot on the cross [who] silently contains everything in himself and imprints on everything His form, the form of the divine mercy, for which it is a matter of sublime indifference whether its glory is manifested invisibly in earthly beauty or in ugliness."[180]

SPIRIT AND BEAUTY IN SERGEI BULGAKOV

The Christological is central to Balthasar's aesthetics, but this centrality does not exclude the work of the Holy Spirit. We have seen that in the negotiation between spirit and matter, it is important to Balthasar not only to protect the integrity of each, but, where appropriate, to specify a distinction between the divine, personal being of the Holy Spirit and what is only the "empty impersonal transcendence of one's own spirit."[181] The preeminent Russian representative of a pneumatological perspective in this analysis, particularly one that is inflected aesthetically,[182] is Bulgakov, with whom Balthasar shares a great deal. It is striking indeed to compare Bulgakov's *The Comforter* (1936) side by side with the third volume of Balthasar's *Theo-Logic, The Spirit of Truth* (1987), whose treatment of common themes—for instance, the Ireanean "dyad" of Son and Spirit,[183] the rather conciliatory take on the *filioque*, a Trinitarian interpretation of *kenosis*, and most germane here, an identification of the Holy Spirit with beauty—suggest that although Balthasar references Bulgakov by name only six times in the volume, his influence is far more pervasive than not.[184]

For Bulgakov, the entire creative process is parsed pneumatologically: as the *only* source of creativity, the Holy Spirit has been long at work in the pagan articulations of poetry and beauty.[185] The Holy Spirit, almost rhapsodically, is "the Artist of the world, the Principle of form and the Form of forms. . . . The beauty of the world is an effect of the Holy Spirit, the Spirit of Beauty; and Beauty is Joy, the joy of being."[186] Balthasar likewise relates the Holy Spirit to beauty, citing Nicholas of Cusa approvingly with respect to the belief that beauty "is the intradivine glory whose authentic place is the Holy Spirit,"[187] although it is the Son (or, sometimes, the entire Trinitarian economy) who seems in Balthasar's account—which has a Christological center and a Trinitarian horizon—to undergird theological aesthetics. For Balthasar, the primary aesthetic role of the Holy Spirit is to assist the perceiver/believer in authentically *seeing*—after all, "it is the Spirit who gives believers eyes to discern God's revelation as an integral, organically differentiated form"[188]—the beauty of the mystery of the Christ-form.[189] For Bulgakov, too, more than capacitating natural or artistic beauty, the Trinitarian role of the Holy Spirit is to reveal the Father not as content (which is for the Son), but as the mode of actualizing the content of the Word of God precisely as beauty.[190]

Furthermore, as was the case with Soloviev, material forms are for Bulgakov ever in the process of being spiritualized by the Holy Spirit through the sanctification (sacramental or otherwise) of "cosmic matter."[191] Bulgakov comments on the sophiological phenomenon of the beauty of natural forms, which, as in his intellectual predecessor Soloviev, await their eventual actualization, or humanization brought about by "spirit-bearing" human being.[192] Nature itself, however, even prior to this transformation, is spirit-bearing itself (Psalm 19:1), having been infused with the "sophianicity" of the Holy Spirit, and as spirit-bearing, "nature is also, in this sense, God-bearing—and it is such not only by its boundless content but also by that ineffable and rationally unfathomable beauty which delights, nourishes, freshens, and fills the soul."[193] For Bulgakov, there is no such thing as a "dead" nature that would resist or be naturally uncongenial to the possibility of material spiritualization, sanctification, the unification of matter and spirit. The human being, after all, is a spirit incarnate in the world, defying any attempt to oppose spirit and matter as competitive principles.[194]

In his reflective piece "The Holy Grail" (1932) Bulgakov renders beautifully the moment at which Christ's side is pierced, when the finite earth itself becomes

> the Holy Grail, for it has received into itself and contains Christ's precious blood and water. The whole world is the chalice of Christ's blood and water; the whole world partook of them in communion

at the hour of Christ's death. . . . One can say that the world that has received Christ into itself, that has received Christ's body and carries him within itself, has *retained* within itself his corporeality after his death and Resurrection with Ascension. And this humanity of Christ's invisibly lives in the world and is inwardly transfiguring the world toward a new heaven and a new earth.[195]

Again, for Bulgakov there is no real sense in which spirit and matter are opposed; rather, through the work of the Holy Spirit, matter itself is already a dynamic force capable of spiritualization (though this capacity does admit of degrees).[196] It is the human flesh of Christ that has transfigured the material of the world in a cooperative activity with the Spirit, continually ratified through Christ's sinlessness (permitting a complete transparence to the Spirit), the descent of the Spirit at baptism, on the mount of Transfiguration, and at the Resurrection.[197] Through this and in participation in the sacraments, the human being receives this matter, this "substratum for divine life . . . [which] is integrated into the fullness of [human] essence, into . . . spiritual and corporeal being."[198] Here, then, finitude is decisively affirmed, which is one of the nonnegotiable desiderata for Balthasar on all fronts.

THE RILKEAN CLAUSE

The aesthetic-eschatological transfiguration of the world toward a new heaven and a new earth, observed in the Russian representatives who write under the mantle of Dostoevsky's claim that beauty must save the world, is hardly a one-sided affair. According to Bulgakov (and Schelling, of course, is not far away), genuine art is something of a frontier, *methorios* phenomenon, lying on the boundary between two realms in its capacity for expressing in concrete terms its perception of nonnative beauty. First, beauty is impotent if its sole purpose is to entertain the senses and not to transfigure the world: evoking Dostoevsky, "if beauty once saved the world, then art must prove itself an instrument of this salvation."[199] In short, for Soloviev, Berdyaev, and Bulgakov, the artistic or creative process is and must be *theurgic*, that is, involving the cooperation of the divine and the human. The status of this cooperative endeavor for each thinker, however, is a bit different.

In his relatively early work *The Philosophical Principles of Integral Knowledge* (1877), Soloviev introduces the term in the context of the authentically mystical objective of genuine art and the creative process, which includes applied art, the fine arts, and the religious, mystical sacralization of matter.[200] In his essay "Art and 'Theurgy,'" however, Bulgakov quibbles with the term as employed by Soloviev for (inadvertently) muddying the waters between the *work of God* or, say, human beings' efforts toward a divine task. For Bulgakov, it is necessary to make a very clear distinction between *God's* work in the world (a condescension, technically *theurgy*) and the *human* response (an ascent, what Bulgakov terms *sophiurgy*).[201] Bulgakov's worry is not without merit: Berdyaev, for instance, interprets the theme of theurgy in terms of the creative power of human beings as applied toward the absolute transformation of the world.[202] Rather than the work of God, it is for Berdyaev "the answer of [the hu]man to the call of God."[203] More than this, for him it is God's *lack* that requires cooperative activity with human beings: in his own words, "the need of God for the creative activity of man, could not be revealed to man by God, it had to be brought to light by the daring of man himself."[204] According to Bulgakov, however, "theurgy is the action of God, the outpouring of his pardoning and saving grace upon humankind. As such, it depends not upon human beings but upon the will of God. In its essence, theurgy is inseparably connected with the incarnation, it is the incarnation itself extended in time and uninterruptedly in process of accomplishment, the unending action of Christ in humanity,"[205] which is accomplished at Pentecost. Any art that attempts through its own Pelagian "technical artistic virtuosity or aestheticist magic" to accomplish the task will seriously err.[206] This concern of misplaced power on a technique that can be mastered is a fundamental worry of Balthasar's in both the early *Apokalypse der deutschen Seele* and later articulations of aesthetics in his trilogy.

The famous last lines of Rilke's poem "Archaic Torso of Apollo," which serve as this chapter's epigraph—"for there is no place / that does not see you. You must change your life"—binds the aesthetic and the ethical in an agreement that loosely unites the Romantics (Schiller, especially), the Russians, and Balthasar. The quality of the Russian religious aesthetic, particularly in Soloviev, is both a vision and a task to incarnate ideal content in the real, for material beauty asymptotically to reflect eschatological promise. For Balthasar, there is likewise in the aesthetic a latent ethical or moral demand. Balthasar makes a double appeal to Origen's Johannine word-mysticism and to Rilke's poetry for the moral quality of beauty in revelation: "For Origen, the moral meaning of revelation is not to be found *alongside* its mystical meaning: the spiritual light proceeding from revelation's depths. For Origen, the 'moral meaning' refers to the urgency with which such light penetrates the beholder's very heart, in a manner described by Rilke in his 'The Archaic Torso of Apollo': 'there is no place in it which does not see you. You must change your life.'"[207] Thus, the ethical is "beauty's inner coordinate axis."[208] It is Balthasar's stated task, especially after Kierkegaard's *Either/Or*, to reconnect the aesthetic and the ethical with a copula rather than a disjunctive.[209] To be confronted with the beauty of God is to present the beholder with an urgent choice, a moral decision, a yes or a no.[210] In this way, as suggested in a subsequent chapter, the enrapturing moment is also apocalyptic.

In this exercise of plotting the aesthetics of Schelling, the Russians, and Balthasar roughly along the axes of dialectical terms, we have observed Balthasar's affirmation of a type of aesthetics structurally and formally similar to Schelling's, insofar as beauty has a mediating function between real and ideal. Categorically not affirmed, however, is an aesthetic of identity between natural and supernatural, which leads to either materialism or monism, subsuming the finite or else making it absolute. This *identitas entis* represents the spectacular failure of aesthetic theology to produce glory. Whereas Berdyaev's aesthetics depreciates the finite, Soloviev's thoroughly Chalcedonian formulation and Bulgakov's pneumatological articulation accord Christ His rightful place as the genuine union between infinite and finite, which indicates concretely the mystery of the Trinity, love, and being as such.

In Balthasar's theological aesthetics, the enrapturing of the beholder is not simply for the pleasure of the senses; rather, the aesthetic anticipates and requires the dramatic, for "no one is enraptured without returning, from this encounter, with a personal mission."[211] The internal, objective evidential power of the beautiful in revelation is existentially transformative for human beings insofar as it communicates not only the phenomena itself, but simultaneously the grace to see love rightly and the freedom to answer in kind.[212] For, with Balthasar, "where a thing of beauty is really and radically beheld, freedom too is radically opened up, and decision can take place."[213] This capacity for a free response on the part of the human being assumes the integrity of finite freedom and creatureliness (in short, a relation of analogy rather than identity) that is not absorbed into the absoluteness of the appearing phenomenon. What is primary for Balthasar, as the next chapter aims to demonstrate in its examination on the nature of freedom, is not the exercise of finite freedom itself, but "that I hand myself over to the deciding reality and thus am resolved, decided, to let myself be marked by the unique encounter offered me."[214]

CHAPTER 3

"DU DUNKELHEIT, AUS DER ICH STAMME"
Ontology, Evil, and Myth at the Root

Schelling, with Böhme behind him, receives in this chapter what might seem to be rather extravagant consideration for a book purporting to be mainly theological in nature. Böhme and Schelling, however, provide a direct line of Western influence to Russian religious thinking,[1] not to mention the fact that Schelling's Romanticism was influential for certain nineteenth-century Roman Catholics of the Tübingen School, especially J. S. Drey.[2] Schelling and Böhme are foregrounded deliberately here because their respective configurations of dialectical metaphysics and theogonic process—wherein gods are "born" in darkness—place division at the root of divinity and of being that ultimately produces the created world, mythology, and human history.[3] This philosophical background deeply and explicitly determines Berdyaev's religious philosophy of freedom, evil, history, and myth, as well as his extra-confessional sophiological commitments; perhaps more important, the direct sites of Berdyaev's influence by Böhme and Schelling are precisely the sites of Balthasar's most vociferous objections to Berdyaev.[4] In short, the primary reason for investigating these discourses, however much their complexity and arcana may tax the patience of even the most indulgent reader, is to see how Balthasar adjudicates these extra-confessional modes when they resurface definitively in speculative Russian religious philosophy. Finally, Schelling's adoption of Böhme in his philosophy of myth is important for our purposes, as Soloviev assimilates a version of the Schellingian potencies in the *Lectures on Divine Humanity*, though Soloviev's version supplements it with more determinately Christian content and thus escapes Balthasar's damning critique. Schelling, then, informed by Böhme, provides the generative grammar for this chapter and the means of tracing central convergences and departures between these thinkers on freedom, evil, temporality, and the relation of myth and history.

The more basic question that arises at this juncture, however, is why Balthasar troubles himself at all with potentially dangerous thinkers such as Berdyaev and Soloviev. It is certainly true that Schelling, the speculative Russians, and Balthasar have a common adversary in the presumptions of modern rationalism. Alike they chafe at the overweening Enlightenment confidence in the power of reason to overcome myth, to derogate freedom (both human and divine), and to treat too casually the problem of evil. Indeed, as already noted, part of the value of certain extra-confessional lines of thinking with which Balthasar engages, particularly that of Böhme–Schelling–Berdyaev, is that they serve as *religious* counterpoints to the excesses of rationalistic modernity. While on this point Balthasar finds the Böhme–Schelling–Berdyaev response comprehensible in its attempts to retain the mythic, preserve human freedom, and take evil seriously, he absolutely does not countenance it. The speculative ontologies embedded in the discourses of this trio of thinkers are the deformative unmaking of an authentically Christian rendition of freedom, myth, and the problem of evil; the Titanic humanism of Romanticism dooms itself. In effect, although Soloviev takes his bearings from Schelling, especially in articulating a version of the three "potencies" of God, his position decisively departs from this line and aligns far more closely with the determinative content of Christian theology, particularly as it is informed and constrained by a common patristic inheritance of East and West: Maximus the Confessor, who according to Balthasar "has drawn from the mystery of Christ a perspective for the whole Christian view of the universe."[5]

Balthasar has rightly characterized Western philosophical history as a long attempt to differentiate that which is necessary, abstract, and universal from that which is contingent, particular, and singular, a discursive mode that follows the fault lines of grandiose rational systems (Hegel looms large) and the dynamic historicity of empirical facts. According to Balthasar, in this negotiation preference has been accorded emphatically to the former over the latter in terms of valuation and philosophical respectability, where particulars are interpreted always as illustrative or emblematic of the larger system of universal, abstract processes. The problem with this model is that the historical process crushes that which is individual and particular, jeopardizing human creativity, personality, and individual freedom.[6] He shares this concern with Berdyaev. This chapter, then, along with the others, can again be understood in the broadest possible terms as a comparative examination of the means by which our religious philosophers—German, Russian, and Swiss—attempt to meet the long-standing philosophical problem of the relation between universals and particulars, infinite and finite.[7] For Balthasar, there are two choices for thinking this difference: either human beings can understand themselves to be defined by the distinction, that is, as finite existents (world) vis-à-vis the infinite Absolute (God), or they can attempt to eradicate the distinction by methodically ignoring the Absolute and operating from a purely immanentist perspective in which possible meaning is restricted to the this-worldly.[8]

The questions that emerge are central for Schelling, the Russians, and Balthasar: Whence comes the temporal, particular, historical, finite, and genuinely developmental existence of the actual world in relation to the oneness, simplicity, and eternity of God? How can relations between finite and infinite, particular and universal, multiplicity and unity, change and permanence be negotiated? Does the absolute, infinite nature of God mitigate the existence and exercise of finite human freedom? How can the created order be said to be good if human beings freely choose themselves over against God? These are indeed what Balthasar calls the "most ancient questions" of human beings, questions that cannot blithely be set aside, "for we cannot deny that we are not nothing, any more than that we are not God; nor can we deny that there exist good and evil and hence created freedom too."⁹ Certainly these are ancient questions, particularly that of the one and the many, traceable to the very roots of Western philosophy. Interestingly, for Balthasar it is Maximus the Confessor's thoroughly Chalcedonian philosophy of Christ as the concrete universal—with which he ultimately alibis Soloviev—that overcomes, in its sophisticated theological reflection on the problem of generality and particularity, "the old Greek suspicion of particularity, the exaggerated preference for the universal."¹⁰

This complex of concerns also provoked Schelling to adopt a version of Böhme's speculative ontology and posit theogonic process, a highly dynamistic doctrine of the origin or birth of God, at the door not only of his metaphysics but also his philosophy of mythology.¹¹ Böhme's theogonic myth—elements of which arise and function as explanatory principles of creation, history, providence, human agency, time, freedom, and evil—resurfaces assertively in this genealogy, first in the speculative ontology of Schelling and then in the Russians, and particularly Berdyaev, but through Schelling also to Soloviev. Thus, in the interest of economy, this chapter focuses on the ways Berdyaev and Soloviev negotiate this line, as well as Balthasar's reception of it, leaving more sustained dialogue with Bulgakov to chapters 4 and 5. Let it be said, however, that Bulgakov, like Balthasar, explicitly recognizes the dangers of a Böhmian line of thinking, especially insofar as it is theogonic, impersonal rather than personal, emanational, insufficient with respect to Trinity, overly rationalistic, and ultimately world-denying.¹² Schelling's Böhmian inheritance thus opens up several mutually implied discursive fields, including metaphysical voluntarism, the possibility of free will, the nature and origin of evil, mythology, progressive religious development, historicity, temporality, and—for the Russians at least—sophiology. This chapter speaks to many of these elements in turn because they are sites of maximally significant conjunctions and disjunctions between Schelling, the Russians, and Balthasar, though some worthy themes (sophiology, for instance) must lamentably but necessarily fall by the wayside.

As already indicated elsewhere, there are many Schellings.¹³ Here the Schelling in play is largely that of the transitional middle period

(1806–1820), especially in the essay on freedom (1809) and the *Ages of the World* (*Weltalter*, 1811–1815), although his 1804 *Philosophy and Religion* is significant in its introduction of the idea of the primordial Fall, which Berdyaev adopts, and as it foreshadows the thematic of freedom and evil taken up more decisively in the 1809 *Philosophische Untersuchungen über das Wesen der menschlichen Freiheit*.[14] It is during this middle period that Schelling's Böhmian heritage (transmitted genetically and, for Balthasar, fatally, to Berdyaev) appears most evident. The tremendous influence of Böhme wanes in the late Schelling. With respect to the middle period, though, Schelling's enthusiastic reception of Böhme's work (after being introduced to it by Franz von Baader) seems clear enough, despite the fact that, even in the 1809 essay on freedom that suggests a debt, Böhme is not acknowledged by name.[15] Though chapter 5 of this volume briefly revisits *The Ages of the World*, it deserves mention here as it both ratifies and expounds upon that which Schelling borrowed from Böhme in the 1809 freedom essay, *Philosophical Inquiries into the Nature of Human Freedom*, and it contains a nascent description of his *Potenzenlehre*, or theory of the potencies. Schelling's *Potenzenlehre* draws upon Böhme's notion of an originary contracting power of bare, free, indeterminate primitive will whose nisus is only ec-static manifestation, which is to say, a divine self-constitution.[16] This triadic doctrine of the potencies reappears more concretely in the late (1842) Berlin lectures on the philosophy of mythology, in which the potencies unfold in nature, in myth, and in history.[17]

WOLLEN IST URSEIN

The question of freedom—both human and divine—is at the very center of the religious philosophy of Schelling and the Russians, as well as the theo-dramatic theology of Balthasar. The question of the meaning of freedom, especially vis-à-vis history, was of particular significance to Schelling (who once wrote that "the beginning and end of all philosophy is—Freedom"[18]). After all, what must the nature of history be if human beings—and God—had real agency to determine or change its course? Berdyaev shares this fundamental interest.[19] And Balthasar's theo-drama absolutely requires the preservation of both finite and infinite freedom, where the deep structures of freedom in the "noumenal life-form"[20] of human being operate as a self-determination that admits of degrees. For Balthasar, human freedom operates on two dimensions, the first of which moves toward a definitive (and, as suggested in chapter 4, apocalyptic) determination of "yes" or "no," and the second "forms a vast, inexhaustible space within which these definite decisions fall."[21] Both dimensions operate on the premise that the individual form and the Absolute are not equated one with the other. Human relation provides an analogy, though, like all analogies, it limps: "When lovers hand themselves over to each other, they do not renounce the greater, inexhaustible realm of freedom: they simply anchor their mutual bond within it."[22] While the genealogical line of Böhme–Schelling–Berdyaev shares with Balthasar an interest in articulating the compossibility of infinite and finite freedom, the monological solution—and the speculative ontology embedded therein—offered by the former is considered by the latter to be entirely bankrupt. Here Berdyaev is indicted, but Soloviev is not. Moreover, as we shall see below, the discourse of freedom becomes of a piece with that of the origin and nature of evil, and Böhme and Schelling likewise variously inform the Russians on the problem of evil.[23]

In *Philosophical Inquiries into the Nature of Human Freedom*, Schelling's task is first to demonstrate that his developing philosophy is capable of accommodating human freedom (especially concerning charges of pantheism made by his former friend Friedrich Schlegel; according to Schlegel, pantheism compromises freedom by its determinism).[24] Significantly, against the regnant philosophical Idealism of his day, Schelling ultimately defines authentic freedom simply as "a possibility of good and evil."[25] Freedom can only exist if the genuine possibility for evil is present. Thus, freedom cannot be thought without reference to the brute facticity of evil. This definition naturally requires Schelling to speculate upon the nature of evil and of the dilemma that emerges: if actual, real evil is admissible, it seems to jeopardize the perfection of the Absolute; but if actual, real evil is inadmissible, the most robust sense of human freedom is likewise jeopardized.[26]

The problem is how to account for the oneness of the Absolute as well as the reality of evil. By this time Schelling has embraced the view, against major currents in Idealism, that evil is an actual spiritual force, not—as in Hegel or Augustine—simply a negation or privation of the good; he does not hold, however, the dualistic premise that evil is an oppositional force co-eternal with God, for everything that exists, exists in God.[27] But, even given this commitment, Schelling does not want to affirm that God wills evil.

It is in the face of this dilemma that Schelling relates the myth of origins, of that which is prior to being, which he borrows substantially from Böhme's theogonic metaphysics of self-generating divinity, a process that suggests the creation of the world is a groundless act of absolute freedom. The practice of telling theogonic myths does not, of course, originate with Böhme; Balthasar places Böhme and Schelling (*The Ages of the World* gets special mention) in a line traced back through Lucretius, Plato's *Timaeus*, and the Eleatic school to Hesiod's *Theogony*, which, like Böhme, coaxes the principle of light from that of darkness in a manner that cannot leave the light unsullied.[28] Indeed, Böhme's origin myth repeats a version of the ancient symbol of the self-eating serpent ouroboros, ever consuming its own tail, symbolic of the perpetual cycle of becoming, of eternity, of primordial unity. *Timaeus* details such a figure, a great circular worm with no eyes and no ears, as there was nothing outside this creature to be sensed, and with no organs, "since there was nothing which went from him or came into him: for there was nothing beside him . . . his own waste provid[ed] his own food, and all that he did or suffered [took] place in and by himself."[29] The ouroboros becomes a central image in Gnostic, hermetic, and alchemical discourses, as well as the poetry of Western Romanticism.[30]

Here a look at Böhme's myth of origins is in order. This account is more summative of his mature position and of necessity flattens out some of the subtleties of the development of his thought from *Aurora* to *De Signatura Rerum* and *Mysterium Magnum*, but as a sketch it will serve current purposes. According to Böhme, prior to being, prior to divinity, prior to good and evil, prior to Divine Trinity, the *Ungrund* of bare nothingness, of uncreated freedom, stirs. The inchoate, undifferentiated will seeks self-expression by (necessarily) going out of itself into actuality, into the "revelation" of sensible media, in order to become not only self-actualized, but also self-aware. At the root of this movement is primal conflict, as the undifferentiated will meets opposition. This instability gives rise to a second will that seeks not eccentric actualization, but a return or contraction to primal unity, while maintaining the seeds of darkness. Unfulfilled longing begets suffering, which begets the dark fire of bitterness, or *Grimmigkeit*. According to Böhme, this *Grimmigkeit* is the first of three principles that emerge from this primordium; it can, as divine wrath, be identified with God the Father, the sharp, astringent principle of "No." The second principle is divine love, or God the Son, the "Yes." As these dialectical principles interact oppositionally, the creative process of the world begins and is sustained by the cooperative movement between "No" and "Yes," between "Father" and "Son": that is, the third principle of the Holy Spirit.[31] Good and evil alike stem from the divine nature. Böhme's God is therefore Janus-faced: "He Himself is all Being, He is Evil and Good, heaven and hell, light and darkness, eternity and time, the beginning and the end; wherever His love becomes hidden in a being there appears His wrath."[32]

Schelling appropriates from Böhme much of this primordial, cyclical process, particularly the dark fundament of irrationality at the root of being, which preforms the universe, and the primordial act of free will that brings the world into being.[33] This dark ground is contained in God, but is not God: *das Dunkle* is God's "nature" (die Natur in Gott), "inseparable from him, to be sure, but nevertheless distinguishable from him."[34] All things have their basis in this bare will, this primordial hunger or desire—prior to divinity—for self-actualization, which is the principle of becoming, of vitality, and of dynamism: "It is the longing which the eternal One feels to give birth to itself. This is not the One itself, but is co-eternal with it. This longing seeks to give birth to God, i.e., the unfathomable unity, but to this extent it has not yet the unity in its own self. Therefore, regarded in itself, it is also will; but a will within which there is no understanding, and thus not an independent and complete will, since understanding is actually the will in willing."[35] From these early stirrings "there is born in God himself an inward, imaginative response" through which for the first time "God sees himself in his own image . . . [which] is the first in which God, viewed absolutely, is realized, though only in himself; it is in the beginning in God, and is the God-begotten God himself,"[36] who alone, as the existent God, abides in pure light. God, then, is the indissoluble identity of the binaries of darkness and light, the will to revelation and the will to love, with the darkness subdued by the light. The concept of the potencies of God is developed at much greater length in his later philosophy of mythology. For Schelling's dialectical metaphysics, and for Böhme, upon whom he relies, the bitter, dark (material) principle is absolutely necessary for God's self-actualization, which, much as in Hegel, requires a self-posited opposition in order to emerge (and eventually reunify the contrary principles).[37] As Schelling writes, "If there were no division of the principles, then unity could not manifest its omnipotence; if there were no conflict then love could not become real."[38] Darkness, for Schelling, is the "necessary heritage"[39] of the created order. Thus, God undergoes development and, in the face of this tremendous dark freedom, is not totally in control.

At the genesis of divinity, then, is the Unground, that indeterminate, dark, premundane freedom invoked by Böhme to explain both the origins of the world and the origins of metaphysical evil, which, again, is decidedly non-privative. Schelling's appeal to Böhme's theogonic conception of this originary self-propelling, self-creating process (imagining it later, in *The Ages of the World* fragments, as in Böhme, like "an unremitting wheel"[40]) that ultimately produces God and the created world—and, with it, presumably, evil—thus permits him simultaneously to maintain the immanence of evil in God and the actuality of evil as a real force, and to exempt God from any responsibility for it, because evil arises before God is, properly speaking, God. The impulse in Böhme and Schelling to identify darkness at the root of being—repeated decisively in Berdyaev and condemned just as decisively by Balthasar—is thus at the first an attempt at theodicy, a response to the pervasive problem of both evil and its origins.[41] To be sure, Balthasar is strenuously opposed to this mode of explanatory theodicy.[42]

ONTOLOGY: RUSSIAN REPETITIONS

This Böhmian and Schellingian heritage is evident particularly in Nicholas Berdyaev. Berdyaev assimilates and makes central to his own religious philosophy the notion that it is the intuitive, the mythic, that is the most adequate mode of truth and perception. Indeed, Berdyaev specifically praises the mystical and the theosophical modes according to which Böhme, the untrained Lutheran shoemaker who privileged immediacy of access to the divine over external rituals, operates. Böhme is, for Berdyaev, practiced in the sort of wisdom that employs myth, vision, and symbol rather than more strictly rational or discursive categories.[43] Berdyaev views him as a mythmaker of remarkable originality, one whose importance and ingenuity rests primarily in the fact that he introduced not only dynamism but also tragedy into God's internal life.[44]

Berdyaev enthusiastically repeats Böhme's notion of a dark root of reality, the theogonic process, and a radical metaphysical voluntarism (some of which is owed to Kant, whom Berdyaev lauds for upholding freedom as the primary principle[45]). Indeed, Berdyaev strongly asserts that "the denial of this theogonic process is a denial of the life of the Godhead."[46] That the will in Böhme and in Schelling is primary to time, to history, and to being itself sets a theme adopted self-consciously by Berdyaev to ensure dynamism: that of metaphysical voluntarism.[47] In fact, Berdyaev's adoption of Böhme's notion of the irrational ground, an originary "meonic" freedom of nonbeing as pure potency prior to God, explicitly provides the condition of the possibility for his central metaphysical and eschatological claims, particularly the phenomenon of becoming as such, the nature of God as life rather than static being, the manifestation of the physical world, and the true nature of evil.[48] Further, Berdyaev's philosophy of history requires a version of Böhme's shadowed ground, with preference to the principle of darkness over the principle of light. As he suggests in *The Meaning of History*, sounding quite a lot like Schelling, "Historical reality implies the existence of an irrational principle which makes dynamism possible. Neither history nor true dynamism is possible without this principle, which is turbulent, mobile, and pliant, and which kindles the conflict between the opposing forces of light and darkness."[49] As in Schelling, the primordial being unfolds in (the objectified, fallen realms of) nature and history, and these two modes of being are in Berdyaev associated with different modes of time, the former with cosmic time and the latter with historical, linear time.[50] According to Berdyaev, human beings must proceed through history in order to break eventually (eschatologically) out of the bonds of what he calls "objectification."[51]

This concept of objectification represents a significant point of convergence between Schelling and the Russians, given the former's notion of a primordial fall *into* time and the phenomenal world. For instance, in the 1804 essay *Philosophy and Religion*, Schelling suggests that the movement from Absolute to actual historical particulars and the sense world is not continuous. Rather, "the origin of the phenomenal world is conceivable only as a complete falling-away from absoluteness by means of a leap (*Sprung*)."[52] This fall is a fall into the nonideal, chaotic, visible world; thus the fall is coincident with the moment of creation. This idea is also shared by Soloviev, though on this point Balthasar again suggests Soloviev is more like Maximus the Confessor than he is like Schelling or Berdyaev.[53]

Recall that Berdyaev advanced a radically dualistic conception of reality that placed the realm of spirit and the realm of nature (rather like the Kantian conception of the noumenal and the phenomenal) in an absolutely oppositional relationship. Following Schelling, the Fall did not occur in the phenomenal world, but actually *caused* it, ejecting human beings from the divine, unified mode of spirit to an objectified realm of temporal, spatial, and historical division and chaos. The Fall was the very "process of exteriorization" itself.[54] This fact gives the observable world an ambiguous, unreal cast: "The natural world of phenomena is symbolic in character. It is full of signs of another world and it is a symptom of division and alienation in the sphere of spirit. There is no natural objective world in the sense of a reality in itself; the only world there is is the world which is divinely and humanly free. The object world is enslavement and fall."[55]

This conception of a primordial fall, which Berdyaev adopts from Schelling, is for Balthasar quite beyond the pale, for it diminishes the sense world and human finitude altogether. Balthasar draws particular attention to this illusory character of human being in the created order, which is necessitated by the appeal to the "multifarious theories of a 'fall' that threaten to devalue the dignity and uniqueness of earthly existence, seeing it as something 'unreal.'"[56] Though he does not mention Berdyaev explicitly in this context, it can be safely assumed that he (or at least Böhme, who forms Berdyaev's thinking) is indeed in Balthasar's sights here. Bulgakov likewise criticizes Böhme precisely on these grounds: the denigration of the finite, what he calls a "metaphysical squeamishness," is the large part of what Bulgakov finds so distasteful about Böhme, who posits, for instance, that sexual and alimentary aspects of human bodies came into existence only after the Fall.[57]

Balthasar also comments on Soloviev's conception of the Fall, although his consistent hermeneutic is more nearly one of charity than not. In the *Lectures on Divine Humanity*, Soloviev writes, "If our natural world, lying in evil, a land of curse and banishment, bringing forth thistles and thorns, is the inevitable *consequence* of sin and the fall, it is clear that the *origin* of sin and the fall lies not here but in that garden of God in which not only the tree of life but also the tree of knowledge of good and evil have their roots. In other words, the *primordial* origin of evil can lie only in the domain of the eternal, prenatural world."[58] Likewise, he indicates in the same lecture that the phenomenal world and those entities that populate it are "only consequences or manifestations of evil."[59] In "Lecture Ten," he says that the world resulted "in the chaotic being of the all constituting the primordial fact."[60] Balthasar, however, in his essay on Soloviev, suggests that in order "to avoid identifying the coming into reality of nature with the Fall, identifying separateness with egotism, we must stick to those texts that are quite clear in tracing the Fall back to a (transcendental) free decision, which establishes the form of fragmentation in cosmic life."[61] There is much, then, to recommend Cyril O'Regan's observation that Balthasar reads Soloviev rather *as if* he were Bulgakov, a Bulgakov by proxy, as it were.[62] Balthasar certainly seems to criticize with a light hand because he is viewing Soloviev through Bulgakov's revisionist reading of him.

For Schelling (and here his Neoplatonic heritage—shared with Balthasar—shows as well), history follows a pattern of *egressus* and return. What separates Schelling from Neoplatonism somewhat, however, is that the fall into finitude as depicted in *Philosophy and Religion* is contingent and sudden, rather than gradual. According to Schelling,

> history is an epic composed in the mind of God. It has two main parts: one depicting mankind's egress from its center to its farthest point of displacement; the other, its return. The former is, as it were, history's *Iliad*; the latter, its *Odyssey*. In the one, the direction is centrifugal; in the other, it becomes centripetal. In this way, the grand purpose of the phenomenal world reveals itself in history. The ideas, the spirits, must fall away from their center and insert themselves into the particularity of nature, the general realm of the falling-away, so that afterward, and as particularities, they may return to indifference and, reconciled with it, may be able to abide in it without disturbing it.[63]

History, then, is the narrative that traces the rehabilitation of human beings from this fall away from God back to rejoin the Absolute. The falling away is the necessary vehicle for the expression of the self-revelation of God, and thus, in a real sense, a felix culpa. It is the principle of dark striving that motors the dynamic of history.[64] For Schelling and for Berdyaev, however, the onus of return rests squarely upon human beings. For Berdyaev, for instance, God must await and is absolutely dependent upon human action to realize the coming of the Kingdom.[65] Further distinguishing Soloviev from Schelling and Berdyaev on this point is that the process of coming to perfection in history is for him accomplished by Christ, and not fundamentally by the work of human beings necessary to supplement the impotence of God.[66]

Especially apropos is the way Schelling's Böhmian metaphysics—which, as shown earlier, functions as rationale for the origin of evil and the character of human freedom—implicates and informs his philosophy of history. Even in Schelling's understanding of history's second "act," the return to God, evil is not converted to good, but is only restored to its proper place of hidden potentiality. Recalling not only Schelling's belief that the suffering hidden in the depths of God is necessary, but also his understanding of the necessity of process for the actualization and subsequent personalization of the living (e.g., not static) God, it is manifestly clear that for Schelling "all history remains incomprehensible without the concept of a humanly suffering God."[67]

According to Schelling, God will continue to follow the course of development, following periods of progressive revelation, and will eventually be all in all. In the freedom essay, which sounds quite Johannine here, the myth of history begins in the first creation, or the naissance of light, which is the ideal principle that stands in opposition to the preceding dark principle; the light is "the creative Word which redeems the hidden life in the depths from non-being, raises it from potency to actuality."[68] The unifying principle of Spirit then arises, subordinating both light and dark "for the sake of realization and personality."[69] The dark principle of striving is required to draw out the good—and the God—to actuality. It is "the primal basis of existence insofar as it strives towards actualization in created beings."[70] In Schelling's philosophy of history, the ultimate stage of the spirit of love is not revealed all at once, but—as permitted providentially by God—moves through a progressive historical series from a primeval golden age characterized by a certain naïveté regarding good and evil, through the age of the gods and the rise and fall of high culture, to the point at which the light is manifest in human form in order to mediate between God and world.[71]

THE CENTER AND THE PERIPHERY

The binary structure of the principles of darkness and light in Schelling's doctrine of God is reflected, as in a mirror, in Schelling's anthropology.[72] That is, human beings inherit the opposition between darkness and light, where the darkness maps onto self-will and light onto reason, and the perversion of evil at the root of being becomes an actual possibility. The production of the light occurs only through the necessary power of the dark principle. As Schelling notes, the warring principles in human beings function as explanatory principles for the origin of evil in the world: "Therefore that unity which is indissoluble in God must be dissoluble in man—and this constitutes the possibility of good and evil."[73] This dissolution of principles not only indicates the possibility of evil, but also the nature of evil: it is a perverse disordering, an unbalancing of the proper distribution of the living nexus of human will(s). Therefore, personality, human and divine, is marked by a complex unity of opposing forces, the dark ground and the light of reason that keeps the dark ground chastened: "Personality is the perpetual actualization of selfhood; it is the conscious and purposive control of irrational underlying potentialities."[74] Following Schelling's argument, if the dark self-will (which desires to exalt and assert itself above the principle of light) predominates, it deviates from its proper place in the depths, upsetting the delicate balance of forces in a complex organism: "But hardly does self-will move from the center which is its station, than the nexus of forces is also dissolved; in its place a merely particular will rules which can no longer unite the forces among themselves as before, but must therefore strive to form or compose a special and peculiar life out of the now separate forces, an insurgent host of desires and passions—since every individual force is also an obsession and passion."[75]

In other words, when the latent dark principle of self-will perversely dominates in human being, the possibility of evil arises. Schelling's account of evil, borrowed here from Böhme, insists that it is something more than absence or privation: it is and must be an actual positive force of perversion, "founded [not merely] on something inherently positive, but rather on the highest positive being which nature contains,"[76] namely, the primordial will. It is particularly notable that Schelling explains this disordering, which gives rise to evil, by the analogous phenomenon of physical disease, the "true counterpart of evil and sin,"[77] which is understood likewise as an unsalutary, equilibrium-defying movement of that which ought to be in the center into the periphery.[78] On this front Schelling found much to appreciate in von Baader, whose account of evil was sufficiently robust for Schelling's thinking and made use of the physical analogy of disease, as well as the sense of perverse disordering from center to periphery.[79] Schelling's freedom essay indicates that thinking evil as this move to the periphery might suggest some rationale for the traditional cultural and literary association of evil with the serpent, which is biologically a circle with no center: that is, the snake is *only* periphery.[80] Like evil, disease is felt as a real force but has a certain liminal status—"a swaying between being and non-being."[81] Soloviev and Berdyaev will characterize the nature of evil in much the same way.

For Schelling, influenced both by Böhme and von Baader, evil is not merely privative or physical, but rather a diabolical force that exists through a primordial act of freedom, woven into the fabric of reality and even divinity itself.[82] Schelling's construal of freedom as the genuine possibility to choose good or evil, however, does not suggest that this is an arbitrary choice. Indeed, according to Schelling, who recurs to the well-worn example of Buridan's ass, which starves to death between two equally appealing piles of hay, "to be able to decide for A or –A without any motivating reasons would . . . only be a privilege to act entirely unreasonably."[83] In order to safeguard human freedom from external determinism without insinuating that human actions are radically contingent and only accidental, Schelling appeals to a higher conception of *inner* necessity, a fully free self-determination, a self-making (recalling Fichte) in accordance with the laws of a given individual nature. Thus, a human act "can follow from its inner nature only in accordance with the law of identity, and with absolute necessity which is also the only absolute freedom."[84] Thus, freedom and necessity are coincident. This is possible only if human beings determine their own natures, constitutional tendencies toward good or toward evil, by their own free act. This act, however, does not take place in time, but is, rather, a preconscious decision in eternity prior to corporealization and being itself.[85] Given the freedom in play for self-determination, and the fact that when human beings from eternity prefer evil to good, darkness to light, it is not only a physical but also a spiritual reality. Schelling, extending Kant, denotes this phenomenon as radical evil.[86] Evil, again, is not a lack; it is not caused by finitude, but is rather a free self-determination.

As Balthasar points out, however, this proto-temporal self-making not only makes the actually experienced phenomenon of religious or moral conversion difficult if not impossible to explain, but also jeopardizes the individual personality of those who choose the good.[87] This sacrifice of the personality is, for Balthasar, a symptom of all forms of Titanism, as the individual "burns to glowing ashes in the belly of the Moloch of the Absolute, be it the 'will' or 'life' or 'death,'" or Hegel's *Geist*.[88] If, as Schelling maintains in the freedom essay, the dark principle is that of ego, of particularity, of differentiation, and the will of God is "to universalize everything, to lift it to unity with light,"[89] how can those who choose the good be distinguished from one another? Any system that privileges the universal at the expense of the personal and particular, flattening out individual freedom, "signals the abdication of drama in favor of a narrative philosophy of history, an epic story of the Spirit or of mankind."[90] Further, Balthasar objects to the overweening absoluteness of finite freedom in Schelling's philosophy: "Although we cannot deny that finite freedom has an absolute aspect, it has power over neither its own ground nor its own fulfillment. It does not possess itself, yet it is not its own gift to itself: it owes itself to some other origin."[91] Balthasar rightly worries with respect to Schelling that when human freedom becomes so incredibly important, even absolute, God (in Balthasar's theatrical metaphor, the "Producer") exists only insofar as the "play" of history is performed.[92]

FREEDOM AND EVIL: RUSSIAN REPETITIONS

Significantly, Schelling's understanding of evil as a positive spiritual force characterized by the aberrant inversion of principles recurs in Soloviev, who was likely also independently influenced by von Baader. His final text, *War, Progress, and the End of History: Three Conversations Including a Short Story of the Anti-Christ* (1899–1900), is a rather fanciful dialogue exploring the manifestations of moral evil in the historical process. It aims, against Tolstoy, to demonstrate that evil is far more insidious than simple defect: it is a real force that must be actively countered. More than this, the question of the nature of evil requires a decisive turn to "a complete system of metaphysics."[93] Five characters participate in the dialogue: the General, the Politician, the Lady, the Tolstoyan Prince, and the religious Mr. Z., whose perspective accords most nearly to Soloviev's own. The expressed aim of the dialogue is to present three different perspectives upon the issue of evil and the meaning of history: the traditionalist General, who represents the view of the past; the progressive Politician, who represents culture contemporary to Soloviev; and the enigmatic Mr. Z., who is identifiable most nearly with prophecy, newness, surprise, and the absolutely religious perspective of the future.[94] Mr. Z. describes the phenomenon of evil in this manner:

> Evil really exists, and it finds its expression not only in the deficiency of good but in the positive resistance and predominance of the lower qualities over the higher ones in all spheres of being. There is an individual evil in the great majority of people. This occurs when the lower side of human beings, their animal and bestial passions, resist the better impulses of the soul, *overpowering them*. And there is a social evil, when the human crowd, individually enslaved by evil, resists the salutary efforts of the few better men and eventually overpowers them. There is, lastly, a physical evil in humanity, when the baser material constituents of the human body resist the living and enlightening power that binds them together into a beautiful form of organism and resist and break the form, destroying the real basis of the higher life. This is the *extreme* evil, called death.[95]

Soloviev's parallels with Schelling (and Böhme and von Baader behind him) on this point emerge perspicuously: evil is a non-privative reality and essentially an unwarranted subordination or inversion of the higher principles to those lower. The same logic is in play here as in his earlier aesthetics, when, for instance, the grounds of nonideality or ugliness are precisely when, either in an artistic composition or in nature, a single part prevails over the others, matter dominates form, disrupting the proper unity. This disproportion is especially offensive in zoological ugliness, where it represents a jarring disconnect between inner complexity and outward form. Soloviev identifies this type of regressive formlessness in slugs, snails, whales, and seals.[96]

Furthermore, Soloviev's 1883 address in memory of Dostoevsky lauds the great novelist for recognizing the extent and the radical depths of the possible perversity of human nature; indeed a solution to this "dark basis of our nature—evil in its exclusive egoism and insane in its striving to realize this egoism, to relate everything to itself and to define everything by itself,"[97] must be aggressively sought. In the *Lectures on Divine Humanity*, Soloviev remarks that evil is the radical egoism that pervades the nature of everything that lives, from blade of grass to human being, the "striving to set up one's exclusive I in the place of everything else, to eliminate everything else."[98] Thus, it must have a metaphysical, not merely a physical origin.[99]

Berdyaev likewise found Schelling's freedom essay very compelling, not only because it affirmed the Böhmian axiom that uncreated freedom is the fundamental principle of reality, prior to both human beings and God, but also in its elaboration of freedom precisely as this capacity for good or for evil. For Berdyaev—responding to Ivan Karamazov's "brilliant dialectic" in the Grand Inquisitor poem—it is far worse for human beings to be good automatons than it is for them to possess a real, often actualized, capacity for evil.[100] He, like Schelling and Soloviev, also objects strenuously to what he considers the weak view of evil as privative, as absence or diminution (Augustine), a view he characterizes in the face of systemic suffering as "anti-Christian and unethical."[101] For Berdyaev it is only by explicit appeal to Böhme that a proper solution to the problem of evil can be had; everything depends on admitting the genuine reality "not only of being, but also of non-being, of the dark abyss which precedes the very identification of being and the very distinction between good and evil."[102] In his panegyric to Böhme in *The Beginning and the End*, Berdyaev further highlights the fact that his vision of this primordial freedom explains the origin of both being and evil.[103] Certainly for Berdyaev, following Schelling, it is nearly impossible to separate what he considers to be the concomitant discourses of freedom and evil.

Balthasar, however, considers the appeal to Böhme and Schelling on the long-standing problem of understanding creaturely freedom vis-à-vis divine freedom and the possibility of evil to be absolutely untenable. Lambasting Berdyaev's positing of the Böhmian *Ungrund* at the root of reality as a patently "absurd idea,"[104] Balthasar notes that despite best and stated intentions, this move actually undercuts the integrity of finite freedom, since the freedom of human beings originates in a poisoned well. Because freedom no longer comes from a good and loving God whose gift of freedom is not only gracious and deliberate, but also comes from a place of divine plenitude rather than lack, the human being is operating not under a divine norm, but rather a norm of irrational nothingness.

Balthasar's riposte to the problem of the compatibility between infinite and finite freedom that so exasperated the Böhme–Schelling–Berdyaev line of thinking is his theological dramatic theory, or "theo-drama," which, like any other drama, requires the possibility of the play of genuine freedoms.[105] Balthasar's dramatics gives a necessary dimension of tension, of act, to the aesthetics discussed in the previous chapter. As suggested in chapter 2, with reference to what we called the Rilkean Clause, the encounter with Beauty as such does not and cannot leave the beholder unchanged. Rather, "where a thing of beauty is really and radically beheld, freedom too is radically opened up, and decision can take place. But what is ultimate here is not my decision but that I hand myself over to the deciding reality and thus am re-solved, decided, to let myself be marked by the unique encounter offered me."[106] To behold rightly, then, is not a specular event above and external to the fray. It is to be transformed, to accept a mission, to be made a witness, and all this freely.

The double question thus arises: first, how can finite freedom genuinely act with respect to infinite freedom without being engulfed by it, and, second, how can infinite freedom retain its infinitude if God makes a space for the action of the finite? For Balthasar, the possibility of a genuine drama between God (as personal) and human beings depends upon a scrupulously maintained distinction between them, a dialogical movement of the characters that assumes their respective freedoms. Indeed, according to Balthasar, the most climactic periods of religious theatre—Greek myth, the mystery plays, Shakespeare, Calderon—appear "where God was able to appear on Stage as a free Someone over against free worldly beings (Titans, humans, angelic powers)."[107] In these dramas, God participates in finite existence in a way that does not threaten the absoluteness of the divine nature. In Balthasar's estimation, then, the blurring of distinction between "I's" is a fatal weakness of Schelling: indeed, the radical self-determination that is finite freedom in Schelling expands to displace God (the play's "Producer") altogether.

Certainly the veracity and poignancy of the dramatic moment in ancient myth is precisely in the fact that it emerged, at its apex, after the waning of the sense that the numinous was only an occasion for fear, but before it had been domesticated so thoroughly that the divine devolved into one aestheticized object among many.[108] In ancient cultic drama, "the risky undertaking of a synthesis between the way man sees himself and his encounter with the divine myth as it manifests itself to him . . . takes place at the dangerous borderline where magic and revelation cannot be told apart."[109] This mythological sense of the not-entirely-safe numinous perdures in the best of dramatic forms. As Rilke suggests in the *Duino Elegies*, "the beautiful is nothing else than the onset of the terrible, which we only just endure, and we admire it, because it calmly disdains to destroy us."[110] When God is conceived monologically, this beautiful danger and surprise, and even drama itself, are simply not possible.

In the face of this problem of the compossibility of finite and infinite freedom, Balthasar does not turn to irrationalism, but rather insists that biblical and philosophical reflection ought to and must be mutually informative. For Balthasar the existence of finite freedom depends entirely upon its participation in infinite freedom, as the latter is both immanent in and transcendent beyond the former. An unexamined view of God often prevails, however, closer to the mythological than not, in which an anthropomorphized divine being exists in heaven simply as one parallel existent, albeit on a higher plane, among other existing beings. This prevailing view cannot account for the hard paradox that the existence and exercise of human freedom does not vitiate God's freedom: "In fact, God shows his almighty power particularly by imparting authentic selfhood to his creatures."[111] Balthasar's doctrine of God, dovetailing with that articulated in the aesthetics, understands God to be not the "Other," over against finite others, but, in language borrowed from Nicholas of Cusa, the "Non-Other." Balthasar's biblically determined reflections insist on two philosophical postulates that make sense of the dramatic arc of the biblical narrative: (1) the Absolute must be free, and (2) the Absolute as

Non-aliud is able, from the source of this infinite freedom, deliberately to bring forth authentically free finite beings such that infinite and finite freedoms coexist oppositionally.[112] Schelling's Böhmian conception of the divine fails on both counts, since in his determined efforts to safeguard finite freedom, God is not able to impart freedom to finite beings.[113]

These philosophical postulates are radicalized by the biblical revelation of Christ: first, the opposition between finite and infinite freedom deepens, insofar as finitude has been compromised by sin, and second, the notion of the Other as non-Other shifts toward a more properly Trinitarian claim of alterity and otherness *in* one divine being.[114] The concrete apex of these two dimensions, where God is "forsaken by God because of man's godlessness," where eternity breaks into time and history, is the event of the cross of Christ.[115] Christ is the mediator, not the mediating principle: Christ Himself is "indispensable and yet beyond all human calculation, in a pact with both warring parties and yet not a traitor to either; epitomizing the living drama in the very 'composition' of his being, torn asunder by his tragic situation and yet, thus torn, healing divisions."[116] Christ "recapitulates" and thereby sublimates in his own person the conflict between the divine "everything" and the human "something."[117]

This dynamic relationship between Christology and Trinity is addressed at more length in chapter 5 in a turn to the "action" proper of Balthasar's theo-drama, which nearly fully appropriates Bulgakov's apocalyptic and kenotic theology of the Lamb as though slain. Suffice it to say, by way of anticipation, that for Balthasar divine nature is coincident with but not emergent from this "action": "Thus the dramatic level becomes ultimate, not to be surpassed; it does not point to some prior 'wisdom' or 'teaching' or 'gnosis' or 'theology' that could then be recounted in the epic mode: it remains at the center, as drama, as the action that takes place between God and man, undiminished in its contemporary relevance."[118] For Balthasar, the dramatic militates against thinking divine or human being in an abstracted manner; nature, essence, and substance simply cannot be thought apart from action.

More ought to be said about the character of finite and infinite freedom in Balthasar. Note that the exercise of finite freedom occurs not in a solitary vacuum, but only in human community, a social dimension, among interrelated, finite freedoms.[119] Speaking purely philosophically at first, Balthasar argues that human beings experience a primordial self-presencing, a fundamental sense of the *cogito sum*, that indicates not only that an "I" exists in absolutely incommunicable uniqueness, but also the great expanse of being as such: "It is precisely in the experience of being 'I' (and no one else) that I pass beyond all limiting knowledge of my nature and touch being (reality) in its uniqueness."[120] With self-knowledge comes the attendant realization that there are others who possess being in the same (incommunicable and mysterious) way. Thus, the mode of individual existence and the realization of universal being are always of a piece, always articulated together, as openness to Being in its totality reveals individual being as one among others.[121] Analogously, all beings participate in God, whose self-communication in plenitude far exceeds the sum of those who participate therein. Human beings, in their finitude and uniqueness, make a space for others to be, just as uniquely, and in this way image the divine nature as Trinity, "*in whom the incommunicability of the hypostases is one with the unity of 'essence' in each of them.*"[122] Finite freedoms encounter one another every day without incorporation or appropriation; the freedom of the other is and must be a moment of self-disclosure.

This imaging suggests the dual structure of finite freedom itself, its first "pillar" being this freedom of self-possession, the *autexousion*, the vantage point of openness to being at the fundament, separate from conscious or unconscious motivations, "that enables us to affirm the value of things and reject their defects, to become involved with them or turn away from them."[123] According to Balthasar, this constitutive freedom (which is given and received) is rather like Ignatian indifference. The second pillar of freedom emerges from the first and is the "freedom of autonomous motion," or freedom of will, freedom to choose. Where the first pillar may be thought as self-possession, the second is self-realization, and the manner of this self-realization in the world—as human beings move from alienation toward relations of mutual openness under the aegis of divine freedom, providence, and love—remains open and autonomous.[124]

The operation of self-realization, if it is not to construe God and others simply as a means of its own self-enjoyment, is "the opportunity to hand itself over to infinite free Being, to the Being who is the Giver of this free openness."[125] Thus finite freedom originates and is fulfilled in infinite freedom, which self-discloses with infinite generosity. (Balthasar employs the somewhat startling metaphor of an opening of the "womb of the Father's divine freedom."[126]) As demonstrated in the final chapter, the infinite freedom of God is a freedom to surrender God's Self, as the Father, Son, and Spirit mutually give of themselves in absolute love. This Trinitarian law of love, of "letting-be," which both characterizes and is the nature of infinite freedom, thereby safeguards the integrity of finite freedom. For Balthasar it is especially the Holy Spirit who frees the finite being to take on its own ultimate freedom through participation in infinite freedom, which is all beatitude.[127] This is no reabsorption of the finite into the infinite, but an affirmation of human finitude, "down to the last detail."[128] Balthasar makes this positive valuation of finitude clear in his monograph on Maximus, which, as noted earlier, anachronistically but profitably puts the Confessor into direct conversation with German Idealism. He quotes a memorable line from Maximus's *Ambigua*: "Whatever has no end (τέλος) to its natural activity is also not complete, not perfect (τέλειου)"[129] In an absorbtionist model, in which finitude disappears into an identification with the infinite, the most significant aspects of the creature are obliterated when true creaturely perfection is, rather, the preservation and perfection of its own unique limitations.

Moving therefore to the problem of evil, though Balthasar certainly recognizes the complexity of the question, he insists on maintaining that God as creator is unequivocally good and just, with no antagonistic principles within the divine essence; that human freedom is subordinate to God; and (against Schelling, Soloviev, and Berdyaev) that evil ought to be understood as a privation of the good.[130] Balthasar is no naïf. He acknowledges that it is impossible for human beings in modernity to pull on those antiquarian "spectacles, lent to him by the Christian faith, through which the spectator once contemplated the world and saw it transfigured."[131] Answering the problem of evil, however, cannot come at the expense of a good God in a proper, oppositional yet noncompetitive relation to human beings: "The emphasis changes when, in modern times, the darkness and fragmentation of creation is projected into the divine ground itself (*Jakob Böhme*) and speculation discovers the element of absoluteness in human freedom (*Schelling* in his middle years, continuing the idea of autonomy in *Kant*). Now it is *God* who bears the contradiction (including hell) in himself, and in the same breath man, with *his* contradiction, moves over into the realm of the absolute. Here, as an equal partner with God, he can accuse the world of being contradictory and existence of being meaningless."[132]

According to Balthasar, the fact that God's omnipotence is compromised on this model requires specifically Berdyaev to "adopt a gnostic tone" and insert tragedy into the inner life of God. This problematic is revisited in chapter 5, which addresses Balthasar's borrowings from Bulgakov on the "powerless-ness" of God through the primordial kenotic mode of the Trinitarian hypostases. Now, however, it is enough to indicate that the corrosive association of Böhme with Berdyaev is both clear and devastating enough in Balthasar.[133]

To summarize, Böhmian ontology, whether undiluted or as repeated by Schelling or the Russians to varying degrees, is for Balthasar quite outside the bounds of licit speculation. Though Balthasar sympathetically recognizes the tendency for human beings, when faced with the tenacious problem of evil and prodigious human suffering, to retroject the abyss onto God, thereby making it more intelligible, it represents a sort of speculation that is dangerous, destructive, and entirely inimical to Christian thought.[134] Balthasar speaks directly against the Böhmian/Schellingian/Berdyevean line of thinking: "The many forms of post-Christian Titanism, which dare to regard man as originating in a divinity that has (demonically) split (Jakob Böhme and those who came after him, right up to the Romantics, to von Baader, Schelling and the Russians) and destined ultimately to redeem this tragic God, are all inconceivable apart from their passage through Christianity. But they also lead to its total perversion."[135] This type of illicit speculation attempts to force its way behind the fundamental

Christian mystery of Christ, who was crucified freely and in love.[136] Further, once the mysterious essence of God is broached, it almost always becomes commoditized as a rationalistic means for explicating anthropology and cosmology.

MYTHOLOGY AND THE *POTENZENLEHRE*

The speculative ontology of divine potencies that was skeletal in Schelling's *Freiheitsschrift* and the *Weltalter* rises up as the bones in Ezekiel's valley and is clothed with tendon and flesh in the Berlin lectures on the philosophy of mythology. Bone by bone, the content of ancient myth covers and animates that which was largely metaphysical and theoretical in the earlier texts.[137] Schelling's *Potenzenlehre* invoked in his understanding of myth is highly original, departing from Hegel particularly in the religious, historical, and ontological weight he gives to myth. For the later Schelling, classic myths were neither simple fictitious stories composed by ancient singular geniuses, nor codified superstition, nor primitive imagistic attempts to grapple with natural phenomena that exceeded ready explanation. They were, rather, manifestations of the deepest structures of existence, expressive of the divine reality of the potencies.[138] Thus, as Edward Beach puts it succinctly, for Schelling "ontology was the core of mythological thought, just as mythology, conversely, was a concrete embodiment of ontology."[139]

According to Schelling, these deep ontological structures were repeated in the deepest layers of human unconscious, which were "not at all the result of conscious reflection, but sprang immediately and unbidden from the deepest regions of the soul."[140] According to Beach, Schelling understood myths to be "concrete historical phenomena, with a nature and morphology of their own"[141] and therefore operating according to a set of perceivable laws governed by the potencies. Myths and progressive religious developments were indicative of an actual theogonic process among the various divinities of various world religions. Most important for present purposes, however, is not the way Schelling handles the concrete, empirical data of ancient myth, cross-identifying certain deities as Moloch, Set, Baal, or Brahma, or the way he suggests that Persephone and Demeter function as the interpretive key to all mythology, but rather the theoretical framework of the *Potenzenlehre* that he offers to undergird his more particular claims.

It is important at the outset to note that Schelling's theory of the three potencies (A^1, A^2, A^3) is remarkably similar to Böhme's thesis of the primal triad of wills that emerges from the primitive, undifferentiated will. Schelling repeats Böhme's positing of an irrational ground in the structure of ontology that comes out in the symbolic or mythic register. In its purely conceptual, pre-actualized state, the first potency (signified as $-A$ or A^1) is undifferentiated pure potentiality, "being-in-itself," (das an sich Seiende, das sein Könnende).[142] It is an unstructured and infinite totality and thereby requires an "other" to provide objective structure and determinate form. Here Schelling recurs to the language of *ouk on* and *me on* (language that Berdyaev also employs, as he places himself in the line of this meonic tradition) with the former indicating absolute nonbeing and the latter indicating a relative nonbeing.[143]

The second potency ($+A$ or A^2) is the principle of pure objectivity and actuality that provides the required order and specific determination to the infinite potentiality of the first potency; it is eccentric being (das außer sich Seiende, das sein Müssende). Whereas A^1 is subjunctive, A^2 is indicative.[144] Further, while the first potency is all will, the second potency has no will of its own, but "constantly strives to satisfy the indeterminate propensities of the first Potency."[145] Because A^1 and A^2 are essentially incompatible with one another, a third potency is required: $\pm A$ or A^3, which mediates the subjectivity of the first potency and the objectivity of the second without (*contra* Hegel) sublating either term. This third potency is "being-with-itself" (das bei sich Seiende, das sein Sollende), which is the highest potency, the harmonization of the *Subjekt–Objekt*, which becomes the teleological goal of history as such. At this stage, these relations are ideal and merely formal.

According to Schelling, however, when the potencies become actualized and the visible universe comes into being, A^1 is violently con-/in-verted to a positive force of chaos and disorder (thereafter signified as "B") in order to explain the chaotic, dark beginning of concrete existence.[146] B operates antagonistically with respect to divine providence; it is a provisionally tolerated force that requires subduing through the processes of history, processes that work to transform B back to its proper state as A^1. It is in these terms—as instantiations of primal conflict between the first and the second potencies—that Schelling suggests ancient mythological religions should best be understood.[147] With respect to religious development, human beings must proceed from a primitive "relative" monotheism (where the first potency dominates) through polytheism to the absolute monotheism of the revealed religions of Judaism, Islam, and Christianity.[148] For Schelling, the submission of B occurs decisively only when mythology passes over into revelation, with the appearance of Christianity in human history, which points ahead to the third potency.[149] The pagan instantiations of A^2 (including Melkart, Osiris, Shiva, and Dionysus) are thus understood as precursors to Christ, who is according to Schelling the true manifestation of the actualized form of the second potency.[150]

Against Enlightenment rationalism and scientific functionalism, Schelling and Balthasar stand together insofar as they take myth very seriously and value it highly, though the latter resists the embedded speculative ontology of the former. As discussed above, Schelling devotes the last stages of his philosophical career to developing a philosophy of mythology (and then revelation); Balthasar gives the fourth volume of his aesthetics, *The Realm of Metaphysics in Antiquity*, over to Homer, Hesiod, Pindar, Aeschylus, Sophocles, and Plato. It is certainly not the case, then, that Balthasar considered myth as such to be a theologically unusable category, though he does reject a pernicious brand of mythologizing that extracts or abstracts ahistorical truths from events in history. Real myth, however, infuses brute facticity with mystery. Indeed, for Balthasar, metaphysics includes myth as revelatory of the meaning of being. Not only is the mythopoetic imagination valuable as a prefiguring of the relationship between God and the world, but biblical revelation "occurs in the same formal anthropological *locus* where the mythopoeic imagination designed its images of the eternal. . . [and] the fulfillment of [the human being's] entire philosophical-mythological questioning."[151] Balthasar leaves open the possibility that the true light of God shines upon myths and speculative philosophy, however slantwise, such that these figures can lead the seeker of truth to the God of revelation. He expresses particular sympathy for and admiration of the Russian religious spirit, which is, somewhat in the spirit of the mythological interests of the later Schelling, not intolerant of an antique, pagan past.[152] For Balthasar, it is not untoward to maintain that Christ "'inherits' the gods of paganism: that is to say, 'inherits' the splendour of the theophanies which now passes over to him, who is the sole Heir and the Wholly Other."[153] With respect to this rather generous posture, Balthasar privileges the East, saying that "in what concerns Christ's authentic heritage, Greek and Russian theology as a rule has a far better understanding than the West. Behind Alyosha and his *starets* the tradition stretches out for a thousand years or more."[154] Christ is the fulfillment of myth, but by this fulfillment myth is not totally vitiated.

Balthasar considers the value of Schelling's philosophy of mythology in particular to be located not only in its "subtlety," "sensitivity," or "philosophical seriousness,"[155] but also in a logic that contravenes the reigning trend of demythologization of biblical revelation. He speaks of a kind of brief flowering in the later Schelling, for whom "the *logoi spermatikoi* of ultimate forms of human and worldly fate which lie scattered in the myth, could be gathered together into the definitive form of revelation of Jesus Christ. Thus genuine art (rooted in the myth) would enjoy a relaxed relationship to what is Christian, for there is no reason why an illuminating and directing light may not fall from the form of revelation upon the significant forms of art which refer to the whole."[156] Indeed, according to Balthasar's assessment, the late Schelling "arrives at the very threshold of the gospel."[157] Though Schelling subsumes both pagan and Christian religion under the same category, Balthasar comments that his tendency to preserve the historical facticity of Christ is laudable.[158] To be fair, the late Schelling of the philosophy of revelation does not interpret Christianity in mythological terms, but asserts, "The true content of Christianity is a history into which the divine enters. . . . The historical element is not accidental to the doctrine, but the doctrine itself."[159] In Balthasar's evaluation of Schelling's late stance, he does admit that "the Incarnation is the truth of the subjective images of myth; it fulfills myth in the act of transcending it."[160] At the end of the day, however, the rationally conceived speculative system, not the historical facticity of Christ, is for Schelling the primary category.

Though it has much to recommend itself, Schelling's philosophy of mythology does not for Balthasar ultimately cross over the threshold. First, not only is it insufficiently determined by Scripture and the Christian theological tradition, it also departs from traditional theology as Schelling posits a Logos who kenotically "renounces this glory in order by his obedient sacrificial death to fulfill all the deaths suffered by the mythical gods and to reconcile the world with the Father."[161] It is *only* at this point of reconciliation that Christ becomes fully divine, a claim that is obviously theologically problematic for Balthasar. Second, according to Balthasar, Schelling's system of mythology stipulates the necessity of paganism as the ground from which Christianity develops.[162] Third, the association of the Trinitarian hypostases with the three potencies gives rise to a modalistic understanding of Trinity, which becomes personal only over a long course of development.[163] Fourth, while Balthasar permits that the late Schelling's formulation of the philosophy of mythology breaks out of the philosophical to be nearly if not totally theological, insofar as it constitutes a "lifting of the vision above the level of being,"[164] he is worried that Schelling simply cannot escape Hegel's gravitational pull toward a materialistic conception of being. Finally, Balthasar deeply resists a pernicious kind of monism (elsewhere ascribed to Georg Friedrich Creuzer, though it could well be ascribed to Schelling, whose mythological research relied heavily upon Creuzer) that would assert an exact correspondence between theology and mythology. Such an identification risks both sacralizing art and aestheticizing religion.[165] For Balthasar, there cannot be a continuous line extending without a break between mythology and revealed Christian faith. Christian revelation is absolutely new; thus, the governing metaphor cannot be that of the Tower of Babel.

The status of myth, for Balthasar, is that which can only intend (but only impotently) toward actualization: myths are beautiful on their own merit, but this aesthetic quality—*contra* the mythologies of Schelling and Berdyaev—is never actualized in human history, making the myth a sort of unfinished gesture or movement that invites completion and functions to indicate fundamentally their own "incapacity to provide salvation."[166] As put forward in chapter 1, the decisive answer to this "philosophical-mythological questioning" of human beings is and must be the Johannine Word who became flesh, very God and very history. The Incarnation of the Logos is the decisive difference between authentic Christianity and myth: the salvation event, which draws human beings into friendship with God, occurs in history, fulfilling the unfulfilled longing of mere mysticism and myth, for "reality is the place and the material within which the living God appears."[167] For Balthasar, Christ is no theory but, as the concrete universal, absolutely attenuates classical mythology as, with the advent of he who is the one true savior, "all the myths and fairytales become transparent to Him and consequently lose their weight."[168] This decisive Christological departure from the mythical imagination is ratified eschatologically by the resurrection of the dead, which is discussed in chapter 4. Further, by way of anticipation of chapter 5, it is particularly Balthasar's appeal (through Bulgakov) to the ur-image in Revelation of Christ as the Lamb as though slain which "must fulfill the inchoate yearnings of *mythos* and, at the same time, banish its uncertainties."[169]

More broadly, Balthasar's own view hearkens back—though again, without invoking him by name—to Bulgakov's excurses on the nature of myth, which are redolent of Schelling but without the drift toward theogony observed in Berdyaev.[170] As in Schelling, myths for Bulgakov are not the product of conscious thought, imagination, or subjective literary invention, but carry an objective meaning in response to some event, some genuine though veiled encounter with transcendence mediated through the Logos.[171] Hegel's view fails on this count for Bulgakov, too, for it accords all of the power of mythmaking to the mythmaker. Bulgakov insists, however, that myth results from religious experience that is theurgic and not simply subjective, a "certain going out of the self into the domain of divine being, some sort of divine operation."[172] As in Balthasar, the singular instance of myth's coincidence with history for Bulgakov is the incarnation, death, and resurrection of God the Word made flesh, such that myth is for the first time truly visible to those with eyes to see.[173]

MYTH: RUSSIAN REPETITIONS

In *The Meaning of History*, Berdyaev weighs in positively on Schelling's philosophy of mythology, calling it an "ingenious theory according to which mythology represents the repetition in the human spirit and consciousness of the processes of nature."[174] Schelling thus becomes incredibly influential on Berdyaev's claim that concrete mythology is the fundament and originary basis of human history. As Berdayev suggests, mythology is "the opening page of a tale about man's terrestrial destiny, which succeeded his celestial one and the prologue which was enacted in heaven,"[175] this prologue being the original freedom and fall into the natural, physical world. These deep structures of myth preexist discursive reason, imprinted as they are on the font of human nature itself.[176] Myth for Berdyaev is not a "naïve or false contrivance,"[177] but the mode in excess of discursive reason that conceals the very greatest mystery of humankind. For him, then, a philosophy of history ought to be based on an identification of history with the mythological. He writes, "History is not an objective empirical datum; it is a myth. Myth is no fiction, but a reality; it is, however, one of a different order from that of the so-called objective empirical fact. . . . [It] transcends the limits of the external objective world, revealing an ideal world."[178] As suggested above, though Balthasar and Bulgakov side with Schelling and Berdyaev, insofar as myth countenances pernicious forces of rationalism and demythologization, they are unprepared to accept the speculative ontologies embedded in their mythological programs. While there is for Balthasar "a real analogy between revelation and the beautiful, both the natural revelation of mythology and the supernatural revelation,"[179] he insists absolutely that the two cannot be collapsed.

With respect to Balthasar's estimations, then, Schelling and Berdyaev do not fare well because they depart too drastically from Scripture and the theological tradition. It goes better for Soloviev, though not as well as it does for Bulgakov, who will be treated more at length in the next two chapters. Soloviev's very early text *The Mythological Process in Paganism* (1873) certainly owes debts to Schelling's own philosophy of mythology.[180] Balthasar recognizes this relation of dependence, noting that the text "takes its bearings from Schelling."[181] Schelling's three potencies—being-in-itself (an sich Seiende), being-for-itself (für sich Seiende), and being-with-itself (bei sich Seiende) resurface definitively in Soloviev's doctrine of God in the *Lectures on Divine Humanity*.[182] In this text Soloviev delineates his Trinitarian doctrine of God, which he considers to be "a doctrine which is at once the crown of pre-Christian religious wisdom and the basic speculative principle of Christianity."[183] Much like Schelling, Soloviev identifies a conundrum at the heart of it: God exists as such, transcending any finite determination. The meaning of God as existent, however, must simultaneously exceed the abstraction of being in general, since "*being* can be conceived only *as the relation of an existent to its objective essence or content*, a relation in which it affirms, posits, or manifests its content, its essence, in one way or another."[184] God possesses all being, all determinate content. At the same time, however, God cannot be a determinate thing among other things. Thus, for Soloviev, as in Schelling and Böhme, God is the Absolute, the super-subsistent All, though Soloviev understands this claim to resist a devolution into naturalistic or idealistic pantheism: "The only possible answer to the question, What is God? is the one already known to us, namely, that God is the all, that is, that the all in the positive sense, or the unity of all things, constitutes God's own content, object, or objective essence, and that God's actual being is the assertion or positing of this content, of this essence, and, in it, of the One who posits, the existent One."[185] God is thus a subject/existent who possesses and manifests the All (that is, divine content or essence): the content of this All is "absolute love, that is, love that equally contains and responds to all . . . precisely that ideal all, that all-integrity that constitutes the proper content of the divine principle."[186]

This relation between God as existent and God's essence is exemplified in three self-positings, which align for Soloviev determinatively with the Trinitarian hypostases. Adapting Schelling,[187] his first positing (God in God's Self) is God as potentiality, as nondifferentiated immediacy, as absolute subject: at this stage the content of God is not actualized, but only latent. Now, according to Soloviev, "for this universal essence to be actual, God not only must contain it *in Himself*, that is, He must affirm it as other, must manifest and actualize it as something distinct from Himself."[188] The second positing (God for God's Self) draws out that which is latent and undifferentiated into objective actuality, expressing through God's own free self-determination (not external necessity) the inner content of the first mode. The third positing (God with God's Self), is the perfect union of the first two positings, a unity that is "already *asserted*, manifested, or mediated, having passed through its own opposite, through a differentiation, and it is thereby *intensified* (potentiated)."[189]

THE ABSOLUTION OF VLADIMIR SOLOVIEV

Soloviev's debts to Schelling—here and elsewhere—are self-conscious and not simply accidental. Indeed, a jotting in one of his notebooks from 1875 is telling, indicating a self-styled alliance to a certain line of esoteric speculative thinking. The entry reads:

> Kabbalah and Neoplatonism.
> Boehme and Swedenborg.
> Schelling and me.[190]

As Balthasar maintains, however, Soloviev's deeply original religious philosophy does not guilelessly repeat Schelling, but rather seeks to broaden and enrich the boundaries of Orthodox thought by opening up the potential resources of Western philosophy. Balthasar's essay on Soloviev is remarkable in this respect, as it consistently provides an alibi—one that is, if not unjust, somewhat peculiar in its insistence— for Soloviev. Balthasar alibis him on several counts, first by putting the accent more on his patristic pedigree, including Maximus, Augustine, and Thomas, than on inheritances from German Idealism and Romanticism. As Balthasar's perhaps too gentle critique suggests, Soloviev's appeals to Schelling are mitigated by his deep formation by biblical texts, especially the Wisdom tradition, the Greek fathers (Maximus the Confessor in particular), and mystical literature. Even the impulse to open up the Chalcedonian tradition to include, for instance, Soloviev's "Godmanhood" has for Balthasar a Maximian imprimatur, as Maximus himself is profiled in Balthasar's monograph as a creative genius, not of a class of "trivial compilers or passive reservoirs . . . [but rather of] creators, who can work, surely with traditional material but who also know how to arrange the pieces according to their own architectural design."[191]

Balthasar's propensity for absolving Soloviev whenever possible is certainly not unwarranted, since, on balance, the departures between Soloviev and Schelling are enormously significant. First, unlike Berdyaev, Soloviev opposes Schelling's understanding of darkness as a constitutive element of divinity. For instance, in *Russia and the Universal Church*, Soloviev avers that "the proper sphere of the Father is absolute light, light in itself, having no relation with darkness,"[192] and further, "in God can be found *no shadow of evil whatsoever*."[193] Even in his triadic scheme in *Lectures on Divine Humanity*, which details the three spheres of primordial divinity, there is no shadowed ground, no bitterness or wrath; the divine being is in all modes "'free from envy,' from exclusiveness," it is "all-one and all-good."[194] Second, Soloviev's triadic scheme is more tightly determined by his Trinitarian commitments. Though Soloviev's conception of the Trinity in *Lectures* has rightly been described as a "curious hybrid of Hegelian dialectic, Schellingean *Potenzenlehre*, and classical Trinitarian theology of the Fourth and Fifth Centuries,"[195] it is remarkable that Balthasar recognizes but is not terribly put off by Soloviev's apparent debts to the esoteric tradition, including Böhme, Swedenborg, and von Baader, beyond those already mentioned. No, according to Balthasar a process of purification takes place in Soloviev's reading of dubious sources: "[He] fully appropriates them for himself, the muddy stream runs through him as if through a purifying agent and is distilled in crystal-clear, disinfected waters, answering the needs of his own philosophical spirit, which (in contrast to that of so many of his speculative compatriots) can live and breathe only in an atmosphere of unqualified transparency and intelligibility."[196] Balthasar's assessment, while perhaps hyperbolic, is not terribly off the mark.[197] Indeed, as explored in chapter 5, Balthasar enthusiastically affirms the theology of Bulgakov, whose more careful work filters out some of Soloviev's excesses. Further, Soloviev's conception of the All as essentially absolute love that freely flowers forth an-Other as well as the created order informs Bulgakov's plural understanding of kenosis, which Balthasar adopts without significant critique.[198] In Balthasar's assessment, though Soloviev shares quite a bit structurally with Schelling, he "fills up the idealistic form with what he considers to be (and wants to be grasped as) Christian content. As the ground of all that is (*quod est*, the subject), God is Father; as paradigm of existing reality (*essential*, the object), he is Son; and as that which unites both (*esse*, identity), he is Spirit or being."[199]

Finally, Soloviev's debts to Böhme and Schelling are displaced by the self-consciously central element of this thinking: the Jesus Christ of historic, revealed religion, who is not simply one case of divine humanity among many others, but rather its "unique and all-transcending peak."[200] What is primary for Soloviev is not—as in Schelling—system building, wherein the particulars of Christianity must stretch to fit a Procrustean bed of speculative, abstract theologizing, but the historical fact of Christ as *the* manifestation of divine humanity. In *Lectures*, Soloviev argues that "the originality of Christianity lies not in its general views but in positive facts, not in the speculative content of its idea but in its personal incarnation."[201] Balthasar certainly understands Soloviev to be a thoroughly Christological and Chalcedonian thinker after the manner of Maximus; though he may take certain language or concepts or logic from Idealism, he is not fatally determined by these debts. As Balthasar suggests, Soloviev's interest in ever-increasing integration "will be bound to take its aspect of formal absoluteness from rational idealism, but the real fullness of substantive historical content from empirical 'materialism.' In Christ, the real and the ideal have become archetypally one."[202] A careful analysis of Soloviev indicates, then, if not a total innocence, a strongly Trinitarian and Christological mooring.

This emphasis on the facticity of Christ thus exceeds the merely mythological. Very broadly speaking, the moderns wanted to reinvigorate the (simply) historical with the mythic. We have seen that for Schelling mythology is the primordial history (Urgeschichte) of human beings, a notion Berdyaev takes up decisively. Though Balthasar recognizes the possibility of the disclosive, truth-giving power of myth and understands Christianity to be functionally hospitable to myth (particularly Greek and Roman), it is never at the expense of this most basic substance of Christian faith: Jesus Christ. Christ—as incarnate and resurrected flesh—is decisively an historical, not a mythical figure. Christianity may appear to be one variant among others, a repetition of the ancient structures of myth, but history is the decisive difference. For Balthasar, the resurrected flesh of Christ mitigates against the mythical: "All Christian teaching proceeds from the experience of the bodily Resurrection of Christ, which is by no means mythical and speculative but sober and historical; and this Resurrection illuminates the truth and meaning of his Cross and, behind it, of his entire Incarnation. . . . In the face of this basic datum, all the vestiges of mythical ideas, of mythical thinking and speaking in the New Testament shrink to purely formal ways of expressing something that is completely new and unique."[203]

This is in no wise to say that for Balthasar extra-confessional discourses such as philosophy and myth have no place in a Christian theology that places the historical Christ at its very center. Soloviev, for instance, points out an "essential kinship" between Neoplatonism and Christianity, but does not consider these resonances to jeopardize the unique content of Christianity as a positive revelation. Though the "same speculative theme, the self-revelation of the all-one Divinity"[204] is sounded, the metaphysical speculations of Alexandrian philosophy are precisely that: speculation. And yet, according to Soloviev, Christians could recognize in these theoretical abstractions that which they had experienced in Christ as "living reality."[205] This living content of biblical revelation makes the difference that gives life to the dry bones of simply formal models.

THIS CHAPTER WAS AN exposition of the modes in which the cluster of themes motivating the theogonic myth of Böhme—creation, theodicy, freedom, the origin and nature of evil, and myth—moved through the thought of Schelling and was then creatively assimilated or repeated in Berdyaev and Soloviev. In his adjudicating these discourses in the Russians, Balthasar considers Berdyaev's repetitions of Böhme to be too literal, more a dull echo than a pleasing riff; his acceptance of *das Dunkle* at the heart of God fatally compromises his theological philosophy of human finitude and his doctrine of God. Soloviev's repetitions, however, attenuate the Böhmian and Schellingian heritage with accents on more traditional sources in the Fathers, particularly Maximus the Confessor. It should be perfectly clear from the foregoing, however, that even in his affirmations of a traditional heritage, Balthasar is constitutively open to other conceptual fields. He has an easy freedom with respect to the limited value of extra-confessional discourses, though he couples this leniency with a capaciously orthodox sensibility that insists upon maintaining the integrity of both God and human being.

CHAPTER 4

"GRÜN WIRKLICHER GRÜNE, WIRKLICHER SONNENSCHEIN, WIRKLICHER WALD"

Anthropological Eschata *and the Logic of Resurrection*

In *The Russian Idea*, Berdyaev quite rightly characterizes Russians as "a people of the end."[1] Both the penultimate and the final substantive chapters of this book thus consider, appropriately, endings. The capacious frontiers of eschatology and apocalyptic, which in their strangeness and beauty determine rather than bookend the theological task, bring many of our previous concerns to a point—both in time and of infinite density—and are the most fertile ground for examining the complex relation between Schelling, the Russian triumvirate, and Balthasar, all of whom are eschatologically and apocalyptically disposed. Again, the task is not strictly to demonstrate a textual genealogy between Balthasar and the Russian Orthodox thinkers, although that is arguable: the stated purpose of this book is to demonstrate homologous content and shared imagination in order to make a fairly simple claim about the fundamental mode and method of Balthasar's theology.

Because eschatological concerns constitutively categorize all the thinkers considered, it will be necessary to narrow the field of inquiry to the most striking convergences between Balthasar, Schelling, and the Russians, namely, (1) the meaning of death and resurrection, and the nature of postmortem existence, with particular attention to what is entailed by the anthropological category of *geistige Körperlichkeit* (spiritual corporeality); (2) the nature of hell as imaginative rather than physical space; (3) the possibility of universal salvation; (4) a shared Johannine register; (5) figurations of Antichrist as a function of religious counterfeiting; and finally (6) the positive connection of paschal Trinitarianism with apocalyptic, the unveiling of which reveals that everything is taken in and contained eschatologically.

How best to begin to accomplish this admittedly daunting task? Within the purview of eschatology, Balthasar makes an important and helpful distinction between anthropological *eschata*, which includes death, judgment, hell, and heaven—perhaps the most traditional understanding of what eschatology considers—and the theocentric, which is the ultimate, and the ultimately determinative Trinitarian horizon. Though in the order of being the anthropological and the theocentric cannot be separated (indeed, Balthasar asserts that the anthropocentric can *only* be understood within the context of the theocentric), this chapter examines the former and chapter 5 the latter, with attention to the deformative lineage of Böhme and Joachim in Schelling, which reappears in the Russians marginally in Soloviev and maximally in Berdyaev, who, like Joachim, parses time into three distinct epochs. This chapter queries human dying and rising, which naturally entails a discussion of theological anthropology (however skeletal), the nature of the final judgment, and the (perhaps unfashionable) subject of hell, which leads ultimately to the threshold of the possibility of universal salvation.

This chapter, like the others, recurs to the formula of imaginatively construing the theological speculations of Balthasar alongside those of Schelling and the Russians (with Bulgakov again having pride of place), a construction that first and foremost is intended diagnostically to indicate the periphery of licit theological conjecture for confessional religious discourse. It is particularly in the context of eschatology, at the frontiers of that which can be known, that Balthasar explicitly recommends pursuing the more speculative questions. This recommendation does not come at the cost of dogmatically defined doctrines, but he does leave to future generations the creative exploration of eschatological questions that admit no pat answers so as to "develop from the core of truth . . . a more extensive and adequate body of speculation."[2] Bulgakov likewise calls attention to the fact that, with respect to eschatology, there are no universally binding dogmatic definitions made by the Church, and thus developments in this area are somewhat provisional and open to "free theological investigation."[3]

With respect to Balthasar's speculative eschatology, the general trend of his evaluation of Schelling—an uneasy mixture of attraction and repulsion—holds. He affirms philosophy's unique contributions to human understanding, which can and ought to be factored into the theological project, but these contributions always fall flat because they are disconnected from the dynamism (and humility) of a living relation to biblical revelation that authentic Christianity provides (and requires). The structural homologies of Schelling's philosophy with authentically Christian revelation, particularly the late adoption of a religious vocabulary that might suggest a greater degree of compatibility with Christian metaphysics than is actually possible, given Schelling's required elision of the genuinely historical to the ideal and the mythical, are actually far more insidious because of the similarities. As Balthasar writes in another context, "Tragically, the attempts that come closest to the truth are usually the most dangerous, because they are the most presumptuous (Icarus and his wings): precisely because they are so sure of success, they fail most fundamentally to grasp the humility of the God who humbles himself in taking the form of man."[4]

In the first volume of his *Apokalypse der deutschen Seele*, Balthasar refers to Schelling as "der wahre theoretische Eschatologe der Zeit"[5] and "der eigentliche Apokalyptiker,"[6] though for Balthasar, Schelling's apocalypse is more Enochian than not in its presumptive unveiling of mystery, a sure demerit given Balthasar's trepidation about intertestamental apocalyptic literature.[7] This reserve is corroborated throughout the Balthasarian corpus, but especially in the sixth volume of *The Glory of the Lord*, where Balthasar criticizes it for falling prey to a tendency toward unrestrained speculative inquiry: "In their inquisitiveness, they press forwards and break through, making inquiries about the heavenly realm *like tourists* and having angels lead them even to the throne of the glory on high."[8] It is this tourism-*cum*-voyeurism that Balthasar finds objectionable: when eschatology is thought outside of an existential register it becomes a morbid spectator sport that reconfigures revelation first as disproportionately anthro-pocentric/morphic and second as overemphasizing the world to come at the expense of the present, earthly world, "forgetting that this is the good creation of God, the place of his covenant and the abiding foun-dation of all the promises."[9] Notably, Berdyaev's eschatology, aligned more nearly with the Enochian apocalyptic tradition than the book of Revelation, suffers from the same defects.[10]

While Balthasar deems Schelling's brand of speculative escha-tology to be insufficient, it is especially striking to compare Balthasar's speculative eschatology in *The Final Act*, the fifth volume of his *Theo-Drama*, with Bulgakov's, which, as we will address in the following chapter, operates like a (heretofore underestimated) subcutaneous musculature that animates Balthasar's paschal Trinitarianism. Further-more, with respect to the question of universal salvation, both take a probative position, though it turns out in (and about) the end that Balthasar is more modest than Bulgakov. In a shared resistance to the Enochian brand of apocalyptic, which presumes to know too much, the governing interpretive principle invoked to constrain speculation in Balthasar and Bulgakov is the fundamental mysteriousness of the end of history, death, afterlife, and so on, though Bulgakov occasion-ally uses this invocation as warrant for pressing further forward.

Balthasar's speculation is circumscribed by an epistemic humility, a tentativeness that dares only to suggest rough sketches or images but not to presuppose the certainty of a science. His tone is not overcon-fident, but rather is characterized by modesty with respect to making definite claims. For instance, he opens one article on eschatology with the bald statement that "concerning the whereabouts and circum-stances of the dead: we know nothing."[11] This epistemic inaccessibility, however, is not a demerit according to Balthasar. Paradoxically, the more inaccessible *ta eschata* are to thought, the more *actual* they be-come; these are not just more "things" continuous with the "things" of the earth.[12] From this posture of tentativeness, Balthasar and Bulgakov alike follow intramural indications latent in the boundaries of Scrip-ture and tradition toward the speculative in their reflections on the postmortem state, reflections that are "nothing more than an aston-ished stammering as we circle around this mystery on the basis of particular luminous words and suggestions of Holy Scripture."[13]

A NOTE ON TEXTS

Because all of these thinkers have a constitutively eschatological orientation, it is not possible to supply a full-bodied treatment of their individual eschatologies as such. With respect to Schelling, these chapters privilege the fragmentary dialogue *Clara, or, On Nature's Connection to the Spirit World*, as well as *The Ages of the World*, with limited attention to the more informal, popular-level 1810 *Stuttgart Lectures* (which went unpublished in his lifetime).[14] Though Berdyaev's entire orientation bears an eschatological stamp, here *The Beginning and the End* and *The Destiny of Man* serve best. Soloviev's *War, Progress, and the End of History* is likewise sufficiently representative, as is Bulgakov's *The Bride of the Lamb*, particularly the final section.[15] In terms of Balthasar's great triptych of *The Glory of the Lord*, *Theo-Drama*, and *Theo-Logic*, from which many eschatological gems can easily be mined, these chapters nevertheless privilege the fourth and fifth volumes of *Theo-Drama*, in which Balthasar's generally uncomplicated profile as apocalyptic theologian—typified as paschal and Trinitarian, and ratified in *Mysterium Paschale* (1970)—emerges most perspicuously. The argument of these texts is underwritten by that of the early *Apokalypse der deutschen Seele*, which executes a wide-ranging critique of the apocalyptic timbre of German philosophy and literature from Idealism and Romanticism onward.[16] With respect to the question of universal salvation in Balthasar's thought, the slim but provocative *Dare We Hope "That All Men Be Saved"?* and its epilogue, "A Short Discourse on Hell," shall certainly come under discussion.

ADRIENNE VON SPEYR AS BIBLICAL COMMENTATOR

Balthasar's apocalyptic "law of heightening" is reflected structurally in the texts of the *Theo-Drama*; after volume 1, *Prolegomena*, come volumes of the anthropological (vol. 2), the Christological (vol. 3), the soteriological (vol. 4), and, finally, the Trinitarian (vol. 5), which is the main vehicle for an exposition of his (thoroughly Trinitarian) eschatology, informed not least by the biblical commentaries of Adrienne von Speyr. A drawing-out of Balthasar's subterranean engagement with Russian, and specifically Bulgakovian, eschatological themes by no means displaces what can only be described as the wholly saturated presence of von Speyr in Balthasar's eschatology. Indeed, Balthasar's decidedly eschatological fourth and fifth volumes of *Theo-Drama* are where von Speyr's presence, particularly through a reliance on her commentaries on John and Revelation, is most felt. These texts of the *Theo-Drama* are an exercise in intertextuality, with lengthy quotations from von Speyr interwoven with Balthasar's own prose in order to indicate their speaking in *una voce*. In those two volumes in particular he speaks *as* von Speyr, weaving his own narrative into quotes from her copious works in order to "show the fundamental consonance between her views and mine."[17] This self-understanding is further corroborated when Balthasar notes that "the greater part of so much of what I have written is a translation of what is present in more immediate, less technical fashion in the powerful work of Adrienne von Speyr."[18]

Despite the strangeness and uncanny nature of some of von Speyr's reported mystical experiences, which make even ardent Balthasarians a little nervous, this kind of self-conscious announcement, compounded by the performance of perhaps superfluous levels of quotation—meant explicitly to ratify von Speyr's status as source and biblical commentator—really ought to be trusted. Other scholars are not so convinced, finding von Speyr's work to be either uninformative or wholly deformative to Balthasar's theological enterprise. For instance, Mongrain suggests that though von Speyr is important for understanding Balthasar psychologically, her influence "was deforming rather than constructive, derived rather than original . . . [and] *completely dispensable* for theologically understanding him."[19] Given Balthasar's own articulation of her positive influence, as well as the abundant level of textual and thematic quotation, Mongrain's claim seems difficult to sustain.[20]

It is certainly fair at the least to construe von Speyr's biblical commentary on Revelation as complementary to Bulgakov's with respect to informing Balthasar's theological project. If Balthasar speaks with von Speyr in *una voce*, however, he speaks with Bulgakov *sotto voce*, and this studied lowering of the voice calls particular attention to an absolutely vital Russian source. One might theorize, particularly in the densely Speyrian passages in *Theo-Drama* 5 (especially "The World is from the Trinity"), that Balthasar is *over*performing, *over*ratifying von Speyr as source, *over*emphasizing for the very sake of normalizing and regulating her as source. To lower the voice, to speak in secret—in theatrical terms, as an aside—is perhaps to draw a special emphasis to what is said and to the method of delivery.

THE THANATOLOGICAL AND THE ANTHROPOLOGICAL

Following traditional accounts of eschatology, the first aspect for consideration is death and the character of the postmortem state. To supply an account of human dying is at the same time to supply an account, however abbreviated, of theological anthropology and the relationship of body, soul, and spirit. For Balthasar, for whom death is both immanent and increasingly imminent, the heartrending riddle of human death is the clearest expression of the central existential paradox of life, the primary instance of expressing the absolute through the relative, the infinite through the finite.[21] In the mortal condition of bodily existence, human beings "are constrained to inscribe things of absolute validity upon a time continuum that is running out."[22] Human beings are liminal, "centaurlike" creatures who constantly must negotiate the absolute in the transient, particularly in confronting their own certain death, which highlights their insoluble existential paradox.[23] Construing a theology of death in terms of the negotiation between finite and infinite elements is a major point of commonality— as well as, perhaps, the site of greatest distance with respect to the ultimate standing of finitude—between Schelling, the Russians, and Balthasar.

In the first volume of *Apokalypse der deutschen Seele*, in which Balthasar treats the eschatological attitude of figures in German Idealism, his essay on Schelling indicates his own discomfort with a posture that is ambivalent at best to the experience of finitude. At the root of Schelling's thought—the ambivalence of which transfers squarely to his eschatology—Balthasar identifies two competing aspects: the ecstatic mystical spiritualist aspect, which locates meaning wholly outside the finite (e.g., in its necessary dissolution of the particular within the infinite Absolute) and the organic-creative aspect, in which finite and Absolute work together to attain the creative realization of the All-Real.[24] The first attitude, in which finite things are *non-esse*, indicates that the particular concrete thing is in the All insofar as it is imbued by and dissolved into the All, which comprises the genuine identity of finite and infinite. This identity of the finite with the infinite, however, requires that the finite cease to be so.[25] Here, on the one hand, is an unmistakably "other-worldly" stance. On the other hand, as Balthasar points out, is the more positive reading that finite beings have no *an-sich-sein* precisely because they are in God and thereby participate in the potencies (A^1, A^2, A^3) of dynamic vitality that move toward *Allsein*.[26] This indicates a radical immanence.

This paradoxical formula, in which the finite and all physical existence are decried as nonbeing apart from its *Auflösung* in the Absolute, and at the same time valorized for their work in realizing *Allsein*, renders the existential attitude of human being as irredeemably ambiguous: both ex-stasis and en-stasis are at the same time recommended.[27] For Schelling, the fundamental characteristic of the material is heaviness, gravity; it is eccentric to being and synonymous with nonlife.[28] This puts human being in a double bind; the human is created and destroyed in the same act.[29] This anthropological ambivalence, again, seeps darkly into Schelling's eschatology.

As has been suggested in previous chapters, the same ambivalence about the finite that Balthasar identifies here is enormously present in Berdyaev. Because of his express reliance upon the Böhmian cosmological myth that begins with a dark, irrational "meonic" freedom prior to God and commitment to the simultaneity of the Fall and the actualization of the phenomenal world, the created order radiates from its root and center a chaotic, poisoned core. As shown in chapter 3, Berdyaev understands the Fall of humanity to be a fall, to put it in Kantian terms, from the freedom of the noumena *into* the objectified necessity of the phenomenal, that is, *into* the natural world, which is explicitly in an antagonistic relation to the world of spirit. For Berdyaev, spirit—

characterized as an existence of freedom, love, and personality beyond objective and subjective reality—is primary; that which is actually concrete, the material world, is secondary and derivative, only "an epiphenomena of spirit."[30]

Though Berdyaev's insistence on existential personalism does separate his view from Schelling's essential monism, human finitude really fares no better in his system. Personality is a spiritual, ethical category, not a genetic or biological one. Berdyaev tries to exempt the form of the human body itself ("and the expression of the eyes"[31]) as elements of the spiritual personality rather than physical, and thus not in antagonistic relation to spirit, but this gesture is weak at best. Furthermore, the thrust of his eschatology anticipates the destruction, not the transformation, of the world, brought about by a final "creative" and cooperative act of God and human beings together, where "the crowning point of world creation is the end of the world. . . . The world must be turned into an image of beauty, it must be dissolved in creative ecstasy."[32] This denigration of the finite Balthasar will not countenance.

DEATH EXPERIENCED: SCHELLING AND *GEISTIGE KÖRPERLICHKEIT*

Schelling himself was no stranger to death. The tragic losses of his wife, Caroline, and her daughter, Auguste (reportedly due to his own peculiar interventions in her medical care), were likely deeply formative in the composition of his philosophical dialogue *Clara, or, On Nature's Connection to the Spirit World*.[33] This text, a fictionalized and fragmentary narrative that begins, appropriately, on All Souls' Day, deals with the question of life after death and the possibility and form of the postmortem perdurance of the human being, which is, as in Augustine, holistic and tripartite; that is, the human being is a unity of body, spirit, and soul. The text reflects this anthropology in its three main characters: the doctor (nature/body), the priest (spirit/mind), and one of the only named characters, Clara (soul/personality). This anthropology reflects Schelling's understanding of God as having three divine potencies: the real and the ideal, and their identity, principles that are correlative to body, spirit, and soul. As the divine is the identity of real and ideal, so too human existence can include the antinomial pairings of the corporeal and spiritual principles, with the soul providing the principle of absolute identity and the bond between body and spirit.

In an important piece of dialogical exposition between Clara and the priest, it comes to light that "the whole person" must be reunited after the separation of death, after which the body and the spirit are united through the power of the soul, which, sharing equally in the nature of both body and spirit, mediates between them.[34] The soul, then, is primary, "the *most noble* of the three, because it alone includes the other two within it."[35] It is the "actual innermost germ of life."[36] Yet, importantly, these elements of human being are not hermetically sealed one from the other, but all contain in themselves something latent of the other. Duality is sublated. Thus, the body does not suddenly *become* spiritual at death: it is rather the case that "the spiritual side of the body that here [i.e., on earth] was hidden and subordinate becomes one that there [i.e., in the "spirit-world"] is manifest and dominant."[37]

For Schelling, the spiritual always already has a corporeal element, and the corporeal always already has a spiritual element, claims that according to Schelling provide the condition of the possibility for spectral reality: animal magnetism, the existence of ghosts, and so on.[38] This idea of *geistige Körperlichkeit*, a shadowy in-between space, emerges first in *Clara* and reappears later in the *Stuttgart Lectures*.[39] According at least to the first part of the dialogue (excluding the so-called spring fragment), Schelling is of the opinion that the body has both inner and outer elements; the former passes over to the spiritual world at death, while the latter is the natural, gross body of flesh.[40] Death, then, at least theoretically, is no horror but "a positive transition into a spiritual condition"[41] and "the release of the inner form of life from the external one that keeps it suppressed."[42] As Clara herself puts it in the dialogue, "To me death always seemed to be something that assembles rather than disperses."[43] For Schelling, the moment of death is a *transcensus* into another life with what was spiritual (daimonic) within the body, and the suppression of that which is merely natural:

> Death is therefore not an absolute separation of the spirit from the body, but only a separation from that element of the body that is in opposition to the spirit . . . of the good from the evil, then, and of the evil from the good. This means that it is not just part of the person that is immortal, but rather the whole person in regard to the true essence—death is a reduction to the essential (*reductio ad essentiam*). In order not to confuse it with the purely spiritual, we would like to give the name 'the daimonic' to the being that is not left behind in death (since what is left behind is a dead body [*caput mortuum*]) but becomes reconstructed, since it is neither simply spiritual nor simply physical but is the spiritual (dimension) of the physical and the physical (dimension) of the spiritual. So the immortal part of a person is the daimonic, not a negation of the physical but rather the physical reduced to its essence.[44]

So the unity of body, soul, and spirit is maintained, though the body as Schelling understands it is an "essentification" of physicality that strips from it all that is *non-esse* (and, though the philosopher doth protest too much, all that is personal).[45] Schelling's anthropology is thus (at best) ambivalent about the status of the finite body as oppositional to spirit, which, as Balthasar points out, always retains something negative even in its so-called transfiguration.[46]

RUSSIAN REPETITIONS: SPIRITUAL CORPOREALITY

The sophiological legacy of Soloviev bears with it a notion of the spiritualization of matter as well, which goes on to feature prominently in Bulgakov's understanding of human "sophianicity" and ultimately in his description of resurrected bodies. In Bulgakov's anthropology, as in Schelling's, human beings are tripartite composites of spirit, body, and soul, the latter two of which belong to the "earth," or created nature.[47] The spirit—which is from God and thus is both uncreated and created—has a "potency of immortality"[48] that is communicated gradually (and ultimately, eschatologically) to the created nature of the body-soul complex.

As in Balthasar's metaphysics of death, death is in Bulgakov's thanatology an unnatural pathology, a horrific minus, an ontologically parasitic "open maw of non-being."[49] Elsewhere he vividly characterizes "pug-nosed" death as a "gaping hole" with "no ontic core."[50] It is, in short, a state of contradiction. And yet it can only temporarily disrupt the tripartite composite of human beings, who are in their fullest potentiality by virtue of the divine origin of the spirit, "God-earth, an incarnate godlike spirit,"[51] which permits personal participation in the divine (not monistic dissolution into the divine, as is the case for Schelling). This is death as "dormition," not annihilation.[52] Because death is ontologically a negative—accidental rather than substantial—it can be comprehended only in the context and as a particular state of life.[53]

In his explication of the dissolving power of death upon the union of the creaturely principles of soul and body from spirit, Bulgakov does not seem to be terribly far from Schelling's notion of spiritual corporeality at play in *Clara*:

> In the tripartite structure of man, death's dividing sickle passes between the spirit and the soul . . . on the one hand and between the spirit and the body on the other. It is very important to take into account this indivisibility of the spirit and the soul in death, for it confirms the principle of creaturely immortality in the continuing connection with this world. The soul is an intermediate principle connecting the spirit with the creaturely world. *The soul is creaturely, like the "blood" that animates the body: The physical body dies and decomposes together with the body. But the supraphysical energy of life, whose substratum is the blood, abides (this can also be expressed by the esoteric notion of the "etheric" or "astral" body).*[54]

Bulgakov, however, appeals to this somewhat peculiar analogue of the astral body in order to safeguard the integrity of human being from death's final victory: if death were to cleave the creaturely principle entirely from the spiritual (the noncreaturely-creaturely), then it would triumph, and the human being "would fall apart into onto-logical dust."[55] While perhaps speculatively brave, his speculations here do not denigrate the finite. Quite the contrary, for Bulgakov, human persons are specified, concretized in the world of bodies, in the created order, and do not lose that connection at death, all in order *not* to dehumanize human being:

> The human hypostasis does not have a spiritual, supramundane being, nor, in this being, an immortality independent of incarna-tion. The human spirit is not created a fleshless spirit, like the angels. No human spirit can exist independently of the world. It therefore does not have abstract, nonhuman immortality. Its very being and, therefore, immortality (insofar as it possesses the latter) are qualified by and inseparably connected with the world. This immortality is a human one, whose realization encompasses both death and resurrection. Both the one and the other, accomplished in Christ and, in Him and through Him, in all humankind, have, so to speak, their ontological place in human nature, fully assumed by the Lord in His incarnation.[56]

Christ's death does not represent a disincarnation; rather, "the connec-tion of His divine spirit with His body also remains, as the pledge of resurrection (this is the basis for the dogmatic doctrine of relics.)"[57] Further, the resurrected spiritual body retains its body-ness, having the property of a certain spatial extension.[58]

In his theology of resurrection, Bulgakov suggests that in human death corporeality is only potentialized, made dormant, until the seed flowers forth at resurrection. According to Bulgakov's theology of res-urrection, this germinative function, the "quickening power," actual-izes that body, which is proper for the soul, with material taken from the natural world. This feature of his thought indicates that resurrec-tion is a restoration of what is already created rather than a new cre-ation.[59] This actualization of the body is in accordance with the ideal, artful image of the body rather than its literal reproduction, which sidesteps the question of the state (sickness, disfigurement, and so on) in which the individual may be raised. This body is incorruptible and, evoking a Nyssan anthropology, not bound by those functions that are most susceptible to the passions, that is, the alimentary and the sexual (though even where he follows Nyssa, Bulgakov resists affirming any version of primal androgyny). In short, the spiritual body is the "icon of the spirit"—not made by hands!—with a perfected degree of transparency to the perfected spiritual condition ("proto-image") of the individual person.[60] Ultimately, the spiritual body is adequate to the originary "proto-image" sketched divinely and thus "clothed in divine beauty . . . [and] resplendent."[61]

Both Bulgakov and Schelling appeal to 1 Corinthians 15 for their respective understandings of spiritual corporeality: "So it is with the resurrection of the dead. What is sown is perishable, what is raised is imperishable. It is sown in dishonor, it is raised in glory. It is sown in weakness, it is raised in power. It is sown a physical body, it is raised a spiritual body. If there is a physical body, there is also a spiritual body" (42–44, NRSV). Bulgakov's more biblically faithful articulation of the resurrected body, however, avoids denigrating the status of human finitude and creaturehood.[62] This stipulation is present likewise in Balthasar, who makes certain to indicate the perdurance of identity between the mortal and the spiritual body.[63] Even in the New Jerusalem, human being is far from removed from the natural world, but rather is, according to Bulgakov's account, "earth" as at the moment of creation from the dust of the ground.[64] Bulgakov thus has an extremely high valuation of human finitude and creatureliness, even (especially) in an eschatological register, in which—contra Berdyaev—the created world is not abolished but saved and transformed by the power of resurrection; "heaven bends down to earth" rather than evacuating the latter.[65] He describes the earth somewhat colloquially as "'God's acre,' a cemetery, preserving bodies for the resurrection."[66] This positive theological value accorded to creatureliness ("not a denigration but the determination given to him by God"[67]) is well in keeping with Bulgakov's commitment to the sophianicity of creation. Because for Bulgakov human death is underwritten by the death (and resurrection) of Christ, the very natural dreadfulness of death has by grace been overcome supernaturally: that dread mortal corridor has been already traversed and is thereby "suffused and illuminated by the fiery tongues of the descent of the Holy Spirit into the world even through the fetters of death."[68] Moreover, death opens up upon future resurrection, which indicates a continuity of life before and after human death.

BALTHASAR'S THEOLOGY OF DEATH

Balthasar's theology of death and resurrection bears several striking similarities to Bulgakov's. As noted, both understand death to be ontologically parasitic. Also, the accent in both theologians falls upon eschatological victory, upon resurrection. Indeed, Balthasar repeatedly affirms the very Johannine trope that in the death of Christ—who in the book of Revelation holds the keys of Death and Hades (1:18)—the Resurrection is already implicit.[69] The pairing in the Gospel of John of suffering with exaltation, death with resurrection, and all these as love indicates too that those who have died live already in the resurrected Lord: "For John, physical death is almost an obsolete phenomenon, since the believer already lives in the Lord, who is the resurrection."[70] This eschatological reality does not, however, lessen the horrors of death: referring to the figure of the triumphant eschatological Christ of Revelation, Balthasar notes, "Even if it be true . . . that the Son of Man holds 'the keys of Death and Hades' (Rev 1:18), he does so only because these things *are* realities."[71]

The implications that follow from thinking of death too blithely (Hegel is also in Balthasar's sights)—namely, a devaluation of creaturehood—is pervasive in the Balthasarian oeuvre. For instance, to recur to an image of the chrysalis in which death happily releases the spirit from the heaviness of its earthly body is to trivialize "the whole tragic paradox of mortality by failing to give due weight to the positive aspect of finitude."[72] Yet certain positive effects can be felt. Recalling Heidegger, Balthasar's theology of death stipulates that it is human mortality—*my own* unavoidable death—that provides meaning for existence, rescuing human beings from the bruteness of "everyday facticity."[73] According to Balthasar, death "is the most lonely encounter

with my I-that-is-no-longer, an encounter that sheds a light of absolute seriousness on everything I am still able to experience in the time
that remains to me."[74] The positive and the negative characteristics of
death are of a piece: in a postlapsarian world, death is at best an ambiguous reality.[75]

To be bodily is to be in a state of being-toward-death, and this
feature of life human being cannot circumvent.[76] Balthasar, despite the
commonly traded shibboleth that his theology is "other-worldly," does
not in point of fact diminish the body.[77] Rather, for him "it is precisely
the body (and with it, the world) that counts, for it is only together
with the body that we are saved."[78] This concern with the bodily is
especially present in his theology of death. On the issue of postmortem
existence, Balthasar underlines the reluctance of the human being to
attribute survival only to the soul, for human beings desire to be "taken
seriously" as flesh and blood.[79] Postmortem existence "is a transformation that certainly cannot be 'de-physicalizing' but (for lack of a better
term) can only be hinted at as 'transfiguration' or 'incorruptibility' or
'the swallowing of death into life.' Redemption is not *from* finitude but
is rather an assumption *of* the finite (and thus of the other) into the
infinite, which must have within itself, in order to be the life of love,
the Other as such (Word, Son) and that which is united with the One
(Spirit)."[80]

A(NOTHER) CHRISTOLOGICAL PROVISO: HOLY SATURDAY

The decisively Christian solution to this constant negotiation between
infinite and finite, to the inscription of death upon the immortal human
soul, and the central tenet of Balthasar's theology of death is simple:
that human dying is undergirded by the dying and rising of Christ,
whose death, and the perfect self-surrender embodied therein, were
perfectly serious. For Balthasar, Christ's self-surrender is always in the
context of the constitutive self-gift of Trinitarian existence, which is
absolute love between, in Johannine language, the One who sends and
the One sent. (Much more on this point is to come in the next chapter.)
This seriousness is heightened by Balthasar's somewhat eccentric un-

derstanding of Christ's non-victorious descent into hell, which also gives greater weight to Balthasar's nondualistic presupposition that it is not just the body that suffers death, but the body-soul complex in its totality.[81] Balthasar's anthropology and thanatology are above all else underwritten Christologically.[82] In the incarnation, the impossible indeed has happened: "If the absolute not only irradiates finitude but actually *becomes* finite, something unimaginable happens to existence: what is finite, as such, is drawn into what is ultimate and eternal; what is finite in its temporal extension, in each one of its moments and their interconnection, and not merely, for instance, in its final result. The finite, because of its insight into the true and the good, was always the recipient of radiance from the absolute; on the other hand, time kept running on."[83] Indeed, again evoking but not invoking Bulgakov, the person of Christ represents the perfect expression of a divinely or- dained equipoise between absolute and relative.[84] According to Bal- thasar, the double-movement of corporalizing the spirit and spiritual- izing the body hangs the human being in an ambiguous suspended middle, and must be ratified Christologically to be theologically (and anthropologically) satisfying:

> The vertical dimension of man reaches without a break from the spirit through the soul and the living body down into matter, and "soul" and "body" are the stages and modes in which spirit takes root in matter, and matter blooms into spirit—a single, ultimate, dually moved life: corporalization of the spirit, spiritualization of the body, neither existing without the other. If the body strove one-sidedly to become spirit, without allowing the spirit corre- spondingly to penetrate the body and become one with it, then man would be striving away from himself into a chimerical self- alienation. But in this dual movement man is suspended in the middle, since neither the Dionysian drive back to the maternal ori- gins, nor the Promethean drive to pure spirit brings him nearer to himself, and the two tendencies cannot be made into one. As a product of maternal earth and paternal heaven he has to turn his face toward both, without being able to see both at once. He cannot find his ground or take his rest in either, or in both at once, but only

in him who has created heaven and earth, spirit and matter, day and night.[85]

For Balthasar, the Christological transvaluation of human death is not symbolic, poetic, or ludic: no, "he bores right through it to the bottom, to the chaotic formlessness of the death cry (Matt. 27:50) and the wordless silence of death on Holy Saturday,"[86] an authentic death that demonstrates enormous solidarity with human beings both in death and in unredeemed separation from God.[87] Indeed, perhaps the most controversial element of Balthasar's theology, if Pitstick's reading is any indication, is his interpretation of Christ's descent into hell, which is not a glorious or triumphant descent but a sinking down in the absolute passivity of true death. This condition of being truly dead not only distinguishes Jesus from "all the other pilgrims into Hades, from Orpheus and Odysseus to Enoch, Jonah, Aeneas and Dante,"[88] but also—by actually bearing to the full extent an ignoble death in loving obedience to the Father, anticipating the theocentric dimension of eschatology treated more at length in the next chapter—transfigures it: "That the death of Jesus, like his Incarnation, was a function of his living, eternal love makes it that special death that 'shatters to pieces the terrifying gates of hell.'"[89] Balthasar surely does not underestimate the seriousness and the reality of the fact that Christ was dead, and dead indeed, a death that, like all other human deaths described in the Sheol of the Old Testament, was marked by inactivity, inability, and profound loneliness, being in contact neither with other souls nor with God.[90] It is this condition of true death that matters to Balthasar, especially insofar as it provides further ratification of Jesus's perfect transparence and surrender to the Father.[91]

What, ultimately, does Holy Saturday mean for Balthasar from an anthropocentric perspective? Fundamentally, it is that there is no place or state where God is not, even the moment of absolute forsakenness of human choosing, for Christ has already willingly gone down to hell: "Anyone who tries to choose complete forsakenness—in order to prove himself absolute vis-à-vis God—finds himself confronted by the figure of someone even 'more absolutely' forsaken than himself."[92] Here Balthasar makes explicit appeal to Dostoevsky, in this case the near conclusion of *The Idiot*, when Prince Myshkin—as a type of Christ—spends a night in close quarters with a feverish Rogozhin, in hiding after his murder of Natasha Philipovna, whose corpse remains in the narrow room with them: "Meanwhile it had grown completely light; at last, he lay down on the cushion, as though now wholly in the grip of helplessness and despair, and pressed his face against Rogozhin's pale and motionless face; tears streamed from his eyes on to Rogozhin's cheeks."[93] Myshkin is present alongside the murderer, just as in *Crime and Punishment* Sonja's presence in Siberia in solidarity with the convicted Raskolnikov begins at last to thaw what first seemed an irrevocably hardened heart.[94] These literary examples are only "remote metaphors for the unimaginable process whereby man, timelessly closed in upon himself, is opened up by the ineluctable presence of Another, who stands beside him, equally timelessly, and calls into question his apparent, pretended inaccessibility. Man's shell is not hard enough, however, for it is formed of a contradiction. Perhaps the man whose shell can be broken open is not yet really in hell but only—in his rebellious attitude to God—turned toward it."[95] Balthasar thus preserves hope. His conviction regarding the possibility of the salvation of all persons is deeply connected to his particular understanding of Christ's radical solidarity with (all) the dead in his descent into hell, in which he was non-victorious, but rather "dead with the dead."[96]

A Northern Renaissance painting here further unites Balthasar with the Russians through Dostoevsky. Hans Holbein's stark painting *The Body of the Dead Christ in the Tomb* (1521), an enormous work that realistically depicts the early stages of putrefaction, absolutely captivated Dostoevsky upon an 1867 visit to the Kunstmuseum in Basel, Switzerland.[97] Later, he has his character Ippolit say in *The Idiot*,

> I believe that painters are usually in the habit of depicting Christ, whether on the cross or taken from the cross, as still retaining a shade of extraordinary beauty on his face; that beauty they strive to preserve even in his moments of greatest agony. In Rogozhin's picture there was no trace of beauty. It was a faithful representation of the dead body of a man who has undergone unbearable torments before the crucifixion, been wounded, tortured, beaten by the

guards, beaten by the people, when he carried the cross and fell under its weight, and, at last, has suffered the agony of crucifixion, lasting for six hours (according to my calculation, at least). . . . I know that the Christian Church laid it down in the first few centuries of its existence that Christ really did suffer and that the Passion was not symbolical. His body on the cross was therefore fully and entirely subject to the laws of nature. In the picture the face is terribly smashed with blows, swollen, covered with terrible, swollen, and bloodstained bruises, the eyes open and squinting; the large, open whites of the eyes have a sort of dead and glassy glint.[98]

Balthasar highlights the actuality of Christ's experience of human death also with reference to the Holbein piece. In it, the cadaver of Christ, on that "empty, wordless pause"[99] of Holy Saturday, is "lying horizontally, putrid blue. This is the death of Him who is priceless. His real death, not his apparent death. It is the victory of nature, which 'as some huge engine of the latest design . . . has senselessly seized, cut to pieces, and swallowed up—impassively and unfeelingly—[this] great Being'; on the day when God Himself is dead, eternal life coincides with eternal death. For Dostoevsky this picture is the symbolic diacritical point between faith and unbelief, between Christianity and atheism: twinned to the point of identification in the most extreme differentiation."[100] Indeed, Christ's true death and descent into Sheol on Holy Saturday is the moment at which a proleptic light of mercy can shine redemptively, "soften[ing] the true lostness to something else."[101] It is the Johannine doublet of humiliation and glory, a traversal that is for Balthasar the condition of the possibility for the theological concept of purgatory.[102]

In *The Bride of the Lamb*, Bulgakov flags the notion of purgatory as a schematized (and in some cases concretely topographized) third "place" in addition to heaven and hell—a contaminated move that he deems "proper to Catholic rigorism"[103]—as a factor that identifies irreversibly the fate of individual persons before the universal judgment.[104] Balthasar, however, does not readily fulfill the stereotype (nor does he allow a distinction between personal and universal judgment as Bulgakov does). In a text absolutely informed by von Speyr's

Objektive Mystik, Balthasar again situates the doctrine of purgatory firmly in the purview of Holy Saturday, such that mercy, love, and hope enter in to temper the state of the "lost." Balthasar's "dialectic of fire," drawn from Origen, is fully operative here; the purgative and the eschatological flames are one and the same, and the fire of wrath becomes a purifying flame.[105]

JUDGMENT, HELL, AND THE PROSPECT OF FINAL DAMNATION

The issue of hell and the prospect of damnation loomed large for Balthasar, as they did for all the Russians, but particularly Bulgakov. Balthasar discusses hell at length in the final, eschatological volume of the *Theo-Drama*, and perhaps most (in-)famously in *Dare We Hope "That All Men Be Saved"?* and its epilogue, "A Short Discourse on Hell." Interestingly, long before the writing of *Dare We Hope*, Balthasar observed that, given the deep sense of community in which everyone is responsible for all, the abhorrence of the doctrine of hell is typically a Russian phenomenon.[106] This observation certainly holds true for Berdyaev, who asserts colorfully that "paradise is impossible for me if the people I love, my friends or relatives or mere acquaintances, will be in hell—if Boehme is in hell as a 'heretic,' Nietzsche as 'an antichrist,' Goethe as a 'pagan' and Pushkin as a sinner."[107] Certainly, too, the theme that all are responsible for all is unambiguously present in Dostoevsky's *The Brothers Karamazov*, in the biography of the Elder Zosima's kind brother Markel, who believed that among all the robbers and murderers, he alone was the worst offender, who said to his mother that "everyone is really responsible to all men for all men and for everything."[108] It is present when Ivan goes mad with this sense of crushing responsibility for his father's murder, and when Dmitri embraces the judgment for a crime he did not commit, saying:

> Even there, in the mines, underground, I may find a human heart in another convict and murderer by my side, and I may make friends with him, for even there one may live and love and suffer. One may resurrect and revive a frozen heart in that convict, one may wait

upon him for years, and at last bring up from the dark depths a lofty soul, a feeling, suffering creature; one may bring forth an angel, resurrect a hero! There are so many of them, hundreds of them, and we are all responsible for them. . . . Because we are all responsible for all.[109]

This sense of moral responsibility present in the classic literature extends in the Russian mind even unto eternity, which anticipates the tendency toward the theological (and, in the case of Dostoevsky, the literary) affirmation of universal salvation.

The speculative points with the highest degree of convergence between Schelling, the Russians, and Balthasar regarding hell and final judgment are as follows: (1) hell can be conceived as an imaginative (but not imaginary) state rather than a physical place; (2) relatedly, the event of final judgment as an "auto-contraction" of being is self-inflicted rather than divinely inflicted; and (3) a qualitative distinction obtains between "eternity" in heaven and "eternity" in hell. These suggestions, most pointedly in Bulgakov and Balthasar, operate as preconditions for their proposal of the possibility of universal salvation for human beings. It bears repeating that on these counts Balthasar walks more softly than Bulgakov. While both claim to operate according to a principle of dogmatic minimalism, having a tentativeness and epistemic reserve that recognizes such claims about the essential mystery of the postmortem state as, at best, only fragments and approximations insoluble in the *theologia viatorum*, it is clear that Bulgakov sounds a surer tone.[110]

First, common to all our religious thinkers is the idea that hell may be understood as an imaginative condition rather than a local place; it is an internal closing in of the self by the self. This is so despite Bulgakov's already observed recalcitrance in persisting in a gross mischaracterization of a homogenized "Catholic" reification of heaven, hell, and purgatory to purely physical phenomena. In *The Holy Grail and the Eucharist*, Bulgakov criticizes Catholicism unilaterally for the ("crude" and "superstitious") view that heaven is an astronomical place, and later ascribes a corporeal sense of hell and purgatory as distinctly Catholic.[111] This naïve "physicalization" of eschatological spaces does not appear in Balthasar. To the contrary, he writes, "Not only must we discard, therefore, any localization of the eschatological 'places' (heaven, hell, purgatory, limbo) in the one world—since that means their transference from a theological cosmos, whose higher and lower regions are the divine and demonic, to a physical—but also cease to regard any 'end of time' (say, of the planet Earth) as an event relevant to theology."[112]

On the possibility of hell as an imaginative space or condition, a torture of the inner state more than of the body, Balthasar gestures toward a fascinating genealogy that not only filters Augustine's *De Genesi ad Litteram XII* through the Platonic Idealism of Porphyry, but also explicitly incorporates elements of Schellingian eschatology.[113] Though Schelling's *Clara* is not as concerned with the question of hell as his *Stuttgart Lectures* are, it is the more significant text for our purposes because Balthasar refers to it directly in this particular context. The mention is cursory but by no means trivial. The relevant point in both Augustine and Schelling is that human being is tripartite, comprised of mind, imagination (*pneuma, spiritus*), and body.[114] While the vision of highest heaven is a function of the mind, for Augustine, "the experience of hell is primarily one of the imagination, which suffers the impress of painful 'material images' (*similitudines corporum*)."[115] It is noteworthy here again that Schelling operates for Balthasar as supplemental (but corrosively so) to Augustine. As in Augustine, Schelling's *Clara* indicates as well that hell is a function of the imagination rather than the body: "If the imagination is indeed generally the tool through which most people sin, shouldn't the imagination be that through which most people are punished—and shouldn't the tortures that await sinners in the other world consist primarily of tortures of the imagination, whose subject would primarily be the previous corporeal world?"[116] Neither is such a condition homogenous, for "that invisible kingdom is not as simple as many think it is; rather, if the saying holds true that each will be done by according to how he thought and acted in his corporeal life, that kingdom must look quite wonderfully diverse."[117]

It is probably the case, however, that on the point of hell as a (highly variable) psychological condition Schelling is more nearly

Swedenborgian than he is Augustinian. That Schelling made use of the visionary Emanuel Swedenborg is not terribly surprising, given Romanticism's interest in the spirit world. Swedenborg's doctrine of correspondences, in which the details of the natural world have precise correspondence in the spiritual (axiomatically, "as above, so below"), indicates that heaven and hell reproduce the imaginative states experienced prior to death, constructed of the same building blocks of sensory data perceived on earth.[118] In the section "Of the Appearance, Situation, and Plurality of the Hells," Swedenborg describes his travels to hell with great gusto, describing such wide and varied hells as like unto caverns, the dens of animals, subterranean mines, the ruins of houses after a devastating fire "in which the infernal spirits skulk,"[119] rude cottages, streets and byways in which people quarrel and bicker, gloomy forests, barren deserts, and so on.

This detour into the peculiar mysticism of Swedenborg is significant, not only because Berdyaev and Soloviev identified Swedenborg as influential for their own thinking, but also because there is evidence suggesting Dostoevsky's novelistic borrowings from Swedenborg, an important link to the Russian ethos. In his essay "Dostoevsky and Swedenborg," which endeavors to demonstrate a modest degree of influence of Swedenborg on Dostoevsky, Czeslaw Milosz connects Swedenborg's catalogue of imaging the various hells as common alleys, dark streets, and so on, to a similar passage in Dostoevsky's *Crime and Punishment*:

> "I don't believe in a future life," said Raskolnikov.
> Svidrigailov sat lost in thought.
> "And what if there are only spiders there, or something of that sort," he said suddenly.
> "He is a madman," thought Raskolnikov.
> "We always imagine eternity as something beyond our conception, something vast, vast! But why must it be vast? Instead of all that, what if it's one little room, like a bathhouse in the country, black and grimy and spiders in every corner, and that's all eternity is? I sometimes fancy it like that."
> "Can it be you can imagine nothing juster and more comforting than that?" Raskolnikov cried, with a feeling of anguish.

"Juster? And how can we tell, perhaps that is just, and do you know it's what I would certainly have made it," answered Svidrigailov, with a vague smile.

This horrible answer sent a cold chill through Raskolnikov.[120]

Likewise, for Bulgakov, there is a great plurality of possible hells as dark counterpoints to the "many mansions" of heaven: "deformities, perversions, monstrosities . . . [characterized by] nakedness, the absence of a wedding garment, the excruciating disharmony between what has been realized and what remains a task to be realized,"[121] which may well have a similar genealogy, albeit filtered through Dostoevsky.

More to the point, there is homologous or at least analogous content in both Bulgakov's and Balthasar's transpositions of the radical spatial narrowing of hell to an ontological and a temporal key: that is, hell is not a place but a state of timeless duration deprived of divine eternity through a self-determined contraction of being.[122] According to Balthasar, if the human being chooses his or her own finite freedom over the infinite freedom of divine reality as the absolute good, there results a state of absolutely devouring self-contradiction as the hellish, infinite "I" presumes to expand—and therefore actually contracts— exponentially: "The formal object that informs it—which is in fact absolute, self-positing freedom—is in constant contradiction with finite freedom's pretentious claim to be infinite. This contradiction, if persisted in, is hell."[123] Notably, this set of convictions also appears in Berdyaev, who articulates the concept of hell in terms of freedom and personality rather than justice. Here, in terms largely parallel to Balthasar and Bulgakov, Berdyaev suggests that hell is a subjective, radical expression of human freedom insofar as the self-containment and isolation is self-made, though he departs fatally from them when he suggests it is the subterranean workings of a Böhmian "dark meonic freedom" that are to blame.[124] Bulgakov too identifies hell as a self-made state, likely recalling Dostoevsky's Underground as he notes that "to want oneself in one's own selfhood, to lock oneself in one's creatureliness as in the absolute, means to want the underground and to be affirmed in it."[125] For Balthasar and Bulgakov, hell is neither a creation of God nor a condition to which God damns forever, but rather the act of human beings themselves, who labor strenuously to inure themselves against a God who is absolute love.[126] Schelling's *Clara* indicates, in common with the theologians, that hell is a self-made state, though the torture in his telling comes not in facing the absolute love and holiness of God, but rather in the individual facing his or her own solitary self.[127] This understanding is no new invention either—in the patristic fathers and in the scholastics, the idea of judgment as concomitant with beholding the light of divine truth appears to some degree in Origen, Basil, Gregory Nazianzen, Ambrose, Augustine, Peter Lombard, and Thomas Aquinas.[128]

This sense that human beings are the primary agents of their own judgment is deeply embedded in the Russian ethos, and particularly in the novels of Dostoevsky. That hell is of our own doing is illustrated concretely in Dostoevsky's parable of the onion, put in the mouth of Grushenka in *The Brothers Karamazov* and recounted here by Balthasar in *Dare We Hope*:

> Once upon a time there was a peasant woman and a very wicked woman she was. And she died and did not leave a single good deed behind. The devils caught her and plunged her into the lake of fire. So her guardian angel stood and wondered what good deed of hers he could remember to tell to God; "She once pulled up an onion in her garden," said he, "and gave it to a beggar woman." And God answered: "You take that onion then, hold it out to her in the lake, and let her take hold and be pulled out. And if you can pull her out of the lake, let her come to Paradise, but if the onion breaks, then the woman must stay where she is." The angel ran to the woman and held out the onion to her. "Come," said he, "catch hold and I'll pull you out." And he began cautiously pulling her out. He had just pulled her right out, when the other sinners in the lake, seeing how she was being drawn out, began catching hold of her so as to be pulled out with her. But she was a very wicked woman and she began kicking them. "I'm to be pulled out, not you. It's my onion, not yours." As soon as she said that, the onion broke. And the woman fell into the lake and she is burning there to this day. So the angel wept and went away.[129]

Balthasar notes that this theme of hell as a self-determination also appears in *The Brothers Karamazov* in Father Zosima's excursus, "Of Hell and Hellfire, A Mystic Reflection," in which he observes that hell is the nonmaterial condition of being no longer able to love by one's own free choice: "Oh, there are some who remain proud and fierce even in hell, in spite of their certain knowledge and contemplation of the absolute truth; there are some fearful ones who have given themselves over to Satan and his proud spirit entirely. For such, *hell is voluntary and ever consuming; they are tortured by their own choice.*"[130] Bulgakov likewise understands (at least individual, preliminary) judgment in this manner. The end of human life is met with a greater degree of self-consciousness in the presence of the absolute God, which manifests itself directly and existentially as "self-knowledge ('trial and tribulation'), self-deepening, and self-verdict."[131]

The direct convergences of Balthasar with Bulgakov on these issues—eternity as having a qualitative rather than temporal quality, hell as self-made, the deep asymmetry between eternity in heaven and "eternity" in hell, even the so-called dialectic of fire drawn from Origen—are striking. For Bulgakov and for Balthasar (both with appeal to Gregory of Nyssa, the latter with pedigree in Aquinas) heaven and hell are two instances of *timeless* duration, "which can become mutually opposed depending on whether there is a participation in, or a depriving of, divine eternity."[132] Eternity in heaven connotes participation and contemplation of the divine rather than, as it is perhaps usually understood, a measure of infinite time.[133] Hell, again, is the absolute narrowing of human being only to the timeless self, described by Balthasar as a kind of Sartrean "total withdrawal of any temporal dimension, by being tightly bound into the most constricted, airless and exitless now."[134] Eternity in heaven is a fullness of participation in the beauty and vitality of the Trinitarian relations; eternity in hell is a desiccated "now," no more than a grimy country bathhouse with spiders in the corners. Berdyaev has something of a similar view, insofar as he understands hell to seem to be an endless duration in time, a "bad infinity," though it is not in fact eternal because, for Berdyaev, "there can be no diabolical eternity—the only eternity is that of the Kingdom of God and there is no other reality on a level with it."[135]

Bulgakov goes on to suggest that *"eternal* fire, *eternal* torment, *eternal* perdition and other synonymous expressions have no relation to *time*. They are not temporal but qualitative determinations. They express the general idea of suffering before the face of God, in God, in God's love. They have a *sophianic* significance in the sense that, having come to know himself in his sophianic *form*, the glorified human being will thereby also know himself in his own *deformity*, will be horrified by himself. And this deformation of his likeness in relation to his proto-image is for him the scourge of love, the burning fire of love."[136] Bulgakov, like Berdyaev, is not shy in his resistance to naming hell as "eternal" in the same way that heaven is eternal. To do so, he believes, is to admit an ontological failure, and this failure would be God's, whose eternal kingdom has by dint of creaturely freedom a co-eternal competitor; the "antisophianicity" of hell seems to triumph over the goodness of the world.[137] As in Balthasar, it is simply not possible to allow the co-eternity of heaven and hell: baldly, in Bulgakov, "heaven and hell cannot be *equally* eternal,"[138] for hell, like evil and death, is ontologically parasitic and fundamentally self-exhausting, whereas heaven is a participation in the inexhaustible, ever-greater life of God.

Thus, both Bulgakov and Balthasar employ a recontextualized sense of eternity as something other than temporal infinity as a means of advancing the banner of some brand of soteriological universalism, though again Balthasar remains in the subjunctive rather than the indicative mood and eschews affirming the Alexandrian postulate of *apokatastasis panton*.[139] For Bulgakov, the existence of hell is the "inner limit of heaven": heaven cannot be fully complete as long as hell—which, given the principle of all being responsible for all, affects all of humanity—exists.[140] Balthasar, Berdyaev, and Bulgakov together resist the idea that once saved, the righteous can forget about the fate of their unsaved counterparts, since the theologians resist construing salvation as significant only for the individual.[141] Moreover, recalling Péguy, authentically Christian hope does not warrant a laissez-faire, spectator approach to the question of eternal salvation: rather, to hope theologically is not an empty gesture but an active engagement purposed to bring "the world with it on its way to God . . . [by] creating conditions apt to promote it."[142]

An egotistic evaluation of salvation stands alien to the spirit of the Church's teaching on redemption and is, according to Balthasar, "at bottom utterly bourgeois and capitalistic."[143] Not every theological position that suggests that the experience of paradise is lessened by the knowledge of hell gets a pass, however, since here, as everywhere, much rests upon motive. After tracing a genealogy of this line of thinking in Protestantism after Schleiermacher, from Alexander Schweizer to H. L. Martensen, Ernst Troeltsch, and Bonhoeffer, up to and including Karl Barth, Balthasar offers this critique: "This whole wave of reaction against Augustinian, medieval and Reformation rigorism is largely the product of a humanistic recalcitrance, an anti-orthodox feeling, a craving for philosophical system or simply an optimism in the Enlightenment manner; *we hardly ever find it undergirded by a sufficiently deep, trinitarian theology.*"[144] Barth and, we may presume, Bulgakov, are the exception to this rule, given their rich doctrines of the Trinity. Fundamentally, though, for Balthasar, the dogma of hell serves precisely as a *constraint* on illicit theological speculation, with the real prospect of eternal catastrophe having a kerygmatic, edifying function rather than reason to indulge in a kind of spectator theology that would presume too much, especially about the condition of the souls of other persons.[145] While Bulgakov's eschatological Trinitarian theology is robust enough for Balthasar, both he and Barth go too far toward affirming *apokatastasis* for Balthasar's comfort. Interestingly, Berdyaev sides with Balthasar in discrediting the doctrine, but he does so not out of concern for observing theological constraints, but rather because he considers it to be an overly rationalistic doctrine that undermines the exercise of human freedom.[146]

Bulgakov is almost certainly in Balthasar's sights when, in *Dare We Hope*, he makes an oblique reference to certain writers, "especially Russian ones and certain figures in Dostoevski" who "tried to enchant us" with visions of *apokatastasis*.[147] On the latter point, recall, for instance, Ivan Karamazov's vision of the devil, who proclaims, "I know that *at the end of things I shall be reconciled*. I, too, shall walk my quadrillion and learn the secret."[148] Balthasar's reluctance to affirm *apokatastasis* marks a significant point of departure between Balthasar and Bulgakov, a place to which Bulgakov travels that is for Balthasar too far to follow, especially as the former argues for not only the fact but also the ontological *necessity* of the salvation of Satan. *Dare We Hope*, while certainly bold in its implications, is a book characterized by an epistemological humility, a tentativeness that would not confuse hope with a certain, secure knowledge.[149] Further, while Balthasar famously defends a robust theological hope for all human beings— "certainty cannot be attained, but hope can be justified"[150]—to hope for the redemption of the satanic is for him thoroughly beyond the pale of licit speculation.[151]

With respect to the language of *apokatastasis*, Bulgakov notes that though the question itself is "dangerous," especially because of the possibility of indulging in "false sentimentality under the pretext of love," this "limit to love" (recalling Saint Isaac the Syrian's "pitying heart") may not be totally uncrossable eschatologically.[152] As the argument goes, because demons are part of God's creation, they have at their core an "indestructible power of being"[153] that remains even when the content of their lives is erased. Bulgakov continues, intrepidly, "Satan's very being, his createdness by the omniscient God, is, so to speak, an *ontological proof of the inevitability of his future salvation*. Even Satan in his madness does not have the power to overcome the fact of his own being, its divine foundation, that is, the sophianicity of all creation, by virtue of which 'God will be all in all.'"[154] Thus, Satan's eventual conversion is mostly a function of Bulgakov's sophiology, which Balthasar does not take up, at least consciously, and indeed intends largely to divest it from his theological reappropriation of Bulgakov.[155]

Moreover, for Bulgakov, the language of hell and heaven, "the sheep and the goats," refers not to a local division of the ultimate destinies of distinct groups of individuals, in which the condemned latter group is cut off from humanity, but rather indicates a line of division *within* each individual person, since there is no one without sin. Heaven and hell are thus *qualitative* measures present in every human being to one degree or another; as in Origen, though God is a consuming fire, the straw is burned and the gold refined by one and the same flame.[156] Interestingly, Bulgakov suggests that all people have within them "the principle of gehennic burning," and, repeating rather strangely the ambiguity of the image of fire, this burning is "ignited by the power of the parousia of Christ in glory."[157] What is more, this "daring" idea that the human being under judgment stands simultaneously to the right and to the left of the judge appears also in Ambrose, and is even referred to approvingly in Balthasar as he draws the "final act" to curtain.[158]

Resisting a dualistic ossification into rigid groups of the saved and the damned among human beings reappears, albeit somewhat differently, in Balthasar's anthropocentric eschatological theology wherein salvation and judgment are simultaneously present.[159] Balthasar must here contend with a complex biblical testimony, and he does so somewhat phenomenologically, presenting the texts in tension as they appear "in all their deliberate starkness."[160] With respect to the question of salvation, Balthasar notes two classes of texts in the New Testament, those which indicate threateningly the presence of hellfire, outer darkness, eternal punishment, unquenchable fire, and so on, and those which indicate God's will for universal redemption, that is, for "all," the former class largely attributed to the pre-Easter Jesus and the latter generally containing post-Easter assertions.[161]

These texts, according to Balthasar, cannot and must not be brought into an overall synthesis or easy systematization: the "cleft" between them that represents the possibility of "both ways" for human postmortem existence must ever be maintained: "It is not for [the human being], who is *under* judgment, to construct syntheses here, and above all none of such a kind as to subsume one series of statements under the other, practically emasculating the universalist ones because he believes himself to have 'certain knowledge' of the potency of the first."[162] Despite the very human urge to systematize, Balthasar recommends that theologians leave these texts unreconciled. This high premium placed on ambiguity also features prominently in his criticisms of intertestamental apocalyptic literature, which by his estimation "hardens into a cosmological system in an apocalyptic *gnosis* about the double outcome of the final judgment."[163]

Balthasar's careful withholding of judgment is related to the ambiguity of the human condition, which is such that it must act and exercise freedom in a state always already compromised by finitude and the horizon of death.[164] As such, Balthasar's position exemplifies a striking degree of compassion for the ambiguities of making one's way in the world. In a reflection on Ivan's tortured relation to faith in Dostoevsky's *The Brothers Karamazov*, Balthasar writes that

> Ivan Karamazov refuses his entrance ticket to heaven so long as innocent children have to suffer in the world. Basically he is relatively unconcerned about the world beyond: what upsets him is the unbearable disorder on earth, for which he makes God responsible. Dostoyevsky implies that Karamazov is thereby entertaining satanic forces; but if we look back at the borderline situations of the world drama, can we really imagine that human beings, living in the impenetrable misery of this world, can be eventually divided into two clear categories—the eternally elect and the eternally damned? How should beings, existing in the contradiction between their attempts at ultimate meaning and the certainty of death, cut their way through the primeval forest toward absolute Good—which proves ever elusive—except by means of compromises? If man refuses, in the face of the world's chaotic state, to find meaning (and hence Providence) and turns to the finite as what alone can be attained, should we brand this as "demonic"? Given the ever-increasing rationalization of the planet, which turns people's attention more and more from an overarching meaning and toward the particular, fragmentary and precarious, is not a life decision for good or evil increasingly problematical? And in view of the shifts of consciousness that emerge in different historical periods, can the Church continue, in good conscience, to present the old judgment-eschatology of the New Testament in unchanged form without first submitting it to a thorough critique?[165]

Ultimately, then, for Balthasar, the question of hell for others at bottom resists theoretical speculation from a spectator's perspective because the question can be seriously entertained only with respect to one's *own* precarious spiritual condition.[166] Berdyaev laudably makes the same point: "I may create hell for myself and, alas, I do too much to create it. But I must not create hell for others, nor for a single living being. Let the 'good' cease being lofty, idealistic avengers."[167] The fact that ambiguity characterizes all of human existence, which operates under the sometimes invisible constraints of unseen, unquantifiable forces, suggests to Balthasar that the best practice is to reserve judgment on others and only to accuse the self, as far as it can be known.

VINDICATING THE POETS: THE LOGIC OF RESURRECTION

Despite the absolute centrality of Good Friday and Holy Saturday in Balthasar's theology, it is truly the glory of Easter that provides the ballast for this Johannine theologian. According to Balthasar, the message of the gospel is not the presentation of two symmetric parts, that is, cross and resurrection, "but is rather the dynamic transition whereby the former makes way for the latter,"[168] thus in their union giving a forward trajectory and dynamism to the mode of Christian—and all human—existence. The resurrection is for Balthasar "the core of the kerygma"[169] and the starting point for ecclesiology. It is not an overstatement to assert that it is the resurrected Christ who for Balthasar provides absolutely the meaning for everything: aesthetics, anthropology, history, the cosmic order, an answer to the mythic imagination, and so on, and it is Christ's resurrection that capacitates the resurrection of human beings, whose finitude (impossibly!) now rests in the "lap" of divine eternity.

With the bodily resurrection of Christ, the transformative power of the Incarnation on human finitude is ratified and broadened by the dialectical movement whereby the conditioned form of Jesus's human existence in space and in time is exchanged for the "'eternal finitude' of Jesus' resurrected flesh [whereby] all that is interior, invisible, spiritual and divine becomes accessible"[170] to human beings. Thus, in keeping with Balthasar's high valuation of the body, it is not simply the immortal soul that is preserved, but the whole range of temporal, finite, embodied human existence.[171] Further, again channeling John's Gospel, this ratification of the "eternity-content and eternal dignity of an existence that is lived and died in bodily terms" is not deferred to the end of time, but rather is realized, having "this quality in the very *midst* of world time and *perpendicular* to it."[172] The fact of the resurrection of Christ is the only thing that can ultimately safeguard the value of the finite and flesh-and-blood bodies. Thus, the extent to which these religious philosophers, whether German, Swiss, or Russian, succeed in maintaining the value of finite human existence is directly related to their respective understandings of bodily resurrection, which must defy absolutely the collapse of finite into infinite: "If there were no such thing as the resurrection of the flesh, then the truth would lie with Gnosticism and every form of idealism down to Schopenhauer and Hegel, for whom the finite must literally perish if it is to become spiritual and infinite. But the resurrection of the flesh vindicates the poets in a definitive sense; the aesthetic scheme of things, which allows us to possess the infinite with the finitude of form (however it is seen, understood or grasped spiritually) is right."[173] The incarnate Christ is no intermediary figure or *daimon*. According to Balthasar, it is the bodily resurrection of Christ that affirms ultimately the goodness of creation, "of the body, of sex, of fellowship, of work. He brings all of this goodness into the ultimate freedom in the presence of God."[174]

As indicated in chapter 3, for Schelling Christ's resurrection is only a required theoretical postulate of the exoteric unfolding of the second potency. Christian orthodoxy is thereby only a supplement to a philosophical datum that does not sufficiently account for the "sober and historical fact" of Christ.[175] Hegel fails spectacularly on the resurrection as well, insofar as on his view, the resurrection of Jesus is not actual and historical, but only communal. To the degree that Hegel and Schelling fail on the question of resurrection, they fail on the body and finitude. Schelling's (thin) version of human resurrection is a gradual, developmental process of spiritualization that begins even before death; as human beings "become more and more perfect, they eventually pass over into God completely, and finally they even disappear within Him."[176] Recall that at death, the "inner side" of the spiritual, "essentified" body becomes more and more unified with the Absolute and thus purer, more whole, while the physical, merely natural or external body is cast aside. The relation of the soul to the Absolute, then, is radically interior rather than in terms of the future, and—according to Balthasar's early critique—the eschatological loses any teleological import to become nothing more than the axiological, the vertical "Now" and nothing more.[177] This peculiar notion of resurrection results in the expressly non-Christian view of the incarnation of God in all of humanity. In Balthasar's analysis of the *Stuttgart Lectures* in the first volume of *Apokalypse der deutschen Seele*, he indicates that on Schelling's view, though human beings are ultimately united into the ideal, God cannot leave nature to ruin absolutely, since God is objectified in nature and seeks God's Self there as in a mirror.[178] Thus we come to Schelling's notion of resurrection wherein the "lange Krankheit der Natur"[179] must finally come to an end, and God is all in all, and all is God. Thus, as Balthasar points out, what now only Christ is, then all human beings will be, expressive of the ultimate meaning of God as the "loving union of nature and spirit."[180]

As it goes with Schelling's paradoxical anthropology, so too goes it with his dialectical eschatology, which must balance between the tremendous mystery of the Absolute in all things and the concomitant sense that human beings eventually realize the eternity of the Absolute in themselves, with the requisite dissolution of the personality. As Schelling wrote in no uncertain terms to Hegel, "Our ultimate goal is the *destruction* of our personality, the transition into the absolute sphere of being."[181] Those who hope to find the eternal beyond the grave ought to ratchet down expectation to a mere continuation of the same, to the "immortality of the mortal,"[182] though as Balthasar argues later, such a prolongation—even if it were only of the pleasant elements of life—would be simply disastrous for human being, who is "like a piece of music which only makes sense in its finite extension; if it were drawn out into infinity it would be unbearable."[183] Schelling's eschatology threatens personal being so decisively that Balthasar hears resounding echoes of a Stoic resignation at the loss of selfhood, though this is weak medicine indeed when the modern philosophers of the experience of death (Heidegger, for instance) "portray death as the most powerful stimulant for utter finitude, enabling it to stand forth, unsupported and unadorned, in nothingness . . . [which] is seen as the true origin of freedom."[184]

Here the Russians and Balthasar (who is not far from Johann Baptist Metz on this point) are something of a united front against Schelling's depersonalizing philosophy of death. All can rally around

Ivan Karamazov's resistance to the commoditization of the dead for the progress of future generations: "Surely I haven't suffered simply that I, my crimes and my sufferings, may manure the soil of the future harmony for somebody else."[185] Indeed, Berdyaev rightfully deems this abiding interest in negotiating the conflict between the world processes and individual personality "very Russian."[186] Balthasar defies the trend that is true of both secular materialist and Idealist views of death, that the individual ought to be satisfied enough with having contributed in some small way to the ultimate destiny of the human race; harmonizing with Schelling's thanatology, the finite/individual surrenders itself to the good of the infinite/collective, which problematically economizes death and the dying.[187] For Balthasar, individuals cannot be exchanged for the sake of societal progress, which would make their deaths generic or anonymous.[188] Analogously, Balthasar's glosses 1 Thessalonians 4:13–18 in this way: "When history's vanguard penetrates into the kingdom, this does not involve forgetting what it has been, as if this were 'building materials' now lost to sight. The solidarity that no form of socialism can know, which is likewise forgotten or undervalued by an existential and a merely historical interpretation of Scripture, hopes first for those who belong hopelessly to the past, and only then for itself."[189] This stress upon the fact that it is the *dead* who are raised first, such that the final generation living have no advantage over them, resists in a productive manner this system of economy, preserving the dignity of the dead.

The logic of resurrection operates decisively in Soloviev, and it is this focus on resurrection that Balthasar finds particularly compelling and salutary in his thought. In *Die Vergöttlichung des Todes*, the third volume of *Apokalypse der deutschen Seele*, Balthasar draws attention to the fact that in Soloviev's *War, Progress, and the End of History*, actual bodily resurrection is at the kerygmatic core of his theological reflection. Importantly, too, Balthasar acknowledges that the resurrection of the dead was always the operative horizon for Soloviev, even at those points in his career that seemed unduly to privilege an unrestrained evolutionary progress.[190] As noted in the previous chapter's discussion of evil and freedom, Soloviev has his own mouthpiece, the "absolutely religious" character Mr. Z., explain the phenomenon of evil as not only the privation of good, but also "the positive resistance and predominance of the lower qualities over the higher ones in all spheres of being."[191] This is the moment at which the soul individually is overcome by the lower passions, or collectively individuals engage in social or structural sin.

Most relevant to the present concern, however, is the way that Mr. Z. explains the final and most extreme manifestation of this phenomenon on the physical plane in death. Echoing Schelling's thanatology, death in Soloviev is defined in the course of the narrative as "when the baser material constituents of the human body resist the living and enlightening power that binds them together into a beautiful form or organism and resist and break the form, destroying the real basis of the higher life."[192] According to Mr. Z., however, in this sustained diatribe against the Prince (a caricature of Tolstoy), if death were simply the end of the story, then evil would triumph most absurdly, and the positive acts of human beings would be all for naught. The *only* remedy against the actual triumph of evil (either moral or physical) is singular: actual, literal bodily resurrection.[193] Mr. Z. again postulates that "the Kingdom of God is the kingdom of life triumphing through resurrection—in which life there lies the real, actual, and final good. In this rests all the power and work of Christ, in this lies his real love toward us and our love toward him; whereas all the other things are only the condition, the path, the preliminary steps. Without faith in the accomplished resurrection of One, and without cherishing the future resurrection of all, all talk of some Kingdom of God remains nothing, but words while, in reality, one finds only the Kingdom of Death."[194] Balthasar affirms this attention to the resurrection of Christ as the "ultimate synthesis of body and soul, idea and manifestation," as Soloviev's solution to the eschatological problem of negotiating finite and infinite is "aimed straight at the point that Dostoevsky circled as the actual core of all eschatology."[195] Surely Dostoevsky's *The Brothers Karamazov* corroborates this theme of bodily resurrection after death and illustrates well the way it sanctifies and joyfully celebrates finitude, given both the epigraph of the novel from John 12:24 and the stirring final conclusion as the grieving boys gather around the grave of the young Ilyusha:

"Karamazov!" cried Kolya, "can it really be true what religion says, that we shall all rise from the dead, and shall live, and see each other again, everyone, and Ilyushechka?"

"Certainly we shall all rise again, certainly we shall see each other and gladly, joyfully will tell each other all that has happened," Alyosha answered, half laughing, half ecstatic.

"Ah, how good it will be!" broke from Kolya.

"Well, now we will finish talking and go to his funeral dinner. Don't be put out at our eating pancakes—it's something ancient, eternal, and there's something good in that," laughed Alyosha. "Well, let us go! And now we go hand in hand."

"And eternally, so, all our lives hand in hand! Hurrah for Karamazov!" Kolya cried once more ecstatically and once more all the boys joined in his exclamation.[196]

An imploring personal letter from Soloviev to Tolstoy, dated August 2, 1894, corroborates the privileged position of this primary theme of resurrection in Soloviev's dialogue. Soloviev was distressed that Tolstoy's positions rebuffed the mystical and metaphysical depth of religion, preferring to understand it only in horizontal, ethical, this-worldly terms. An earlier (1880) letter from Tolstoy to another friend indicates in no uncertain terms that he held this position:

I and all the rest of us live like animals, and will die the same way. To escape from this excruciating situation, Christ offered us salvation. Who is Christ: A God or a man? He is what he says he is. He says he is the Son of God, he says he is the Son of Man, he says, "I am what I tell you I am. I am the truth and the life . . . " And from that moment they began to mix it all up together and say he was God and the second person of the Trinity, the result was sacrilege, falsehood, and nonsense. If he were that, he would have been capable of saying so. He offered us salvation. How? By teaching us to give a meaning to our lives that is not destroyed by death. . . . For me, the foundation of his teaching is that to achieve salvation it is necessary, every day and every hour of every day, to think of God, of one's soul, and therefore to set the love of one's neighbor above mere bestial existence.[197]

In Tolstoy's position (again, represented by the Prince in Soloviev's dialogue), the spiritual depths of the faith are evacuated; Jesus's divinity, a genuine resurrection of an eternal body and soul, and salvation as anything other than from material or social conditions of hunger, poverty, and the like are jettisoned. In Soloviev's letter to Tolstoy, intended to encourage him to adopt more orthodox Christian views, Soloviev persuasively argues that the rationale for hope in the Resurrection is already contained in three certain principles that Tolstoy already holds: first, that the world and the forms therein are progressively moving from a lower state to the higher; second, that there is a relation of interdependence between the inner condition of human being and the material condition; and third, that spiritual perfection is achieved to the extent that the spiritual controls and conditions the physical life. Again, death is put in terms of the eventual victory of the "alien material principle"; it is the victory of "non-sense over sense, of chaos over cosmos."[198] And again, for Soloviev, bodily resurrection is the only therapy: "If a struggle with chaos and death constitutes the heart of the world-process, in which the luminous, spiritual side ever tends to gain the upper hand, though slowly and gradually, then the Resurrection—the actual and final victory of a living being over death—is a necessary stage in this process."[199] Moreover, Christ's spiritual power and perfection indicate that the spiritual principle in him simply cannot have been overtaken by the lower principle.[200]

Bulgakov's thoroughly Chalcedonian explication of the resurrection of Christ, in which the finite and the infinite are coexistent, accords with Soloviev's and Balthasar's. Though discussion of the Trinitarian implications that emerge in his treatment of Christ's resurrection as a continuation of the kenotic moment are deferred to the next chapter, suffice it to say by way of anticipation that Bulgakov parses resurrection in terms of a dual agency of Father and Son, thereby highlighting resurrection as a synergistic divine-human act.[201] What is more apropos for this discussion on safeguarding human finitude is Bulgakov's philosophical reflection concerning the possibility of corporeal form abiding in the Trinity. As noted above, despite its transparence to spirit, Christ's resurrected flesh is precisely that— flesh—with spatial and corporeal properties; how then can it be said that the post-Ascension Christ now abides at the right hand of the Father, if God is incorporeal? Bulgakov presents the paradox:

> On the one hand, disincarnation is inconceivable, but on the other hand, there is no place for the body of flesh, even if glorified, in the kingdom of the pure absolute Spirit, which Divinity is. A body can only be spatial, but no spatiality is compatible with spiritual being. If we attempt to evade this aporia by referring to the spirituality of the glorified body, we must remember that even this *spirituality* of the body does not signify the revocation or total abolition of corporeality and thus of spatiality. . . . We arrive at a *contradictio in adjecto*, at a contradictory definition: a spiritual body understood as a *noncorporeal* body, or simply as a *nonbody*.[202]

He attempts to break this impasse by making a distinction between the state of the resurrected body of Christ as "supra-earthly" and, after the Ascension, "supramundane, although not extramundane,"[203] a state which is not heaven, but rather the summit of the world upon which there is "a ladder between earth and heaven that has been climbed down and up and has forever united heaven and earth."[204] Christ's ascended body thereby exceeds the body present at the incarnation as its ideal image or energy. Here Bulgakov's sophiology is very much at work: "In Christ, in His Divine-Humanity, the total sophianization of creation and, in this sense, the identification of the creaturely Sophia and the noncreaturely Sophia are attained. . . . Thus, the 'spiritual body' in which Christ abides at the right hand of the Father is nothing other than this *connection of identification* of the Divine Sophia and the creaturely Sophia. And so, the spiritual body is the creaturely Image of the eternal Proto-Image in their identity, and this spiritual image can be realized in the flesh of the world."[205] Ultimately, then, in Bulgakov the value of the "flesh of the world" is scrupulously maintained, and, despite what may appear sophiologically as a heterodox innovation, it is actually parsed in the quite traditional terms of ecclesiology and sacrament evocative of Origen. Christ's true spiritual body, the "*Body of the body*," is present finally in the Church and in the Eucharistic elements.[206] Moreover, for Bulgakov the resurrection of Christ has cosmic, universal efficacy irrespective of a personal relationship to or knowledge of Christ's saving work: by this "universal resurrection" the world is transfigured, though in a qualitative rather than temporal interpretation of certain Scriptures, followers of Christ are resurrected differently from those who are not.[207]

For all human beings, however, this universal resurrection is an ongoing synergistic "ripening" of individuals that—importantly for Bulgakov's tendency toward universalism—continues into the afterlife.[208] For Bulgakov, the state of the dead, even in hell, is neither static nor passive, but is, rather dynamic and organic and pedagogical, a "spiritual school" in which self-creative activity takes place: "Every individual must, in his own way, ripen spiritually to this resurrection and determine himself with finality both in good and in evil."[209] This rather probative point marks a perhaps surprising degree of convergence with Balthasar, who, although again far more tentative epistemically than Bulgakov, suggests parenthetically something quite along these lines, namely, that the bodily resurrection of Christ is efficacious for ongoing perfection, a process operative both on earth and beyond it: "The bodily risen Lord, precisely through his exaltation and as an expression of his glorification, has granted freedom and space for his members who remain on earth to continue their journey toward perfection. (Why should this not apply, by analogy, to other risen saints?)."[210]

This attitude coincides with Balthasar's presupposition of a genuine theological hope for (but not certainty of) the universal power of the efficacious love of Christ, which on his accounting persisted in the East—for instance, Gregory of Nyssa and Maximus the Confessor—far more vigorously than in the West.[211] It is the double logic of resurrection, as both final object and efficient cause, which guarantees true Christian hope: the seed of certainty is planted already with the Resurrection of Christ the Lord.[212] Importantly, this boundless expansiveness of hope—hearkening Balthasar's muse Charles Péguy, the poetic champion par excellence of the Christian virtue of hope—is for Balthasar all that remains to the believer after the eventual failure of speculative systems.[213]

THIS CHAPTER HAS undertaken the task of tracking prominent nodes of connection between Schelling, the Russians, and Balthasar, specifically with respect to traditional eschatological questions posed from an anthropocentric perspective, namely, those dealing with the phenomenon of death, the nature of postmortem existence, judgment, and (at least the hope of) universal salvation. Questions of eschatology and anthropology are also seen to be of a piece. In Balthasar's judgment, the poisoned heart of the speculative ontologies that mark the thought of Schelling and Berdyaev ultimately malign and discredit the finite existence of human beings, while Soloviev and Bulgakov's fundamental accent on the bodily resurrection of Christ, the decisive concrete co-existence of finite and infinite, underwrites both the theological virtue to hope for the salvation of all human beings and the extraordinary goodness of creation. This extensive discussion has demonstrated Balthasar's direct and constitutive affirmation of bodiliness, contravening an unfortunate but prevalent impression of Balthasarian theology as being otherworldly or constitutively nonconcrete.

Furthermore, this construction highlights those instances in which Balthasar permits theological speculation, in both his assessment of the Russians and his own experimental theologizing, including hell as a self-made subjective state of the imagination, Christ's radical solidarity with the dead, the efficacy of the resurrection of Christ for both the living and the dead, and the possibility of universal salvation, all of which accord with what has appropriately been called Balthasar's "ontology of generosity."[214] It indicates as well the boundaries of theological speculation beyond which Balthasar refuses to go, including the theorem of *apokatastasis* and—particularly relevant with respect to anthropocentric eschatological matters—the de-evolution of the speculative into the spectatorial. The "last things" of human being, that ever-darkening horizon of life—the end of time, the immanence of dying, the resurrection of the body that breaks in as hard reality (as in Rilke's poem "Death Experienced," which gives this chapter its name), through a fissure that reveals the "green of real green, real sunshine, real forest," are marked ultimately not by closure but rather by dis-/closure, by the constitutional openness of the book.[215] Indeed, common to Balthasar, the Romantics, and the Russians is an openness, a receptivity toward that which is only potential, an expectant posture toward the not-yet-emergent, though the degree to which this future may become reified in each thinker (perhaps in the manner of Joachim) remains to be seen, whether something of the order of gnosis rather than the order of mystery and love. This presumptive tendency of peering into the internal life of God—with what Balthasar calls the "stony and incontestable gaze of the Sibyl"[216]—is especially prevalent in Schelling and in Berdyaev, and it anticipates the content of the next chapter, which widens eschatology from the anthropocentric purview to include the broader vista of the theocentric, properly Trinitarian horizon.

CHAPTER 5

"DENN ARMUT IST EIN GROßER GLANZ AUS INNEN"

The Theocentric Horizon

This book is ultimately an exercise in gauging proximity and distance: in particular, it attends to Balthasar's mode of sifting out the proverbial wheat from the chaff with respect first to the salvageable contributions of modern German philosophy and second to his reading, which often allows wheat and weeds to grow together for a time, of speculative Russian religious philosophy that is formed, informed, or deformed by the lineage of thinking that includes Böhme, Joachim, Schelling, and Hegel. The Russian appropriation of extratraditional sources and the way that these sources are adapted in each appropriation once again provides the heartiest grist for the mill; as shown in chapter 3, the degree to which the Russians corrosively adopt the legacies of Böhme, Joachim, Schelling, and Hegel is approximately the degree to which Balthasar indicts them as (illicitly) speculative. Berdyaev again takes dubious top honors. Ultimately, Balthasar gives a positive reading of Soloviev's apocalyptic theology, which is for him somehow inoculated against heterodox forms, and again both affirms and appropriates Bulgakov, particularly his dramatic, eschatological Trinitarianism, which employs a robust form of kenosis, both Christological and Trinitarian.

While the last chapter attended largely to the anthropocentric eschatological horizon—that is, questions of death, judgment, and the resurrected body—this chapter turns to the broader "theocentric" horizon, the necessary context in which the anthropocentric ought to be understood. It is categorized in the main by Trinitarian and thus more (licitly) speculative concerns. It treats (1) a shared Johannine register, which includes such features as a "realized" eschatology, a dialectic of unveiling and concealment, the symbol of the slain Lamb, and the polarizing apocalyptic doublet of light and darkness that necessitates from the human being a yes or a no; (2) figurations of Antichrist as a function of religious counterfeiting, which puts Balthasar in proximity to Soloviev (and to Dostoevsky); and, finally (3) the positive connection of paschal Trinitarianism with apocalyptic by Russian appropriations of Schellingian kenosis, which reappears in a more purified form in Balthasar through the radicalized and profoundly original ur-kenoticism of Bulgakov.[1] This chapter's epigraph from Rilke— "poverty is luminous from within"—thus gestures toward the counterintuitive richness, power, and luminosity of this divine self-gift.[2]

It is on the point of apocalyptic Trinitarianism that Balthasar's borrowings from Bulgakov are most clear and also at greatest distance from both Schelling's ambivalent Trinitarianism and Hegel's thoroughly deformed Trinitarianism. Balthasar is against both Schelling, whose trinity is only thinly conceived, and Hegel, for whom the immanent trinity is exhausted totally in the economic. The robust Trinitarianism that characterizes Balthasar and Bulgakov's thickly apocalyptic theology is only spectrally present in Schelling's wan trinity of Father (eternal), Son (finite), and Spirit (infinite), and not at all in Hegel. Consider, for instance, Bulgakov's decisive and withering critique of the excessive rationalism found in Schelling's emaciated version of the Trinity:

> For all his profundity and exegetical skill one has to acknowledge that Schelling introduces opinions about Divinity and the holy Trinity that are completely inadmissible for Christianity, and his whole "deduction" of trinitarity is a sad attempt of presumptuous speculation, of that same treacherous "mystical rationalism" with which he rightly reproaches Böhme. Schelling wants "to explain," and "to deduce" that which the voice of religious feeling and philosophical criticism equally enjoin to *accept* as the fact of divine life,

established in religious experience and revelation. . . . This is rationalistic lack of taste, which one would least of all want to see in
Schelling, and he is paid for it not only with heresy but also with
contradiction of his own self.[3]

Balthasar and Bulgakov, informed as they are by the determinate content of Catholicism and Orthodoxy respectively and committed to
receiving mystery as a positive good, posit God as triadic being, but
for them God is a "trihypostatic personality," with each hypostatic
center possessing a weight, a density that is absent in both Schelling
and Hegel, whose rationalistic deductions of the Trinity verge toward
Sabellian modalism.

   Balthasar explicitly borrows from Bulgakov the rhetorically rich
concept of the primal drama operative between Father, Son, and Spirit
in the "drama of the 'emptying' of the Father's heart, in the generation
of the Son that contains and surpasses all possible drama between God
and a world."[4] Balthasar's (and Bulgakov's) Trinitarian theology and
eschatology are of a piece: each is the condition of the possibility for
the other. The theocentric mode of eschatology is a highly integrative
discourse, drawing protology, cosmology, aesthetics, the mythical, a
theology of history, thanatology, Christology, and Trinitarian discourse all into its long reach.[5]

READING REVELATION, READING JOHN: A DECISIVELY
JOHANNINE HERMENEUTIC

An attraction to the Johannine—characterized broadly as that which
is visionary, mystical, Trinitarian, and paschal—unites Schelling, Balthasar, and the Russians, who all to some degree privilege textually
the Gospel of John and the Apocalypse. There is indeed an operative
Johannine hermeneutic across the board, so much so that it is tempting
to consider this chapter as an exercise in biblical hermeneutics in a decidedly Johannine key. As already noted, Balthasar views Schelling as
fundamentally "an apocalyptic figure for whom all is arranged around
revelation, around the disclosure of mystery, around breakthrough

into the mysteries of God."[6] By sins of commission and omission, however, the Schellingian Johannine hermeneutic is thoroughly warped, by
both its Prometheanism and its replacement of the Gospel of Jesus
with the gospel of the self, and, at least by Bulgakov's lights, the same
"mystical rationalism" condemned in Böhme. According to Balthasar,
Schelling's brand of apocalyptic actually stands "eye-to-eye" with that
of John himself, save the most important element: in the choice of the
"two gods," Schelling fatally chooses Dionysius over Christ.[7] That is
to say, although Schelling does invoke Johannine visionary literature,
especially in the *Philosophy of Mythology* and the *Philosophy of Revelation*, his version of "Dionysian" theogonic apocalyptic fails to cross
the threshold into the genuinely Christian insofar as it accords human
beings a status that belongs properly only to God. Thus, unpacking the
self-understanding of each thinker—Russian, German, or Swiss—as
Johannine hermeneut demands sober consideration.[8]

First, Balthasar demonstrates a clear preference for a distinctively
Johannine "realized" eschatology. Balthasar is careful to qualify this
designation, however, underscoring the fact that it must be understood
not from the anthropocentric perspective alone, but rather from the
theocentric, which encompasses and conditions the former.[9] John's eschatology is first a vertical irruption of Christ in the present before it
is a horizontal process. Further, a choice for John is not a choice against
the synoptics, as Balthasar considers Johannine eschatology to function, in Ireanean terms, recapitulatively rather than oppositionally.[10]
For Balthasar, eschatology proper—from the theocentric view—does
not indicate some class of events relegated to a far and distant future:
it is *nun*, "now," "today," in the expression of the colocation of time
and eternity.[11] Balthasar's interpretation of the biblical sense of "today"
requires a kind of temporal acrobatics that maintains the simultaneity
of the historically pastness of the Christ-event with its eternal presence, as well as an inbreaking on the horizon, an always-coming-
toward.[12] Hence, the present moment has a significance always that
exceeds itself. It connotes simultaneously "the 'eternal present' of the
'Lamb as though it had been slain'" as well as "the increasingly mo-
mentous irruption of the reality of time into that of eternity."[13]

In the Gospel of John, which again for Balthasar does not contradict but rather develops the thought of the synoptics, "the Christ-
event, which is always seen in its totality, is the vertical irruption of the
fulfillment into horizontal time; such irruption does not leave this
time—with its present, past and future—unchanged, but draws it into
itself and thereby gives it a new character."[14] Christ's entrance into time
as an historical person who suffers and dies does not evacuate his person of the character of eternity; rather, time and transience are affected
by Christ's eternity.[15] Thus, the "I am" sayings of Jesus in the Gospel
of John, particularly the very present claim in the narrative of the rais-
ing of Lazarus that "I *am* the resurrection and the life" (11:24–25),
contemporize a deferred hope to the theologically significant moment
of *Now*. In this way, the "realized," primarily vertical theo-drama, especially in the fifth volume of Balthasar's *Theo-Drama*, ought to be
understood in a manner that is primarily Christological and therefore
ultimately eschatological before it is anthropological.[16]

The theocentric framework, both the Christological and, more
originary, the Trinitarian, is the absolutely necessary context for understanding Johannine and therefore Bulgakovian and Balthasarian
eschatology. As Balthasar points out, this "realized" eschatology is not
in an antithetical relation to futurist eschatology, but rather a way of
drawing the latter into the former by way of Christology and Trinitarian reflection.[17] Both present and future elements are present. As
suggested in chapter 4, authentically Christian hope is a theological
virtue that is possible based on what has already been done, in the
bodily resurrection of Jesus, and, underlying this, the life of the divine
Trinity. It is precisely the relations between Father, Son, and Spirit that
give Balthasar a stake in this modified "realized" eschatology; that is,
his constitutively open/future orientation is possible because there is
in the present moment the promise of love, which is parsed Christologically and pneumatologically. Balthasar is adamant first that emphasizing the explicitly Christological hub and rationale of eschatology is
necessary to save eschatological discourse from being ghettoized to the
domain of the obscure and the marginal. Far from being comprised of
idle speculations, the fundamental thrust of Balthasar's eschatology
hearkens back to Augustine's theme: "Ipse [Deus] post istam vitam sit

locus noster." In the hereafter, God's Self is our place: "Gained, he is heaven; lost, he is hell; examining, he is judgment; purifying, he is purgatory. He it is to whom finite being dies, and through whom it rises to him, in him."[18] Furthermore, he associates the Spirit directly with the creation and opening of a thickly conceived future marked by love, "not an empty future, but one that continually fulfills itself and, in fulfilling, promises anew."[19] Again following the marvelous poet Péguy, Balthasar challenges the hegemony of the merely chronological future, opening up the vertical dimension, the now, to the eschatological horizon: as small children in their play tirelessly cover the same ground over and over again, so the "earthly future is inserted into an ever-new 'now' that is a gift of divine grace."[20]

Furthermore, both Bulgakov and Balthasar read the Gospel of John in tandem with Revelation, which, according to O'Regan's incisive analysis of Bulgakov's *Bride of the Lamb*, complements rather than competes with Matthew 24 through 25 and 1 and 2 Thessalonians.[21] To read Revelation properly is determinative, but not overdetermined or totalizing: the text is first and foremost "a book of vision, opening up perspectives that, once opened, can never be shut."[22] Balthasar and Bulgakov both understand the function of apocalyptic symbolism primarily as preventing the proverbial door from closing all the way, resisting an interpretation that would univocally concretize or historicize the violent images of Revelation. That is, there is no sense in which it is appropriate in reading John's Apocalypse to assign particular historical analogues to what is a highly imagistic literary figuration.[23]

Indeed, evoking Origen, the images themselves are an irreducible, mysterious "dogmatics" intended to keep the reader from the sense that the Christian faith is the sort of thing that might be mastered, interpretively or otherwise.[24] The symbolic, spiritual nature of the text, gesturing to God as the ever-greater "eternal surprise,"[25] suggests an infinite creative novelty that exceeds human knowledge and invites human participation in that which is always coming toward us.[26] Given his dramatic orientation, as well as his commitment to the absolute freedom of the divine, Balthasar places a high premium on the possibility of surprise. As he puts it, "as one who loves, [the believer] does not ask at all how much of what is to come he perceives in advance, thanks to love, and how much he does not perceive. He allows himself to be surprised again and again by the divine love in such a way that, since he knows how God delights in surprising, he is ready to be surprised again in a definitive way and as it were for the very first time."[27] Certainly because of this element of the divine character, and particularly with respect to Spirit, human being is ever on the cusp of something; there is an openness and a promise and a hope that constitutively structure being: "everything that exists is a 'not yet' of what it can be, ought to be, perhaps will be."[28] The positive value of the ungraspable, the openness of all that exists, marks a departure from Berdyaev, whose Schellingian and Joachimite heritage shows as he attempts to fill out the content of the "Age of the Spirit" with the certainty of a science.

Balthasar is resolutely anti-Joachimite, insofar as the inevitable ossification of the latter's view simultaneously sunders and presumes to know too much about the Trinity, although he tempers his criticism of Joachim himself, who intended, in Balthasar's reading, only to offer "homage" to the Spirit.[29] There is also in Schellingian eschatology, particularly *The Ages of the World*, a dangerous tendency toward presumptive and audacious gnosis, a presumption to know the "'unbekannten' Gott," both of the present and of the future, a theme that is incurably repeated in Berdayev's own temporal genealogy. As suggested in chapter 3, with respect to his acceptance of the Böhmian–Schellingian *Ungrund*, Berdyaev's eschatological philosophy is too heavily determined by the outer limits of speculative heterodox apocalypse for Balthasar's comfort. As O'Regan suggests, Joachim is "one of Balthasar's declared enemies. Balthasar endorses totally de Lubac's genealogy in which Joachim is at the origin of the Reformation, its speculative translation, a presence in Romanticism and Idealism, which deepens the derailment of Christianity given in the Enlightenment in and by a Christian repackaging in which only what is marginal to the Christian theological tradition is allowed to speak."[30] It is striking that when Balthasar makes this genealogical point, tracing the history of effects from Joachim through the Franciscan Spirituals to Idealism, he also indicts certain "sophiological triadic systems of the philosophy of history."[31] It is almost certain, especially given Balthasar's criticisms of Berdyaev as both Schellingian and Gnostic in *Apokalypse der deutschen Seele*, that he has him firmly in mind again here.[32]

Following Joachim's general schematic, Berdyaev posits three epochs of divine revelation: the Age of the Father, the Age of the Son, and the Age of the Spirit. We can conjecture that the general structure of Berdyaev's temporal chronology is indeed borrowed from Joachim, although Berdyaev's analysis is more developed than Joachim's as he also posits three principal temporal forms: the cosmic, historical, and existential.[33] According to Berdyaev's adaptation of Joachim, the Age of the Father is associated with the Old Testament and with revelation in nature; the Age of the Son with the New Testament and revelation in history; and the Age of the Spirit with apocalyptic expectation. The Age of the Spirit is the third epoch of religious history, marked by existential time, "which is akin to eternity . . . [in which] the eternal accomplishment of the mystery of spirit takes place."[34]

As in Böhme, Joachim, and the Schelling of *The Ages of the World* (which pays its debts to both Böhme and Joachim), the Trinitarian complex of serial temporal existence is sundered one from the other. The notion of the Spirit considered apart from Father and Son is absolutely unacceptable both for Balthasar, whose pneumatology affirms precisely that "the medium in which the Spirit moves is the 'We,' the eternal dialogue between the Father and the Son,"[35] and for Bulgakov, whose pneumatology is even more robust than Balthasar's even as it likely motivated Balthasar's turn to the Spirit.[36] There is no case in which the Spirit can surpass, move beyond, or sever itself from Son and Father, for "there arrives only what already existed: nothing truly new is still to be awaited. We know the Christ who comes, indeed, we already know his transfigured, risen form."[37] The Spirit does not surpass what is indicated at the cross of Christ. For both Balthasar and Bulgakov, we know the Spirit precisely as the Spirit of Christ with whom, in the "dyad" of revelatory hypostases, the Father, or the revealed hypostasis, is made known to us.[38]

Epistemic humility notwithstanding, the literal reading of apocalyptic (*apokalypsis*) is "unveiling," and thus it is a disclosure of *something*. It is fair to assert that for Balthasar, as well as Bulgakov, while it is far from comprehensive, this unveiling can be said to be of a determinate content. For Bulgakov, all of human history is the apocalypse, or revelation, of Christ.[39] For both Bulgakov and Balthasar, the principle that if Christological, so too Trinitarian, more or less holds across the board. Apocalyptic is thus a disclosure of the Trinity, as much as an essential mystery can be said to be unveiled or disclosed. According to Balthasar, the elements of the faith to which Revelation speaks "are truly open, for, after all, what we are dealing with is *apokalypsis*; yet they remain only significant hieroglyphs that, however legible, conceal their ultimate meaning in the mystery of God."[40] This quality of dialectical veiling and unveiling in Balthasar and Bulgakov is a dark vision akin to that of Gregory of Nyssa; it does not proclaim certitude for itself. Exceeding this reserve, however, is the assertion that unresolved mystery and hiddenness is a positive category that is "theologically fundamental and therefore essential."[41] Jesus's passion and resurrection did not annul his "essential hiddenness," the unveiling of which is left to the Holy Spirit and to the Church, "who can 'reveal' him, interpret him and make him known to the world later on only *as the one who is hidden*."[42] This dramatic union of hiddenness and revelation is most balanced in the Gospel of John, in the fundamentally eschatological tension between already and not-yet, between the present glory of Christ in the Church and the future glory of the kingdom.[43]

Analogous to the tension between revelation and hiddenness is the further Johannine theme of light and darkness that thoroughly characterizes Balthasar's reading of Revelation as operating according to the dramatic rhythm of a "law of heightened resistance."[44] The trope of ever-ratcheting stakes is present also in Schelling, as Balthasar observes.[45] Certainly, the similarities with Schelling on this point are striking, particularly in the freedom essay:

> Feeling, in advance, the coming of light, the gathering of the deep grows constantly more apparent, and at once draws all forces from indetermination to meet light in full opposition. As the thunderstorm is brought on by the mediation of the sun, but immediately through an opposing force of the Earth, so the spirit of evil . . . is aroused through the approach of the good, not by means of a participation but rather through a partition of forces. Thus it is only

with the decisive coming of the good that evil too becomes manifest decisively and as such (not as though it only now arose, but because the contrast is only now given in which it can appear in its totality and as itself).[46]

According to Balthasar, the very presence of Jesus as the "disclosure of absolute, causeless love"[47] provokes forces of evil and opposition to come out into the open; this opposition is not simply hostile to Christianity but in fact its precise opposite, its anti-.[48] Indeed, in the apocalyptic literature of Revelation, the "No" to God's "Yes" intensifies: this marks the culmination of the riddle of evil, whereby human beings exercise freely the choice to refuse God.[49]

FIGURATIONS OF ANTICHRIST AS COUNTERFEIT

This apocalyptic trope of the ever-increasing polarization between light and darkness in Balthasar is both suggestive of Soloviev's pseudo- or counterfeit figurations of Antichrist and emphatic of the very Solovievian sense that apocalyptic disclosure is always the occasion for free human decision and self-determination, for yes or for no.[50] Here we pick up the thread dangling from the discussion in chapter 3, which examined Soloviev's final text, *War, Progress, and the End of History*, with respect to what bearing the phenomenon of moral evil has upon the meaning of history. In keeping with the epistemic reserve of Balthasar and Bulgakov is Soloviev's ultimate genre modulation in *War, Progress, and the End of History*, from what had theretofore been philosophical dialogue to a fantastical prophetic apocalypse that breaks off abruptly, indicating formally the impossibility of articulating with any certainty the end of history.[51] As suggested in previous chapters, Soloviev's theological perspective, characterized by great optimism concerning the ongoing progress of humanity toward the realization of the kingdom of God upon the earth, is ultimately an evolutionary one, which Balthasar elsewhere indicts as empty, infinite, and therefore hopeless. This criticism is qualified somewhat by Soloviev's emphasis on bodily resurrection and nearly invalidated by his late turn to apocalyptic.

Christianity is different because it possesses a certain "explosiveness," having within its resources a breakthrough of God into the cosmos.[52] Balthasar thereby denies any possibility of a "gradual realization of the eschaton."[53] He goes on to state that "all the evolution and work of the world will not suffice to bring in the kingdom of God."[54] Along with these reservations, Balthasar finds Soloviev's turn to the apocalyptic in "A Short Story of the Antichrist" to be an implicit forfeiture of a thoroughly teleological theory of history and a "salutary counterpoise to his evolutionism" (especially vis-à-vis Teilhard).[55] Of primary importance to Balthasar is Soloviev's apparent renunciation of the "idea that the process comes to perfection within history."[56] Thus, in Balthasar's judgment with respect to theologians such as Soloviev, whose theological project is characterized by progress and development, the apocalyptic is a necessary capstone insofar as it interrupts a primarily evolutionary trajectory. Balthasar suggests that

> whoever takes the idea of the development of the spirit seriously—which cannot be anything other than increasing integration—as Vladimir Soloviev does, following Schelling and Hegel, must, if he is to go on thinking in a Christian way, reach the increasing apocalyptic alternative, which the "story of the Antichrist" presents symbolically. The Christian fact within history is, through its existence, the cause of the fact that the "noosphere closing itself" expressly places itself under the sign of "anti." The profundity of Christ's words becomes clear when he says that when called by God a man is placed in an either-or situation.[57]

For both Soloviev and Balthasar, then, the densely symbolic apocalyptic genre functions panoptically, as the manifold eyes of the cherubim turn their gaze upon the individual, threatening the safe distance of the spectator. Balthasar suggests,

> The apocalyptic view of things offers the assurance that history as history (and not only as the sum of individual lives) has before God a completely clear and overwhelmingly magnificent sense. The translation of this sense into an aesthetic or symbolic view is the best way in which man, still struggling within history, can share in

this vision. . . . It can be accomplished only in images which do not have as their content the reporting of decisions, but are themselves, in their form, like the parables of the gospel, images of decisions: images, which from their latent presence, demand a *yes* or a *no*.[58]

For Balthasar, then, apocalyptic images function a bit like koans in that they both provoke decision and are themselves the enactment of decision.

In Soloviev's apocalyptic discourse, too, the metaphysical and existential stakes are high. The main purpose of the third conversation in Soloviev's final apocalyptic work is to bring to light the error of Tolstoyanism, represented by the Prince insofar as he is engaged in a kind of Harnackian project that would flatten the thickness of the Gospel, reducing it down to the kernel of an ethical message apart from the metaphysical basis that gives it life. In Soloviev's dialogue, this ethical reduction is not simply objectionable from a Christian perspective; it is—perhaps worse!—lethally boring, because it does not and cannot elicit either a vigorous yes or no in response to it. As the General says, attributing this dreary development to demonic forces, "Even in the past, Christianity was unintelligible to some and hateful to others. But it remained to our time to make it either repulsive or so dull that it bores people to death."[59] As a rejoinder to the Prince's Tolstoyanism, which resisted the idea that evil is a powerful, real force that must be actively opposed, Soloviev has his Mr. Z. relate the apocalyptic story of the Antichrist.[60] This move is significant because it again modulates genre from dialogue to embedded narrative, and also because it contravenes a purely evolutionary reading of history.

Soloviev's Antichrist represents not only a force inimical to Christianity, "not a mere infidelity to or a denial of Christianity, nor simply the triumph of materialism or anything similar to it, but . . . a religious *imposture*."[61] With respect to the idea of anti-Christianity as primarily a counterfeiting, corrosive force, Soloviev and Balthasar speak in one voice, especially the latter in his tracing out of the "law of heightened resistance" in the book of Revelation, which draws out "a demonic trinity, namely, the primal devil, a pseudo-incarnation and a pseudo-spirit."[62] Soloviev's robust understanding of evil is at least an implicit critique of Hegel, not only as far as Hegel considered evil to be a necessary element of the dialectical unfolding of history, but also his thought that evil might in the process of sublation be overcome. This critique recalls Balthasar's own criticisms of Hegel. With respect to Soloviev's truncation of evolutionary progress with the interrupting moment of apocalyptic, Balthasar says,

> Here the total opposition between Hegel and Soloviev comes out into the open, between Hegel's dialectic of absolute knowledge (which again first takes flight—as the "owl of Minerva"—in the twilight of the end of history) and Soloviev's Christian programme of integration. For the former evil can be no more than Socratic ignorance; for the latter, it is a clearly acknowledged act of saying No to love. And this contradiction shatters any systematic clarity in the cosmic "process"; it explodes into a battle to the death, a battle of mounting intensity, that, in Soloviev's eschatological consciousness, could not be other than directly imminent. And so it is into this fiery inferno [of apocalyptic] that his entire system flows.[63]

Not unrelated here is Balthasar's provocative suggestion in the second volume of *Apokalypse der deutschen Seele* that Dostoevsky—who because of personal and literary relationship and mutual influence might stand proxy for Soloviev—is engaged also in a deliberate resistance to Hegel.

Whereas the discussion in chapter 4 engaged primarily with the first two "days" of dialogue presented in *War, Progress, and the End of History*, featuring the General's views on war on the first and the statesman's views of "progress" and modernity on the second, the third and final day is given over to the enigmatic Mr. Z., who suggests the ultimate manifestation of evil in a figuration of the Anti-Christ in Soloviev's original fantastical literary apocalypse.[64] The "Third Conversation" of the third "day" includes Mr. Z's reading of the fictitious manuscript of one Father Pansophius, namely, "A Short Story of the Anti-Christ." The manuscript is set in the twenty-first century, where out of the democratic nations that joined together as the "United States of Europe" there emerged a popular leader, a "super-man," a young man of thirty-three with "irreproachable morals and exceptional genius."[65]

Though this man believed in God, "in the depths of his soul he involuntarily and unconsciously preferred himself,"[66] coming to think of Christ only as a preliminary to himself, and indeed, himself as superior to Christ, for he was to be a peaceful benefactor rather than a divisive reformer, a leader who preferred distributive justice over retributive. Readers of Dostoevsky will associate this rightly with the embedded narrative of the Grand Inquisitor in *The Brothers Karamazov*, in which the Inquisitor supplies bread to the hungry but gives allegiance to the devil rather than to Christ. In Soloviev, the thought of bowing before Christ ("as some Russian peasant" or "old Polish woman") filled the young super-man with such despair, rage, and envy that he cried out, "It is I, it is I, and not he! He is dead—is and will ever be! He did not—no, did not rise! He is rotting in the grave, rotting as the lost."[67] On this evening he was met by a strange figure who likewise decried "that crucified beggar," telling the young man, "I have no other son but thee. Thou art the sole, the only begotten, the equal of myself. I love thee, and ask for nothing from thee. Thou art so beautiful, great, and mighty. Do thy work in *thine own* name, not mine."[68]

From that day on, his work (particularly the nearly vacuous book *The Open Way to Universal Peace and Prosperity*) was met with accolades and uncomplicated acceptance, and he—now known as "The Coming Man"—was elected president for life of the United States of Europe and then Roman Emperor. This Superman Emperor was absolutely beyond reproach: highly connected in military circles, a wealthy philanthropist, and a vegetarian, advocating a platform of peace and prosperity, and without much difficulty achieving a solution to *all* social and economic problems. These reforms were not the end, however, as the Emperor also had it in mind to achieve final unity among the churches and settle the religious question once and for all.

At an ecumenical council convened at his request, the Emperor asks a large delegation what the most precious thing in Christianity is. When an answer is not immediately forthcoming, he makes his own suggestions (an exercise of freedom-limiting power that again calls to mind Ivan Karamazov's Grand Inquisitor, who abolishes free choice, preferring satisfied automatons). To the Catholics, he promises that the papacy will be restored to Rome; to the Orthodox he promises a world museum in Constantinople that would house ancient religious artifacts of the Eastern Church; to the Protestants he promises a well-funded institute for biblical research.

Most delegates accept the terms, but three delegates resist: from the Catholics, Pope Peter II; from the Protestants, Professor Ernst Pauli; and from the Orthodox, the peripatetic monk John. When asked what they desire, Elder John rises and, evoking Colossians 2:9, quietly says,

> What we value most in Christianity is Christ himself—in his person. All comes from him, for we know that in him dwells as fullness the Godhead bodily. We are ready, sire, to accept any gift from you, if only we recognize the holy hand of Christ in your generosity. Our candid answer to your question, what can you do for us, is this: Confess now and before us the name of Jesus Christ, the Son of God, who came in the flesh, rose, and who will come again— Confess his name, and we will accept you with love as the true forerunner of his second glorious coming.[69]

At this, the Emperor can barely contain his rage, and the monk John recognizes him for what he is. He calls out, "Little children, it is Anti-Christ!" This confession unleashes an epic battle between the followers of the Anti-Christ and the remnant of all the Christian faithful, which culminates in a quiet unification of the churches under the cover of darkness.

Balthasar affirms the counterfeit figurations of evil that appear in Soloviev and in Dostoevsky, which culminate in the presentation of Antichrist as a great humanist who perversely but plausibly counterfeits the good.[70] This deformative parody recalls Luca Signorelli's painting *Preaching of the Antichrist*, in which Antichrist appears from a distance to be the Christ in all respects except that his ear is inclined to the devil figure's whispers.[71] According to Balthasar's reading of Soloviev, the true identity of Antichrist is hidden "under the last mask to be stripped away, the mask of what is good and what is Christian."[72] Soloviev's attractive Antichrist figure runs on a platform of social change, reform, social justice, and economic and material betterment, which again resonates deeply with Dostoevsky's Grand Inquisitor narrative in *The Brothers Karamazov*, as well as Balthasar's apocalyptic speculations that the Antichrist will have earthly, political power.[73] This power, even if used for the good, is, as in Soloviev's story (aimed straight at Tolstoy), actually corrosive, insofar as it reconfigures positive aspects of Christianity (liberation, social reforms, community among human beings) as if they originated in and are totally the purview of human beings rather than an "insight into the heart of God."[74]

As suggested above, the apocalypse is for Balthasar the moment in which the human being is offered two competing freedoms: the freedom of mundane self-determination, which is the same as alienation from God, and the Christomorphic freedom of self-gift in free obedience to the free self-disclosure of God.[75] Again, this point of decision is for Balthasar *the* eschatological moment: "The Christian eschaton, glimpsed in anticipation, sheds such a light of decision on to history that from now on one can only say 'yes' or 'no' to it."[76] To say no is to buy into the deceptive grab for a counterfeit power that refuses freedom and existence itself as gift. That power, such as it is, is restricted to the world and is indeed a servitude to the world; by this presumptive exercise of autonomy those who say no are by their own decision robbed of the capacious freedom of participation in Trinitarian love. The assumption of absolute power represents for Balthasar the "complete Antichrist, endowed with total power, as the No to Christ's total powerlessness."[77] The true power of the yes is actually that which appears to be a kind of powerlessness, to surrender the fiction of the absolute autonomy of finite freedom for self-determination.

For Balthasar, therefore, what is most provocative about the message of Christ vis-à-vis Antichrist is that it reveals apocalyptically the kenotic manifestation of divine character, the appearance in Jesus of "the glory of divine power in lowliness, defenselessness and a self-surrender that goes to the lengths of the eucharistic Cross . . . [that] unveils a totally unexpected picture of God's internal, Trinitarian defenselessness."[78] This principle, namely that the mode of self-emptying present in Christ's incarnation and death on the cross is expressive of the mutual self-emptying of the persons of the immanent Trinity, is at the center, not the periphery, of Balthasar's theocentric, Trinitarian eschatology. Indeed, this notion of Trinitarian kenosis borrowed from

Bulgakov, whose presupposition and grounding is the Ur-kenosis of the Father's generation of the Son, becomes a fundamental organizing principle of his entire theological work.[79] There, indeed at the center, we find a wounded little Lamb, luminous in its poverty.

BATTLING MEONIC ONTOLOGY

A preliminary examination of Schelling's understanding of God as dynamic and self-emptying is crucial here for getting at the interrelated questions of divine immutability and kenosis, and for tracking the lineage from Böhme to Schelling to the Russians, as well as to certain of the nineteenth-century kenoticists with whom Balthasar deals on the question of revising immutability.[80] Schelling's philosophy (as Hegel's) has in its own way attempted to grapple with conceiving an eternal God vis-à-vis the temporal processes of nature, time, and history. Schelling's fragmentary *Ages of the World* provides an example of an attempt, however unsuccessful, to conceive within the figure of an eternal God a rationale for the gratuitous existence of the world. It is no accident that Schelling ultimately parses this relationship kenotically. Schelling's potencies of the Absolute (which are replicated in all that which exists) include the first force, that which is in itself, is met by that which strives toward eccentric existence, and is united by the third. This triad is not static but dynamic.[81] Recall the discussion from chapter 3 of Schelling's formulation of the triad of potencies, in which the second potency, the Son, is differentiated from the first potency through kenotically assuming determinate being. Bulgakov and then Balthasar make analogous moves (though they are only analogous, as their departures from Schelling function deliberately to correct him).

Though not fully fleshed out until the Berlin mythology lectures, Schelling's ontology is sketched out in *Ages of the World* in the theory of the triadic potencies that Soloviev will eventually take up. This speculative ontology was treated at some length in chapter 3. To review, the *Potenzenlehre* asserts that God contains within God's own being the capacity to self-posit an "Other." In the *Weltalter* Schelling postulates a God/Absolute whose being is comprised of the union of two oppositional forces, that which contracts and that which expands. This conception is informed by Böhme's positing of a dialectical relation between the negative potency and positive potency, no and yes, *Ungrund* and *Urgrund*, a version of which reappears decisively in Berdyaev's own theogonic conception of the Trinity.[82] Only in the unconscious combination (but not sublation) of these contradictory forces in the theogonic process does God's being as Trinitarian emerge or actualize.[83] Undifferentiated nonbeing therefore passes into differentiated actuality. More importantly, neither pole dominates the other, such that there is in divine being no necessity.[84] In Schelling's rather convoluted prose,

> the unconditioned can express itself as what-is and as being, and it can refrain from expressing itself as both; in other words, it can be both, or it can let both alone. Free will is just this ability to be something along with the ability to not-be it. But further, the Highest can be what-is, and it can be being; it can express itself as this thing-that-is, and as this being. That is, it can express itself or posit itself as *existing*. For existence (*Existenz*) is precisely the active unification of a definite thing-that-is with a definite being. Put most succinctly: the Highest can exist, and it can also not-exist; this is to say it has all conditions of existence in itself, but what matters is whether or not it draws upon these conditions, whether it uses them as conditions.[85]

This absolute freedom is operative in the creation of the world. Here Schelling is laudably attempting to contravene Hegelian necessity. In this text, the creation of the world in Schelling—and this is important with respect to Bulgakov, as well as Balthasar's appropriation of Bulgakov—is the external expression, the finite replication in matter, of the ontological structure of divine essence such that there is an internal coherence and not external necessity.[86] Schelling rhapsodically describes the non-necessary interaction of these two forces, the eternal and the will, as the "first pure joy of mutual finding and being found . . . [bound] only by the inexhaustible pleasure of having and feeling the presence of each other, [which] is the freest life, the life that plays with itself . . . filled with ceaseless excitement and bursting with its own renewed vitality."[87]

While this dynamic vitality of Schelling's quintessentially Romantic reflection on the divine may be an attractive feature for the Russians and for Balthasar, the reception of his ontology is certainly more uneven. For Balthasar's dramatic theory, it is important to maintain a dynamism original to the immanent Trinity, a drama that is present regardless of the exigencies of the created world. Again, the primal drama is eternal, but not static or self-enclosed; it is eternal action in which all other temporal things take place.[88] Balthasar, however, will not countenance the speculative, theogonic ontology that underwrites this dynamism in Böhme, Schelling, or Berdyaev. As already shown, Berdyaev explicitly acknowledges his debts to Böhme vis-à-vis not only the necessity of a divine dark side, but also the theogonic process out of which God is born. Berdyaev requires an irrational freedom prior to God in order to absolve God from responsibility for evil: "Out of the abyss, out of the Divine Nothing is born the Trinitary God and He is confronted with meonic freedom."[89]

Crucially, Bulgakov, like Balthasar, does not accept this meonic ontology that corrodes Berdyaev's theological credibility. Appealing again to Johannine literature—"God is light, and in him is no darkness at all" (1 John 1:5)—Bulgakov underlines that in God there can be nothing unconscious, nothing impersonal, "no meonal darkness, no nocturnal twilight of half-being"[90] prior to or above God. This commitment is in keeping with the Bulgakovian principle that in God, everything is hypostasized.[91] That is, there is no nature outside the hypostases, and no hypostases outside nature. Bulgakov, insofar as he *is* influenced by Schelling's metaphysics of creation, does refer to the creation of the world as the material expression of divine being, but this is not an exhaustive "inner *self-positing of Divinity*"[92] but rather a free work of a benevolent God reflective of the ecstatic, absolutely free love that the Trinity itself is. As he puts it,

> the creation of heaven and earth, as an act of God's love flowing beyond the limits of the proper divine life into the world, is, in relation to Divinity itself, a voluntary self-diminution, a metaphysical

kenosis: Alongside His *absolute* being, God establishes a *relative* being with which He enters into an interrelation, being God and Creator for this being. The creative "let there be," which is the command of God's omnipotence, at the same time expresses the sacrifice of Divine love, of God's love for the world, the love of the Absolute for the relative, in virtue of which the Absolute becomes the Absolute-Relative.[93]

For Bulgakov, this sense of creation as a kenotic act of God is bracketed within an all-encompassing kenotic Trinitarianism. As suggested in chapter 3, Balthasar rejects in no uncertain terms this entire meonic tradition, which understands God to be exteriorizing God's Self in that which is opposite.[94]

The central element of eschatological Trinitarianism in Balthasar and Bulgakov's shared visionary theological profile does not, as with Schelling and Hegel, compound the esoteric with the esoteric, the abstracted with the abstract: rather, the *concrete* relations between Father and Son and Spirit, and especially the relationship of obedience of Christ to the Father, are understood to be absolutely regulative of apocalyptic discourse. The regulating image central to this discourse for both theologians is the little slain Lamb of John's Apocalypse (Revelation 13:8), which provides an iconic shorthand of the enduring gift of love that is at the same time a freely kenotic gifting of the Father and a freely kenotic being given by the Son, a being given that is pure self-abandonment, the hypostatic figuration of kenosis itself.[95] For Balthasar, the dense symbol of the Lamb whose wounds do not heal both signifies and is God's relation to the world, which is to say, a relation of beautiful, gracious, perfectly sacrificial love.[96]

The open wound, in contrast to the blasphemous "pseudo-miracle" of the healing of the beast's wounds in Revelation, manifests "the truth of the defenseless nature of the divine, Trinitarian love."[97] The Johannine principle that suffering and glory are of a piece, forming a single reality, prevails in Balthasar: "He who really *was* 'dead,' yet now lives 'for evermore' (Rev. 1:18) takes his pierced heart with him to heaven; on God's throne he is 'the Lamb as it were slain.'"[98] That the Lamb is slain and yet victorious indicates also that this form of love governs (and is) power; apocalyptic need not include gratuitous violence, and those who follow the Lamb can and must fashion their weapons into ploughshares (Isaiah 2:4) in an attempt to image the kenotic self-gift of Trinity.[99]

For Balthasar, it is nearly impossible to separate the theological enterprise of articulating precisely what is meant by kenosis from a discussion of the close relation between the economic and the immanent Trinity. It is therefore no surprise that Balthasar's primary interlocutors on the issue of kenosis are Hegel, Rahner, and Jürgen Moltmann, all of whom treat the relation in their own distinct (and, according to Balthasar, variously unsuccessful) ways. Balthasar takes to be inadequate theological attempts to meet Lessing's infamous question of the impossibility of continuity between contingent facts of history and necessary truths of reason (for instance, in the work of Rudolf Bultmann or Schleiermacher that, on Balthasar's interpretation, attenuates the historical existence of Jesus of Nazareth). Balthasar is deeply concerned with maintaining a robust link between the concrete life of Jesus as attested in the Scriptures and the inner life of the Godhead. In this respect, then, Balthasar's Christological starting point is decisively "from below," from the empirical data of salvation history, although he remains open to the probability that relevant data may well come "from above," that is, beyond the events of recorded salvation history. Balthasar is very concerned to relate the historical Jesus to the immanent Godhead and so wants there to be an organic connection between economic and immanent. For him, it is only through that which is revealed in the economic—particularly the absolute love manifest in the cross of Jesus, the Lamb slain before the foundation of the world—that it is possible to "feel our way back" to claims about the nature of the immanent Trinity. The Son is the visible translation of the Trinity, a rendering in the language of the temporal and the corporeal the eternal relation with God the Father.[100] It is especially in the cross, and, more radically, in the Son's passive descent into hell, that the "drastic counterposing of the divine Persons in the economy becomes visible" through the peculiar (theo)logic of identity in contradiction.[101]

Balthasar, however, expresses no small degree of anxiety about the dangers implicit in an uncritical equation of the events of salvation history with the inner life of the Trinity. He does not want to reduce the immanent Trinity down to the interplay of events on the plane of salvation history alone, or equate the immanent and the economic in a relation of strict identity. This commitment notwithstanding, he asks whether this economic involvement and suffering on the cross affects God in some way. Coincident with the question of kenosis, and the fertile ground in which it often emerges, is thus the question of divine immutability. With the Incarnation and the cross-event, in what way(s) and to what degree can God be said to change, or, more to the point, to suffer? Can this change, particularly in the divine entry into the ebb and flow of human history, be brought about without compromising God's transcendence? What theologically responsible option—one that at the very least retains a transcendent element and does not succumb to an out-and-out ascription of mutability to God—remains to speak to a genuinely free self-divestiture (in creation, Incarnation, passion, or in the events of history) that is not tantamount to a thoroughly mythic "noughting" of the Divine? In short, can there be a *Gottlosigkeit* that is *not* a Nought?

ENGAGEMENT WITH NINETEENTH-CENTURY KENOTICISTS

Consideration of these questions requires a turn to nineteenth-century kenotic theory in German Lutheranism, which both Balthasar and Bulgakov engage directly.[102] These views, especially that God must make God's Self finite in nature and history in order to be actualized, were certainly influenced by the speculative Idealism of Hegel (whose premier critic, Isaak Dorner, was certainly influenced by Schelling).[103] These kenoticists attempted to maintain in most cases at least a semblance of fidelity to traditional Chalcedonian "two-nature" Christology along with the thoroughly modern commitment to a psychological understanding of Jesus's personality and historical experience. The primary representative of this group of thinkers is surely Gottfried Thomasius, whose *Christi Person und Werk* provided the first systematic strategy to account for continuity of the Logos and the historical person of Jesus (and, in so doing, to account for a strong relationship between economic and immanent, between the events of salvation history and the inner life of the Godhead).[104] What differentiates modern thinkers such as Thomasius from patristic thought on kenosis is that in the traditional view, Christ took on the "veil" of human flesh, which masked his divine glory, and that the suffering he experienced while upon the earth was only qua human nature, leaving the Logos untouched.

The nineteenth-century kenoticists, however, stringently resisted the distinction between the simple possession and use of divine properties and attributed an actual diminution (of both possession and exercise of attributes) to the divine nature, to the Logos, a move that Balthasar finds helpful. The primary motivation for this version of kenosis is to work out a scheme that could account for the presence of the divine in Jesus of Nazareth that would not vitiate his actual humanity, which must accord with human nature at every point (except, of course, for sin). For example, the nineteenth-century kenoticists found the notion of an infant Jesus being omnipotent, omniscient, and omnipresent, with full knowledge of his status as divine, ruling the world from the manger in Bethlehem, a ridiculous claim, particularly because it did violence to the integrity of Jesus's real human nature, which must develop naturally, gradually, and, above all, humanly. In his effort to suss out the relation between immanent and economic, and to stay faithful to robust claims about the preservation of Jesus's genuine humanity, Thomasius made a distinction (which, it must be noted, Balthasar evaluates decisively as "wholly unworkable"[105]) between relative and immanent/absolute divine attributes, the former being the category that was divested at the Incarnation. The relative attributes had to do with the qualities of God's *relation* to the world, namely, omniscience, omnipotence, and omnipresence. These would vitiate humanity if present in the psychical function of a person and are not essential for God to be God. The absolute attributes of absolute holiness, truth, and love do not vitiate true humanity and are essential for God to be God. These attributes were retained by Jesus at the Incarnation.

The most radical nineteenth-century kenoticist, Wolfgang Gess, goes quite beyond the pale (to what one commentator humorously referred to as a total "kenosis of reason"[106]) in his suggestion that the

Logos was first divine, then human, that is, that the Christ on earth was not in any way divine, and that in his absence from heaven the Father gave his administrative, world-ruling duties to the Spirit. More bizarrely, for Gess, during the time of the Incarnation the Spirit ceased to proceed from the Father and the Son and proceeded from the Father alone. The *filioque* disagreement notwithstanding, Bulgakov weighs in on Gess's theory as "compromisingly absurd, since such a supposition would signify nothing other than the total self-abolition of the Second hypostasis (as well as of its kenosis)."[107] This move, while certainly preserving Christ's humanity, does great violence to Trinitarian claims. Although Balthasar, himself uncomfortable with the idea that kenosis is only qua human nature, appreciates the impulse that leads these thinkers to claim some kenosis of the Logos itself, a kenosis that does indicate some event or change of state or condition in the Trinity, the various solutions of the nineteenth-century kenoticists—who, despite their best intentions, were not able to break the Hegelian logic of kenosis—are for Balthasar wholly inadequate to cogent Trinitarian thinking.

For Balthasar, rather, "the *paradox* must be allowed to stand: in the undiminished humanity of Jesus, the whole power and glory of God are made present to us."[108] The desiderata for an adequate solution would thereby include the preservation of robust Trinitarian claims to equidivinity, not divide God's attributes into "parts," not implicate the Incarnation as an alien imposition, not attribute pain to the divine, and ultimately preserve the absolute freedom of God. Moreover, one must be able to claim that God has grounded the world process, but in perfect liberty, freedom, and sovereignty. Further, there can be no sense of process or the need for actualization in God. In the preface to the second edition of *Mysterium Paschale*, Balthasar calls for a negotiation between these twin dangers inherent in kenotic thought with regard to the relation between the immanent and the economic. Balthasar sets out what he understands to be problematic tendencies in the history of kenotic reflection that veer dangerously toward some variant of theopaschism—for instance, the "crucified God" of Moltmann, who accepts Hegel's premise that suffering is necessary to ratify the seriousness of divine love—or strive to maintain (largely by the assertion that kenosis ought to be circumscribed to Christ's assumption of human nature) a traditional divine immutability in which God is unmoved by human suffering.[109] For Balthasar, the former implicates God as dependent on necessary world processes, and the latter is challenged by the biblical record and ordinary human experience.

With respect to the first undesirable, theopaschism, Balthasar resists the claim that there is pain or suffering in God; indeed, as in Hegel's speculative Trinitarianism, one *must* ascribe pain to God for God to be God, to account for becoming as such as well as the seriousness of the immanent Trinity.[110] On this point, Balthasar tellingly indicts Berdyaev in the very same breath as he does Hegel: "Over and over, down to Hegel and Berdyaev, this speciously deep thought was to haunt Christian metaphysics: that love without pain and guilt remains simply a joke, a game."[111] Certainly, Balthasar's opposition to those regimes in which a tragic God must necessarily and without remainder enter exhaustively into the processes of the world as fully and exhaustively immanentized (those in which "the mystery of the Cross [is converted] into a piece of philosophy"[112]) comes through perspicuously. Balthasar objects strenuously to Hegel's inscription of the pain and suffering of God as a *necessary* postulate in order for this love to become "serious." In the preface to the *Phenomenology of Spirit*, Hegel writes, "It is quite possible to regard the life of God and the divine knowledge as love playing with itself; but this idea, deprived of the gravity, the pain, the patience and the agonizing of the negative within it, sinks to the level of tasteless pious sentiment."[113] This positing that without the pain and suffering of God love is only insipid, sportive play is objectionable to Balthasar in part because God is absolute and self-sufficient; on Hegel's view, God would need the world as a kind of proving ground upon which God is required to act out a tragedy in order to demonstrate concretely and materially the solemn depths of divine love.[114] Hegel's Trinitarian speculation problematically proceeds according to a principle of lack in which the immanent Trinity is immediately sublated and exhausted (and thus erased), insofar as it is expressed completely in the finitude of nature, time, and history.[115]

Moltmann's attempt to identify the immanent and the economic Trinity is also disqualified on Balthasarian grounds because it is marked

by both Hegelianism and Whiteheadian process thought that effectively collapses the distinction between the immanent and economic,
making creation functionally or ontologically necessary for God to be
God. Moltmann is indicted because his view considers the cross as not
only the moment of the highest self-revelation of the Trinity, but also
the moment of its very self-actualization or realization. According to
Balthasar, Moltmann's construal of God as participating in the cross-
event to the degree that even the Father dies and is forsaken "entan-
gles" God in the world, making God "tragic" and "mythological."[116]

   With respect to traditional divine immutability, Balthasar resists
the claim that the Incarnation of the second hypostasis did not in any
way affect the immanent Trinity (or, for that matter, the divine nature
of Christ). In order to be sufficiently dramatic, there must be the possibility for a genuine interplay between the freedom of God and that
of human beings. God "cannot function . . . as a mere Spectator,"[117]
presiding, unmoved, over a world full of suffering. Though Balthasar
wants to claim some kind of event in God, he does not wish to suggest
that there was a substantial change in God as such. In sum, Balthasar
wishes to retain the traditional language of immutability, but also to
complexify it with a Trinitarian and kenotic inflection borrowed directly from Bulgakov.[118]

UR-KENOSIS AND PASCHAL TRINITARIANISM: THE SLAIN LAMB
OF THE APOCALYPSE

Balthasar, interested both in guarding the integrity of the relation between the immanent and the economic and permitting the immanent
Trinity to be understood as gratuitously grounding the world process
in the mode of absolute love without being mired necessarily within
it, wants to chart a middle way.[119] It is constituted by an appropriation
of Bulgakov's expansive reading of kenosis as a Trinitarian event, particularly as formulated in the 1943 *Du Verbe Incarné: Agnus Dei*. Again,
the symbol of the Lamb "slain before the foundation of the world"
regulates the discourse. The figure of the slain Lamb indicates that the
"'slaying' is in no sense conceived in a Gnostic manner, as a heavenly

sacrifice independent of that of Golgotha, . . . [but] rather, the eternal aspect of the historic and bloody sacrifice of the Cross."[120]

This figuration of the cross does give Balthasar occasion to register a bit of nervousness about Bulgakov's perceived drift toward Gnosticism. In *Lamb of God*, Bulgakov writes that the incarnation is the "*metaphysical* Golgotha of the self-crucifixion of the Logos in time. The *historical* Golgotha was only a *consequence* of the metaphysical one,"[121] an ascription that Balthasar suggests is Gnostic in *Mysterium Paschale*.[122] A decade later, however, at the writing of the *Theo-Drama*, Balthasar is much less nervous about Bulgakov. In several major texts, Balthasar explicitly calls upon Bulgakov's kenotic theory, although he ostensibly distances himself from the "excesses" of his sophiology:[123]

> It is therefore preferable to be guided by some of Bulgakov's fundamental ideas (while avoiding his sophiological excesses), and to take the "selflessness" of the divine persons, as of pure relations in the love within the Godhead, as the basis of everything: this selflessness is the basis of a first form of kenosis, that lies in creation (especially in the creation of man who is free), for the creator here gives up a part of his freedom to the creature, in the act of creating; but this he can dare to do only in virtue of his foreseeing and taking into account the second and truest kenosis, that of the cross, in which he makes good the uttermost consequences of creation's freedom, and goes beyond them. In this, kenosis—as the surrender of the "form of God"—becomes the decisive act of the love of the Son, who translates his being begotten by the Father (and in this, his dependence on him) into the expressive form of creaturely obedience, but the whole Trinity remains involved in this act, the Father by sending out the Son and abandoning him on the cross, and the Spirit by uniting them only in the expressive form of the separation.[124]

For Bulgakov, then, kenosis is primordially and originarily the eternal divine processions within the self-donative life of the immanent Trinity, in which the Father gives himself ecstatically and fully in the generation of the Son as consubstantial, uncreated Other, in the "receptivity" and "thanksgiving" of the Son's own emptying, and the bond of the Holy Spirit who is absolute love.[125] In God, the divine hypostases are eternally co-posited (never posited alone, which would be tritheism), each in the other, in a mode that is ecstatic, sacrificial, and free. For Bulgakov, the generation of the Son is thoroughly Trinitarian, as there can be no consubstantiality without the Father, no "We" without the Spirit. The Father's possession of divine nature is always in a mode of dispossession. The Son responds to this self-evacuation in a mode of receptivity and thanksgiving, permitting himself to be generated. The Son, too, possesses the divine nature always already in a mode of self-sacrificial kenosis. The Spirit's kenosis is its lack of substantive individual content, witnessing to the love between Father and Son.[126]

Although he is constitutionally opposed to causal origination in the Trinity, Bulgakov does assert that there is a hierarchy in the Trinity. This claim is not to be thought of in terms of cause or origination, but rather in terms of *taxis*, or (logical but nonchronological) ordering.[127] In his system, the Father is the source, the font, and the subject of revelation. The reason that the Father is the subject and thus the "first" is precisely that the Father does not reveal the other hypostases, but only "himself": the Father is properly the *revealed* hypostasis, whereas the dyad of Son and Spirit are the *revealing* hypostases, God's "two hands," as it were, to borrow from Saint Irenaeus. The Father is not hypostatically revealed in the world; the Father is revealed *only* through the Son and the Spirit, who go into the world, revealing not only themselves but the Father (principally) as well. Though it can be said in the Bulgakovian system that the Father is first, and that the Son and the Spirit are *not* the first, there is no further hierarchical relation between Son and Spirit. In fact, as we see with Bulgakov's "trinitarian inversion" taken over by Balthasar, there is rather an instability, an openness to reversal with respect to ordering the Son and Spirit, insofar as in the immanent Trinity, the Son is the condition of the Spirit's procession, and in the economy, it is the Spirit who gives power to Christ.[128]

Bulgakov continues his grammatical metaphor to speak to the revealing hypostases of Son and Spirit. Whereas the Father is the subject of revelation, the Spirit and the Son are the one "bi-une" revelation or dyad of the Father: they are, respectively, the "copula" and the "predicate."[129] According to Bulgakov, the dyad of Son and Spirit does not sunder the Trinity, protected as it is by the principle of the monarchy of the Father. The Spirit is copula—emptied of content of its own in a kind of "hypostatic annulment"—because it bears witness to the (free, ecstatic, joyful, and sacrificial) love shared between Father and Son.

So, if Fatherhood is essentially giving away what is proper to self (exhaustively) to Son and Spirit, the Son is always already eternal kenosis, receptivity, thanksgiving, the *content*, or what, of revelation, and the Spirit is the union between them, absolute beauty, the how of revelation. There is no instance of Christ's work in the world that does not involve the Spirit, and the Spirit too is intimately related to acts of Christ in the world, although these hypostases are absolutely non-reducible to one another. The Spirit is the accomplishing hypostasis, completing the work of Father and Son. The dyad is the predicate of the Father, the subject of revelation: it reveals God's Self fully in the world in revelation. The Word is the word of the Father, who is silent except to speak through the dyad or biune predication of Son and Spirit.[130]

For Bulgakov, this first (ontological, not chronological), Ur-kenosis of the Trinitarian processions is the primal drama that prefigures and undergirds all ensuing kenotic modalities in the economy, including the Incarnation, the creation of the world up to and including the paschal mystery, Christ's descent into hell, and the silence of Holy Saturday. Repeating Bulgakov (as well as evoking the Scholastic premise that the inner-Trinitarian relations are the condition of the possibility for creation), Balthasar likewise sees creation as a second kenosis and the events of Incarnation and paschal mystery to follow this kenotic trajectory similarly.[131] These economic events are the legible "consequences" of the pure immanent relations of the Trinity.[132] Hence, on the Balthasarian–Bulgakovian model, kenosis is not a rigidly Christological doctrine, but rather has been transposed to a Trinitarian key with a plurality of referents that indicate the essential self-donation of the Persons.

When the Father generates the Son, the Father does not give that which he possesses, but rather gives that all he is, "for in God there is only being, not having."[133] For Balthasar, then, the Father substantially and essentially *is* the *Hingabebewegung*, the pure loving self-dispossession without remainder: God "*is* this movement of self-giving that holds nothing back."[134] In Balthasar's own, deliberately provocative terms, the Father presents as a divine "God-lessness"[135]—a privative that nevertheless does not connote self-extinction but rather is *constitutive* of divine personhood: there is no time at which the person of the Father existed apart from this movement of self-surrender; rather, the Father substantially *is* the kenotic dynamism of the generation of the Son as Other. Again, the Father "possesses" power only in this dispossession of it, such that power actually coincides paradoxically with powerlessness. As Balthasar follows Bulgakov here, the Father's eternal self-evaculation in the consubstantial generation of the Son demonstrates a "unity of omnipotence and powerlessness";[136] the "risks" of God are "undergirded by, and enabled by, the power-less power of the divine self-giving."[137]

These relations presuppose the "letting-be" of a Trinitarian ontology, in which "each Hypostasis can only be itself insofar as it 'lets' the others 'be' in equal concreteness."[138] The risk factor is mitigated by an equal self-gift, even on the part of the Father. According to Balthasar's understanding of Trinitarian kenosis, personhood itself— human and, perhaps surprisingly, divine—is a gifted existence, an "incomprehensible having-been-gifted-ness"[139] that is mutually constituted. It is not a quality that can be possessed, but is "a unique and irreducible identity received in relations of love and freedom that can only be labeled as *kenotic*."[140] Significantly, for Balthasar "Fatherhood" is also, then, in a manner of speaking, a received existence: "The Father, too, owes his Fatherhood to the Son who allows himself to be generated, and he also owes his power of 'spiration'—of 'breathing forth' the Spirit—to the Spirit who allows himself to be breathed forth by Father and Son."[141]

Turning to Bulgakov specifically, this movement in love and self-gift toward ecstatic existence—begetting—is for him the very definition of Fatherhood itself, which is "precisely the form of love in which the loving one desires to have himself not in himself but outside himself, in order to give his own to this other I, but an I identified with him. . . . [T]he Father actualizes *His own*, His own hypostatically transparent nature."[142] Sonship is for Bulgakov a self-depletion on behalf of the Father, a being-begotten, "already *eternal kenosis*,"[143] "hypostatic obedience to the commands of the Father."[144] Apart from the Spirit, these mutual relations of self-depletion would be tragic. Yet it is the Spirit who is "the *joy* of sacrificial love, the bliss and actualization of this love,"[145] which identifies the Father and Son as the Holy Spirit proceeds from the Father through the Son. Again, the lack of particular content of the Spirit is the fact of the Spirit's kenosis: "He is the Spirit of Truth, not Truth itself. In Him and through Him the depths of God become transparent as all-real Truth and Beauty."[146] For Bulgakov, the Trinity accomplishes the Incarnation and the paschal mystery, which is kenotic not only for the Son but also for the Father and the Spirit.[147] Balthasar repeats this virtually without change or criticism.[148]

How does the suggestion of Urkenosis provide an adequate solution to the question of the relation between the economic and the immanent? This mode of perfect, absolute, self-sacrificial, and ecstatic love, which is constitutive for divine personhood, is that which substantially and essentially is divinity. To sound a Johannine theme, God *is* love. For Bulgakov and Balthasar, kenosis takes place at the level of form (*morphe*), not eternal essence (*ousia*) (as is the case in Schelling, Hegel, and the nineteenth-century kenoticists). Because both Bulgakov and Balthasar hold that this eternal self-donation is essential to the life of the Trinity, it becomes a defensible premise that the Incarnation and death of Christ on the cross do not represent a change in God from earth to heaven, time to eternity, but is rather a continuation of the substantial modality of self-giving love at the core of divine being, which is ordered toward human salvation. As Bulgakov has it, "Christ's cross is inscribed in creation at its very origin, and in its initial act the world is already called to received Divinity into its depths."[149] There is thus no measurable change in God and therefore no relative separation between immanent and economic. Though there is no measurable change, this does not indicate that there is no vitality or dynamism in God. Rather, according to Balthasar,

> Within God himself there is the original of that of which man's relationship to God is a copy: room for love between Father and Son—

for God in the mode of creative giving and for God in the mode of created receiving and giving back in full measure—in the unity of the Spirit of love which alone emerges from the double fount of love and, as the eternal fruit of love, unites and distinguishes the Father and the Son. These unplumbable depths of the springs of life in the eternal God are seen as the only sufficient condition for the historical appearance of the Son of God and of Man.[150]

The economic is latent in the immanent; the (very real, not Gnostic, bloodless, or heavenly) sacrifice of Christ on the cross is a concrete expression of the same mode of kenotic love, which, as it turns out, is the only (free) "necessity" in God. The apparent powerlessness of God is in fact a display of great omnipotence, because nothing is more powerful than gift. The creation of the world is the same expression of this substantially kenotic love.

Even the horrors of the cross and the ultimate distance of the descent into hell on Holy Saturday, where Jesus was "dead with the dead," are moments of revelation of this perfect obedience and self-squandering love.[151] Here, too, Balthasar is in Bulgakov's debt for centralizing the descent into hell motif, especially in connection with a more expansive reading of kenosis. In *The Lamb of God*, Bulgakov suggests that the descent unto the dead in hell continues the kenotic trajectory in solidarity with the deceased "in order that He might continue to serve men even beyond the grave."[152] For Bulgakov, as in Balthasar, the three days in the grave when Christ was in the afterlife state are a silence, "the extreme of self-devastation . . . [in which] only receptive passivity remains."[153] Bulgakov understands the so-called preaching in hell as a symbolic way of designating Christ's mysterious presence in the afterlife state, which is, significantly, part of the kenotic sacrifice of the high-priestly ministry rather than the more triumphant royal ministry.[154] Likewise, for Balthasar, the mode of proclamation operative in Christ's descent is the very absence of speech.

According to this model, the horrors of death and hell do not contradict the nature of God but are, rather, "the revelation of the highest positivity of trinitarian love."[155] Indeed, the "doctrine of the Trinity [i]s the ever-present, inner presupposition of the doctrine of the Cross."[156]

Rather than being an aberration, the cross of Christ and the silence of Holy Saturday are for Balthasar moments of genuine apocalypse that is, however stark, the unveiling of the logic of Trinitarian relations in both difference and sameness, identity in non-identity.[157] Indeed, the cross becomes the greatest, most poignant revelation of the interior life of the Godhead, as it demonstrates both the distinction between persons and their unity (capacitated by the Spirit, who maintains their unity without destroying their separation).[158] For Balthasar, moreover, the eternal relation of free but yielding obedience of the Son to the Father is exposed, a relation so radical that it can rightly be called "the obedience of a corpse," a turn of phrase borrowed from Saint Francis of Assisi.[159] In Christ's "being dead with the dead, the attitude and stance of the divine Logos has been stripped away, as it were. For it was in the extremities of this death that the Logos found the adequate expression of this divine stance: letting himself remain available for the Father in everything, even in the ultimate alienation. The stripping away of the man Jesus is the laying bare not only of Sheol but also of the Trinitarian relationship in which the Son is entirely the one who springs forth from the Father."[160] Indeed, the first order of this Trinitarian Urkenosis highlights the difference, the distance between the hypostases, which is then the condition of the possibility for every other instance of "distance"—up to and including the cross and the "silence" (which is the last resounding word!) of Holy Saturday, which is the expression of absolute love.[161]

To revisit a theme sounded in chapter 3, Balthasar's valuation of alterity as an absolute good reaffirms the finite, which is a notable element missing from Berdyaev, where alterity and otherness are an unfortunate result of the Fall. For Balthasar, though, as the Father generates the Son as a consubstantial, co-eternal "Other," introducing the precondition for loving communion, so too does this diastasis function as precondition for the drama between creature and Creator and as presupposition for finite, human others. This "hiatus" within God is a set of brackets wherein "'kenotic' space is made for the recognition of the 'other' as other,"[162] the condition of the possibility for the created order itself, even for physical bodies interacting in the world.[163] Conversely, Berdyaev's unremitting apocalypticism both implicates and seeks to extinguish time—and all that is "nailed to the cross of time," including contingency, the phenomenal world, language, progress, and ontology—as a fundamental disruption and "objectification" of the primordial spiritual unity of human beings. *Contra* Berdyaev, Balthasar suggests that the "'otherness' of the new aeon is a making other, a making new, of the old; it is not a matter of throwing over the created world and making another, quite different one in its place."[164] Further, for Balthasar, the enormous difference between God and the world is "neither a fated 'defection' nor (what would be the same thing) an 'out-flow' of God, both of which would stamp the world in its deepest reality as a region of doom and mere physical laws. Rather, the world's position has been freely willed and is one that gives to the world its inner stamp of freedom. Thus the finite is meant to exist through infinite freedom so that it might have the freedom for infinite freedom."[165]

According to Balthasar, "all the contingent 'abasements' of God in the economy of salvation are forever included and outstripped in the eternal event of Love."[166] This feature is consonant with the Balthasarian conviction that the mutual, free self-donation of hypostases within the Trinity is first and foremost a soteriological doctrine.[167] God as self-surrendering *Ungrund* is the "gulf" of absolute love into which all the "distances" of the sinful world—including the cross of Christ—can be taken.[168] This suggestion is not wholly different from the Hegelian ascription of distance, death, and suffering in the Godhead (reappearing in Moltmann), but Balthasar's conscious framing of it in terms of gratuity, non-necessity, love, and identity preserves the freedom of God, challenging Hegel directly, as well as those critics who ascribe Hegelianism to Balthasar based on only structural similarities.[169]

The event of the cross affects the inner life of God—at least insofar as there is some element in God that can "develop" into suffering, for instance, when the absolute love is met with the creaturely no of a calculated self-preservation—yet he does not speak like Moltmann or Hegel in the language of pain or suffering in or as constitutive of God.[170] The cross-event as a moment in the economy of salvation does indicate a distance between the Father and the Son, but this distance is not original to the cross: it actually indicates a *preexistent* distance within the immanent Trinity. Because both Bulgakov and Balthasar hold that eternal self-donation is essential to the nature of the

Trinitarian relations, the Incarnation and death of Christ on the cross do not represent a change in God or a contradiction of the divine nature, but are rather a continuation and continuous ratification of the substantial modality of inscrutable self-giving love that remains ever at the core of divine being.

Even though Balthasar asserts that the kenotic modes in the economy are revelatory of the inner nature of the Trinity—indeed, that they provide the fundamental instance of the unveiling or "apocalypse" of the Father's originary love—this principle cannot be deduced in advance or considered to be a necessary premise: "No necessity, no philosophical law of the structure of the created world, empowers us either to deduce the sovereign freedom of the decision of grace that is the kenosis of God, or to extend it to become a universal law."[171] To universalize the principle as necessary is to render it gnostically or idealistically: any ascription of necessary is always inadequate to the radical freedom of the love of God.

Balthasar's elaboration of the different forms of Trinitarian kenosis borrowed from Bulgakov—and the symbol of Urkenosis in particular—enables him to maintain a unitive (nonreductive) account of the relation between economic and immanent, without succumbing to problematic ascriptions of Hegelian necessity or Schellingian or Böhmian seeds of darkness in God or to claims (as in the nineteenth-century kenoticists) that compromise the integrity of Trinitarian persons. In Balthasar's critical reappropriation of Hegel, God is all fullness and all plentitude: there is no lack. No actualization or process takes place, because all is love and self-gift. The hypostases are thoroughly "themselves" in the kenotic mode of free, ecstatic love, not simply moments in the Hegelian actualization of *Geist*. The economy is all gift of love, and an expression of the same mode of love that characterizes essentially the immanent Trinity.

THE CAPACIOUS HORIZON OF ESCHATOLOGY

Both Bulgakovian and Balthasarian eschatology are thus characterized by a dramatic soteriological kenoticism that requires a Trinitarian grounding. In his scriptural interpretation, Bulgakov connects explicitly the prologue to the Gospel of John with the fundamental kenosis text of Philippians 2. On his (typically Russian) antinomial reading, when the "Word was made flesh" (John 1:14), the Word-God became "not God" without ceasing to be both Word and God.[172] The absolute Creator enters into creatureliness, assuming creaturely being as a voluntary self-humiliation, the meaning of which exceeds Incarnation and ignominious death but also indicates the relations of the Trinity. For Bulgakov, Philippians 2 "talks not only about an earthly event occurring within the limits of human life but also about a heavenly event occurring in the depths of Divinity itself: the kenosis of God the Word."[173] As is the case in Balthasar, too, the kenoticism of the cross opens up upon and is itself a kind of glory; this union of suffering and exaltation is, of course, deeply Johannine.

With this more expansive assessment of the eschatological, there is no sense in which eschatology can be disconnected from protology; according to Balthasar's organic metaphors, eschatology proper is no more than the long ripening of protology, "the way protology blossoms out,"[174] "the estuary into which protology flows."[175] This understanding of eschatology is also the reason why the anthropocentric horizon is only intelligible in the context of the theocentric. Being itself is structurally conditioned by gratuitous Trinitarian love, and the whole of eschatology can be distilled into the originary principle of the divine decision "to nestle the created world, with [human beings] at its center, in [the Trinity's] own endless inner life at the world's 'end.'"[176] For Balthasar the ultimate goal of eschatology is the "participation in the very surging life of God,"[177] an initiation into the self-giving dynamism of the depths of the Trinitarian mystery to which human beings are already introduced proleptically. At bottom, "the mutual gifts of the Trinity are the creature's place and home."[178] For Balthasar (and also Bulgakov) eschatology, soteriology, and Christology cannot be separated: "God is the 'last thing' of the creature. This he is, however, as he presents himself to the world, that is, in his Son, *Jesus Christ*, who is the revelation of God and, therefore, the whole essence of the last things. . . . Eschatology is, almost more even than any other *locus theologicus*, entirely a doctrine of *salvation*."[179]

The Trinity is thus for Balthasar the last horizon of eschatology, as well as its beginning, and the true name of Being itself: "The real 'last thing' is the triune life of God disclosed in Jesus Christ. Naturally this Omega also implies the Alpha; it is what is present, first and last, in every 'now.' And what is this but Being itself? For apart from Being there is 'only nothing,' while within it there is that mysterious vitality disclosed through Christological revelation, so that everything that comes from absolute Being must bear its seal, with revelation giving us access to the fount of God's life."[180] This Trinitarian ontological principle operates doubly: it is both the beginning and the end of all things, the Alpha and the Omega, providing the fertile ground of possibility for the kenotic movement of the divine in creation, Incarnation, and the cross. It is at the deepest heart of Balthasar's theocentric eschatology, wherein the principle of Trinitarian love, which is the substance of Being itself, is visible in Jesus Christ. Here is the most explicit of Balthasar's borrowing from Bulgakov. This Johannine structure of the Alpha and Omega (Revelation 1:8, 1:18, 22:13; John 1), expressed eschatologically and Trinitarianly, corresponds well with Balthasar's theology of history, in which Christ provides the framework for, the bracketing of, the entire drama of history and the end of history.[181] Indeed, as suggested in chapter 4, this Johannine principle of beginning and end is the condition of the possibility for there being a theology of history at all.[182] Within these Trinitarian brackets is also inscribed an invitation for human beings to participate in the ever-greater, ever-deeper, ever-new event of the mystery of Trinitarian love, whatever comes.

IN KEEPING WITH OUR original hypothesis, in the test cases of the Russians Balthasar can and does tolerate as well as enact an experimental, probative mode of theologizing, but, like Bulgakov, his profound devotion to and respect for the tradition are what allow him to do so. His speculative *Tendenz* is indicated perhaps nowhere more clearly than his adoption of the Russian kenotic hypothesis, which, as it appears in Bulgakov, is shorn of its Böhmian, Schellingian, and Hegelian excesses, but which also, in an effort to preserve God's capacious Trinitarian freedom, ambiguates the classical conception of divine immutability.[183] This liveliness in God that Bulgakov and Balthasar affirm is all dynamism, movement, surprise, openness, the "livingness" of the divine rather like that propounded by the Romantics. This openness and dynamism, even playfulness, informs their shared allegiance to a *zhivoe predanie*, or "living tradition," which permits—nay, requires—the adoption of the same "audacious creativity" in the mode of the Spirit that characterizes and enlivens the early Fathers. Theological discourse thus becomes "the expression of an expression, on the one hand an obedient repetition of the expression of revelation imprinted on the believer, and, on the other a creative, childlike, free sharing in the bringing-to-expression in the Holy Spirit—who is the Spirit of Christ, of the Church and of the believer—of the mystery which expresses itself."[184] It is to the nature of this living tradition and the theological method it necessitates that we now turn.

CONCLUSION

The foregoing chapters of this book, in tracking Hans Urs von Balthasar's engagement with the proximate discourses of three figures of the nineteenth-century Russian school, as well as Schelling, upon whom they rely, have endeavored to provide material proof for profiling the Balthasarian theological method as more experimental than nostalgic, with an underacknowledged speculative *Tendenz* evocative of the patristic figure of Origen. The substantial analytic chapters, in their treatment of theological aesthetics, freedom, myth, evil, and eschatology, both anthropocentric and theocentric, have demonstrated concretely not only the phenomenon of Balthasar's unselfconscious ecumenical retrieval of non-Catholic, nonmagisterial sources, but also the fact that he comes even to the most dangerous extra-confessional discourses with an open hand. This analysis of both the generosity and the limitations of Balthasar's reception of the Russians influenced by German Romanticism suggests that there are two divergent roads when operating in the speculative mode, of which one is illicit and deformative for theology and the other is licit and salutary. This investigation indicates in Balthasar perhaps a surprising latitude with respect to speculation. He allows the highest measure of potential contribution from all sides, and yet, in matters that are compromised, for example, by Promethean Titanism, untoward presumptuous rational conjecture, derogation of the finite, ascription of evil or darkness to

God, or the conflation of natural and supernatural, he is as relentlessly uncompromising as he is generous.

A statement of general protocols for licit speculative theology that emerges from this study might include the following: first, speculation should preserve rather than raid the mystery of God. As Balthasar suggests in a different context, "the Christian can know not only too little but also too much."[1] Balthasar, as shown throughout this investigation, is constitutively opposed to the reductive rationalism of purely logical speculation that is spectatorial in nature, especially damaging in Böhmian ontology, in Berdyaev, and in Romanticism and Idealism. Balthasar is particularly resistant to a type of "epic-narrative" speculation that assumes an external, journalistic, and disinterested perspective outside the drama that "will quite logically assume the role of judge over the events and their actualization."[2] The dramatic dimension that infuses Scripture and tradition, rather, draws *all* would-be spectators into the action.[3]

In terms of their resistance to excessive rationalism in theology, Balthasar and Bulgakov are substantially in agreement, even given the proviso that the latter occasionally is more declarative than inquisitive in some of his positions. Bulgakov certainly recommends epistemic humility for the theological task, saying:

> *Not everything is understandable*, but God is in everything and in this is the great joy of faith and submissiveness. We draw near to the abyss where the fiery sword of the archangel again bars to us the further path of cognition. *It is so*—religious experience tells us about this entirely firmly; even religious philosophy needs to accept this as the original definition—in the humility of reason, for the sacrifice of humility is demanded from reason too, as the highest reasonableness of folly. The unutterable, unnameable, incomprehensible, unknowable, unthinkable God is revealed to creation in a name, a word, a cult, theophanies, incarnation. Glory to your condescension, O Lord![4]

It is the essential nature of both the theological discipline and religious experience to resist coarsening into a rigidly logical system of

discursive knowledge. This understanding of what constrains speculative theology requires an unpretentious acknowledgment that God,
the director and producer of the theo-dramatic "play," is unknowable
mystery, eternal surprise, that which human thought cannot presume
to master. A *speculum* is, in the most literal sense, a mirror: it reflects.
In the case of speculative theology, however, reflections of God are
necessarily through a glass darkly, such that the reflected images can be
only refractions, bending away from the exact reality and thus always
only constituting an approximation. These theological reflections *cum*
refractions, however, cannot be refractory, but rather accord themselves humbly to the faith in responsiveness to the essential and very
present mystery of God. It is not that theological reflection can say
nothing, but rather that it must demonstrate epistemic reserve in the
face of a divine presence whose plenitude exceeds and transcends all
conceptual categories.

THIS ACKNOWLEDGMENT that knowledge can be and often has been
overasserted does not mean that gnosis is unimportant for speculative
theology. The second corollary protocol that emerges regarding licit
speculation might be, then, that this knowledge of God should always
be located in its properly Christian context, which is its true north and
home. Balthasar and Bulgakov alike oppose the posturing of a speculative gnosis that would mulishly forge ahead not only without the three
that "remain"—that is, faith, hope, and love (1 Corinthians 13:13)—
but, even more disastrously, as an alternative to them. As seen in Origen, however, the biblical, contemplative gnosis of the spiritual exegete
is continuously constrained by *pistis* and Johannine love, and is, moreover, exercised in an ecclesial and sacramental context. It is only this
simultaneous commitment to personal holiness, fidelity to a living tradition, and reception of what is gifted in the self-expression of God the
Logos in the revelation of Scripture and tradition that gives life and
dynamism to formal and logical systems. Indeed, speculation cannot
be abstracted or disconnected from revelation but must receive it in
faith and love.

The manner in which Balthasar goes about his theologizing is far
from monolithic, which suggests a third protocol for licit speculative

theology: it indulges but does not always readily sanction a plurality of voices.[5] For Balthasar, the truth of God is "great enough to allow an infinity of approaches and entryways."[6] This feature is shown not least in his presentations of the twelve "styles" of theology in volumes 2 and 3 of *The Glory of the Lord*, both clerical and lay, which accords Soloviev—an eccentric choice by all counts—a place alongside pillars of Catholic tradition including Irenaeus, Augustine, Denys, Anselm, and Bonaventure. Their modes of theologizing—and those of other theologians—have different formal objects, including "God in himself," "God's revelation," the "synthesis of God and the world," and finally a formal object that capacitates the human mediator to be transparent to the Holy Spirit. This "engagement of the Spirit of God with the spirit of man in the Spirit of Christ is what ultimately bestows form,"[7] as in Joachim de Fiore, Hegel, Schleiermacher, early Möhler, and "a number of Russians."[8] This emphatic inclusion of Soloviev, as well as the presence of Bulgakov in Balthasar's pneumatology and apocalyptic eschatology, is one witness to his constitutive affirmation of plurality.

In terms of adjudicating these multiple voices, there may be guilt, but for Balthasar there is no guilt by *mere* association. This analysis has demonstrated that he is not terribly prudish about discursive purity in particular, and he is untroubled by the critical approximation of "impure" sources, although sources are certainly not unimportant. The proximate source material of Berdyaev, for example, is Gnosticism, Schelling, Böhme, and Joachim, while that of Bulgakov, Balthasar's authorized Russian, is Scripture and Orthodox tradition; Soloviev is a mixed bag, with sources ranging from Schelling to Darwin to Aquinas to Maximus. There is a myopic, insufficient brand of critique that judges thinkers only by the company they keep; this is not so with Balthasar. As has been shown, particularly with respect to Soloviev, reliance upon unstable philosophical discourses is not necessarily fatal, provided the proper Christological parsing is in place.

RELATED IS A FOURTH PRINCIPLE of generosity toward the often ambiguous cultural contributions of the world, as Balthasar sanctions the mediatory or revelatory capacity of cultural products: music, art, drama, prose literature, and poetry, even those not explicitly or exceptionally Christian. Like Origen, Balthasar has a strong sense of the presence of the Logos invisibly infusing all of creation. He suggests that "however secular this human word may seem as culture, art, philosophy, pedagogy and technology, it can yet be a response to God's call, and so a bringing back of man and the world to God. Thus in responding to God's Word man will also be enabled to 'redeem' *the word lying deeply hidden in the nature of things*, to say what each thing says."[9] Here, perhaps, we might cast a backward glance toward Rilke, whose poetry has accompanied each level of this excavation of Balthasar's critical appropriation of Russian school religious philosophy and might serve as but one example of Balthasar's notable hermeneutic of generosity with respect to permitting the nontheological cultural to inform and even to enrich the theological project.

It is not insignificant that the first two books of Rilke's *The Book of Hours: Prayers to a Lowly God*, "The Book of the Monkish Life" and "The Book of Pilgrimage," are marked by a distinctly Russian mode of mystic spirituality, the imprint of his two journeys to Russia in 1899 and 1900. In these poems Rilke adopts the persona of a Russian artist-monk who enjoins a prayerful dialogue with God. Balthasar, however, considers this work to be no more than "a monologue in dialogical form," for the poems merely "cover a post-Christian core with classical and Christian clothing."[10] Though imperfect in its scope, Rilke's final turn to concrete instances of the Italian poor in "The Book of Poverty and Death" indicates for Balthasar a luminosity and a kind of glory in which "the poor man, the man without resources, the cast-out leper is the place where kenotically the divine dwells."[11] As noted in chapter 5, Balthasar recognizes and appreciates the Johannine character of the synonymity of poverty and glory in this singular line from *The Book of Hours*: "For poverty is luminous from within." According to Balthasar, Rilke here "brushes very closely against the mystery that lies at the heart of Christianity,"[12] that is, the self-emptying kenosis of God in Trinity, creation, and, fundamentally in the paschal mystery, but does not ultimately enter the fold. Despite the fact that Rilke is not "in" in any uncomplicated way, there are intimations in his poetry that get at something authentically Christian and that Balthasar affirms without compunction.

Moreover, the divine excess that is the true subject of theology not only permits but actually requires a panoply of genres to name it, however asymptotically. Discursive, scientific, and rational modes of language alone are insufficient and must be joined by poetry, narrative, confession, prophecy, praise, rhapsody, contemplations, and prayer. Hand in hand with the givenness of revelation, then, is a multiplicity, even a playfulness, a child's game of a plenitude of expressive forms, as in the multiple, nowhere near inevitable genres of the witness of the Scriptures—prose, poetry, hymn, prayer, law, wisdom literature, and so on—a game that "in no way expresses contempt on the part of the divine spirit for the limitations of secular forms of expression," for the Logos incarnate "proves the opposite: an absolute acknowledgment and sanctioning of the created vessels of expression, a total harmonization of content and form, and this precisely in the making manifest of the divine freedom."[13]

Finally, licit speculation is Trinitarian, privileging the Christological and the pneumatological together, a fundamental posture that does not foreclose but rather remains open to infinite content, to the depths of a hidden mystery. This faith is expansive rather than confining insofar as it is "a mode of hearing *that never issues in final vision*, but [is] a progression without end, a progression ultimately dependent, in its scope, on the Holy Spirit."[14] This fundamental invocation of the Holy Spirit—arguably another significant locus of influence of Bulgakov upon Balthasar's theology, which a comparison of the former's *The Comforter* to the latter's *The Spirit of Truth*, volume 3 of *Theo-Logic*, will certainly bear out—programmatically resists closure or systematization. Balthasar's confidence in the Spirit's authorship and inspiration of all things revealed constitutes his dynamic view of revelation and provides a secure mooring that capacitates a freedom of play. As Balthasar suggests in *The Spirit of Truth*, very likely following Bulgakov's lead, "an authentic theology, however simple or learned it professes to be, can only be developed *in* the Holy Spirit."[15] Elsewhere, Balthasar could not be clearer in his positive association of the Spirit with the preclusion of religious dogma hardening into dogmatism:

> The truths that come into new prominence can never contradict the old, but nevertheless the Spirit can in every age blow where he will,

and in every age can bring to the fore entirely new aspects of divine Revelation. What is entirely intolerable is the notion that the "progress of dogma" gradually narrows down the unexplored area of divine truth, continually allowing less and less space to the free play of thought within the Faith, as though "progress" consisted in first of all establishing the main outlines of the Faith, and then proceeding to the more and more detailed work required to complete the edifice until finally—shortly before the Last Judgment, perhaps?—the structure would stand there complete, consisting in all its aspects of fully "used up," defined dogma. This dreary picture is the very opposite of the truth. The Spirit mocks all human attempts to delimit him. Upon those who are truly poor, who truly thirst after it, the Spirit pours out the consolation of his truth in such breathtaking, ever-increasing abundance that the very notion of "using it up," if it ever occurred to them, could only strike them as ludicrous blasphemy. . . . The Church's knowledge, dogmatic knowledge . . . is subject to the paradox which applies to all Christian truth, that the content of what is given always overflows to an infinite degree the vessel into which it is poured.[16]

This rather lengthy extract indicates that *in* the Holy Spirit, theology swells rather than narrows. As observed with Origen's spiritual exegesis, the exuberant superabundance of the divine content of Word and Spirit floods out and runs over any "vessel" of finite expression. The excess of the divine is mirrored in the Scriptures, which themselves are, insofar as the *gramma* points beyond itself to the *pneuma*, "a vessel that is too small" (John 21:25).[17]

It might be said, then, that for Balthasar the theological task is simply to be as capacious as the Holy Spirit. It is structurally open, fundamentally creative, resolutely brave, and certainly not precious. This book has aimed to exemplify concretely this mode of deeply pneumatic theologizing with what Balthasar calls "a living spirit."[18] What Balthasar has performed in his critical appropriations of the Russian school theology is a daring theological creativity that operates in a largely pneumatic register. Indeed, the Spirit blows where it will.[19] As Bulgakov indicates, "there cannot be a 'Philokalia' for creative activity, for the latter is outside of law and regularity."[20] For Balthasar (and

Bulgakov) the creative agency of the Holy Spirit cannot be contained: "It knows no slavish cleaving to the *littera* and shows its own freedom at the same time the vitality of the word of God itself, which from the beginning is more than the letter and, therefore, cannot be imprisoned in any book, even an inspired one (John 20, 30; 21, 25). The same Spirit, however, which reveals the inner connections of the word of revelation and by comparing the spiritual with the spiritual (*'spiritualibus spiritualia comparantes'* 1 Cor. 2, 13, for Origen the basic concern of theological investigation) produces new spirit, shows in that its freedom and inexhaustibility."[21]

In its conception of tradition, Balthasar's view is fundamentally consonant with that of Bulgakov, whose essay "The Church as Tradition" articulates a dynamic vision of the tradition of the Church that eschews construing it statically as a "sort of archeology, which by its shadows connects the present with the past."[22] Analogous to Drey's distinction between the "fixed" and "mobile" aspects of Church tradition with which this book began, Bulgakov distinguishes between elements of Church tradition as "lex credenda or lex orandi, or lex canonica or lex ecclesiastica"[23] that have been fixed, and those which have not been defined and can admit further dogmatic development. Because the Church tradition is the expression of the one Spirit of God, it is always identical with itself, or, in Balthasar's language, reflective of a "single entelechy which remains true to itself," even vis-à-vis developments that are "gnoseologically new."[24]

The evident resistance to narrow dogmatism cannot be mistaken for a resistance to dogma itself, for Balthasar or indeed for Bulgakov, who observes that a "pusillanimous and barely conscious" rejection of dogma as such is just as dogmatic as dogmatism itself.[25] Bulgakov and Balthasar's conceptions of dogmatic and conciliar statements are understood in the main to cordon off the "edges" of the mystery of God, to "point from the farthest edges of what is sayable into a region no one may enter."[26] Inside these limits, however, there is room for exploration, even that which is speculatively daring. Bulgakov describes the "fence" of dogma as defining

> that external boundary beyond which it is impossible to deviate, but it is not adequate to dogma at all, it does not exhaust its content;

first of all because every dogmatic formula . . . is only a logical
schema, a sketch of integral religious experience, its incomplete
translation into the language of concepts; and then because it usually arises because of heresy. . . . [I]t pursues for the most part
critical goals and hence has sometimes even a negative character:
"unmingled and indivisible," "one Divinity and three hypostases,"
"unity in Trinity and Trinity in unity," *Omnis definitio est negatio*
[All definition is negation]. This formula of Spinoza is especially
applicable to dogmatics, for here *negatio*, hewing dogmas like
sparks from a stone, more often is the occasion for *definitio*: the
quantity of *possible* dogmatic definitions in Christianity could be
significantly greater than those that are formulated at councils.[27]

This "positive" or "possible" contribution is exactly and explicitly
what occurs in both Bulgakov's speculative parsing of the traditional
creedal concept of *ousia* as "Sophia" and Balthasar's startling and
original interpretation of the harrowing of hell.

To recapitulate, the present work attended to Balthasar's rich set
of texts, from the early *Apokalypse der deutschen Seele* to his trilogy
(aesthetics, dramatics, logic), to other, more occasional writings with
an eye toward explicit or implicit convergences with Berdyaev, Soloviev, and Bulgakov, and Schelling below them, and at a deeper layer
Jakob Böhme. According to this analysis, Berdyaev is convicted, Soloviev is alibied, and Bulgakov, though through a veil of anonymity, is
largely absolved. For Balthasar, Berdyaev's religious philosophy can
be said to be valuable, at least insofar as it attempts to take myth, freedom, and evil seriously. Ultimately, however, it is determined far too
heavily by the illicitly speculative meonic line of Böhme–Schelling,
which becomes evident in his denigration of finitude and the created
order, explanatory theodicy, and presumptive Gnostic importation of
tragedy into the inner life of God. These divergences between Berdyaev and Balthasar illustrate concretely that which lies beyond the
boundaries of licit theological speculation.

Soloviev fares better because, although he uses the grammar of
Idealism and Romanticism, particularly Schelling's, to articulate his
own aesthetic and religious philosophy of *bogochelovechestvo*, he is a
genuinely Christological thinker informed most deeply by Scripture

and the Fathers, particularly Maximus the Confessor. His apocalyptic shift at the end of his career, informed by the bodily resurrection of Christ, moderates any tendency toward unrestrained evolutionism and preserves the goodness of the finite. Finally, Balthasar finds much to appreciate in the Russian enunciation of Antichrist as religious imposture, epitomized in Soloviev's short fiction, which rhymes thematically with Dostoevsky's embedded tale of the Grand Inquisitor in *The Brothers Karamazov*.

Finally, Bulgakov is absolutely formative for Balthasar, notably in his unusual interpretation of Christ's descent into hell, sustained attention to the theology of Holy Saturday, interest in the universality of human salvation, Trinitarian understanding of the symbol of Ur-kenosis that includes within it the creation of the world as the exteriorization and kenotic expression of God, dyadic action of Son and Spirit, apocalyptic symbol of the Lamb as though slain from the book of Revelation, and the decisive turn to pneumatology. Needless to say, Bulgakov elicits high praise, both explicitly and performatively, as Balthasar incorporates many of Bulgakov's reflections into the heart of his own theology. Balthasar worries, however, that with respect to the universality of salvation Bulgakov speaks too assuredly, in a mood indicative rather than optative. That notwithstanding, the central Johannine image of the slain Lamb, privileged by both Balthasar and Bulgakov and functioning as shorthand for the kenotic Trinitarianism at the heart of their shared dramatic soteriology, demands the exercise of epistemic humility in the theological task.

Attention to the regulative Christological image of the slain Lamb and the pneumatologically governed openness to the ever-greater adopted from Bulgakov helps to frustrate the shibboleth that Balthasar is constitutively overreaching in his speculative theology. The depths of eternal, luminous mystery of God, of self-giving Trinitarian love concretely expressed on the cross of Christ, defies a systematic method; *methodos*, for Balthasar, is at bottom "the pursuit of a way, and when One claims to be the way and we believe him, method could be translated as *sequela*, following."[28] If method is to be determined by the object of inquiry, the most important rule of engagement is that there can be no closure, but only a following after an ever-greater God who is all exceeding glory.

NOTES

CHAPTER 1

"Der Seelen wunderliches Bergwerk"

1. Rainer Maria Rilke, "Orpheus. Eurydice. Hermes": "It was the souls' strange mine. / Like silent silver ore they wandered / through its dark like veins. Between roots / the blood welled up that makes its way to men, / and it looked hard as porphyry in the dark. / Nothing else was red." *New Poems*, trans. Edward Snow (New York: North Point, 2001), 140–41. For text of the full poem with English translation alongside, see 140–47.

2. See Alexander Schmemann, "Russian Theology: 1920–1972, An Introductory Survey," *St. Vladimir's Theological Quarterly* 16 (1972): 172–94; Schmemann originally designated these figures as such. See also Paul Valliere, *Modern Russian Theology: Bukharev, Soloviev, Bulgakov: Orthodox Theology in a New Key* (Grand Rapids, MI: Eerdmans, 2000), esp. 1–15.

3. Theodore Ziolkowski, "The Mine: Image of the Soul," *German Romanticism and Its Institutions* (Princeton: Princeton University Press, 1990), 18–63.

4. Hans Urs von Balthasar, *The Glory of the Lord: A Theological Aesthetics*, vol. 7, *Theology: The New Covenant*, trans. Brian McNeil, C.R.V., ed. John Riches (San Francisco: Ignatius Press, 1989), 10. All volumes of *The Glory of the Lord* noted after first reference as *GL*.

5. Though I have retained this language as a way of marking certain methodological distinctions between Vladimir Soloviev, Pavel Florensky, and Sergei Bulgakov from the "Neopatristic" thought of Georges Florovsky and Vladimir Lossky, I do so somewhat hesitantly and with the acknowledgment that recent Orthodox thought has rightly challenged the ossification of mod-

ern Russian theology into these two groups as mutually exclusive. See Aristotle Papanikolaou's entry, "Eastern Orthodox Theology," in the *Routledge Companion to Modern Christian Thought*, ed. Chad Meister and James Beilby (New York: Routledge, 2013), 538–48, in which he argues compellingly both that Sergei Bulgakov is more "neo-patristic" than not, and that Vladimir Lossky's thought is formed by Bulgakov's theology rather than an absolute departure from it. Paul Gavrilyuk's brilliant *Georges Florovsky and the Russian Religious Renaissance* (Oxford: Oxford University Press, 2014) similarly challenges this standard narrative of contrast by providing an incisive analysis of Florovsky's use of Soloviev and Bulgakov.

6. Balthasar's position on the Russians—even Soloviev and Bulgakov, whom he later seems to affirm quite heartily—is not univocally enthusiastic. He is, for instance, much more dubious of the Russians in his 1941 monograph *Kosmische Liturgie*, available in English as *Cosmic Liturgy: The Universe According to Maximus the Confessor*, trans. Brian E. Daley, S.J. (San Francisco: Ignatius Press, 2003), than he is later in *The Glory of the Lord*. See also his *Presence and Thought: Essay on the Religious Philosophy of Gregory of Nyssa* (San Francisco: Ignatius Press, 1995), in which he asserts that Gregory "prepares the ground in some ways for that Gnostic dynamism of the Byzantine philosophies, which end up logically in the gnosis of Dostoevsky, Soloviev and Berdyaev" (118–19n46).

7. Hans Urs von Balthasar, "The Place of Theology," *Explorations in Theology*, vol. 1, *The Word Made Flesh* (San Francisco: Ignatius Press, 1989), 159–60. See David S. Yeago, "Literature in the Drama of Nature and Grace: Hans Urs von Balthasar's Paradigm for a Theology of Culture," and Virgil Nemoianu, "Hans Urs von Balthasar and the Traditions of Christian Humanism," both in *Glory, Grace, and Culture: The Work of Hans Urs von Balthasar*, ed. Ed Block Jr. (New York: Paulist Press, 2005), 88–106 and 127–49.

8. Balthasar acknowledges both Soloviev and Bulgakov explicitly as "certain of [Schelling's] Russian followers" during his discussion of Louis Bouyer's *Le Consolateur: Esprit Saint et Vie de grace*, in *Theo-Logic: Theological Logical Theory*, vol. 3, *The Spirit of Truth*, trans. Graham Harrison (San Francisco: Ignatius Press, 2004), 53. All volumes of *Theo-Logic* noted after first reference as *TL*.

9. Hans Urs von Balthasar, *The Glory of the Lord: A Theological Aesthetics*, vol. 5, *The Realm of Metaphysics in the Modern Age*, trans. Oliver Davies, Andrew Louth, Brian McNeil, C.R.V., John Saward, and Rowan Williams, ed. Brian McNeil, C.R.V. and John Riches (San Francisco: Ignatius Press, 1990), 26–27.

10. Hans Urs von Balthasar, *Theo-Drama: Theological Dramatic Theory*, vol. 4, *The Action*, trans. Graham Harrison (San Francisco: Ignatius Press, 1994), 458–59. All volumes of *Theo-Drama* noted after first reference as *TD*.

11. Balthasar, *GL*, 5:26–27. Also see Hans Urs von Balthasar, *The Moment of Christian Witness*, trans. Richard Beckley (San Francisco: Ignatius Press, 1994), 99.

12. Hans Urs von Balthasar, *My Work: In Retrospect* (San Francisco: Ignatius Press, 1993), 89.

13. Henri de Lubac, "A Witness of Christ in the Church: Hans Urs von Balthasar," in *Hans Urs von Balthasar: His Life and Work*, ed. David L. Schindler (San Francisco: Ignatius Press, 1991), 272.

14. See Erich Przywara, *Analogia Entis: Metaphysics: Original Structure and Universal Rhythym*, trans. John R. Betz and David Bentley Hart (Grand Rapids, MI: Eerdmans, 2014).

15. Hans Urs von Balthasar, *Dare We Hope "That All Men Be Saved"?*, trans. David Kipp and Lothar Krauth (San Francisco: Ignatius Press, 1988), 19–20.

16. See Medard Kehl, "Hans Urs von Balthasar: A Portrait," in *The Von Balthasar Reader*, ed. Medard Kehl, S.J., and Werner Löser, S.J. (New York: Crossroad, 1982), 4–6; and Kevin Mongrain, *The Systematic Thought of Hans Urs von Balthasar: An Irenaean Retrieval* (New York: Crossroad, 2002), 12–15.

17. Alyssa Lyra Pitstick, *Light in Darkness: Hans Urs von Balthasar and the Catholic Doctrine of Christ's Descent into Hell* (Grand Rapids, MI: Eerdmans, 2007), 346.

18. Ibid. For a catalogue of more particular criticisms about Balthasar's method with respect to his arriving at a rereading of *decensus* theology, see Pitstick, *Light in Darkness*, 323–37, which ultimately claims that Balthasar "sets Scripture against that very Tradition and ends up concluding something contrary to the Tradition he received and in which he claims to stand" (337).

19. See Ben Quash, "'Between the Brutely Given, and the Brutally, Banally Free': Von Balthasar's Theology of Drama in Dialogue with Hegel," *Modern Theology* 13, no. 3 (July 1997): 293–318; "Drama and the Ends of Modernity," in *Balthasar at the End of Modernity*, ed. Lucy Gardner, David Moss, Ben Quash, and Graham Ward (Edinburgh: T&T Clark, 1999), 139–71; and *Theology and the Drama of History* (Cambridge: Cambridge University Press, 2005). For a similar but less developed attribution of Hegelianism to Balthasar, see Karen Kilby, *Balthasar: A (Very) Critical Introduction* (Grand Rapids, MI: Eerdmans, 2012), 61–62. Kevin Mongrain challenges Quash's reading in *Systematic Thought*, 225n1, as does Cyril O'Regan, *The Anatomy of Misremembering: Von Balthasar's Response to Philosophical Modernity*, vol. 1, *Hegel* (New York: Crossroad, 2014), especially 616n11. O'Regan also takes a rather critical stance in his review of Quash's monograph in *Modern Theology* 23, no. 3 (April 2007): 293–96.

20. Karl Rahner, *Karl Rahner in Dialogue: Conversations and Interviews 1965–1982*, ed. Paul Irnhoff and Hubert Biallowons, trans. Harvey D. Egan (New York: Crossroads, 1986), 126–27; italics added.

21. Kilby, *Balthasar*, 14.

22. Ibid. Note that Kilby does acknowledge certain passages that suggest "the limited nature of our knowing, the need for epistemic humility, the inescapability of mystery" (ibid.).

23. Ibid., 149–50n2. Kilby takes the central image of the symphony in Balthasar further:

> Perhaps for the most part, because we can catch only a bit in the middle, or because we are seated too close to the drums, or because of the simple limitations of our hearing, we cannot entirely make sense of what we hear, can only perceive it as incomplete, unresolved, even at times perhaps discordant. Revelation, one might say, allows us to catch *something* of the music, and to trust that there is indeed a whole symphony, but it does not allow us to *hear* the whole. Balthasar, however, is not inclined to take the image in such a direction. (151)

24. See Hans Urs von Balthasar, *The Glory of the Lord: A Theological Aesthetics*, vol. 3, *Studies in Theological Style: Lay Styles*, trans. Andrew Louth, John Saward, Martin Simon, and Rowan Williams, ed. John Riches (San Francisco: Ignatius Press, 1985), 289.

25. For a solid treatment of Soloviev's early dissertation, see Valliere, "The Critique of Abstract Principles," in *Modern Russian Theology*, 117–41.

26. Sergei Bulgakov, *The Lamb of God*, trans. Boris Jakim (Grand Rapids, MI: Eerdmans, 2008), 321. He argues, for instance, that the divine nature (*ousia/Sophia*) not only funds all of life but also is "the absolute content of absolute life with all its 'properties,' the property of all properties. It is proper for this content to include All, for no limitations are applicable to Divinity; furthermore, this All should be understood not as an aggregate or series of an infinite number of elements of the All but as their organic inner integrity, as integral wisdom in union. This is the All as unity and unity as All, *All-unity*" (102). Cf. 104, 107–8 of the same volume.

27. Hans Urs von Balthasar, *The Glory of the Lord: A Theological Aesthetics*, vol. 1, *Seeing the Form*, trans. Erasmo Leiva-Merikakis, ed. Joseph Fessio, S.J., and John Riches (San Francisco: Ignatius Press, 1982), 31.

28. Hans Urs von Balthasar, *Theo-Logic: Theological Logical Theory*, vol. 1, *The Truth of the World*, trans. A. J. Walker (San Francisco: Ignatius Press, 2000), 8.

29. Ibid., 49, 128.

30. Ibid., 186.

31. Balthasar, *GL*, 1:18; italics added.

32. Hans Urs von Balthasar, *Apokalypse der deutschen Seele: Studien zu einer Lehre von letzten Haltungen*, vol. 1, *Der deutsche Idealismus* (Freiburg: Johannes Verlag Einsiedeln, 1937), 204–51.

33. Louis Roberts, *The Theological Aesthetics of Hans Urs von Balthasar* (Washington, DC: Catholic University of America Press, 1987), 209; cf. Thomas O'Meara, *Romantic Idealism and Roman Catholicism: Schelling and the Theologians* (Notre Dame, IN: University of Notre Dame Press, 1986), 11.

34. See Stephan van Erp, *The Art of Theology: Hans Urs von Balthasar's Theological Aesthetics and the Foundations of Faith* (Leuven: Peeters, 2004), for a study that puts Balthasar in dialogue with both Schelling and Nicholas of Cusa, particularly with attention to these sources for Balthasar's aesthetics. For a broader treatment of Balthasar on Hegel and Heidegger, see O'Regan, *Anatomy of Misremembering*, vol. 1, *Hegel*; and vol. 2, *Heidegger* (New York: Crossroad Publishing Company, forthcoming).

35. Balthasar, *Apokalypse der deutschen Seele*, 1:206.

36. Hans Urs von Balthasar, "Revelation and the Beautiful," *Explorations in Theology*, 1:125.

37. Hans Urs von Balthasar, *The Glory of the Lord: A Theological Aesthetics*, vol. 2, *Studies in Theological Style: Clerical Styles*, trans. Andrew Louth, Francis McDonagh, and Brian McNeil, C.R.V.; ed. John Riches (San Francisco: Ignatius Press, 1986), 15.

38. Cf. O'Meara, *Romantic Idealism*; and John E. Thiel, *Imagination and Authority: Theological Authorship in the Modern Tradition* (Minneapolis: Fortress Press, 1991). Also see James Turnstead Burtchaell, C.S.C., "Drey, Möhler and the Catholic School of Tübingen," in *Nineteenth-Century Religious Thought in the West*, ed. Ninian Smart, John Clayton, Patrick Sherry, and Steven Katz, 3 vols. (Cambridge: Cambridge University Press, 1985), 2:111–39.

39. V. V. Zenkovsky, *A History of Russian Philosophy*, trans. George L. Kline, 2 vols. (New York: Columbia University Press, 1953), 1:212. Cf. Valliere, *Modern Russian Theology*, 9.

40. F. W. J. Schelling, *The Grounding of Positive Philosophy: The Berlin Lectures*, trans. Bruce Matthews (New York: State University of New York Press, 2008).

41. Thiel, *Imagination and Authority*, especially 20–24.

42. Valliere, *Modern Russian Theology*, 295.

43. Ibid., 296.

44. Ibid.

45. Johann Sebastian Drey, *Brief Introduction to the Study of Theology with Reference to the Scientific Standpoint and the Catholic System*, trans. Michael J. Himes (Notre Dame, IN: University of Notre Dame Press, 1994),

§203, 77–78; §256, 170. For secondary treatments of Drey on the development of doctrine, see John Thiel, *Senses of Tradition: Continuity and Development in Catholic Faith* (Oxford: Oxford University Press, 2000), especially 61–63; and Bradford Hinze, *Narrating History, Developing Doctrine: Friedrich Schleiermacher and Johann Sebastian Drey* (Oxford: Oxford University Press, 1993).

46. Drey, §260, 173.

47. See, for instance, Hans Urs von Balthasar, *The Glory of the Lord: A Theological Aesthetics*, vol. 4, *The Realm of Metaphysics in Antiquity*, trans. Brian McNeil, C.R.V., Andrew Louth, John Saward, Rowan Williams, and Oliver Davies, ed. John Riches (San Francisco: Ignatius Press, 1989), 36. For a concise, elegant statement of Bulgakov's perspective with respect to the decidedly nonarcheological, organic elasticity of ecclesial tradition, see Sergei Bulgakov, "The Church as Tradition," in *The Orthodox Church* (Crestwood, NY: St. Vladimir's Seminary Press, 1988), 9–35.

48. Balthasar, *Presence and Thought*, 12.

49. Balthasar, "The Place of Theology," *Explorations in Theology*, 1:157.

50. Balthasar, *GL*, 5:443, 564. For a classic articulation of Böhme's influence on Schelling, see Robert Brown, *The Later Philosophy of Schelling: The Influence of Boehme on the Works of 1809–1815* (Lewisburg, PA: Bucknell University Press, 1977).

51. Cyril O'Regan, *Gnostic Return in Modernity* (Albany: State University of New York Press, 2001), 33. O'Regan also indicates there that Soloviev and Berdyaev's dependence on Schelling and Böhme, along with a "sense of the necessity of a narrative ontotheology with the suffering of the cross at the center," suggests that the Russians considered here "are prime candidates for analysis [of some ascription of Gnostic return], given their complex weave of myth, Idealism and the Eastern orthodox tradition" (35–36). We do not presume to continue O'Regan's project by demonstrating a full-fledged Gnostic haunting of these modern Russian discourses by their association with German Idealism and Romanticism, Böhme, or Schelling. Our interest, again, lies more with the analysis of the way these Russian narratives are evaluated explicitly in *Balthasar's* theology, with the suggestion that for Balthasar, Soloviev and Bulgakov supply successive sites of sanitization of Schelling's and Böhme's potentially corrosive influence.

52. Balthasar, *GL*, 1:102–4.

53. Balthasar, *GL*, 5:297. Also see Hans Urs von Balthasar, "Titanisms," in *Theo-Drama: Theological Dramatic Theory*, vol. 2, *The Dramatis Personae: Man in God*, trans. Graham Harrison (San Francisco: Ignatius Press, 1990), 420–26.

54. Balthasar, *GL*, 5:547–48.

55. The ecclesiological similarities between Schelling and the Russians, though beyond the scope of the present study, are worth exploring. Soloviev's

Three Dialogues, especially the "Short Story of the Antichrist," ultimately suggests an idealized, ecumenical version of Christianity — the *Petrine* (Roman Catholics), *Pauline* (Protestants), and *Johannine* (Russian Orthodox). According to Valliere, "Soloviev's threefold scheme derives partly from the end of Schelling's *Philosophy of Revelation*, where Schelling envisions an ecumenical church of the future incorporating Petrine, Pauline and Johannine principles. Schelling does not figure Orthodoxy into the equation, however. His Johannine church is pure futurity, the ideal synthesis of Roman Catholic, Protestant and philosophic principles. See F. W. J. Schelling, *Philosophie der Offenbarung 1841/42*, Paulus Nachschrift, ed. Manfred Frank (Frankfurt am Main: Suhrkamp Verlag, 1977), pp. 314–25." Valliere, *Modern Russian Theology*, 217–18n36. Balthasar's ecclesiology uses the same categories, with the addition of James and attention to the undergirding Marian disposition.

56. Soloviev's emphasis on Christology as the center of the doctrine of God and ontology resurfaces in Balthasar and Bulgakov (as well as in Barth). See Brandon Gallaher, "The Christological Focus of Soloviev's Sophiology," *Modern Theology* 25, no. 4 (2009): 617–46. For a nice treatment of Schelling's later more theological commitments, see Frederick C. Copleston, *A History of Philosophy*, vol. 7, pt. 1, *Fichte to Hegel* (Garden City, NY: Image Books, 1965), 157–82.

57. Vladimir Soloviev, "Lecture Five," *Lectures on Divine Humanity*, ed. Boris Jakim (Hudson, NY: Lindisfarne Press, 1995), 64; italics original. Also see "Lecture Four" of the same volume: "For the *all* to be the content of the absolute principle this all must have determinate content" (51).

58. Sergei Bulgakov, *The Philosophy of Economy*: *The World as Household*, ed. and trans. Catherine Evtuhov (Yale University Press, 2000), 93. Bulgakov is quick to note, however, that his creative adaptation of Schelling for a philosophy of economy is not wholesale; it "must be free of any Schellingian dogmatism" (93). For a relatively sustained treatment of Schelling's philosophy of identity by Bulgakov in this volume, see 85–94. For these and other points of influence from Schelling to Bulgakov, see Valliere, *Modern Russian Theology*, 257, 260–61, 265–66, 270n41, 274, 295–96. This notable presence of Schelling in the economic philosophy lessens in Bulgakov's properly theological reflections in later years.

59. See especially Balthasar's discussion in "Revelation and the Beautiful," where he presents the world as locus of the mystery of God revealed, *Explorations in Theology*, 1:120.

60. I consider the sophiological metaphysics of Sergei Bulgakov's thought in dialogue with Balthasar in "The 'Whence' and the 'Whither' of Balthasar's Gendered Theology: Rehabilitating Kenosis for Feminist Theology," *Modern Theology* 31, no. 2 (2015): 211–34. Sophiology is the rather difficult doctrine in the Silver Age of Russian religious thinking that has been

put somewhat in the more mainstream theological limelight with John Milbank's provocative claim that Russian sophiology is "perhaps the most significant theology of the two preceding centuries." John Milbank, "Sophiology and Theurgy: The New Theological Horizon," in *An Encounter between Eastern Orthodoxy and Radical Orthodoxy: Transfiguring the World through the Word*, ed. Adrian Pabst and Christoph Schneider (Aldershot: Ashgate, 2009), 145. For a response to (an earlier version of) Milbank, see Brandon Gallaher, "Graced Creatureliness: Ontological Tension in the Uncreated/Created Distinction in the Sophiologies of Solov'ev, Bulgakov and Milbank," *Logos: A Journal of Eastern Christian Studies* 47, no. 1–2 (2006): 163–90. See also Michael Martin, *The Submerged Reality: Sophiology and the Turn to a Poetic Metaphysics* (Kettering, OH: Angelico Press, 2015). It is exceedingly difficult to present a clear, consistent picture of how "Sophia" is understood in the Russians, or even in the father of the discourse—Soloviev himself—who employed multilayered presentations in poetry and philosophical prose in his attempt to articulate who or what Sophia is. A full evaluation of Russian sophiology is well beyond the scope of the present work, as is an assessment of the pastiche of traditions that inform it, including the Christian Scriptures, Neoplatonism, Gnosticism, Kabbalah, the Russian iconographical tradition, Böhme, and Romanticism, as well as Soloviev's own reported mystical visions. Böhme's sophiology, however, is certainly not absent from Soloviev's many articulations, particularly the claim that Sophia is the corporeal principle for divinity, the dwelling place of God, and especially the metaphor of Sophia as the "mirror of the divinity." See Jacob Böhme, *The Way to Christ*, trans. Peter Erb (New York: Paulist Press, 1978). Judith Deutsch Kornblatt draws attention to those texts (particularly in the poetry) in which Soloviev repeats Böhme's association of Sophia with mirrors in "Who Is Solovyov and What Is Sophia?" in Vladimir Soloviev, *Divine Sophia: The Wisdom Writings of Vladimir Solovyov*, ed. Judith Deutsch Kornblatt, trans. Boris Jakim, Judith Deutsch Kornblatt, and Laury Magnus (Ithaca: Cornell University Press, 2009), 72–73. Something similar appears in Schelling's version of Sophia: see Thomas Klibengajtis, "Sophia in Schelling's Work: From Divine Wisdom to Human Science," *Transcultural Studies* 4 (2008): 13–26. For general influence of Böhme on Soloviev's developing sophiology, see Kornblatt's introduction to Soloviev, *Divine Sophia*, 71–76, and Zdenek V. David, "The Influence of Jacob Boehme on Russian Religious Thought," *Slavic Review* 21, no. 1 (March 1962): 43–64, particularly 61–63. Soloviev's doctrine of Sophia is influenced but not absolutely determined by this dubious line, and Balthasar consistently alibis Soloviev's conception of Sophia in his essay in *GL* 3. We can assume that he has Bulgakov's more sanitized version of sophiology in mind here. Berdyaev, on the other hand, is far less concerned with maintaining an orthodox conception of Trinity and thus has no compunction, following Böhme, of introducing Sophia as a fourth hypostasis: see Nikolai Berdyaev, "Studies Concerning Jacob Boehme: Etude II. The Teaching about Sophia and the Androgyne: J. Boehme and the Russian Sophiological Current," *Put'* 21 (April 1930): 34–62. For Balthasar's worries about Berdyaev's sophiology, see *Apokalypse der deutschen Seele: Studien zu einer Lehre von letzten Haltungen*, vol. 2, *Im Zeichen Nietzsches* (Einsiedeln: Johannes Verlag, 1939), 344. Also see Balthasar, *Cosmic Liturgy*, 190, 346, for early worries about the orthodoxy of Russian sophiology in general.

61. Balthasar, *GL*, 5:548, 627. As is well known, it is here especially that the influence of Erich Przywara is felt.

62. The failure of German Idealism's metaphysics of identity for a theological aesthetics that has "glory" rather than a philosophy of art at the root of it will be discussed in more detail in chapter 2.

63. Balthasar, *GL*, 5:655.

64. Ibid., 627.

65. Balthasar, *My Work*, 83.

66. This claim may be somewhat ironic in light of the critique that Berdyaev offers of Soloviev in Nicolas Berdyaev, *The Beginning and the End: Essay on Eschatological Metaphysics* (London: Geoffrey Bles, 1952), that his "doctrine of Godmanhood assumed too evolutionary and optimistic a character and was not sufficiently free from the influence of Hegel and Schelling" (26).

67. Balthasar, *Moment of Christian Witness*, 71. Of course this attribution is hardly a compliment, especially in this context, where later in the argument he draws connections between the evolutionary Christology of Soloviev and the theology of Karl Rahner (105–7), which is subject to a rather biting critique here.

68. Balthasar, *GL*, 5:553–54.

69. Gerard Manley Hopkins, "That Nature Is a Heraclitean Fire and of the Comfort of the Resurrection," *Poems* (London: Humphrey Milford, 1918). Cf. O'Regan, *Anatomy of Misremembering*, 606n8.

70. Mongrain, *Systematic Thought*, 36.

71. Mongrain does make the wise caveat that his "asserting the presence of a massive Irenaean influence on von Balthasar is not meant to eclipse the importance of . . . other figures on his thought," including Gregory of Nyssa, Augustine, Dionysius, Maximus, and Origen (ibid., 28). The claim, however, that these other patristic thinkers "are for [Balthasar] only moons to Irenaeus's sun" (27) seems slightly overstated.

72. Hans Urs von Balthasar, "Geist und Feuer: Ein Gespräch mit Hans Urs von Balthasar," *Herder Korrespondenz* 30 (1976): 72–82.

73. Balthasar, *My Work*, 11.

74. Ibid., 26. Of course, Balthasar has monographs on both of these figures.

75. Ibid., 89.

76. Pitstick, *Light in Darkness*, 345.

77. Hans Urs von Balthasar, introduction to *Origen: Spirit and Fire: A Thematic Anthology of His Writings*, ed. Hans Urs von Balthasar, trans. Robert J. Daly, S.J. (Washington, DC: Catholic University of America Press, 1984), 8.

78. Ibid., 4.

79. Ibid., 5.

80. See, for example, "Mission as a Basic Concept" in Hans Urs von Balthasar, *Theo-Drama: Theological Dramatic Theory*, vol. 3, *The Dramatis Personae: Persons in Christ*, trans. Graham Harrison (San Francisco: Ignatius Press, 1992), 149–63, especially 153. This Johannine register undergirds all of Balthasar's theology, including its cosmic scope. Correlatively, "there can be no cosmic return without this very specific 'I am the way . . . , no one comes to the Father except by me' (Jn 14:6). If the world is to return to its origin, the trail must be blazed by him who has already completed, emphatically and archetypically, the circle of coming forth and return." (*TL*, 3:436–37).

81. Balthasar, *TL*, 3:331.

82. *GL*, 5:548–49.

83. Hans Urs von Balthasar, preface to *Origen: An Exhortation to Martyrdom, Prayer, and Selected Works*, The Classics of Western Spirituality, by Origen, trans. Rowan A. Greer (Mahwah, NY: Paulist Press, 1979), xi–xiv.

84. See Balthasar, introduction to *Origen: Spirit and Fire*, 3.

85. Ibid., 10. See also Balthasar, preface to *Origen: An Exhortation to Martyrdom*, xii.

86. Origen, *On First Principles*, preface I, trans. G. W. Butterworth (Gloucester, MA: Peter Smith, 1973), 1.

87. Balthasar, preface to *Origen: An Exhortation to Martyrdom*, xiii. For Balthasar as anti-Marcionite, see Anthony C. Sciglitano, *Marcion and Prometheus: Balthasar against the Expulsion of Jewish Origins from Modern Religious Dialogue* (New York: Crossroad, 2014).

88. Balthasar, "The Place of Theology," *Explorations in Theology*, 1:149.

89. Balthasar, "The Word, Scripture, and Tradition," *Explorations in Theology*, 1:11–26.

90. Though O'Regan's *The Anatomy of Misremembering* has rightly identified the Teutonic/Romantic strain in Balthasar's conception of the fragment, including Goethe, Schlegel, Hamann, and so on in the genealogy of this concept, I will set this aspect aside in order to develop the Christological element—which I identify as Bulgakovian—more deeply.

91. Hans Urs von Balthasar, *A Theological Anthropology* (Eugene, OR: Wipf and Stock, 2010), 3. Balthasar suggests too that in book 12 of the *Confessions* Augustine's interpretation of the Genesis creation account is a breaking up into a multiplicity of possible interpretations. Augustine dismantles the sentence into "this vast profusion of bits of meaning" (13), which then must be gathered together. Again in the context of Augustine's reading of the Scriptures, Balthasar writes, "What does 'in the beginning,' or 'heaven,' or 'earth' mean? The interpretations so pile up that it is as if a single sentence of God and Moses undergoes the same process of fragmentation as everything else, and even in the same half-clear way. It is a process of breaking up into pieces, since our clouded intellect can only perceive images and reflections of the one truth, and thus one interpretation follows another. But the process involves also a *divinely dispensed* multiplication of the one truth calling men back, through many different forms, to unity" (13).

92. Ibid., 233.
93. Ibid., 63.
94. Ibid., 100.
95. Ibid., 95.
96. Ibid., 279.
97. Ibid., 280.
98. Ibid., 284–85.
99. Ibid., 285; cf. 289.
100. Ibid., 294.

101. As Balthasar puts it somewhat colloquially, "Knowing of the house built up in grace for him with God, he can cheerfully inhabit his tumbledown hut and free himself through time. Assenting to his secret deprivations in favor of a beyond he cannot reach, he also assents to the secret rewards that come to him from there. He acquires strength when he thought he had none left; wings can bear him up. What is given into his hands to administer is more than he can ascribe to himself: he can therefore only distribute it as something from elsewhere which has mysteriously come into his possession" (*Theological Anthropology*, 101).

102. Balthasar, *TL*, 1:52.

103. Balthasar could not be clearer here: "True, we may get to see only minute fragments of the plan as a whole. We may repeatedly have to *refrain from judgment and evaluation* because we lose sight of the individual thread in the tangled web of the whole design" (*TL*, 1:184; italics added).

104. Ibid., 128.
105. Balthasar, *Theological Anthropology*, 96.
106. Ibid., viii.
107. Ibid., 101.
108. Thiel, *Senses of Tradition*, 197.

109. For example, consider Balthasar's treatment of the "dyad" of Son and Spirit in the act of revelation in *TL*, which prioritizes the "biblical aspect" over the "speculative aspect" (3:167–84). Not unincidentally, it is informed not only by Irenaeus's expressive notion of "the Father's two hands," but also deeply by Sergei Bulgakov's *The Comforter*, trans. Boris Jakim (Grand Rapids, MI: Eerdmans, 2004).

110. See, for instance, Hans Urs von Balthasar, *Theo-Drama: Theological Dramatic Theory*, vol. 5, *The Last Act*, trans. Graham Harrison (San Francisco: Ignatius Press, 1998), 13–14. It asserts Balthasar's intent to construct theological claims on the articles of the faith, and not vice versa. The upper boundary of speculation intervenes where "pseudo-logical speculations have been shown to lead only into an abstract void or to superfluous lists of what is forbidden" (14).

111. Balthasar, *TD*, 3:508.

112. Balthasar, *TL*, 3:429. See also *TD*, 2:419.

113. Balthasar, *GL*, 5:207–9; italics original.

114. In Balthasar's narrative it is Meister Eckhart who, unbeknownst to himself as a sympathetic "friend of God," sounds the terrible gong of identity between divine and human, the "infinite" I and the "finite" I, a sound that reverberates out to Hegel's own speculative Idealism. See *GL*, 5:44–50.

115. Balthasar, *Moment of Christian Witness*, 66–67.

116. Balthasar, *GL*, 5:248.

117. Sergei Bulgakov, *The Unfading Light: Contemplations and Speculations*, trans. Thomas Allen Smith (Grand Rapids, MI: Eerdmans, 2012), 171. Cf. 153 and 201 in the same volume.

118. Balthasar, "The Word, Scripture, and Tradition," *Explorations in Theology*, 1:21.

119. Mongrain, *Systematic Thought*, 30.

120. Balthasar, *GL*, 1:134–35; italics added.

121. Ibid., 135.

122. Balthasar, introduction to *Origen: Spirit and Fire*, 9.

123. Balthasar, *GL*, 1:136.

124. Ibid., 137.

125. Ibid., 39.

126. Ibid., 490.

127. Ibid., 75.

128. Ibid., 77.

129. Ibid.

130. Rowan Williams notes this as well in "Origen: Between Orthodoxy and Heresy," in *Origeniana Septima: Origenes in den Auseinandersetzungen des 4. Jahrhunderts*, ed. Wolfgang A. Bienert and Uwe Kühneweg (Louvain: Leuven University Press, 1999), 3–14, writing that for Origen, "more needs to

be said about the criteria for recognizable continuity and unity in the Church than a straightforward appeal to bishop or canon" (7). Cf. 9.

131. Balthasar, *GL* 1:138–41. Sciglitano's *Marcion and Prometheus* characterizes Balthasar well on this point: "Christian *gnosis* is not a movement away from the symbolic language of faith, but rather a grasp of its meaning and its interconnectedness so that *gnosis* passes beyond mere acceptance of authority or knowledge of individual pieces of Christian truth to a contemplation of the dynamic pattern (*Gestalt*) of revelation, and, finally, to the stage of personal expropriation for a mission of service. Thus, the goal of the genuinely Christian Gnostic is not to reach beyond faith to knowledge, but to attain a more profound and holistic grasp of the *Vorstellungen* of faith in their meaning, their interrelation, and their significance for self, community, and cosmos" (28).

132. Balthasar, preface to *Origen: An Exhortation to Martyrdom*, xiii. Cf. Balthasar, *My Work*, 31, on the mutually enriching relation between theology and holiness.

133. Balthasar, preface to *Origen: An Exhortation to Martyrdom*, 9.

134. Ibid., 8; italics added.

135. Balthasar, *GL*, 7:15. Correlatively, Soloviev argues that it is the Trinity that is "the basic speculative principle of Christianity." Soloviev, *Lectures on Divine Humanity*, 77.

136. Balthasar, "Revelation and the Beautiful," *Explorations in Theology*, 1:97–98.

137. Balthasar, *GL*, 5:228.

138. As Origen famously wrote in his homilies on Luke, "But I hope to be a man of the Church. I hope to be addressed not by the name of some heresiarch, but by the name of Christ. I hope to have his name, which is blessed upon the earth. I desire, both in deed and in thought, both to be and to be called a Christian." Origen, Homily 16, *Homilies on Luke* (*The Fathers of the Church*), trans. Joseph T. Lienhard, S.J. (Washington, DC: Catholic University of America Press, 1996), 67. Balthasar selects this passage as the epigraph for *Origen: Spirit and Fire* and mentions it also in the preface to *Origen: An Exhortation to Martyrdom*. See also Henri de Lubac, "Origen, Man of the Church," *History and Spirit: The Understanding of Scripture According to Origen*, trans. Anne Englund Nash (San Francisco: Ignatius Press, 2007), 51–102.

139. See Hans Urs von Balthasar, *A Short Primer for Unsettled Laymen*, trans. Sister Mary Theresilde Skerry (San Francisco: Ignatius Press, 1985), 54. Balthasar's mode of theologizing seems very much in the spirit of John Paul II's 1998 encyclical *Fides et Ratio*, which cautions against a "latent fideism" that can "appear in the scant consideration accorded to speculative theology, and in disdain for the classical philosophy from which the terms of both the

understanding of faith and the actual formulation of dogma have been drawn" (55). The language and methods of philosophy—submitted in humility to the *regula fidei*—are of great value for addressing

> the use of language to speak about God, the personal relations within the Trinity, God's creative activity in the world, the relationship between God and man, or Christ's identity as true God and true man. . . . It is necessary therefore that the mind of the believer acquire a natural, consistent and true knowledge of created realities—the world and man himself—which are also the object of divine Revelation. Still more, reason must be able to articulate this knowledge in concept and argument. Speculative dogmatic theology thus presupposes and implies a philosophy of the human being, the world and, more radically, of being, which has objective truth as its foundation. (66)

It is certainly not irrelevant that John Paul II recognizes both Vladimir Soloviev and Pavel Florensky as exemplary in this context (74). See also Balthasar, *GL*, 1:165.

140. Hans Urs von Balthasar, *Prayer*, trans. Graham Harrison (San Francisco: Ignatius Press, 1986), 79.

141. Several dissertations have thoughtfully drawn Rilke into the theological conversation. See Anne Carpenter, "Theo-Poetics: Figure and Metaphysics in the Thought of Hans Urs von Balthasar" (Ph.D. diss., Marquette University, 2012), available at http://epublications.marquette.edu/dissertations_mu/191/; and Leonard James DeLorenzo II, "Those Who Hear Will Live: A Theological Explication of the Communion of Saints" (Ph.D. diss., University of Notre Dame, 2014), especially chapter 2.

CHAPTER 2. "Denn da ist keine Stelle, die dich nicht sieht"

1. For a reputable "thick description" introduction, see Aidan Nichols, O.P., *The Word Has Been Abroad: A Guide through Balthasar's Aesthetics* (Washington, DC: Catholic University of America Press, 1998). Also see James Voiss, "Rahner, von Balthasar and the Question of Theological Aesthetics," in *Finding God in All Things: Celebrating Bernard Lonergan, John Courtney Murray, and Karl Rahner*, ed. Mark Bosco and David Stagaman (New York: Fordham University Press, 2007), 167–81. Also helpful is Nichols's succinct article "Von Balthasar's Aims in his Theological Aesthetics," *Heythrop Journal* 15 (1999): 409–23. For a monograph that connects Balthasar's aesthetics with his reading of the Scriptures, see W. T. Dickens, *Hans Urs von Balthasar's Theological Aesthetics: A Model for Post-Critical Biblical Interpretation* (Notre Dame, IN: University of Notre Dame Press, 2003).

2. See Victor V. Bychkov and Oleg K. Bychkov, "Russian Aesthetics: Religious Aesthetics," in *Encyclopedia of Aesthetics*, ed. Michael Kelly (Oxford: Oxford University Press, 1998), 199. Pavel Florensky, whose interest in icons and in the central mystery of the hypostatic union brings theological content to an essentially antinomial perspective, is on the short list of figures immediately following Soloviev who also contributed to modern Russian religious aesthetics associated with Neoorthodoxy, especially insofar as his thinking may influence Bulgakov. Indeed, it has been suggested that Bulgakov "largely continues Florensky's tradition in aesthetics" (ibid., 200). Furthermore, it is impossible to consider Solovievian aesthetics without at least some acknowledgment of his relationship with Dostoevsky. Soloviev and Dostoevsky, both of whom proffer aesthetic systems that emerge from German Romantic Idealism with a Christologically specified foundation, enjoyed a productive friendship that influenced the work of both. On this complicated relationship of influence, see Rowan Williams, *Dostoevsky: Language, Faith, and Fiction* (Waco, TX: Baylor University Press, 2008), especially 209–10, which is somewhat skeptical of Soloviev's influence on Dostoevsky. According to Marina Kostalevsky, although there is much textual evidence of Soloviev in Dostoevsky's great novel *The Brothers Karamazov*, "the nature of their affinity for each other cannot be grasped simply by studying the text of Dostoevsky's last novel; it has to be viewed within the context of the entire legacy of both writers and the historical and philosophical ambience of the times." *Dostoevsky and Soloviev: The Art of Integral Vision* (New Haven, CT: Yale University Press, 1997), 2. Like Soloviev, Dostoevsky was deeply influenced by German Romantic aesthetics through the mediation of his teacher I. I. Davydov. The influence of Schelling and Schiller on Dostoevsky is documented in the literature: see Kenneth Lantz, "Aesthetics," in *The Dostoevsky Encyclopedia* (Santa Barbara, CA: Greenwood, 2004); Joseph Frank, *Dostoevsky: A Writer in His Time* (Princeton, NJ: Princeton University Press, 2009), esp. 35; Heinrich Stammler, "Dostoevsky's Aesthetics and Schelling's Philosophy of Art," *Comparative Literature* 7, no. 4 (1955): 313–23; and Donna Tussing Orwin, *Consequences of Consciousness: Turgenev, Dostoevsky, and Tolstoy* (Palo Alto, CA: Stanford University Press, 2007), esp. 51. For Dostoevsky on icons, see Sophie Ollivier, "Icons in Dostoevsky's Works," in *Dostoevsky and the Christian Tradition*, ed. George Pattison and Diane Oenning Thompson (Cambridge: Cambridge University Press, 2001), 51–68. For a programmatic rather than novelistic treatment of aesthetic themes in Dostoevsky, see "Mr. ---bov and the Question of Art," in *Dostoevsky's Occasional Writings*, ed. and trans. David Magarshack (Evanston, IL: Northwestern University Press, 1963), 86–137. For Balthasar's explicit linking of Dostoevsky and Soloviev, see *GL*, 3:294–96. For Balthasar's recurrence to his treatment of Dostoevsky in the second volume of *Apokalypse der deutschen Seele*, see *GL*,

7:72–74. For a nice treatment of Dostoevskian aesthetics in the context of the literary phenomenon of the "holy fool," see *GL*, 5:188–201.

3. Schelling's influence is neither total nor exclusive. Soloviev's aesthetic theory bears the imprint of a diverse cloud of witnesses, including both Platonic and German Idealism, as well as Neoplatonism, Aristotle, Aquinas, Darwin, and Dostoevsky. See Vladimir Wozniuk's introduction to Vladimir Soloviev, *The Heart of Reality: Essays on Beauty, Love, and Ethics*, ed. and trans. Vladimir Wozniuk (Notre Dame, IN: University of Notre Dame Press, 2003), xi, xiii, xiv. Nor is Hegel absent (cf. Balthasar, *GL*, 3:283–84). Christopher Bamford's foreword to Bulgakov's *Sophia: The Wisdom of God* also associates Paracelsus, Böhme, Johann Georg Gichtel, John Pordage, Jane Leade, Gottfried Arnold, Emmanuel Swedenborg, and Franz von Baader, as well as Valentinus, in Soloviev's intellectual genealogy. See Sergei Bulgakov, *Sophia: The Wisdom of God*, trans. Christopher Bamford (New York: Lindisfarne Press, 1993). Also see Paul M. Allen, *Vladimir Soloviev: Russian Mystic* (Blauvelt, NY: Steiner Books, 1978), 50–51, for a similar list.

4. Balthasar, *GL*, 1:506.

5. Rainer Maria Rilke, "Archaic Torso of Apollo": "We did not know his legendary head, / in which the eyeballs ripened. But / his torso still glows like a candelabrum / in which his gaze, only turned low, / holds and gleams. Else could not the curve / of the breast blind you, nor in the slight turn / of the loins could a smile be running / to that middle, which carried procreation. / Else would this stone be standing maimed and short / under the shoulders' translucent plunge / nor flimmering like the fell of beasts of prey / nor breaking out of all its contours / like a star: for there is no place / that does not see you. You must change your life." *Translations from the Poetry of Rainer Maria Rilke*, trans. M. D. Herter Norton (New York: W.W. Norton & Company, 1938), 180–81.

6. Balthasar, *GL*, 1:68.

7. Helpful here is Oleg Bychkov's working definition of aesthetics in *Aesthetic Revelation: Reading Ancient and Medieval Texts after Hans Urs von Balthasar* (Washington, DC: Catholic University of America Press, 2010) as "transcendental sensibility," which he outlines as "something that involves the senses or analogies with the senses, but at the same time has an 'elevating' or 'advancing' function of going beyond the senses or even human cognitive powers. Aesthetic experience thus understood is (1) sensing, or making us aware of, some hidden principles of reality and therefore (2) orienting us toward higher spiritual, intellectual, or moral goals" (324). However, "not all sensory (*aisthetic*) experiences are revelatory and not all revelatory experiences are sensory (*aisthetic*)" (326). This dual sense of the scope of the field helps not only to narrow the designation *aesthetics* by restricting it to that which is revelatory (and not just surface-level sensual pleasure) but also make sense of

what may seem at first blush to be inconsistencies in the ancient philosophical aesthetic tradition. For instance, Plato, for whom beauty is so central, banishes "artists" or "poets" from the ideal *polis*; on this, see Bychkov *Aesthetic Revelation*, 169–74, suggesting the possibility that "artists" here ought to be taken as "craftsmen" only, producing art that does not contribute toward or point beyond *to kalon*, thus failing the second criteria for authentic aesthetic experience.

8. Balthasar, *GL*, 1:10. Cf. *GL*, 4:407–8.

9. Balthasar, *TD*, 2:422.

10. Balthasar, *GL*, 5:567.

11. See Emil L. Fackenheim, "Schelling in 1800–1801: Art as Revelation," in *The God Within: Kant, Schelling, and Historicity*, ed. John Burbidge (Toronto: University of Toronto Press, 1996), 50–74; Terry Pinkard, *German Philosophy 1760–1860: The Legacy of Idealism* (Cambridge: Cambridge University Press, 2002); David Simpson, ed., *German Aesthetic and Literary Criticism: Kant, Fichte, Schelling, Schopenhauer, Hegel* (Cambridge: Cambridge University Press, 1984); Thomas O'Meara, "Schelling's Religious Aesthetics," in *Reform and Counterreform: Dialectics of the Word in Western Christianity since Luther*, ed. John C. Hawley (Berlin: Mouton de Gruyter, 1994), 119–38; John Shannon Hendrix, *Aesthetics and the Philosophy of Spirit: From Plotinus to Schelling and Hegel* (New York: Peter Lang, 2005); and Kai Hammermeister, *The German Aesthetic Tradition* (Cambridge: Cambridge University Press, 200), 2, 62–86.

12. F. W. J. Schelling, *System of Transcendental Idealism*, trans. Peter Heath (Charlottesville: University Press of Virginia, 1978), 219–36.

13. For a more detailed analysis of each of Schelling's aesthetic works in sequence, see Hendrix, *Aesthetics and the Philosophy of Spirit*, 36–121. Also see van Erp, *Art of Theology*, 201–15.

14. According to Balthasar, "what Kant takes in with his philosophical mother's milk, he passes on to the generation of Schiller and Fichte, Hegel and Schelling, whose views of the world culminate always in a form of aestheticism in one way or another, in a radiant, eschatological 'world of spirits'" (*GL*, 5:482). Although Kant's successors (with Schelling as first among equals) do not add anything substantial to Kantian aesthetics, there are some modifications, particularly that Schelling carries on neither the polarity between beautiful and sublime nor the strong link between aesthetics and ethics; see Bychkov, *Aesthetic Revelation*, 27n31. Both Kant and Schelling, while departing from Baumgarten's notion of aesthetics as a specifically rational faculty, nevertheless consider it to be a "quasi-cognitive domain"; see Michael G. Vater, "Schelling, Friedrich Wilhelm Joseph von (1775–1854)," in *Encyclopedia of Aesthetics*, ed. Michael Kelly (Oxford: Oxford University Press, 1998), 220–24. Kant, particularly in the *Critique of Judgment* (1790), is less interested in

the work of art as such than in an appeal to the aesthetic faculty to ensure the unity of pure reason and practical reason and facilitate mediation between sense and cognition; see Hammermeister, *German Aesthetic Tradition*, 21.

15. See Bychkov, *Aesthetic Revelation*, 29; Bychkov indicates that for Balthasar, Schelling "can support a theological aesthetics no better than the systems of other 'monists' such as Hegel" (29n36).

16. Copleston, *History of Philosophy*, 7:99.

17. Balthasar, *GL*, 5:565; italics added.

18. Schelling and (officially) Hegel, *Fernere Darstellungen*, *Werke*, 4:362, quoted in Frederick C. Beiser, *German Idealism: The Struggle against Subjectivism, 1781–1801* (Cambridge, MA: Harvard University Press, 2002), 580. Schelling is not the first or only philosopher to invoke "intellectual intuition" (against Kant) for undergirding metaphysical systems and capacitating philosophy as a discipline. Fichte, Hegel, Hölderlin, Novalis, and Friedrich Schlegel also appeal to this faculty: although they may preserve the terminology of *intellektuelle Anschauung*, it is understood quite differently. For a reliable account of intellectual intuition in Fichte, who developed the concept first in his *Eigene Meditationen über Elementarphilosophie*, see Beiser, *German Idealism*, 294–301; in Hölderlin, 392–97; in Novalis, 413; in Schelling, 580–84; in Schlegel, 451–52, 457. Cf. Schelling, *System of Transcendental Idealism*, 72–82. Schelling eventually abandoned the language of "intellectual intuition" but retained the sense that intuition is a more sophisticated mode of thought than discursive reason. It is especially significant to note Soloviev's appeal to *intellektuelle Anschauung* as "the primordial form of true knowledge, a form that is clearly distinguished from sense perception and experience, as well as from rational, or abstract thinking" (Soloviev, "Lecture Five," *Lectures on Divine Humanity*, 60). It is no less significant that he appeals in this context to the process of artistic creation and to the superiority of artistic forms, which "necessarily requires an inner union of perfect individuality with complete generality or universality" (62).

19. Schelling, *System of Transcendental Idealism*, §3, 10.

20. Ibid., 11; italics original.

21. Ibid.

22. Ibid., 12; italics original. Cf. 67: "This *third* activity, *at once* both ideal and real, is undoubtedly this producing activity inferred in section I, wherein activity and passivity were to be reciprocally conditioned by each other."

23. Ibid.

24. Ibid. For a similar passage, cf. 231: "It is self-evident that art is at once the only true and eternal organ and document of philosophy, which ever and again continues to speak to us of what philosophy cannot depict in external form, namely the unconscious element in acting and producing, and its original identity with the conscious."

25. See Schelling, *System of Transcendental Idealism*: "An intuition must therefore be exhibitable in the intelligence itself, whereby in *one and the same* appearance the self is at once conscious and unconscious *for itself*, and it is by means of such an intuition that we first bring forth the intelligence, as it were, entirely out of itself; by such an intuition, therefore, that we also first resolve the entire [the supreme] problem of transcendental philosophy (that of explaining the congruence between subjective and objective)" (217–18).

26. Hendrix, *Aesthetics and the Philosophy of Spirit*, 44. The passage Hendrix quotes here is from Schelling's *Bruno*, 328.

27. Ibid., 52, 74. The potencies are addressed further in chapter 3.

28. Schelling, *Philosophy of Art*, §16. Also see Hendrix, *Aesthetics and the Philosophy of Spirit*, 56.

29. Schelling, *Philosophy of Art*, §11.

30. Ibid., §22.

31. Schelling, *System of Transcendental Idealism*, §2, 225.

32. "For art this opposition is an infinite one in regard to *every single object*, and infinity is exhibited in every one of its products. For if aesthetic production proceeds from freedom, and if it is precisely for freedom that this opposition of conscious and unconscious activities is an absolute one, there is properly speaking but one absolute work of art, which may indeed exist in altogether different versions, yet is still only one, even though it should not yet exist in its most ultimate form. . . . Nothing is a work of art which does not exhibit an infinite, either directly, or at least by reflection" (Schelling, *System of Transcendental Idealism*, 231).

33. Hendrix, *Aesthetics and the Philosophy of Spirit*, 56.

34. Schelling, *Philosophy of Art*, §18; cf. §63.

35. Schelling, *System of Transcendental Idealism*, 225.

36. Ibid., 231.

37. Ibid., 221; italics added.

38. Berdyaev, *The Beginning and the End*, 9.

39. Ibid., 96.

40. Ibid., 58–59.

41. Ibid., 12.

42. Nicolas Berdyaev, *Dream and Reality: An Essay in Autobiography*, trans. Katharine Lampert (New York: Collier Books, 1962), 209.

43. Nicolas Berdyaev, *The Meaning of the Creative Act*, trans. Donald A. Lowrie (New York: Collier Books, 1962), 219–20.

44. See Berdyaev, *The Beginning and the End*, 181; cf. *Meaning of the Creative Act*, 209–32.

45. Berdyaev, *Meaning of the Creative Act*, 209.

46. Berdyaev, *The Beginning and the End*, 174–75. See also Berdyaev, *Dream and Reality*, 210.

47. Ibid., 96.

48. Balthasar, *GL*, 3:299.

49. Vladimir Soloviev, *The Philosophical Principles of Integral Knowledge* (Grand Rapids, MI: William B. Eerdman's Publishing Company, 2008), 34. Cf. Balthasar, *GL*, 3:342.

50. Soloviev, "Beauty in Nature," *Heart of Reality: Essays on Beauty, Love, and Ethics* (Notre Dame, IN: University of Notre Dame Press, 2003), 32.

51. Ibid., 38; italics original.

52. Ibid., 39.

53. Ibid; italics original.

54. Ibid.

55. Ibid., 31–32.

56. Ibid., 36. See Hendrix, *Aesthetics and the Philosophy of Spirit*, 82–92, for Schelling on light as "the essence of the absolute . . . the source of the in-difference of the real and ideal in the real" (82), especially as demonstrated in chiaroscuro in painting (with Correggio as the obvious master, particularly *Holy Night (Adoration of the Shepherds)*. It would be an interesting exercise to investigate convergences of Schelling and Soloviev with the aesthetic/optic theory of Robert Grosseteste.

57. Ibid., 37. See also Soloviev, "Beauty in Nature," *Heart of Reality*, 44.

58. Ibid., 36; italics original.

59. Soloviev, "The Universal Meaning of Art," *Heart of Reality*, 73.

60. Ibid., 73–74. Soloviev goes on to explain that it is this feature which distances his own aesthetic theory—in which essence exceeds the discrete phenomena and gives rise to ever greater actualizations of essence—from Hegelian aesthetics. Balthasar affirms Soloviev's distance from Hegel (and lauds his thinking as on the "same level" as Hegel's, *GL*, 3:281) insofar as Hegel's ("Protestant") negative dialectic is replaced with the "catholic '*integration*' of all partial points of view and forms of actualization into an organic totality that annuls and uplifts (*aufhebt*) all things in a manner that preserves that which is transcended far more successfully than in Hegel." Balthasar, *GL*, 3:283–84.

61. See, for instance, Edith Clowes's analysis of certain of Soloviev's poems, which on her reading suggest that the material world is something to be escaped, more so than his essays indicate; Edith W. Clowes, "The Limits of Discourse: Soloviev's Language of *Syzygy* and the Project of Thinking Total-Unity," *Slavic Review* 55, no. 3 (Autumn 1996): 566.

62. Soloviev, "Beauty in Nature," *Heart of Reality*, 66.

63. Soloviev, "The Universal Meaning of Art," *Heart of Reality*, 68, 75.

64. Ibid., 68.

65. On this point, see Hendrix's analysis of the *Bruno*, *Aesthetics and the Philosophy of Spirit*, 39.

66. Soloviev, "The Universal Meaning of Art," *Heart of Reality*, 75.

67. For Balthasar on the coincidence of aesthetics and eschatology in Soloviev, see *GL*, 3:284, 296, 341. For this notion in Bulgakov, see "Religion and Art," in *The Church of God: An Anglo-Russian Symposium*, ed. E. L. Mascall (London: Society for Promoting Christian Knowledge, 1934), esp.178.

68. Balthasar, *GL*, 5:528.

69. Balthasar, *GL*, 3:283. This evocation of eroticism and its relationship to the aesthetic in both Balthasar and the Russians is a theme worth exploring elsewhere. Consider, for instance, parallels between Balthasar's appeal to marriage as a form which makes real the ideal (*GL*, 1:27) and Soloviev's essay "The Meaning of Love" (also *GL*, 3:347–49). Further, Balthasar references Soloviev (along with Pierre Teilhard de Chardin, for whom Soloviev functions as a corrective; see *GL*, 3:290, 296) as a theologian who exemplifies the movement from chaos to eros to cosmos (*GL*, 5:254–55n23). On the limits of Platonic eros for Soloviev, see Balthasar, *GL*, 3:286. On the coincidence of eros and agape in Soloviev, see Balthasar, *GL*, 3:345, and *TD*, 4:114. See also Balthasar, "Eros: The Glory of Melancholy," *GL*, 5:264–84, and the discussion of the aesthetic meaning of metaphysical eros in *GL*, 5:608–10, as well as eros as the first fundamental energy of historical forces in *TD*, 4:106–7. For the notion of creative activity as the result of erotic longing, see Bulgakov, both *The Comforter* and excerpts from *The Unfading Light*. For instance, "*Methexis*, the participation of matter in ideal form, is also *eros*, the desire of 'earth' for 'heaven'. The ideal form or entelechy is at once both a datum, the 'root' of being, so to speak, and a project, a reaching forward towards the limits of realization. It is a painful struggle, the individual thing seeking its own ideal and eternal essence, a self-creation and self-generation. The soul goes in search of itself, like the Shulamite [in the Song of Songs] wandering through the streets of the city in search of her beloved" (*Unfading Light*, 137). Also consult Bulgakov's "The Meaning of Bodily Existence," *Unfading Light*, 141–46; and his exploration of erotic love in *Comforter*, 321–41.

70. Balthasar, "Improvisation on Spirit and Future," *Explorations in Theology*, vol. 3, *Creator Spirit* (San Francisco: Ignatius Press, 1993), 136.

71. "Beautiful reality, or this realized beauty, constitutes only a very insignificant and feeble part of all our far-from-beautiful reality. In human life artistic beauty is only a symbol of a better hope, a momentary rainbow against the dark background of our chaotic experience." Soloviev, "Beauty in Nature," *Heart of Reality*, 30.

72. Ibid., 76; italics original.

73. Wozniuk, introduction to Soloviev, *The Heart of Reality*, xiii; he also refers to the formative influence of Aquinas on Soloviev on xi, xiv, and xv.

74. Soloviev, "Beauty in Nature," *Heart of Reality*, 29.

75. Soloviev, "A First Step towards a Positive Aesthetic," *Heart of Reality*, 13.

76. Soloviev, "Three Addresses in Memory of Dostoevsky," *Heart of Reality*, 16. For the coincidence of the transcendentals in Soloviev, also see "Beauty in Nature," *Heart of Reality*, 39–40, and "The Universal Meaning of Art," *Heart of Reality*, where he writes that "beauty is only an embodiment in sensory forms of the same ideal content that, up until the time of such an embodiment, is called truth and the good" (68).

77. Bychkov, *Aesthetic Revelation*, 328.

78. Ibid. On the quality of *dukhovnost'* in Russian literature, see David Bethea, "Literature," in *The Cambridge Companion to Modern Russian Culture*, ed. Nicholas Rzhevsky (Cambridge: Cambridge University Press, 1998), 161–204.

79. Balthasar's *GL* 5 attends to the specifically classical experience of glory, whereas treatment of biblical *doxa* is reserved for volume 6 (Hans Urs von Balthasar, *The Glory of the Lord: A Theological Aesthetics*, vol. 6, *Theology: The Old Covenant*, ed. John Riches, trans. Erasmo Leiva-Merikakis [San Francisco: Ignatius Press, 1991]) through volume 7.

80. Balthasar, foreword to *GL*, 1:9. Cf. *GL*, 1:117.

81. See Balthasar's important essay "The Theological *Apriori* of the Philosophy of Beauty," *GL*, 4:317–412, in which he treats such figures as Boethius, Cassiodorus, Benedict, Gregory the Great, John Erigena, the Victorines (Hugh and Richard), the School of Chartres (Alan de Lille, Gilbert de la Porrée, Robert Grosseteste), Francis of Assisi, Alexander de Hales, Albert, Ulrich of Strasbourg, Mechtild of Magdeburg, and, finally Thomas Aquinas. Bonaventure is extremely important for Balthasar. Interestingly, Balthasar notes also that Grosseteste's reflections on optics and light as "self-begetting" prefigure the line of Schelling, Soloviev, and Teilhard (*GL*, 4:369). For more on Grosseteste's notion of light as a creative potency, and for similarities on this front with Bonaventure, see Umberto Eco, *The Aesthetics of Thomas Aquinas*, trans. Hugh Bredin (Cambridge, MA: Harvard University Press, 1988), 108–11.

82. Balthasar, *GL*, 4:317.

83. Ibid., 318, 320. Balthasar elaborates on three fundamental themes of the classical world that cross the threshold almost without alteration into the Christian vocabulary: (1) the pattern of *egressus-regressus* of creatures from God and back to God, which appears, for instance, in Origen, Aquinas, and the Johannine literature; (2) the eros of the finite entity for the infinite, transcendent divine (recurring, for example, in Gregory of Nyssa's *epektasis*, in Augustine's unquiet heart of the *Confessions*, in Bernard, William of St. Thierry, Richard of St. Victor, and more broadly in Dante, Petrarch, Marsilio Ficino, and Michelangelo; and (3) the phenomenon of the beauty of the spiritual soul, which culminates in an eschatological wedding (a concept originating in Plato and Plotinus, and continuing in the Song of Songs) (*GL*, 4:321–24).

84. Balthasar, *GL*, 5:12. Balthasar also lauds Aquinas for establishing God over being (and thus contravening pantheism), "secur[ing] at the same time for the concept of glory a place in metaphysics" (*GL*, 4:375). For Thomas, the primary aesthetic conception is one of proportionality between comparative relations: "all order in the cosmos . . . is at once immanent and transcendent" (*GL*, 4:409).

85. Balthasar, *GL*, 5:13. As noted in chapter 1, in this respect Eckhart—despite his best intentions and own deeply religious commitments—functions for Balthasar as the gatekeeper for Idealism. Its legacy includes "Luther, but also Nicholas of Cusa, Spinoza, Böhme, Kant, Fichte, Schelling, and Hegel" (*GL*, 5:30; cf. 45.). For a lengthier treatment of Eckhart, see the section "Being as God," *GL*, 5:29–47.

86. Ibid., 46.

87. Mark C. Taylor, *Hiding* (Chicago, IL: University of Chicago Press, 1997), 11. For Balthasar's profile of the aesthete who dispenses with the depth of meaning for the play of images alone, see Balthasar, *TL*, 1:143–45.

88. Balthasar, *GL*, 4:19; cf. *GL*, 1:22.

89. See, for instance, Balthasar, "Revelation and the Beautiful," *Explorations in Theology*, 1:96; *GL*, 1:18; *GL*, 4:35; and *GL*, 5:598–99, 609. The question of how Balthasar diagnoses when and how aesthetics became a ghettoized, autonomous discipline (and hence unsuitable for theology) is not unimportant. Balthasar asserts that this view is fully formed in Schopenhauer (and later in Nietzsche) "after early moves in this direction by Schiller, Schelling, Goethe, and by early German and classical English Romanticism" (*GL*, 1:50). Insofar as Schleiermacher, Schelling, Hegel and Schopenhauer, and others of their sort uncoupled beauty from the true and the good is the extent to which the "perilous" door is opened for "the beginning of an 'estheticization' of the beautiful" (Balthasar, "Revelation and the Beautiful," *Explorations in Theology*, 1:95–96). Bychkov, however, asserts that for Kant, Schelling, and others, aesthetics was *always* considered in the service of something else, even if only for reasons of practicality, logistics, or convenience. For Bychkov, even Kant does not actually advocate the notion of aesthetics as purely autonomous and "disinterested" even though he uses that language, which Bychkov suggests ought to be interpreted as "in the sense of having no immediate practical interest" since Kant himself "assigns to it an important role of 'linking up' all areas of human experience by providing a 'transcendental' insight into the nature of reality." Bychkov, *Aesthetic Revelation*, 324. See also 163–64n80.

90. Balthasar, *GL*, 5:598.

91. Ibid., 507. See also *TD*, 2:29–30.

92. Balthasar, *GL*, 4:38.

93. See Bulgakov, *Comforter*, 204–5; for the possibility of even the beauty of nature itself becoming, through the corrupt exercise of human freedom, a "coefficient" of evil, see 203. Also see *Unfading Light*, 275 and 484n89.

94. Balthasar, *GL*, 5:190.

95. Balthasar, *GL*, 4:19–20.

96. Balthasar, *GL*, 1:79–80; italics added.

97. Ibid.

98. Balthasar, *GL*, 4:323–24. Interestingly, Bychkov's analysis of antique and medieval aesthetic texts in dialogue with Balthasar indicates that "there is no gap . . . but an essential continuity between ancient and modern revelatory or 'transcendental' aesthetics. . . . Revelatory aesthetics can therefore be considered a fundamental feature of Western European thought" (323).

99. Bychkov notes this commitment elegantly, placing Balthasar in line with Gadamer and Heidegger, among others. *Aesthetic Revelation*, 51–77.

100. Balthasar, *TL*, 1:142.

101. Ibid., 118; cf. *GL*, 4:28–39.

102. Balthasar, foreword to *GL* 1.

103. For Balthasar on Bonaventure, see especially *GL*, 2:260–362. With respect to the question of medieval aesthetics, Eco, *Aesthetics of Thomas Aquinas*, is absolutely invaluable.

104. Balthasar, *GL*, 1:20.

105. Ibid.

106. Balthasar, *GL*, 1:21. See also Balthasar's "Revelation and the Beautiful": "The beauty inherent in things is susceptible of degrees from the lower to the higher, from the purely material and functional to the organic and sensible, and so from that of symmetry, proportion and harmony to that shown in vital tension and power, in the alternation of disclosure and concealment, in all the forms of interaction both inside and outside the erotic with its beguiling qualities" (*Explorations in Theology*, 1:105); see also *GL*, 1:444: "We ourselves are spirit in nature, and because all the expressive laws of the macrocosm are at work in ourselves," a phrasing that certainly evokes a Romantic (and Russian) ethos.

107. And, as shown in a subsequent section, Bulgakovian as well. For Bulgakov, human sensation is not at all antithetical to the spirit:

> On the contrary, it belongs to the spirit as one of the forms of its life, although one that does not exhaust this life. To deprive the spirit of sensation would be to disincarnate it, that is, to abolish man's very essence. . . . The spirit is not opposed to man's psychical and corporeal life; rather, it lives in the psychical and the corporeal, determining them and being determined by them. Matter melts, as it were, losing its inertia and impenetrability; it becomes transparent for the spirit and spirit-bearing . . . it is brought into the life of the spirit, which "conquers" nature. This, the life of the spirit slumbers in nature, and it must be awakened. (*Comforter*, 346)

Further, "at the very threshold of the creation of the world, there is manifested the express relation of the Holy Spirit to what is usually considered to be diametrically opposite to him—His relation to *matter*" (*Comforter*, 194).

108. Balthasar, *GL*, 1:172.

109. Ibid., 164–65, 172; *GL*, 2:27–28.

110. In a kind of reprisal of Schelling's *Naturphilosophie*, Bulgakov also draws attention to the synthesis of freedom and necessity, but his parsing of it is more economic than aesthetic. See Bulgakov, "Economy as a Synthesis of Freedom and Necessity," *Philosophy of Economy*, 196–222. For Soloviev's claim that "freedom is but one of the species of necessity," see "Lecture Two" of *Lectures on Divine Humanity*, especially 20–22.

111. Hans Urs von Balthasar, "Why I Am Still a Christian," in *Two Say Why: Why I Am Still a Christian*, by Hans Urs von Balthasar and Joseph Ratzinger, trans. John Griffiths (Chicago: Franciscan Herald Press, 1971), 20–21.

112. Balthasar, *GL*, 2:26–27; italics added. Cf. *GL*, 1:164.

113. Bychkov makes this point as well, suggesting in a footnote that "Schelling's phenomenological description of aesthetic experience is precisely that upon which theological aesthetics after the fashion of von Balthasar draws" (31n43). Later in the text Bychkov similarly comments that the phrasing of Balthasar's assertion in the section on Augustine that "only the one who loves the finite form as revelation of the infinite is both 'mystic' and 'aesthete'" (*GL*, 2:114) has the ring of nineteenth-century Romantic aesthetic theories (217).

114. Balthasar, *GL*, 1:431; see also 1:151: "Visible form not only 'points' to an invisible, unfathomable mystery; form is the apparition of this mystery, and reveals it while, naturally, at the same time protecting and veiling it. Both natural and artistic form has an exterior which appears and an interior depth, both of which, however, are not separable in the form itself. The content (*Gehalt*) does not lie behind the form (*Gestalt*), but within it."

115. Balthasar, *GL*, 5:548. For the *analogia entis* as the principle of creatureliness vis-à-vis God, see Balthasar, *TD*, 4:116. For a sophisticated and spirited defense of the *analogia entis*, see John Betz, "Beyond the Sublime: the Aesthetics of the Analogy of Being (Part One)," *Modern Theology* 21 (2005): 367–405; and "Beyond the Sublime: the Aesthetics of the Analogy of Being (Part Two)," *Modern Theology* 22 (2006): 1–50.

116. Or, in Betz's analysis, the preservation of both the beautiful and the sublime in a noncompetitive relation: "For it is analogy alone, I would argue, in the fullest sense of the word, that guarantees not only the determinate actuality of the creature (the beautiful), but a real infinite and a real transcendence (the sublime). Indeed, it turns out that analogy, rather than compromising difference, actually makes it possible; and that the sublime, rather than overturning the analogy of being, in fact demands it" (376).

117. Balthasar, *GL*, 5:453. See also Balthasar's explanation of the means by which aesthetics can be divorced from theology "by means of a 'dialectical system' which would conceive of God as exteriorizing himself in nothingness

and in that which is his opposite, a God who, therefore, contains his nothing-ness and his opposite within himself. Jakob Böhme, Schelling, and Hegel elaborated such a view (in a misuse of the mystical tradition)." Balthasar, *GL* 1:49.

118. Balthasar, *GL*, 1:168.

119. Ibid., 170.

120. Ibid., 549. See also "Aesthetics as Science," in *GL*, 5:597–610. For Balthasar, the philosophical premise for aesthetics to be understood strictly as a science is nihilism, where the beauty of the world is—in the manner of Nietzsche's radicalized aesthetics, a violent, totalizing despotism which is for him the *only* grounds for philosophizing—a deception for blind will to power. Arthur Schopenhauer, Richard Wagner, Eduard von Hartmann, Thomas Mann, Max Scheler, early Heidegger, and Sartre are implicated as well (*GL*, 5:598). Also cf. *GL*, 5:415.

121. Balthasar, *GL*, 5:557, 559–60.

122. Ibid., 209. Treatment of Balthasar's critiques of Schelling's phi-losophy of mythology is reserved for chapter 3. For a succinct analysis of the limitations of Schelling's philosophy of art for articulating a theological aes-thetics of glory, see Balthasar's essay on Schelling in *GL*, 5:557–72. For a solid treatment of this essay, which draws out Balthasar's employment of Nicholas of Cusa as a foil for Schelling, see van Erp, *Art of Theology*, especially chap-ter 7, "Friedrich Wilhelm Joseph Schelling: The Absolute in Art," 195–227.

123. See Balthasar's essay on Anselm in *GL*, 2:211–59.

124. Balthasar, *GL*, 2:227.

125. Balthasar, *GL*, 1:488.

126. Ibid., 417. Also see Balthasar, *GL*, 1:36–37:

> It appears impossible to deny that there exists an analogy between God's work of formation and the shaping forces of nature and of man as they generate and give birth. We can post as many question marks and warning signs as we will all along the length and breadth of this analogy, but they will only apply to the ever-present possibility of misusing the analogy, and not to its rightful use. Misuse of the analogy consists in simply sub-jugating and subordinating God's revelation with its own form, to the laws not only of metaphysics and of private, social, and sociological ethics but also of this-worldly aesthetics, instead of respecting the sovereignty which is manifested clearly enough in God's work.

127. Balthasar, *GL*, 1:117.

128. Nichols, *The Word Has Been Abroad*, vii.

129. Balthasar, *GL*, 3:281.

130. Ibid., 284; italics added.

131. Ibid., 285.

132. Balthasar, *GL*, 2:19.

133. Balthasar, *GL*, 3:287. Also see Balthasar's profile of Soloviev (along with Maximus, Nicholas of Cusa, and "in all essentials" Aquinas) as a theologian who considers God "the one who has found the culmination of his self-being in the other, in man, in Jesus Christ" (*GL*, 2:23). Finally, see Balthasar, *My Work*, in which it is clear that Soloviev represents a kind of continuation of Maximus's cosmic Christology (27).

134. Balthasar also comments on the constructive influence of Hegel's universalism, which would also help to contravene a kind of nationalistic Russian particularism: "Hegel's all-embracing intellectual structure in its systematic as well as its historical aspects has been of invaluable service to Eastern Christianity, a means for it to transcend its national limitations, leading it back to its true identity." Balthasar, *GL*, 3:282.

135. Vladimir Soloviev, "Maksim Ispovednik," *Entsiklopedichesko slovar Brockhaus-Efron X* (St. Petersburg: Brockhaus-Efron X, 1896), 598. Cf. Balthasar, *GL*, 3:288n19. Aidan Nichols speaks briefly to this in *The Word Has Been Abroad*, 115.

136. Balthasar, *Cosmic Liturgy*, 162–64.

137. Ibid., 207.

138. There are others, not least of whom are Denys and John Damascene.

139. See especially Balthasar, *GL*, 3:288n21. Also cf. Balthasar's "The Form of Revelation," *GL*, 1:435–62.

140. Balthasar, *GL*, 3:285.

141. Ibid., 291.

142. *Syzygy* here is an appropriation of a Gnostic concept. For a feminist perspective that is more linguistically inclined, see Clowes, "The Limits of Discourse," 552–66.

143. Balthasar, *GL*, 3:308.

144. Ibid., 307–8.

145. Ibid., 293.

146. Balthasar, *GL*, 5:120, in the context of his assessment of Pierre de Bérulle. Further, "The pantheistic *Tat tvam asi* ['This art thou'] . . . can be resolved only by virtue of the unity between God and man in the Son, who is both the *ars divina mundi* and the quintessence of actual creation . . . and by virtue of the Holy Spirit, who proceeds from this incarnate Son in his unity with the Father." Balthasar, *GL*, 1:195.

147. Balthasar, *GL*, 5:569.

148. Balthasar, *GL*, 1:432.

149. Balthasar, *GL*, 2:290; italics added.

150. Stammler, "Dostoevsky's Aesthetics," 317. He goes on to note that it is only with this Christological proviso (which Dostoevsky provides) that it is "possible for man to see nature in her innermost reality, not merely as a system of mathematically established relationships, but as transfigured by the

infusion of God's infinite ideality into reality, as Schelling had described it" (319). Balthasar recognizes that Schelling's late systems of mythology and revelation come much closer to affirming the historical quality of Christ, which is addressed in chapter 3.

151. Balthasar draws attention approvingly to the profound Christological commitment in Dostoevsky in *GL*, 5:190.

152. Balthasar, "Revelation and the Beautiful," *Explorations in Theology*, 1:117.

153. Ibid., 104.

154. See Balthasar, *GL*, 1:155. See also *GL*, 3:346: "Only in the resurrection of the body is the inwardly necessary goal of the world process achieved, the resurrection as the complete illumination of chaotic matter by the loving spirit; but only God can bring this to perfection."

155. Balthasar, *GL*, 1:18.

156. Mongrain, *Systematic Thought*, 61–62, 90.

157. Balthasar, *GL*, 1:90.

158. Ibid., 102–3.

159. Ibid., 103.

160. Ibid., 104. Matthias Scheeben, particularly in his distinction between nature and supernature, serves for Balthasar as the turning point from aesthetic theology to theological aesthetics (though he does not escape critique). Cf. *GL*, 1:105–10.

161. Mongrain, *Systematic Thought*, 62.

162. Berdyaev, *Dream and Reality*, 109. If pressed, however, Berdyaev characterizes his own philosophical approach as more Romantic than not. Berdyaev finds classicism wanting because its emphasis upon the possible perfection of finite form betrays "its characteristically anti-eschatological attitude" (210). He goes on to praise Romanticism, which he elsewhere in the same autobiographical volume criticizes, because it tends to fall victim "to illusions, falsehood, insincerity, to high-pitched and spectacular emotionalism, to aestheticism and to self-indulgence in the imaginary depths of life" (108), and for its "pervading sense of the insufficiency of all achievement within the finite, in its longing for an aspiration to the infinite, or, to be more precise, to the trans-finite" (210). Cf. Berdyaev, *The Beginning and the End*, 188–94.

163. See T. E. Hulme, "Romanticism and Classicism," in *Speculations: Essays on Humanism and the Philosophy of Art*, ed. Herbert Read (London: Routledge & Kegan Paul, 1924), 111–40, for a classic take on the differences between Classicism and Romanticism, in which Classicism is "absolutely identical with the normal religious attitude" (117), while Romanticism is likened to an upturned container of (overly emotive and very sticky) treacle: in his words, "spilt religion" (118). According to Hulme, Romanticism is concerned with the infinite and the human capacity for infinitude, but the classical

poet "never forgets this finiteness, this limit of man. He remembers always that he is mixed up with earth" (120). For a nice treatment of Hegel's distinctions between symbolic, classical, and romantic art forms (Hegel finds Romantic art superior to Classical), see Terry Pinkard, "Symbolic, Classical, and Romantic Art," in *Hegel and the Arts*, ed. Stephen Houlgate (Evanston, IL: Northwestern University Press, 2007), 3–28. Schelling, though he does distinguish between Classical and Romantic, ultimately "dissolve[s] the distinction into a single continuum, the growth toward the revelation of the absolute. . . . The ancient and the modern, Classical and Romantic art, participate in the same dialectic toward a synthesis as do the ideal and real, and universal and particular. Absolute beauty must be found in a synthesis of the two, one which has yet to be achieved." Hendrix, *Aesthetics and the Philosophy of Spirit*, 52.

164. Balthasar, *GL*, 1:118–19; italics added.

165. See, for instance, Balthasar, *Apokalypse der deutschen Seele*, 1:407–514; and *GL*, 5:339–416, especially 408–9. For a concise summation of the Goethe essay in *Apokalypse der deutschen Seele* 1, see Aidan Nichols, *Scattering the Seed. A Guide through Balthasar's Early Writings on Philosophy and the Arts* (Washington, DC: Catholic University of America Press, 2006), 98–108. For secondary sources that treat the relationship between Balthasar and Goethe, see Ulrich Simon, "Balthasar on Goethe," in *The Analogy of Beauty: The Theology of Hans Urs von Balthasar*, ed. John Riches (Edinburgh: T & T Clark, 1986), 60–76; Edward T. Oakes, *Pattern of Redemption: The Theology of Hans Urs von Balthasar* (New York: Continuum, 1994), 72–101, especially 94–98; and David C. Schindler, *Hans Urs von Balthasar and the Dramatic Structure of Truth: A Philosophical Investigation* (New York: Fordham University Press, 2004), esp. 12–14, 168–76, 247.

166. Balthasar, *Apokalypse der deutschen Seele*, 1:407.

167. Balthasar, *GL*, 1:65. The revisiting of classicism could have only been a successful rehabilitation, according to Balthasar, "if antiquity had been understood as an Advent-like openness looking to Christianity, not as a comprehensive ('cosmic-religious') form in which Christianity was embedded as a potentiality." Balthasar, *GL*, 5:451. See also *GL*, 1:514.

168. Balthasar, *GL*, 5:249. Similarly, Balthasar notes that "classicism provided the images, while idealist Romanticism—the real creator of modern aesthetics—constructed the theory. However, once Marx and Tchernischevsky (1855) have left behind Hegel's philosophy and aesthetics, once God and the spiritual have been banished from the universe and its laws, the only choice left is between materialistic and atheistic aesthetics." Balthasar, *GL*, 5:189.

169. Ibid., 189.

170. Ibid., 205.

171. Ibid., 141.

172. Ibid., 152–204.

173. Ibid., 143.

174. Ibid., 81.

175. Georges de Schrijver, *Le merveilleux accord de l'homme et de Dieu: Etude de l'analogie de l'être chez Hans Urs von Balthasar* (Leuven: Leuven University Press, 1983), 79, quoted in Nichols, *Scattering the Seed*, 37.

176. Van Erp, *Art of Theology*, 56.

177. Balthasar, *GL*, 1:124.

178. Balthasar, *GL*, 5:648.

179. Balthasar, *GL*, 1:460. For Balthasar on the notion of the beautiful and the ugly as in a complementary relation, see "Revelation and the Beautiful," *Explorations in Theology*, 1:105; *GL*, 4:28–29; and *GL*, 5:647–48. Cf. Mongrain, *Systematic Thought*, 66–67.

180. Balthasar, *GL*, 5:204.

181. Ibid., 53.

182. For more on Bulgakov's aesthetics, see "The Unfading Light," in Sergei Bulgakov, *Sergii Bulgakov: Towards a Russian Political Theology*, trans. Rowan Williams (London: T&T Clark, 1999), 133–61. See Patrick Sherry, *Spirit and Beauty: An Introduction to Theological Aesthetics* (London: SCM, 2002), which puts Balthasar and Bulgakov in a larger dialogue vis-à-vis aesthetics and the Holy Spirit that begins with patristic forebears Irenaeus, Clement of Alexandria, and Augustine.

183. Bulgakov, *Comforter*, 177–218; Balthasar, *TL*, 1:165–218.

184. Also see Balthasar, *TL*, 3:53 on the development of a "Catholic Spirit Christology" and a linking of Schelling and the Russians, citing Louis Bouyer, *Le Consolateur: Esprit Saint et Vie de grace*:

> Two themes emerge: the first is a kind of transposition into theological terms of Schelling's later philosophy concerning mythology and revelation and of certain of his Russian followers (Soloviev, Bulgakov). According to him, in world history and salvation history we discern the operation of Irenaeus' "two hands of God the Father"—Logos and Spirit—an operation that is common to them, yet distinct in each case, and that is moving toward a point of convergence. The pagans had "intimations of the Spirit" in myth, poetry, and inspiration, which constituted a confused and obscure premonition of the Logos; in the Old Testament this mythology is clarified and becomes genuine prophecy in the Spirit of wisdom, in which the divine Word comes close and exercises its purification, right up to the point where both of them meet in the Virgin Mary, who, as the highest flowering of the Spirit's wisdom, is ready to receive into herself the Word who is drawing near. (Balthasar, *TL*, 3:53; cf. 60)

185. Bulgakov, *Comforter*, 233–43. He writes, "All that is creative in human life is accomplished by natural inspiration, which is sophianic by its essence. And all great creators have in their sophianicity this creative force

238 Notes to Pages 73–75

from the Spirit, for the very capacity for inspiration is already a sophianic spirituality, and there is simply no other source of creative life" (243). Also see *Comforter*, 341. For more on human creativity and the sophianic principle in Sergei Bulgakov, particularly with an apocalyptic cast, see *Sophia: The Wisdom of God*, 141–43.

186. Ibid., 201. It is not unimportant here that Bulgakov supplements his point by quoting a line of Schiller's poetry, demonstrating an affinity for the Romantics shared with both Balthasar and Soloviev.

187. Balthasar, *GL*, 5:218.

188. Balthasar, *TL*, 3:203.

189. Cf. Balthasar, "Revelation and the Beautiful," *Explorations in Theology*, 1:126.

190. Bulgakov, *Comforter*, 182. See also "The Meaning of Bodily Existence," *Unfading Light*, 141–46.

191. Ibid., 343. In another context of addressing the Spirit's pervasive presence in the material world, Bulgakov admits without embarrassment to panentheism, what he terms "a pantheism, but an entirely pious one" (*Comforter*, 199). Cf. Sergei Bulgakov, *The Bride of the Lamb*, trans. Boris Jakim (Grand Rapids, MI: Eerdmans, 2002), 44. Compare this to Balthasar's provocative early statement in "Katholische Religion und Kunst," *Schweizeriche Rundschau* 27 (1927): 44–54, that "aesthetic panentheism" is fully capable of being brought into the Catholic fold. Cf. Balthasar, "There have been numerous attempts to recognize, in this One that sustains the Many, the final, all-embracing reality. . . . We should not be too quick to dismiss these attempts at 'pantheism.' In the end all these expressions are only the different facets of an ultimate drive on the part of world being in its thought process (*des denkenden Weltseins*), unable to envisage any higher goal than the unity of its origin— which by no means implies that the whole movement of coming forth and return (*egressus-regressus*) has been meaningless and nugatory." Balthasar, *TL*, 3:434–35.

192. Bulgakov, *Comforter*, 202.

193. Ibid.

194. Bulgakov, *Comforter*, 343–44. Also see Bulgakov, "The Meaning of Bodily Existence," *Unfading Light*, 141–46, and "The Destiny of the Body," *Unfading Light*, 146–49.

195. Sergei Bulgakov, *The Holy Grail and the Eucharist*, trans. Boris Jakim (Hudson, NY: Lindisfarne Books, 1997), 44–45; italics original.

196. Bulgakov, *Comforter*, 344–45. Also see Sergei Bulgakov, *Die Tragödie der Philosophie* (Darmstadt: Reichl, 1928).

197. Bulgakov, *Comforter*, 346–47. Cf. *The Holy Grail and the Eucharist*, 131–32.

198. Bulgakov, *Comforter*, 346.

199. Sergei Bulgakov, "Art and 'Theurgy,'" *Unfading Light*, 153–54. Cf. Bulgakov's essay "The Destiny of Creation": "Beauty, as the unceasing force that strives within every being towards the realization of its own *logos*, its eternal life, is the inner law of the world, the force that forms the world, the demiurge of the cosmos. It holds the world in being, uniting both its static and its dynamic elements; and in the fullness of time its victory will be accomplished, and it will indeed 'save the world'" (*Unfading Light*, 140). Also see Bulgakov, "Religion and Art," in *The Church of God*, ed. E. L. Mascall, 191. See also Soloviev, "Beauty in Nature," *Heart of Reality*, 29–30, for a statement on beauty's transformative power to improve actual reality.

200. Soloviev, *Philosophical Principles*, 52–53.

201. Bulgakov, "Art and Theurgy," *Unfading Light*, 155. Cf. *Unfading Light*, 382–404.

202. Berdyaev, *The Beginning and the End*, 192.

203. Ibid.

204. Ibid., 193. Cf. 252.

205. Bulgakov, "Art and Theurgy," *Unfading Light*, 156.

206. Ibid., 157.

207. Balthasar, *GL*, 1:23.

208. Ibid., 22–23.

209. This position is argued forcefully in Balthasar's essay "Revelation and the Beautiful," *Explorations in Theology*, 1:95–126. For Balthasar, Charles Péguy is the poet able to reconcile aesthetics and ethics most successfully. See Balthasar's lengthy essay on Péguy in *GL*, 3:400–517. Also see a more popular-level treatment of Péguy's role in theological aesthetics and Christology in general in Jennifer Newsome Martin, "Our Neighbor and Our God: Christology in an Aesthetic and Poetic Register," *Church Life: A Journal for the New Evangelization* 2, no. 1 (Winter 2013): 35–46.

210. Balthasar, *GL*, 1:23; cf. 34, 466. Cf. *TD*, 2:30–31.

211. Balthasar, *TD*, 2:31.

212. Balthasar, *GL*, 1:481–82.

213. Balthasar, *TD*, 2:31.

214. Ibid.

CHAPTER 3. "Du Dunkelheit, aus der ich stamme"

1. See David, "Influence of Jacob Boehme," which attempts to highlight potentially neglected sources in Soloviev's intellectual formation. Though David's claim that Soloviev relies *chiefly* upon Western mystical and theosophical sources (Böhme, Swedenborg, Paracelsus), which were then translated to intellectual currents of pre–World War I Silver Age Russia, is a bit of

an overstatement, the article helpfully traces the means of Böhme's transmission in Russia and provides an overview of his fundamental teachings. David also downplays Schelling's influence as primary for Soloviev (60). For the influence of Böhme on post-Kantian Idealism, see Kurt Leese, *Von Jacob Boehme zu Schelling* (Erfurt: K. Stenger, 1927). See also Paola Mayer, *Jena Romanticism and Its Appropriation of Jakob Böhme: Theosophy, Hagiography, Literature* (Montreal: McGill-Queen's University Press, 1999). For a more general account, see Ernst Benz, *The Mystical Sources of German Romantic Philosophy*, trans. Blair R. Reynolds and Eunice M. Paul (Eugene, OR: Pickwick Publications, 1983). For Böhme himself, the classic source is Alexandre Koyré, *La philosophie de Jacob Boehme* (Paris: Vrin, 1929).

2. See O'Meara, *Romantic Idealism and Roman Catholicism.*

3. Here the relevance of this chapter's epigraph from Rilke's poem, "Du Dunkelheit, aus der ich stamme," from *The Book of Hours*, emerges: "You, darkness, of whom I am born— / I love you more than the flame / that limits the world / to the circle it illumines / and excludes all the rest. / But the dark embraces everything: shapes and shadows, creatures and me / people, nations—just as they are. / It lets me imagine / a great presence stirring beside me. / I believe in the night." *Rilke's Book of Hours: Love Poems to God*, trans. Anita Barrows and Joanna Macy (New York: Riverhead, 2005), 57.

4. For instance, see Hans Urs von Balthasar, *Apokalypse der deutschen Seele: Studien zu einer Lehre von letzten Haltungen*, vol. 3, *Vergöttlichung des Todes* (Einsiedeln: Johannes Verlag, 1939), 425–34, where Balthasar invokes the Böhme–Silesius–Schelling line with respect to Berdyaev.

5. Balthasar, *Cosmic Liturgy*, 153.

6. Hans Urs von Balthasar, *A Theology of History*, 2d. ed. (San Francisco: Ignatius Press, 1963), 9–11.

7. This theme absolutely dominates the thought of Schelling. He identifies the "riddle of the world" (das Räthsel der Welt) as this question: "How is the Absolute able to come out of itself and posit a world opposite itself?" F. W. J. Schelling, *Philosophische Briefe über Dogmatismus und Kriticismus* (Philosophical Letters on Dogmatism and Criticism, 1795), in *Friedrich Wilhelm Joseph von Schellings Sämmtliche Werke*, ed. K. F. A. Schelling, 10 vols. (Stuttgart: J. G. Cotta, 1856–1861), 1856ff., 1:310.

8. Balthasar, *TD*, 2:41.

9. Ibid., 63.

10. Balthasar, *Cosmic Liturgy*, 161.

11. See Edward Allen Beach, *The Potencies of God(s): Schelling's Philosophy of Mythology* (Albany: State University of New York Press, 1994), 62.

12. See Bulgakov, *Lamb of God*, 97, 120, 134; *Comforter*, 44, 59, 361, 392; and especially *Unfading Light*, 170–79, 186, 190.

13. For a nice study of the evolution of Schelling's thought, see Dale E. Snow, *Schelling and the End of Idealism* (Albany: State University of New York Press, 1996).

14. Note that *The Ages of the World (Weltalter)* is fragmentary and in several scattered drafts, so all that is treated with any depth is the past. I consulted both the second and the third drafts of this text. For a translation of the second 1813 draft, see F. W. J. von Schelling, *The Abyss of Freedom/Ages of the World*, trans. Judith Norman (Ann Arbor: University of Michigan Press, 1997). For a translation of the (handwritten) third 1815 draft, see F. W. J. Schelling, *The Ages of the World (Fragment), from the Handwritten Remains (c. 1815)*, trans. Jason M. Wirth (Albany: State University of New York Press, 2000). Also see D. C. Schindler, *The Perfection of Freedom: Schiller, Schelling, and Hegel between the Ancients and the Moderns* (Veritas) (Eugene, OR: Wipf and Stock, 2012).

15. Despite the rather spurious claims of Harald Holz, whose *Spekulation und Faktizität, Zum Freiheitsbegriff des mittleren und späten Schelling* (Bonn: Bouvier, 1970) attempts to contravene the far more widely held view that Schelling was indeed in Böhme's debt, the parallels in their respective philosophical theories as well as Schelling's own claims cannot be ignored. For treatment of Böhme's influence on Schelling, see James Gutmann's introduction to Schelling's *Philosophical Inquiries into the Nature of Human Freedom* (La Salle, IL: Open Court, 1936), xliv–lii, which provides a sense of Schelling's high valuation of Böhme's contributions—especially vis-à-vis St. Martin—as original, dynamic, even "a miracle in the history of humanity and especially in the history of the German mind" (xlvii). Also see Beach, "Three Formative Influences on Schelling: Böhme, Baader, and Hegel," in *Potencies of God(s)*, 69–91; and Brown, *Later Philosophy of Schelling*. Also useful, especially with respect to identifying the various positions scholars have taken regarding Schelling's debts to Böhme, the complex relation between Schelling and Neoplatonism, and the nature of evil, is Paola Mayer, "Idealism, Human Freedom and the Problem of Evil: F. W. J. Schelling," *Jena Romanticism*, 179–221. Berdyaev also speaks briefly to the convergences between Böhme and Schelling, especially in the latter's *Philosophical Inquiries into the Nature of Human Freedom*, although according to Berdyaev, Schelling "does not always understand Boehme exactly" (Nicholas Berdyaev, "Unground and Freedom," introduction to *Six Theosophic Points and Other Writings*, by Jacob Boehme, trans. John Earle [Ann Arbor: University of Michigan Press, 1958], xxvii.) This is not to exclude other sources, however, as Platonic and Neoplatonic sources are also in the mix for Schelling. His work on the *Timaeus* is especially notable, especially with respect to Plato's theory of the relation of chaotic matter to God. See F. W. J. Schelling, "Timaeus" (1794), ed. Hartmut Buchner (Stuttgart-Bad Cannstatt: Frommann-Holzboog, 1994). See also Werner Beierwaltes,

"Plato's *Timaeus* in German Idealism: Schelling and Windischmann," in *Plato's* Timaeus *as Cultural Icon*, ed. Gretchen J. Reydams-Schils (Notre Dame, IN: University of Notre Dame Press, 2003), 267–89. Plato is also extremely important for Soloviev, who in 1898 wrote a long essay called *The Life Drama of Plato*. See Tatjana Kochetkova, "Vladimir Solov'jov's Theory of Divine Humanity" (Ph.D. diss., University of Nijmegen, 2001), as well as *The Search for Authentic Spirituality in Modern Russian Philosophy: The Perdurance of Solov'ev's Ideal* (Lewiston, NY: Edwin Mellen Press, 2007) by the same author. For the influence of Platonic and Neoplatonic sources on Soloviev, also see Soloviev, *Divine Sophia*, 39–48.

16. "In the non-natural, uncreaturely Godhead (*Gottheit*) there is nothing more than a single will, which is also called the One God, who wants nothing else except to find and grasp himself, to go out of himself, and by means of this outgoing to bring himself into visibility (*Beschaulichkeit*). This *Beschaulichkeit* is to be understood as comprising the threefold character of the Godhead, as well as the mirror of his wisdom and the eye by which he sees." Jakob Böhme, *On the Election to Grace*, vol. 4 of *The Works*, Law ed., paragraphs 10–13, pp. 155–56, quoted in Beach, *Potencies of God(s)*, 71. Also see Beach, *Potencies of God(s)*, 37, 72, 133, 267n15, and 277n58.

17. F. W. J. Schelling, *Historical-Critical Introduction to the Philosophy of Mythology*, trans. Mason Richey and Markus Zisselsberger (Albany: State University of New York Press, 2007).

18. Schelling, *Sämmtliche Werke* (1859), 1:177, quoted in James Gutmann's introduction to Schelling, *Philosophical Inquiries*, xxxiv.

19. See Berdyaev, *Meaning of History*.

20. Balthasar, *TD*, 2:37.

21. Ibid., 38.

22. Ibid.

23. For Berdyaev's comments on Böhme on evil, see "Unground and Freedom," x–xi.

24. See F. Schlegel, *Über die Sprache und Weisheit der Indier: Ein Beitrag zur Begründung der Altertumskunde* (Heidelberg, 1808). Indeed, Schelling's own growing uneasiness was that absolute systems could not account for genuine freedom and the unpredictability of the human personality. Berdyaev makes this point as well with reference to Schelling's *Philosophy of Revelation*. See Berdyaev, "Unground and Freedom," xxvii.

25. Schelling, *Philosophical Inquires*, 26. Balthasar problematizes this definition of freedom in "Infinite and Finite Freedom," *TD*, 2:189–334. Also see *TD*, 4:150, in his discussion of Blondel and de Lubac.

26. Schelling, *Philosophical Inquires*, 26.

27. Ibid., 28. Dualism, for Schelling, is "a system of self-destruction and the despair of reason" (ibid.).

28. Balthasar, *GL*, 4:78–84.

29. Plato, *Timaeus*, 33. For Balthasar on Plato, see *GL*, 4:284ff.

30. H. B. de Groot, "The *Ouroboros* and the Romantic Poets: A Renaissance Emblem in Blake, Coleridge, and Shelley," *English Studies* (Amsterdam) 50 (1969): 553–64.

31. Beach, *Potencies of God(s)*, 72–73; also see Mayer, *Jena Romanticism*, 200ff.

32. Quoted without citation in Berdyaev, "Unground and Freedom," xxvi–xxvii.

33. Whether this movement into the sense world ought actually to be understood as upward or downward—that is, victorious ascent or cosmic fall—may be debatable. The conventional reading of Schelling here is that the sense world is the product of a movement *away* from God, and that the exercise of freedom is tragic and antagonistic. Berdyaev certainly accepts this view, making the finite world the result of a cosmic fall. For the sense world as result of a primordial fall, see Schelling, *Philosophy and Religion*, trans. Klaus Ottman (Putnam, CT: Spring Publications, 2010), 26, 46. See also Mayer, *Jena Romanticism*, 192, 194; and Fackenheim, *God Within*, 98, who more conventionally reads the originary act of freedom as a cosmic fall. Žižek suggests, however, that this negative figuration is inadequate. He challenges the more standard interpretation that for Schelling the emergence of time was a "Fall"; rather, it ought to be understood as a "triumphant ascent, the act of decision/ differentiation by means of which the Absolute resolves the agonizing rotary motion of drives and breaks out of its vicious circle into temporal succession" (*The Abyss of Freedom*, 30).

34. Schelling, *Philosophical Inquiries*, 32.

35. Ibid., 34. Cf. Berdyaev, "Unground and Freedom," xix–xxi. The language of a contentless will clearly has its roots in Böhme.

36. Schelling, *Philosophical Inquiries*, 35.

37. Schelling likens it to the "surging billowing sea" of Platonic matter: *Philosophical Inquiries*, 35.

38. Ibid., 50. For a similar passage, see 54.

39. Ibid., 34.

40. From the third draft of the *Weltalter* (1815), with respect to the potencies: "There is neither a veritable higher nor a veritable lower, since in turn one is the higher and the other is the lower. There is only an unremitting wheel, a rotary movement that never comes to a standstill and in which there is no differentiation. Even the concept of the beginning, as well as the concept of the end, again sublimates itself in this circulation" (*Ages of the World [Fragment]*, 76). As shown in chapter 5, in the *Weltalter* the binary principles of negation and affirmation are plotted along rotary lines as contraction and expansion, and their reconciliation.

244 Notes to Pages 87–88

41. Berdyaev in particular sounds the theme of theodicy as a, if not *the* fundamental task of Christian theology. For instance, in his efforts to address the theodicy problem in "The Origin of Good and Evil," Berdyaev appeals explicitly to Böhmian philosophy, asserting, "Out of the Divine Nothing, the *Gottheit* or the *Ungrund*, the Holy Trinity, God the Creator is born. The creation of the world by God the Creator is a secondary act. . . . Freedom is not determined by God; it is part of the nothing out of which God created the world" (and, notably, out of which God arises as well). Nicolas Berdyaev, *The Destiny of Man* [1931], trans. N. Duddington (New York: Harper & Row, 1960), 25. Also see Berdyaev, *The Beginning and the End*, 151.

42. See Jacob H. Friesenhahn, *The Trinity and Theodicy: The Trinitarian Theology of von Balthasar and the Problem of Evil* (Burlington, VT: Ashgate, 2011). Balthasar's eccentric interpretation of Christ's descent into hell, discussed in subsequent chapters, helps alleviate the problem of theodicy, as it is indicative of the radical lengths to which God will go in response to the human abuses of the gift of freedom; cf. Aidan Nichols's introduction to Balthasar, *Mysterium Paschale: The Mystery of Easter*, trans. Aidan Nichols, O.P. (San Francisco: Ignatius Press, 1990), 7.

43. Berdyaev, "Unground and Freedom," v. See also Berdyaev, *The Beginning and the End*, 110, where he suggests that Böhme's evocative use of symbol and myth provides unique access to truth not available to discursive reason. As O'Regan has suggested, however, the profile of Böhme as unlettered aboriginal thinker is more a "Romantic fiction" than not; see Cyril O'Regan, *Gnostic Apocalypse: Jacob Boehme's Haunted Narrative* (Albany: State University of New York Press, 2002), 4. For an example of Schelling's preference for unschooled divine intuition over more sophisticated but highly rational modes of discourse, see his defense of the so-called *Schwärmer* against Fichte's critiques in the 1806 "Exposition of the True Relationship of the Philosophy of Nature to the Improved Fichtean Doctrine." It is notable, however, as Mayer points out in *Jena Romanticism*, that Schelling marshals this defense on behalf not of Böhme but rather of Kepler and Leibniz (195).

44. Berdyaev, "Unground and Freedom," xiii.

45. Berdyaev distinguishes Böhme's recommendation of a theogonic process from Fichte and Hegel in that Böhme "did not mean . . . that God is born within a temporal process, but that God's interior and eternal life manifests itself under the form of a dynamic process, of tragedy within eternity, of battle against the darkness of nonbeing" ("Unground and Freedom," xviii). Berdyaev's essay "Unground and Freedom" also tends to conflate the concept of the Unground with that of divine nature; for Böhme the Unground is actually prior to the generation of nature (the three powers). For a subtle and learned presentation of the theogonic narrative of Böhme, see O'Regan, *Gnostic Apocalypse*. Also note that Kant was not beyond reproach for Berdyaev,

who objected to Kant's emphasis on universal law over the individual personality (see *Destiny of Man*, 81) as well as the sense that the universal law was
always socialized and thus implicated fatally in the fallen world, the "realm of
the herd-man, *das Man*" (92–93).

46. Berdyaev, *The Beginning and the End*, 105.

47. See, for instance, Berdyaev, "Unground and Freedom," where Berdyaev lauds Böhme for being "the first man in the history of human thought
to recognize that the foundations of being, prior to being, are unfathomable
freedom" (xx). See *The Beginning and the End*, 105–17, for Berdyaev's explicit
affirmations of Böhme. Also see Berdyaev, *The Fate of Man in the Modern
World* [1935], trans. Donald A. Lowrie (San Rafael, CA: Semantron Press,
2009), where he describes the *Ungrund* as "the pure potentiality of being, the
negative ground essential for the realization of the novel, creative aspects of
existence" (132).

48. Berdyaev asserts that becoming depends upon nonbeing, writing in
The Beginning and the End that "if we concede being only, there will be no
becoming or development of any sort" (161). Elsewhere in this text he approvingly reports that for Schelling, God is not being but dynamic life (97).
Further, his eschatological metaphysics is meant to destabilize traditional
ontological categories (99). He also explicitly affirms freedom as the most
fundamental category of reality (for example, see *Fate of Man*, 136–37). Cf.
Berdyaev, "Unground and Freedom," xiv.

49. Berdyaev, *Meaning of History*, 43.

50. Berdyaev, *The Beginning and the End*, 114, 166, 206–207. See also
Nicholas Berdyaev, *Slavery and Freedom*, trans. R. M. French (London:
G. Bles, 1947), 257–65.

51. Berdyaev, *The Beginning and the End*, 115.

52. Schelling, *Philosophy and Religion*, 6:38, 1804. This is an odd text,
written in response to K. A. Eschenmayer's *Die Philosophie in ihrem Über-
gang zur Nichtphilosophie*. It was hastily written and understood even by
Schelling to be a transitional work between his so-called negative and positive
philosophies (Snow, *Schelling and the End of Idealism*, 188). The "positive
philosophy" emerges from the doctrine of God as the primal origin of the
universe in the potencies, proceeds through the philosophy of mythology, and
culminates in his philosophy of revelation. Balthasar too writes that, especially
vis-à-vis the *Bruno, Philosophy and Religion* "breathes a totally new atmosphere." Hans Urs von Balthasar, *Theo-Drama: Theological Dramatic Theory*,
vol. 1, *Prolegomena*, trans. Graham Harrison (San Francisco: Ignatius Press,
1988), 570. The theme of the fall becomes important again for Schelling in the
Weltalter in terms of articulating his somewhat esoteric metaphysics of time
and eternity.

53. See Balthasar, *GL*, 3:310–11.

54. Berdyaev, *The Beginning and the End*, 214.

55. Ibid., 59.

56. Balthasar, *TD*, 4:118. Also see *TD*, 1:570.

57. Bulgakov, *Unfading Light*, 275. Bulgakov's heavily gendered theology consciously resists, to some degree, such theories of primal androgyny because they do not lend enough credence to sexual difference. See Martin, "The 'Whence' and the 'Whither' of Balthasar's Gendered Theology."

58. Soloviev, "Lecture Nine," *Lectures on Divine Humanity*, 126.

59. Ibid., 125.

60. Soloviev, "Lecture Ten," *Lectures on Divine Humanity*, 136.

61. Balthasar, *GL*, 3:318.

62. O'Regan, *Anatomy of Misremembering*, 310–14.

63. Schelling, *Philosophy and Religion*, 44–45.

64. On the relation between the fall, history, and myth, Fackenheim says, "Man's existence after the fall is determined by his contradictory relation to God. His divine descent makes him an incomplete and therefore a god-seeking being. But by reason of the fall he cannot find God. This contradictory existence is mythological existence. Man has fallen under the domination of the cosmic powers which are not God but which he, as a god-seeking being, perforce deifies. This mythological existence is the universal fate of fallen man. If it remains unrelieved and unaltered, then man has no more a history than the rest of fallen creation" (*God Within*, 104).

65. See, for instance, Berdyaev, *The Beginning and the End*, 251–52.

66. See Balthasar, *GL*, 3:352.

67. Schelling, *Philosophical Inquiries*, 84.

68. Ibid.

69. Ibid.

70. Ibid., 55.

71. Ibid., 56–57.

72. For Balthasar's critical recapitulation of the middle Schelling, with accents on Schelling's anthropology, which emerges in the main in the freedom essay, *Clara*, and the *Stuttgart Lectures*, see *TD*, 1:566–77.

73. Schelling, *Philosophical Inquires*, 39. See also 58.

74. Fackenheim, *God Within*, 98.

75. Schelling, *Philosophical Inquiries*, 41.

76. Ibid., 45. Cf. Beach, *Potencies of God(s)*, 79–82; and Fackenheim, *God Within*, 96–99.

77. Schelling, *Philosophical Inquiries*, 41.

78. Ibid., 42.

79. Here Schelling cites von Baader's "On the Assertion that there can be no bad use of Reason," in the *Morgenblatt*, 1807, no. 197; and *Concerning Solids and Liquids*, in *Annals of Medicine as Science* 3, no. 2.

80. Cf. Schelling, *Philosophical Inquiries*, 42–43n1, 53n1.

81. Ibid., 42.

82. Schelling, *Philosophical Inquiries*, 66–67. As discussed below, Schelling's understanding of freedom as self-determination evolves and deepens in the *Weltalter*, particularly in relation to conceptions of time and eternity as "proto-temporal." See Beach, *Potencies of God(s)*, 64–65. For a brief introduction to the associations of von Baader and Schelling, see O'Meara, *Romantic Idealism and Roman Catholicism*, especially 79–84.

83. Schelling, *Philosophical Inquiries*, 60.

84. Ibid., 62. Cf. 70.

85. Ibid., 63–65. This conception of freedom as pretemporal self-determination implies a rather esoteric metaphysics of time and eternity, of fundamental concern in his *Weltalter*, which brings the resources of the freedom essay to bear upon the question of time and history.

86. Ibid., 67. Cf. John Laughland, "The Metaphysics of Evil," *Schelling versus Hegel: From German Idealism to Christian Metaphysics* (Burlington, VT: Ashgate Publishing, 2007), 61–91; and Slavoj Žižek, "Selfhood as Such Is Spirit: F. W. J. Schelling on the Origins of Evil," in *Radical Evil*, ed. Joan Copjec (London: Verso, 1996), 1–29. See also David A. Roberts, "An Historical Introduction: Kant and Schelling on Radical Evil," chapter 1 of *Kierkegaard's Analysis of Radical Evil* (London: Continuum, 2006), 1–22.

87. Balthasar, *TD*, 1:574. See also *TD*, 2:40–41.

88. Balthasar, *TD*, 2:423.

89. Schelling, *Philosophical Inquiries*, 58.

90. Balthasar, *TD*, 2:40. Here Balthasar particularly names Hegel, Marx, and Teilhard, but Schelling is not far away.

91. Balthasar, *TD*, 4:139. For more on the giftedness of the self, see *TD*, 2:285–91.

92. Balthsaar, *TD*, 1:181–84, 192.

93. Soloviev, author's preface to *War, Progress, and the End of History: Three Conversations, including a Short Story of the Anti-Christ* (Hudson, NY: Lindisfarne Books, 1990), 15.

94. Soloviev, *War, Progress, and the End of History*, 20.

95. Ibid., 147–48; italics original.

96. See Soloviev, "Beauty in Nature," *Heart of Reality*, 58; see also 37–38. It is likewise significant that these warring principles are delineated along the axes of light and life and their opposite, "the unrestrained manifestation of the chaotic principle, defeating or repressing again the ideal form, naturally produc[ing] an acute impression of ugliness" (37). Moreover, the primal chaotic principle is necessary for natural manifestations of beauty: for instance, "the aesthetic value of phenomena such as a stormy sea depends namely on the fact that beneath them stirs chaos" (45).

97. Soloviev, "Three Addresses in Memory of Dostoevsky," *Heart of Reality*, 21. The third address, originally delivered in February 19, 1883, was published first in *Rus'*, no. 6 (1883).

98. Soloviev, "Lecture Nine," *Lectures on Divine Humanity*, 123.

99. Ibid., 126. Compare with Bulgakov, *Unfading Light*, 187–88 and 266–70.

100. For Berdyaev on the Grand Inquisitor legend, see Berdyaev, *Dostoievsky*, trans. Donald Attwater (New York: Sheed & Ward, 1934).

101. Berdyaev, *The Beginning and the End*, 142. Bulgakov will disagree. See "The Nature of Evil," *Unfading Light*, 266–73, which argues for the metaphysical nothingness/nonbeing of evil.

102. Berdyaev, *The Beginning and the End*, 143; cf. 144, where he appeals to Böhme directly.

103. Ibid., 110. Also see his essay "Unground and Freedom," in which he praises Böhme for his "particularly sharp and strong feeling for the evil in the life of the world . . . [seeing] everywhere a pitched battle between contrary principles, between light and darkness" (ix).

104. Balthasar, *TD*, 4:149.

105. Aidan Nichols provides an excellent summary of the *Theo-Drama* in *No Bloodless Myth: A Guide through Balthasar's Dramatics* (Washington, DC: Catholic University of America Press, 2000). Also see Ed Block Jr., "Hans Urs von Balthasar's *Theo-Drama*: A Contribution to Dramatic Criticism," in *Glory, Grace, and Culture: The Work of Hans Urs von Balthasar*, ed. Ed Block Jr. (New York: Paulist Press, 2005), 175–98.

106. Balthasar, *TD*, 2:31.

107. Ibid., 189.

108. Balthasar, "Revelation and the Beautiful," *Explorations in Theology*, 1:106.

109. Balthasar, *TD*, 1:260.

110. Rilke, *Duino Elegies*, quoted by Balthasar in "Revelation and the Beautiful," *Explorations in Theology*, 1:106.

111. Balthasar, *TD*, 2:192.

112. Ibid., 190.

113. Ibid., 201.

114. Ibid., 194.

115. Ibid.

116. Ibid., 196.

117. Ibid., 195.

118. Ibid., 49.

119. Ibid., 203–206.

120. Ibid., 209.

121. Ibid., 211.

122. Ibid., 210; italics original.

123. Ibid., 211.

124. Ibid., 216–27. Here Balthasar's emphasis on providence as divine pedagogy demonstrates his Irenaean profile in terms of content, which Mongrain has drawn to the fore. Balthasar likewise appeals to the theme of the operation of finite freedom in the context of providence in Origen and in Gregory of Nyssa (217).

125. Ibid., 228.

126. Ibid., 229.

127. Ibid., 230.

128. Ibid., 254.

129. Maximus the Confessor, *Ambigua*, PG 91, 1220 A, quoted in Balthasar, *Cosmic Liturgy*, 155.

130. Balthasar, *TD*, 1:48.

131. Ibid., 49. Cf. "Man without Measure ('Post-Christian')," *TD*, 2:417–29.

132. Balthasar, *TD*, 1:48–49; italics original.

133. For Balthasar's negative evaluation of Berdyaev, see *Apokalypse der deutschen Seele* 3:424–30. O'Regan has neatly drawn out the associations of Böhme and Berdyaev in *Anatomy of Misremembering*, helpfully enumerating a quadrant of fundamental overlap including (1) the theogonic process, which is "predicated on an excess of potentiality in the divine over actuality," (2) a principle of origin prior to immanent and economic Trinity, about which (3) it is not clear that it can be understood as tri-personal. Finally, (4) the function of Sophia as a fourth is mediatory between God and world (607n15). For more on this pairing of Böhme and Berdyaev, see also 313, 340, 600n75, and 601n77.

134. See Balthasar, *TD*, 2:419–20.

135. Ibid., 420.

136. Ibid., 419.

137. Žižek is not impressed, as he thinks the late Schelling is overdetermined and too rationalistic: see *Abyss of Freedom*, 36–37.

138. Beach indicates that though the young Schelling of the essay "Über Mythen, historische Sagen und Philosopheme der ältesten Welt" (1793) had allowed for the possibility of myths originating as hyperbolic, allegorical, and idealized descriptions of the lives and deeds of cultural heroes, as well as naïve attempts to explain natural phenomena in symbolic terms, by the time he systematically treated the status of myth in *Philosophy of Revelation* he had effectively reversed his position on both fronts. See Beach, "Schelling's Earlier Treatment of Mythology," *Potencies of God(s)*, 30–34.

139. Beach, *Potencies of God(s)*, 95.

140. Ibid., 35.

141. Ibid., 5.

142. Here and in what follows immediately I rely heavily upon Beach's account of Schelling's *Potenzenlehre*, especially *Potencies of God(s)*, 116–46.

143. For Bulgakov's analysis of negativity, which appeals to this Greek distinction between *ou* and *me*, see *Unfading Light*, 188–92 and 460n119. He is critical of Böhme in this context.

144. Beach, *Potencies of God(s)*, 121.

145. Ibid., 123.

146. Ibid., 131–36.

147. Ibid., 212. Also see Paul Valliere, "Solov'ev and Schelling's Philosophy of Revelation," in *Vladimir Solov'ev: Reconciler and Polemicist*, ed. Will van den Bercken, Manon de Courten, and Evert van der Zweerde (Leuven: Peeters, 2000); Valliere explains that "mythological religion is the product of the second potency while still in the shadow of the first; it is the religion of irrational nature struggling for liberation" (122).

148. For this, but with particular attention to the activity of the second potency, see Paul Tillich, *The Construction of the History of Religion in Schelling's Positive Philosophy: Its Presuppositions and Principles*, trans. Victor Nuovo (Lewisburg, PA: Bucknell University Press, 1974). Also see Thomas F. O'Meara, "'Christianity is the Future of Paganism': Schelling's Philosophy of Religion, 1826–1854," in *Meaning, Truth, and God*, ed. Leroy S. Rouner (Notre Dame, IN: University of Notre Dame Press, 1982), 216–35.

149. Beach, *Potencies of God(s)*, 242. Also see Valliere, "Solov'ev and Schelling's Philosophy of Revelation," 122.

150. Particularly unusual in Schelling's account is his claim that the passion of Christ actually begins long before his incarnation, as the ec-statically posited second potency. Balthasar is none too friendly to this suggestion. See Beach, *Potencies of God(s)*, 242.

151. Balthasar, *GL*, 1:145. See also "Revelation and the Beautiful," *Explorations in Theology*, 1:109.

152. Balthasar, *GL*, 1:156, 502.

153. Ibid., 501. Balthasar makes a similar point in *Theological Anthropology* with respect to the *spolia Aegyptiorum*, noting that "the adoption and Christianization of pagan wisdom cannot be a profanation of divine wisdom, but only the harvesting of what belonged originally to the true Logos and could be understood only from it and the bringing of it back home" (161).

154. Balthasar, *GL*, 1:502.

155. Hans Urs von Balthasar, *Theo-Logic: Theological Logical Theory*, vol. 2, *Truth of God*, trans. Adrian J. Walker (San Francisco: Ignatius Press, 2004), 257, 261.

156. Balthasar, *GL*, 4:32.

157. Balthasar, *TD*, 1:566–67.

158. Balthasar, *TL*, 2:259.

159. Schelling, *Sämmtliche Werke* 2, 3.195, quoted in Fackenheim, 106.

160. Balthasar, *TL*, 2:260.

161. Ibid.

162. As Xavier Tilliette has remarked, "One cannot help thinking that the preexisting subject—'neither God nor man'—has been invented in order to produce an ingenious connection between pagan fantasy and Christianity" (*Schelling: Une Philosophie en devenir*, 2 vols [Paris: Vrin, 1970], 2:467–68), quoted by Balthasar in *TL*, 2:261.

163. Balthasar, *TL*, 2:261.

164. Balthasar, *GL*, 4:301n354. Here is a gesture toward Schelling's influence by Neoplatonism.

165. Ibid., 36.

166. Balthasar, *Theological Anthropology*, 53.

167. Ibid., 66.

168. Balthasar, *GL*, 5:153. See also Balthasar's suggestion that "the drama of Christ is the recapitulation and the end of Greek tragedy" (*TD*, 2:49).

169. Balthasar, *TD*, 2:62.

170. Bulgakov, *Unfading Light*, 63–79.

171. Ibid., 65, 77.

172. Ibid., 70.

173. Ibid.

174. Berdyaev, *Meaning of History*, 78.

175. Ibid., 78–81.

176. Berdyaev, *The Beginning and the End*, 176.

177. Berdyaev, *Meaning of History*, 50.

178. Ibid., 31.

179. Hans Urs von Balthasar, *The Grain of Wheat: Aphorisms* (San Francisco: Ignatius Press, 1995), 106.

180. See Maxime Herman, *Vie et oeuvre de Vladimir Soloviev* (Freibourg: Editions Universitaires, 1995), 24, which identifies in this early work all the major themes that will develop over the course of Soloviev's career, including in the positing of a singular religious principle that operates as a basis for human history. Also see Jonathan Sutton, *The Religious Philosophy of Vladimir Solovyov: Towards a Reassessment* (New York: St. Martin's Press, 1988), esp. 102–5. See also Valliere, "Solov'ev and Schelling's Philosophy of Revelation," 123.

181. Balthasar, *GL*, 3:297.

182. For Soloviev on progressive religious development, see *Lectures on Divine Humanity* 1–6, as well as "Lecture Ten," which traces out three epochs—the astral, the solar, and the tellurian (145)—and follows through early pagan myths to the revelation of Jesus Christ. Also see Valliere, "Solov'ev and Schelling's Philosophy of Revelation." Valliere also identifies the adoption

of the Schellingian triad in Soloviev's philosophy of history articulated in *Russia and the Universal Church*, in which the process of "universal history" is construed as the threefold "perfect woman, or divinized nature, the perfect man or the God-man, and the perfect society of God with human beings—the definitive incarnation of divine Wisdom." Vladimir Soloviev, *La Russie et l'Eglise Universelle*, 4th ed. (Paris: Librairie Stock, 1922), 259; quoted in Valliere, "Solov'ev and Schelling's Philosophy of Revelation," 123. This particular text of Soloviev's is formed (though perhaps not deformed) in some respects by the cosmogonic speculation of Böhme and Schelling, as well as Platonic notions about the World-Soul, which functions to connect real and ideal as the "body" of Sophia. It was published in French initially, in 1889, as *La Russie et l' église universelle*, for fear of censorship, and translated to Russian in 1911, after his death. For an excellent treatment of Soloviev's adoption of Schellingian language of the potencies to elaborate his own Christologically specified doctrine of Godmanhood, see Brandon Gallaher, "The Christological Focus of Vladimir Solov'ev's Sophiology," 617–46. Also see Frederick Copleston, *Philosophy in Russia: From Herzen to Lenin and Berdyaev* (Notre Dame, IN: University of Notre Dame Press, 1986), 223–24.

183. Soloviev, "Lecture Six," *Lectures on Divine Humanity*, 77.

184. Ibid.; italics original.

185. Ibid., 78. Also see "Lecture Four," 45–46.

186. Soloviev, "Lecture Four," *Lectures on Divine Humanity*, 53.

187. But, maddeningly, hardly ever citing. While Soloviev distances himself from the early Schelling, he does explicitly recognize in *Svet nevečernij* (1917) affinities with Schelling's positive philosophy (Valliere, "Solov'ev and Schelling's Philosophy of Revelation," 120).

188. Soloviev, "Lecture Six," *Lectures on Divine Humanity*, 79.

189. Ibid., 83.

190. Soloviev, *Polnoe sobranie sochinenii i pisem v dvadtsati tomakh* (Moscow: Nauka, 2000–2001), 2:355, quoted in Soloviev, *Divine Sophia*, 82. For the influence of Schelling on Soloviev, see Valliere, "Solov'ev and Schelling's Philosophy of Revelation," 119–29. See also Manon de Courten, *History, Sophia and the Russian Nation: A Reassessment of Solov'ev's View of History and His Social Commitment* (Bern: Peter Lang, 2004), 258–66.

191. Balthasar, *Cosmic Liturgy*, 57.

192. Soloviev, *Russia and the Universal Church*, 168.

193. Ibid., 169.

194. Soloviev, "Lecture Nine," *Lectures on Divine Humanity*, 129, 130.

195. Gallaher, "The Christological Focus of Vladimir Solov'ev's Sophiology," 627. Also see Michael Aksionov Meerson, *The Trinity of Love in Modern Russian Theology: The Love Paradigm and the Retrieval of Medieval Love Mysticism in Modern Russian Trinitarian Thought (from Solovyov to Bulgakov)* (Quincy, IL: Franciscan Press, 1998), 21–47.

196. Balthasar, *GL*, 3:292.

197. Balthasar's positive assessment of Soloviev is affirmed by Gallaher, who comments on the skill by which Soloviev is able to transfigure his sources. As he suggests in "The Christological Focus of Vladimir Solov'ev's Sophiology," "Unlike Hegel and Schelling, where Christ as the God-Man is either not intrinsic to the system (Hegel) or Christ as wholly God is completely denied (Schelling), in the case of Solov'ev, his system is founded principally on the notion of Godmanhood. Solov'ev, furthermore, is quite different from Boehme precisely because his system acknowledges the Chalcedonian definition as the matrix in which private metaphysical illumination must be interpreted and not vice-versa" (638).

198. Discussed in chapter 5. For Balthasar on Soloviev's Christology as essentially kenotic, see *GL*, 3:322–25.

199. Balthasar, *GL*, 3:305.

200. Ibid., 322.

201. Soloviev, "Lecture Six," *Lectures on Divine Humanity*, 76.

202. Balthasar, *GL*, 3:291.

203. Balthasar, *TD*, 5:52; cf. 53ff.

204. Soloviev, "Lecture Six," *Lectures on Divine Humanity*, 57–56.

205. Ibid., 75. Cf. Balthasar, *GL*, 3:322.

CHAPTER 4. "Grün wirklicher Grüne, wirklicher Sonnenschein, wirklicher Wald"

1. Nicolas Berdyaev, *The Russian Idea* (New York: Lindisfarne Press, 1992), 208.

2. Balthasar, "Some Points of Eschatology," *Explorations in Theology*, 1:258.

3. Bulgakov, *Bride of the Lamb*, 379.

4. Balthasar, *TD*, 4:110.

5. Balthasar, *Apokalypse der deutschen Seele*, 1:205.

6. Ibid., 206.

7. With respect to Schelling, Balthasar writes, "Man ist versucht, an jenen Henoch der altjüdischen apokryphen Apokalypsen zu denken, der den Gipfel des Weltgebäudes erstiegen hat und von ihm aus die Mysterien der ewigen Ankunft Gottes schaut und verkündet" (*Apokalypse der deutschen Seele*, 1:206).

8. Balthasar, *GL*, 4:324; italics added. Cf. Balthasar, *GL*, 4:321–24, 342–43; *Theology of History*, 135, 145–48; and *TD*, 4:427; *TD*, 3:37; *TD*, 2:88, and *TD*, 1:156–57.

9. Balthasar, *GL*, 6:330; cf. 331–38.

10. See Cyril O'Regan, *Theology and the Spaces of Apocalyptic* (Milwaukee, WI: Marquette University Press, 2009), 136n14.

11. Hans Urs von Balthasar, "The Descent into Hell," *Explorations in Theology*, vol. 4, *Spirit and Institution*, trans. Edward T. Oakes, S.J. (San Francisco: Ignatius Press, 1995), 401.

12. Cf. Balthasar, 'Some Points of Eschatology," *Explorations in Theology*, 1:259–60n4, which quotes Yves Congar approvingly.

13. Balthasar, *TD*, 5:13. Consider a similar statement of Bulgakov's, that postmortem existence "remains transcendent and largely unknowable for us (which is why excessive curiosity about it is spiritually unhealthy, sidetracking Christian thought into the domain of 'spiritual gnosis' or occultism). Nevertheless, we can establish essential features of this life which follow from the fundamental elements of our faith" (*Bride of the Lamb*, 358).

14. *Clara* will be more important here; we have dealt sufficiently with *The Ages of the World* in chapter 3, though it will be important again in the next chapter. For a succinct presentation of the issues regarding situating one text to the other—whether or not, for instance, *Clara* should be understood as a preliminary sketch for *The Ages of the World*, see Fiona Steinkamp's introduction to her translation of F. W. J. Schelling, *Clara, or, On Nature's Connection to the Spirit World*, trans. Fiona Steinkamp (Albany: State University of New York Press, 2002), particularly x–xiii. Many of Schelling's texts were continually rewritten, edited, and deliberately left unfinished or fragmentary. For instance, though its publication was heralded on numerous occasions, *The Ages of the World* was redrafted ad nauseam and ultimately left unfinished, as marginalia continually ambiguated what had been already written. Soloviev's thought has also been characterized as continually self-revising. Even the fictitious manuscript of the "Short Story of the Antichrist" included in his *War, Progress, and the End of History* breaks off in medias res with the untimely death of Father Pansophius (191). For the phenomenon of Romantic apocalypses deliberately left unfinished or fragmentary, see Alice A. Kuzniar, *Delayed Endings: Nonclosure in Novalis and Hölderlin* (Athens: University of Georgia Press, 2008).

15. Also see Bulgakov's final commentary on the book of Revelation, *Apokalipsis Ioanna: opyt dogmaticheskogo istolkovaniia* (Paris: YMCA-Press, 1948), published posthumously.

16. The first volume of Balthasar's *Apokalypse der deutschen Seele, Der deutsche Idealismus*, originally published under the title *Prometheus*, sets out the scope of the project and consists of individual analyses of Lessing, Herder, Kant, Fichte, Schelling, Novalis, Hölderlin, Schiller, Goethe, Hegel, Jean Paul (otherwise known as novelist Johann Paul Friedrich Richter), and Wagner, among others. Volume 2, *Im Zeichen Nietzsches*, is most pertinent to our interests, containing a long comparison of Nietzsche and Dostoevsky (202–419). This structural and thematic juxtaposition of these "hostile brothers" appears

not only in Henri de Lubac's "Dostoevsky as Prophet," *The Drama of Atheist Humanism*, trans. Edith M. Riley (Cleveland, OH: Meridian Books, 1963), 161–246, but also in all cases of our Russian religious philosophers (not to mention Lev Shestov and Dmitrii Merezhkovskii). Volume 3, *Die Vergöttlichung des Todes*, takes aim in the main at Heidegger. For a wonderful summary *en briefe* of this very intimidating work (Balthasar himself called it, half-jokingly, his "giant child"), see Nichols, *Scattering the Seed*.

17. Balthasar, *TD*, 5:13.

18. Balthasar, *My Work*, 105.

19. Mongrain, *Systematic Thought*, 11–12; italics added.

20. For a far more sympathetic interpretation of Speyrian influence, see Michael P. Murphy, *A Theology of Criticism: Balthasar, Postmodernism, and the Catholic Imagination* (Oxford: Oxford University Press, 2008): "It is Speyr—who had no formal training in theology—who served as Balthasar's most influential teacher, a flesh-and-blood tutor in matters of mystical theology, ecclesiology, and, most vitally, prayer" (33). See also Cyril O'Regan, "I Am Not What I Am Because Of . . . " in *How Balthasar Changed My Mind*, ed. Rodney A. Howsare and Larry S. Chapp (New York: Crossroads, 2008), 155–56.

21. Balthasar, *TD*, 4:95. Also see Balthasar, *Theological Anthropology*, 48–49.

22. Balthasar, *TD*, 4:100.

23. Balthasar, *Theological Anthropology*, 49.

24. Balthasar, *Apokalypse der deutschen Seele*, 1:229–30.

25. Ibid., 218–19.

26. Ibid., 219–20.

27. Ibid., 223.

28. Ibid.

29. Ibid., 230.

30. Berdyaev, *The Beginning and the End*, 154; cf. 96.

31. Ibid., 104.

32. Ibid., 174.

33. For Balthasar's explicit mention of the dialogue *Clara*, especially with respect to anthropology, see *TD*, 1:570, 576–77.

34. Schelling, *Clara*, especially 33–50.

35. Ibid., 35; italics original.

36. Ibid., 36.

37. Ibid., 39.

38. For an interesting riff on Schelling's spectral Real with respect to cinema, see Slavoj Žižek, "Everything You Always Wanted to Know about Schelling (But Were Afraid to Ask Hitchcock)," in *The New Schelling*, ed. Judith Norman and Alistair Welchman (London: Continuum, 2004), 30–42.

39. It is likely, as Friedemann Horn has aptly demonstrated in *Schelling and Swedenborg: Mysticism and German Idealism*, trans. George F. Dole (West Chester, PA: Swedenborg Foundation, 1997), that Schelling's notion of spiritual corporeality has its origin in and draws heavily from the work of Swedenborg. Direct textual parallels can certainly be found with Swedenborg's *Heaven and Hell*: "For when man enters the spiritual world or the life after death, he is in a body as he was in the world, with no apparent difference, since he neither sees nor feels any difference. But his body is then spiritual, and thus separated or purified from all that is earthly." Emanuel Swedenborg, *Heaven and Hell*, trans. George F. Dole (Indianapolis: New Century Publishing, 2009), ¶461; cf. ¶433 also. Balthasar mentions Alois Dempf (presumably for his *Theoretische Anthropologie* of 1950) as one who successfully reappropriated this Romantic-Idealist anthropology for Catholic metaphysics. "Some Points of Eschatology," *Explorations in Theology*, 1:276.

40. Horn makes a case that Schelling's eschatology changes drastically in the latter sections of *Clara*, marking a clean break from Swedenborg, whose eschatological reflections Schelling found to be too far outside the Christian fold. It is certainly the case that toward the end of the dialogue nature and the corporeal are afforded greater value (see 76–81), and in the spring fragment (which does not appear with earlier versions), it is said that "the merely spiritual life [*Geisterleben* or *Geistesleben*, depending on the text consulted] doesn't satisfy our heart . . . as the artist does not find peace in thinking about his work, but only when he has represented it physically, and as anyone fired by an ideal wants to find or reveal it in a physical-visible form, the goal of all longing is likewise the very perfection of corporeality as a reflection and mirror of perfect spirituality" (*Clara*, 80). Horn (Schelling and Swedenborg, 95–114) indicates that the apparent shift in Schelling's thinking in *Clara* (corroborated in the later *Stuttgart Lectures*) suggests a *total* abandonment of Swedenborgian influence (95).

41. Schelling, *Clara*, 37.

42. Ibid., 41. Also see 45–46.

43. Ibid., 49. An echo of this line of thinking is found in Schelling's personal correspondence as well. In a personal letter Schelling writes, "Even death, which may cause us to curse our dependence on nature and which fills a human soul's first impression almost with horror against this merciless violence, and which destroys even the most beautiful and best without mercy when her laws demand it, even death, when grasped more deeply, opens up our eyes to the unity of the natural and the divine" (quoted in Fiona Steinkamp, general introduction to *Clara*, xxx).

44. Schelling, *Stuttgart Lectures*, 476.

45. One passage in *Clara* suggests, but unconvincingly, that even complete unity with the divine would not require the sacrifice of particular iden-

tity: "For the drop in the ocean nevertheless always is this drop, even if it isn't distinguished as such" (52).

46. Balthasar, *TD*, 1:577.

47. Bulgakov, *Bride of the Lamb*, 447.

48. Ibid., 351.

49. Ibid., 353.

50. Bulgakov, *Unfading Light*, 187.

51. Bulgakov, *Bride of the Lamb*, 352. See also 355.

52. Ibid., 356. Cf. 360.

53. Ibid., 350.

54. Ibid., 354.

55. Ibid., 355.

56. Ibid., 355.

57. Ibid., 357. For more on relics, particularly as anticipations of the resurrected body, see Bulgakov, *Bride of the Lamb*, 443. Also see *Lamb of God*, 378; *Unfading Light*, 266; and finally, Sergei Bulgakov, *Relics and Miracles: Two Theological Essays*, trans. Boris Jakim (Grand Rapids, MI: Eerdmans, 2011).

58. Bulgakov, *Lamb of God*, 393–94.

59. Bulgakov, *Bride of the Lamb*, 439–40.

60. Ibid., 448.

61. Ibid., 452.

62. See Bulgakov, *Unfading Light*, 261–65.

63. Balthasar, *TD*, 5:359.

64. Bulgakov, *Bride of the Lamb*, 523.

65. Ibid., 519.

66. Bulgakov, *Unfading Light*, 265.

67. Ibid., 521. Also see *Unfading Light*, 273–83.

68. Ibid., 353. For the Christological transvaluation of death—since loving and voluntary—also see Bulgakov's sermon "Having Trampled on Death by Death," in *Ultimate Questions: An Anthology of Modern Russian Religious Thought*, ed. Alexander Schmemann (New York: Holt, Rinehart and Winston, 1965), 307–9.

69. Balthasar, *TD*, 5:341–42. Cf. *GL*, 7:227–28.

70. Balthasar, *TD*, 5:356.

71. Balthasar *TD*, 4:118. In something of a poetic turn, Balthasar writes also that "the only reason that hearts do not constantly rebel against the dark omnipotence of death is that its fateful wind has always bent the trees of the soul toward it, that the powers of infidelity, of injustice, of betrayal, of spiritual debility and physical illness and infirmity are familiar to us from childhood in all their destructive strength. They are forces that are not only above us, but in us, with whom we seem inexplicably to have made a compact,

voluntarily, yet against our will, at a time and place we can no longer remember (*Theological Anthropology*, 49).

72. Balthasar, *TD*, 5:324. Also see *TD*, 4:118, for materially the same point. The relentless affirmation of the theologically positive status of creaturehood and the finite is a central concern in Balthasar's theology. For a reliable secondary account, see Werner Löser, "Die Positivität des Endlichen," *Im Geiste des Origenes: Hans Urs von Balthasar als Interpret der Theologie der Kirchenväter* (Frankfurt: Knecht, 1976).

73. Balthasar, *TD*, 5:323. Cf. Balthasar, *TD*, 4:121ff. For the relationship between Balthasar and Heidegger, see Cyril O' Regan, "Hans Urs von Balthasar and the Unwelcoming of Heidegger," in *The Grandeur of Reason: Religion, Tradition and Universalism*, ed. Peter M. Candler Jr. and Conor Cunningham (London: SCM Press, 2010), 264–98.

74. Balthasar, *TD*, 4:122.

75. According to Balthasar, after the Fall, "the positive and negative aspects of death cannot be unraveled" (*TD*, 5:324).

76. Cf. Balthasar, *GL*, 7:513.

77. For one example of this critique, see Gerard F. O'Hanlon, "The Jesuits and Modern Theology: Rahner, von Balthasar and Liberation Theology," *Irish Theological Quarterly* 58 (1992): 25–45; "May Christians Hope for a Better World?" *Irish Theological Quarterly* 54 (1988): 175–89; and *The Immutability of God in the Theology of Hans Urs von Balthasar* (Cambridge: Cambridge University Press, 1990), 170.

78. Balthasar, *GL*, 7:513. Cf. *Theological Anthropology*: "No, reality is the place and the material within which the living God appears" (66).

79. Balthasar, *TD*, 4:130.

80. Balthasar, *Epilogue*, trans. Edward T. Oakes, S.J. (San Francisco: Ignatius Press, 2004), 38. For more on the relation of eschatology and bodiliness in Balthasar, see "The Word Becomes Flesh," *Epilogue*, 99–108; on the connection between body and resurrection, see *TD*, 5:358–59; 394–401; "From Original State to Final State," *The Christian State of Life*, trans. Mary Frances McCarthy (San Francisco: Ignatius Press, 2002), 67–129. See also "Some Points of Eschatology," *Explorations in Theology*, 1:261–62, where Balthasar talks about the phenomenon of ambiguating death in terms of straightforward mortal/immortal distinction, as well as the "anti-Platonist" cast of much of modern eschatology.

81. Balthasar, *TD*, 4:130. Balthasar's view of Christ's descent into hell is discussed only briefly in this chapter; a more lengthy discussion, with respect to the Trinitarian horizon, is deferred until the next.

82. One representative passage among many: "For every human being [death] is the brutal leveler, the ravager of all things, and yet death itself inescapably confronts one with a mystery: God's death, the death He died out of love." Balthasar, *GL*, 5:147.

83. Balthasar, *TD*, 4:132.

84. Ibid., 110.

85. Balthasar, *Theological Anthropology*, 224.

86. Ibid., 242.

87. Balthasar, *Mysterium Paschale*, 160–68. Note also Balthasar's distinction between Hades and Hell, 177.

88. Balthasar, "The Descent into Hell," *Explorations in Theology*, 4:407–8.

89. Ibid., 411–12.

90. Ibid., 408. For a similar reading of Christ's descent into hell that was surely influenced by Balthasar's interpretation, see Joseph Ratzinger, *Introduction to Christianity*, trans. J. R. Foster and Michael J. Miller (San Francisco: Ignatius Press, 2004), especially 293–301.

91. Bulgakov also emphasizes the authenticity of the death of Christ as a death similar to the death of any human being. Yet there is a distinction, insofar as the death of Christ "was not accompanied and could not be accompanied by the definitive separation between the Divine Spirit and Christ's body." Bulgakov, *Lamb of God*, 378.

92. Balthasar, *TD*, 5:312. Cf. Balthasar, "Eschatology in Outline," *Explorations in Theology*, 4:456–57.

93. Fyodor Dostoevsky, *The Idiot*, trans. Constance Garnett (New York: The Modern Library, 1942), 714. Cf. Balthasar, *GL*, 5:312.

94. Balthasar, *TD*, 5:313.

95. Ibid., 314.

96. Balthasar, "The Descent into Hell," *Explorations in Theology*, 4:411. It is notable that for Schelling also hope is not abandoned in hell:

> Yes, isn't it conceivable that the more the spiritual breaks through in this external life, the less the underworld has power over the dead; or shall we consider even those words carried down from Christ about victory over the ancient kingdom of the dead as completely empty, general figures of speech . . . ? Only when He, through whom in the beginning all things were made, lowered Himself into that sunken and now mortal and transitory nature in order to become, once again, a tie between the spiritual and the natural life even within nature, only then did heaven or the true spirit world become open once more to everyone, and for the second time the bond between earth and heaven was sealed. As He died, the sole light left to man in external nature was extinguished as a sign of the greatest power that death had now exerted . . . the power of death had been overcome. (Schelling, *Clara*, 61)

97. On this encounter, see de Lubac, *Drama of Atheist Humanism*, 173ff.

98. Dostoevsky, *Idiot*, 446–47.

99. Balthasar, *Explorations in Theology*, 4:401.

100. Balthasar, *GL*, 5:193–94; cf. 198–99.

101. Balthasar, *GL*, 7:231.

102. Balthasar, *Mysterium Paschale*, 178.

103. Ibid., 361.

104. Bulgakov, *Bride of the Lamb*, 367.

105. Balthasar, *TD*, 5:360–69. See also *Dare We Hope*, 242–44; *Mysterium Paschale*, 178–79; and the introduction to *Origen: Spirit and Fire*, 12–13.

106. Balthasar, *Apokalypse der deutschen Seele*, 3:427. Also, in his monograph *Bernanos*, Balthasar lists the usual suspects:

> In the first place, Bernanos is concerned with making eternal damnation palpable to an existential faith and to do this by means of the possible experiences of damnation and perdition to be found within the temporal world. Here Bernanos is doing in the Christian camp the same thing as Sartre, Camus, and Kafka (to name but three) are doing on the non-Christian side. He then undertakes to test the social problematic of damnation critically and appropriate it, an endeavor in which he follows Péguy above all, but also Dostoevsky and the Russians. Finally, Bernanos seeks to consider hell in the light of Christ's Cross, his descent into the netherworld, and his Resurrection; in other words, he puts the problem of hell within a soteriological context, which is where it must be approached like all other mysteries of revelation without exception.

Hans Urs von Balthasar, *Bernanos: An Ecclesial Existence*, trans. Erasmo Leiva-Merikakis (San Francisco: Ignatius Press, 1996), 443.

107. Berdyaev, *Destiny of Man*, 276.

108. Fyodor Dostoevsky, *The Brothers Karamazov*, 2d ed., ed. Susan McReynolds Oddo, trans. Constance Garnett (New York: W.W. Norton, 2011), 250.

109. Ibid., 499.

110. In *Bernanos*, Balthasar writes, "It is obvious that all of this cannot be more than an essay and an approximation, for one cannot speak 'systematically' about hell. We can only deal with aspects of it, as indeed revelation itself does" (443).

111. Bulgakov, *The Holy Grail and the Eucharist*, 101–2. See also *Bride of the Lamb*, 374–75 and 477n55.

112. Balthasar, "Some Points of Eschatology," *Explorations in Theology*, 1:259.

113. Balthasar also mentions Johannes Scotus Eriugena, Nicholas of Cusa, and Marsilio Ficino in this capacity (*Mysterium Paschale*, 163).

114. Balthasar also notes a structural homology in the theological anthropology of Schelling and Augustine in the first volume of *Apokalypse der deutschen Seele*, though to make the comparison itself simultaneously indicates proximity and remoteness. According to Balthasar's analysis, both Schelling and Augustine posit that it is the indwelling of the Spirit of God that

enlivens and perfects the soul. For Schelling, however, for whom the finite and the infinite are mutually dependent, the soul is the necessary condition for the Spirit of God, "as it were, a vessel in which [God] rises" (*Apokalypse der deutschen Seele*, 1:225), a claim with obviously troubling implications theologically.

115. Balthasar, *Dare We Hope*, 127. Cf. Augustine, *De Genesi ad litt.* 12:32, 61 (PD 34, 481).

116. Schelling, *Clara*, 58.

117. Ibid., 55.

118. Milosz, "Dostoevsky and Swedenborg," *Emperor of the Earth: Modes of Eccentric Vision* (Berkeley: University of California Press, 1977), 127.

119. Swedenborg, *Heaven and Hell*, §586.

120. Milosz, *Emperor of the Earth*, 129–31. To consult the original passage from *Crime and Punishment* in context, see Fyodor Dostoevsky, *Crime and Punishment*, trans. Richard Pevear and Larissa Volokhonsky (New York: Random House Modern Library, 1994), 335.

121. Bulgakov, *Bride of the Lamb*, 487.

122. Balthasar quotes C.S. Lewis to further underscore the point:

"Do you mean then that Hell—all that infinite empty town—is down in some little crack like this?"

"Yes. All Hell is smaller than one pebble of your earthly world. . . . For a damned soul is nearly nothing; it is shrunk, shut up in itself. . . . Their fists are clenched, their eyes fast shut."

C. S. Lewis, *The Great Divorce* (1946; repr. Glasgow: Collins, 1986), 113–14; quoted by Balthasar in *TD*, 5:307n12.

123. Balthasar, *TD*, 5:301. See also Balthasar, *Dare We Hope*, 81.

124. Berdyaev, *Destiny of Man*, 266–83, here 277.

125. Bulgakov, *Unfading Light*, 187.

126. Balthasar, *Dare We Hope*, 165. Cf. 51–58, which indicates similar views in Chrystostom, Augustine, and Origen, as well as 90–92. For Bulgakov, see *Bride of the Lamb*: "Hell itself consists of unfulfilled love for God, which, because of spiritual limitation, is expressed in enmity toward Him, theomachy, or in spiritual sleep. The state of hell is, in essence, antinomic, because it combines the revelation of God and the abandonment by God; and it is this antinomic character that imparts to hell an eternal character. God Himself does not reject creation. It is creation that, in its desolate emptiness, rejects God" (487–88).

127. "So, I said, how torturous must the impure person find his own presence, in now being alone with himself and reaping what he has sown, when he passes on to a similar condition after death, or at least to one approaching it. If every evil desire and endeavor can take on a kind of personality, and if every sinful deed carries on living within the person like an evil

spirit, how sorely must the soul feel this impure retinue that the soul takes with it into that life!" (Schelling, *Clara*, 59).

128. Balthasar, *TD*, 5:291–92.

129. Balthasar, *Dare We Hope*, 57. Cf. Dostoevsky, *Brothers Karamazov*, 303.

130. Dostoevsky, *Brothers Karamazov*, 278–79; italics added.

131. Bulgakov, *Bride of the Lamb*, 360.

132. Balthasar, *TD*, 5:306. Cf. Thomas Aquinas, *S.Th.* I, 10, 3 ad 1, ad 2. See also *Dare We Hope*: "In hell, there is no true eternity but rather time" (125).

133. Nor is Franz von Baader absent from this genealogy: he writes, "To suffer the torment of eternity is not the same as to suffer eternal torment," in a letter to Hoffmann, January 10, 1837. Franz von Baader, *Sämmtliche Werke* (Leipzig: Bethmann, 1850–1860), 15:552. Cf. Balthasar, *TD*, 5:561. Also, "We must be careful to distinguish *duratio finita* (time as objectively fixed), *duratio indefinita* and *duratio infinita*: the first refers to purgatory, the second, hell, and the third, heaven" (Balthasar, *TD*, 5:307n13).

134. Balthasar, *Dare We Hope*, 129; cf. Balthasar, *TD*, 5:306.

135. Berdyaev, *Destiny of Man*, 269.

136. Bulgakov, *Bride of the Lamb*, 487; italics original.

137. Ibid., 483. Also see 500–1.

138. Ibid., 490.

139. For direct statements in which Balthasar rejects *apokatastasis*, see *Dare We Hope*, 94, 154, 166, 197, 225–54; and *TD*, 5:269.

140. Bulgakov, *Bride of the Lamb*, 489.

141. Balthasar, *Dare We Hope*, 169–70, 198–203, 211–13. Origen has made the same point: "But your full joy will only come when not one of your members is lacking. Wherefore you must wait for the others, just as others have waited for you. Surely, too if you who are a member have not perfect joy as long as a member is missing, how much more will he, our Lord and Savior, consider his joy incomplete while any member of his body is missing." Origen, *Homilies on Leviticus* (The Fathers of the Church Series), trans. Gary Wayne Barkley (Washington, DC: Catholic University of America Press, 1990), 7.2.

142. Balthasar, *TD*, 5:176. Cf. Berdyaev, *Destiny of Man*, 276.

143. Balthasar, *GL*, 3:407. Cf. Bulgakov, *Bride of the Lamb*, 514.

144. Balthasar, *TD*, 5:319; italics added.

145. Balthasar, *Dare We Hope*, 198–99; and *Epilogue*, 122–23.

146. Berdyaev, *Destiny of Man*, 273, 280.

147. Balthasar, *Dare We Hope*, 94.

148. Dostoevsky, *Brothers Karamazov*, 545.

149. Balthasar, *Dare We Hope*, 13, 113, 166. See also "Some Points of Eschatology," *Explorations in Theology*, 1:266.

150. Ibid., 187.

151. Ibid., 144. Also see Balthasar: "We have to be aware of the limits of human speculation here—we have already said that the widest attainable horizon is the 'hope that all will be redeemed'—but at the same time it would be wrong timidly to lag behind the boldness of this hope, while bearing in mind that the question of the fate of demons is insoluble in a *theologia viatorum* and must therefore be excluded" (*TD*, 5:508). See Paul Gavriluk, "Universal Salvation in the Eschatology of Sergius Bulgakov," *Journal of Theological Studies* 57, no. 1 (April 2006): 110–32, which criticizes Bulgakov as being guilty of the very kind of "dogmatic maximalism" (129) that Balthasar eschews, for maintaining that universal salvation bears with it ontological necessity.

152. Bulgakov, *Bride of the Lamb*, 513.

153. Ibid., 505.

154. Ibid., 517; italics added.

155. See, for instance, Balthasar, *Mysterium Paschale*, 35. I argue elsewhere that Balthasar may actually import more from Bulgakov's sophiology than he admits, particularly vis-à-vis constructions of the feminine as answering and receptive, and the importation of gender into the Trinitarian relations. See Martin, "The 'Whence' and the 'Whither' of Balthasar's Gendered Theology."

156. Bulgakov, *Bride of the Lamb*, 500, 515. Cf. 497. See Origen, *In Jer. hom.* XX (19) 3. Balthasar discusses this at length in *Dare We Hope*, 241–44.

157. Bulgakov, *Bride of the Lamb*, 484.

158. Balthasar, *TD*, 5:321. Cf. Ambrose, *In Ps.* 118, sermon 20, 58 (PL 15, 1502).

159. See also Balthasar, *TD*, 5:194–203. This line of thinking is paralleled in the Apocalypse, which allows the juxtaposition of "pure penal justice and the vision of a reality transfigured," liturgy and judgment both together. Cf. *TD*, 4:18–19, 36.

160. Balthasar, *TD*, 5:279.

161. Balthasar, *Dare We Hope*, 20–21. Balthasar lists as representative of the condemnatory New Testament passages Matthew 5:22 and 29f, 7:23, 8:12, 10:28, 11:20ff, 12:31, 18:21ff, 21:33ff, 22:11ff, 23:33, and 25:12, 30, 41, and 46; Mark 9:43; and Revelation 19:20, 20:10, 21:8. See also *TD*, 5:285–90. Biblical texts that ought to be classified among this sort—that is, those that privilege the salvation of "all"—are 1 Timothy 2:1–6; John 12:32, 17:2; and Romans 5:12–21, 11:32. See also Balthasar, *TD*, 5:279–82.

162. Balthasar, *Dare We Hope*, 23; cf. 29, 44, 48, 177 of the same volume, as well as Balthasar, "Some Points of Eschatology," *Explorations in Theology*, 1:267–68.

163. Balthasar, *GL*, 6:339. See also Balthasar, *TD*, 5:143–44.

164. Balthasar, *TD*, 5:295.

165. Ibid., 192. Cf. *TD*, 1:413–24.

166. Balthasar, *TD*, 5:299. Also Balthasar, *Dare We Hope*, 248–51.

167. Berdyaev, *Destiny of Man*, 282; cf. 276.

168. Balthasar, *GL*, 7:493.

169. Balthasar, *Theological Anthropology*, 64.

170. Balthasar, *GL*, 1:155.

171. Balthasar, *TD*, 4:120, cf. 134–35. See also Balthasar, "Some Points of Eschatology," *Explorations in Theology*, 1:275.

172. Balthasar, *TD*, 4:134; italics original.

173. Balthasar, *GL*, 1:155.

174. Balthasar, *GL*, 7:519.

175. "All Christian teaching proceeds from the experience of the bodily Resurrection of Christ, which is by no means mythical and speculative but sober and historical; and this Resurrection illumines the truth and the meaning of his Cross and, behind it, of his entire Incarnation." Balthasar, *TD*, 5:52.

176. Schelling, *Clara*, 52.

177. Balthasar, *Apokalypse der deutschen Seele*, 1:231–32. This critique is interesting with respect to Balthasar's own parsing of eschatology as "realized," an aspect of his thought that will be left until the next chapter.

178. Ibid., 245.

179. Ibid.

180. Ibid., 246.

181. Cited by Balthasar in *Apokalypse der deutschen Seele*, 1:233; italics added.

182. Ibid.

183. Balthasar, *TD*, 4:130.

184. Balthasar, *TD*, 4:125. Cf. Balthasar, *Apokalypse der deutschen Seele*, 1:233.

185. Dostoevsky, *Brothers Karamazov*, 211.

186. Berdyaev, *The Beginning and the End*, 148. Also see the introduction to Soloviev's *War, Progress, and the End of History*, in which Milosz suggests that "one certainty—death—was central to Solovyov's thought. He did not agree with those who, wishing to assuage the cruelty of biological laws, invoked eternal rebirth in Nature; there is no rebirth in Nature because this particular ant, this particular bird, this particular flower lives only once and gives a new beginning not to itself but to other individuals. Death is sufficient proof of universal corruption, the stigma of the Devil in the universe. Man is confronted with one all-important either/or: either Christ was resurrected and thus victorious over the powers of Hell, or he was not resurrected" (23).

187. Balthasar, *TD*, 4:128.

188. See Balthasar, *Theological Anthropology*, 100–1.

189. Balthasar, *GL*, 7:508–9.

190. Balthasar, *GL*, 3:341.

191. Soloviev, *War, Progress, and the End of History*, 147.

192. Ibid., 148.

193. Ibid. Cf. 155.

194. Ibid., 149.

195. Balthasar, *Apokalypse der deutschen Seele*, 3:38; translation is my own.

196. Dostoevsky, *Brothers Karamazov*, 646.

197. Henri Troyat, *Tolstoy* (Garden City, NY: Doubleday, 1967), 395.

198. "Vladimir Solovyov's Letter to L. Tolstoy on the Resurrection of Christ" [1894], *Sobornost* 1 (March 1935): 9.

199. Ibid.

200. Ibid., 10.

201. See Bulgakov, *Lamb of God*, 379–88.

202. Ibid., 394; italics original.

203. Ibid., 395.

204. Ibid.

205. Ibid., 396. Also see Bulgakov, *Comforter*, 346–47. The point that the resurrection of Christ decisively affects the whole of creation, including the natural world, is made more poetically and pastorally in Bulgakov's 1938 sermon "Meditations on the Joy of the Resurrection":

> The rays of the light of Christ's Resurrection penetrate *the whole of creation*. For us, the departed too are alive in this world, and we send our Easter greetings to them, the news of the Resurrection which, each one in his own way, they already know. It is not only animate and rational creation which receives the power of resurrection, rather, the whole of creation rises in Christ's Body, crying out exultantly with the joy of Easter. . . . [T]he unbridled joy of Easter is plain in nature even to the naked eye: the sun is "playing," the air, the water, and growing things are bathed in the rays of divine gladness. The human spirit—as it rises to life—can find no part of nature that is dead and not rising to life with it, and it summons all of nature to the Resurrection of Christ.

Bulgakov, "Meditations on the Joy of the Resurrection," in *Ultimate Questions*, ed. Alexander Schmemann, 302–3.

206. Bulgakov, *Lamb of God*, 396.

207. Bulgakov, *Comforter*, 348. He mentions in particular Matthew 24:31, 1 Corinthians 15:22–23, 1 Thessalonians 4:16–17, and John 5:28–29. Cf. Bulgakov, *Bride of the Lamb*, 433–4.

208. Bulgakov, *Bride of the Lamb*, 372–73. Cf. *The Lamb of God*, 375. Bulgakov later indicates that the separation of "sheep and goats" is only the beginning, only the first eschatological event, for both "the judgment and the separation must be understood not as a static unchangeability but as a dynamic striving beyond their limits, on the pathways to universal deification or salvation. Only deification is capable of justifying creation. It is the only theodicy" (*Bride of the Lamb*, 501).

209. Bulgakov, *Bride of the Lamb*, 363. Also, "even in the afterlife, human souls experience and acquire something new, each in its own way, in its freedom" (363). See also 365–56, 498. For Bulgakov, a permeable boundary between "heaven" and "hell" makes sense given the Orthodox belief in the efficacy of prayers for the dead. Cf. 367, 499.

210. Balthasar, *TD*, 5:359.

211. Ibid., 317–19. Cf. *Dare We Hope*, 178.

212. Balthasar, *TD*, 5:144–52.

213. Ibid., 321.

214. David L. Schindler, "Modernity and the Nature of a Distinction: Balthasar's Ontology of Generosity," in *How Balthasar Changed My Mind*, ed. Rodney A. Howsare and Larry S. Chapp, 224–58.

215. R. M. Rilke, "Death Experienced," *New Poems*, ed. Edward Snow: "We know nothing of this going-hence / that so excludes us. We have no grounds / for showing Death wonderment and love / or hate, since it wears that age-old mask // of tragedy that hopelessly contorts it. / The world is full of roles—which we still act. / As long as we keep striving for acclaim, / Death also acts a part—though always badly. // But when you went, a streak of reality / broke in upon the stage through that fissure / where you left: green of real green, real sunshine, real forest. // We go on acting. Fearful and reciting / things difficult to learn and now and then / inventing gestures; but your existence, / withdrawn from us and taken from our piece, // can sometimes come over us, like a knowledge/of that reality settling in, / so that for a while we act life / transported, not thinking of applause" (95).

216. Balthasar, *Apokalypse der deutschen Seele*, 1:240.

CHAPTER 5. "Denn Armut ist ein großer Glanz aus Innen"

1. See Schelling, *Philosophie der Offenbarung*, 25th lecture. Bulgakov mentions this connection in *Unfading Light*, 346 and 498n64. For secondary treatments of Balthasar on kenosis, see Thomas Dalzell, *The Dramatic Encounter of Divine and Human Freedom in the Theology of Hans Urs von Balthasar* (Bern: Peter Lang, 2000), 162–71; Anne Hunt, *The Trinity and the Paschal Mystery: A Development in Recent Catholic Theology* (Collegeville, MN: Liturgical Press, 1997), 57–90; O'Hanlon, *The Immutability of God*; Graham Ward, "Kenosis: Death, Discourse and Resurrection," in *Balthasar at the End of Modernity*, ed. Gardner et al., 15–68. Also see Katy Leamy, "A Comparison of the Kenotic Trinitarian Theology of Hans Urs von Balthasar and Sergei Bulgakov" (Ph.D. diss., Marquette University, 2012). For secondary sources on Bulgakov's kenotic theory, see Nadejda Gorodetzky, *The Humiliated Christ in Modern Russian Thought* (New York: Macmillan, 1938),

esp.156–74; and Paul Gavrilyuk, "The Kenotic Theology of Sergius Bulga-kov," *Scottish Journal of Theology* 58, no. 3 (2005): 251–69.

2. R. M. Rilke, *The Book of Hours*, trans. Susan Ranson and ed. Ben Hutchinson (Rochester, NY: Camden House, 2008), 178–79.

3. Bulgakov, *Unfading Light*, 201–2.

4. Balthasar, *TD*, 4:327. For several of Balthasar's explicit appeals to Bulgakov on this point, see Balthasar, *TD*, 4:278, 313–14, 323, 338; *Mysterium Paschale*, 35, 46; and *GL*, 7:213–14.

5. See Nicholas J. Healy, *The Eschatology of Hans Urs von Balthasar: Being as Communion* (Oxford: Oxford University Press, 2005), for a book-length treatment of Balthasar's understanding of eschatology as ultimately concerned with the Trinity and the very structure of being as one of Trinitarian love. On Healy's own telling,

> I will argue that the ultimate form of the end, and thus the measure of all that is meant by eschatology, is given in Christ's Eucharistic and pneumatic gift of himself—a gift that simultaneously lays bare the mystery of God's trinitarian life and enables Christ to "return" to the Father in communion with the whole of creation. Insofar as Christ reveals the trinitarian life *and* the mystery of creation in their dramatic interplay, he establishes the form of eschatology as a participation in God's engagement with the world. Under the sign of the Holy Spirit, Christian eschatology involves a sharing in Christ's double movement into the world and, together with the world, into God. For those who would follow Christ with eschatological definitiveness, the path back to God is into the heart of the world. (3)

There are very rich and concrete possibilities in Balthasar's eschatology for political theology as well, especially considering Balthasar's late text *Tragedy under Grace: Reinhold Schneider on the Experience of the West*, trans. Brian McNeil, C.R.V. (San Francisco: Ignatius Press, 1988), on the antiwar German poet and novelist Reinhold Schneider (1903–1958).

6. Balthasar, *Apokalypse der deutschen Seele*, 1:206.

7. Ibid.

8. For an elegant exposition of Balthasar as a reader of Revelation, see O'Regan, *Theology and the Spaces of Apocalyptic*, especially 46ff.

9. Balthasar, *TD*, 5:56–57.

10. See Balthasar, *GL* 7, which indicates a kind of Ireanean hermeneutic of the New Testament, especially 33–76. Balthasar is attempting to rescue John from marginalization vis-à-vis the synoptics, but he wants always to understand the fourth Gospel in relation to the others. This relationship can best be understood as summative and clarifying; in short, an appropriation of Irenaeus's notion of recapitulation as an interpretive tool for understanding the New Testament.

11. See Balthasar, *TD*, 5:28–29.

12. Ibid., 147.

13. Balthasar, *TD*, 4:29; *TD*, 5:93; and Hans Urs von Balthasar, "Improvisation on Spirit and Future," *Explorations in Theology*, vol. 3, *Creator Spirit*, trans. Brian McNeil, C.R.V. (San Francisco: Ignatius Press, 1993), 167–68.

14. Balthasar, *TD*, 5:25.

15. See Balthasar, *Theological Anthropology*, 35.

16. Balthasar, *TD*, 5:29–30, 48.

17. Ibid., 26, 182.

18. Balthasar, "Some Points of Eschatology," *Explorations in Theology*, 1:260. Cf. Balthasar, *TD*, 5:368. Thus, the eschatological is tantamount to the soteriological. Here Balthasar is not far from Barth, who asserted in his *Epistle to the Romans* that "a Christianity which is not wholly eschatology and nothing but eschatology has nothing to do with Christ" (Karl Barth, *The Epistle to the Romans*, 6th ed., trans. Edwyn C. Hoskyns [Oxford: Oxford University Press, 1933], 314).

19. Balthasar, "Improvisation on Spirit and Future," *Explorations in Theology*, 3:166–7. See also Balthasar, *Theology of History*, 44–45.

20. Balthasar, *TD*, 5:187. Péguy's lines from his narrative poem "The Portal of the Mystery of Hope," follow: "Children walk exactly like little puppies. / (Moreover, they play like puppies too) / When a puppy goes for a walk with his masters / He comes and he goes. He comes back, he leaves again. He goes ahead, he returns. / He makes the trip twenty times. / Covers twenty times the distance. / It's because as a matter of fact he's not going somewhere. . . . What he's interested in is precisely making the trip" (108).

21. O'Regan, *Theology and the Spaces of Apocalyptic*, 54.

22. Balthasar, *TD*, 4:19.

23. Ibid., 28, 38, 42; Balthasar, *Theological Anthropology*, 144ff.

24. Balthasar, *TD*, 4:46.

25. Balthasar, *TD*, 5:400. Also cf. *TD*, 5:90, and *GL*, 7:526.

26. Bulgakov, *Bride of the Lamb*, 348. Cf. O'Regan, *Theology and the Spaces of Apocalyptic*, 48–58. Also cf. Balthasar, *TD*, 5:56.

27. Balthasar, *GL*, 7:526.

28. Balthasar, "Improvisation on Spirit and Future," *Explorations in Theology*, 3:135.

29. Ibid., 147. Elsewhere, Balthasar speaks in terms of Joachim's "slight distortion" (*Theological Anthropology*, 133).

30. O'Regan, *Theology and the Spaces of Apocalyptic*, 122–23.

31. Balthasar, "Improvisation on Spirit and Future," *Explorations in Theology*, 3:148.

32. For Balthasar's critical assessment of Berdyaev, see *Apokalypse der deutschen Seele*, 2:344 and 3:424–30, esp. 429. Also see *TD* 4, where Balthasar

indicates Berdyaev's "gnostic tone" when speaking in terms of tragedy within God (149).

33. Berdyaev, *The Beginning and the End*, 206.

34. Ibid., 207.

35. Balthasar, "Improvisation on Spirit and Future," *Explorations in Theology*, 3:168.

36. See Bulgakov, *Comforter*. For further corroboration of the suggestion that Balthasar's pneumatology builds on Bulgakov's, see O'Regan, *Anatomy of Misremembering*, 621n42.

37. Balthasar, "Improvisation on Spirit and Future," *Explorations in Theology*, 3:142; cf. 156. See also *TD* 4: "We are not expecting a 'Third kingdom' of the Spirit" (66).

38. See, for instance, Balthasar, "Improvisation on Spirit and Future," *Explorations in Theology*, 3:151–54, 166; and Bulgakov, *Lamb of God*, 110. The similarities between Balthasar and Bulgakov are particularly striking in Balthasar's analysis of the dyad of Son and Spirit in *Theo-Logic* 3, especially the section "The Father's Two Hands," 167–218.

39. Bulgakov, *Lamb of God*, 431; cf. 424.

40. Balthasar, *TD*, 4:47.

41. Balthasar, *GL*, 7:219.

42. Ibid., 219; italics added.

43. Ibid., 220. Balthasar understands this tension to engender movement, a dynamism that is concretely expressed in the Church, "which essentially is an institution that never rests for a single moment, but must always be breaking off and setting out" (*GL*, 7:485). See especially the whole section "Setting out towards God," *GL*, 7:485–543.

44. See Balthasar, *TD*, 5:56–58; 199–203.

45. For Balthasar on the phenomenon of escalating stakes in Schelling, see *Apokalypse der deutschen Seele*, 1:244: "Die Versuchung des Grundes muß immer heftiger werden, je mehr Gottes Geist siegt, denn die Kraft der Versuchung ist ja die Kraft des göttlichen Grundes selber."

46. Schelling, *Philosophical Inquires*, 57.

47. Balthasar, *TD*, 5:202.

48. See Balthasar, "The Provocation Offered by Jesus," *TD*, 4:433–52. Also see *TD*, 5:271, and "Improvisation on Spirit and Future," *Explorations in Theology*, 3:142.

49. See Balthasar, *TD*, 5:502–4.

50. Here see O'Regan, *Anatomy of Misremembering*, 389 and 617n13.

51. Paul Valliere is very helpful here:

> By appending such a fantastic story to a carefully constructed philo-
> sophical dialogue Soloviev implicitly concedes the limits of a teleological
> theory of history. An idea of the end of things is needed to orient human

action, yet no theory of the end—Mr. Z.'s or anyone else's—can be verified on the basis of present-day realities because the end by definition is not yet given. A teleology of history cannot be consummated *in medias res* except in visions, intimations, presentiments or parables of some kind. Accordingly Mr. Z.'s contribution to *Three Dialogues* ends not in reasoned dialectic but with a prophetic parable. (*Modern Russian Theology*, 214)

52. Balthasar, *GL*, 7:509.

53. Ibid., 514.

54. Ibid., 518–19.

55. Balthasar, *GL*, 3:290.

56. Ibid., 352.

57. Balthasar, *Theological Anthropology*, 192.

58. Ibid., 144.

59. Soloviev, *War, Progress, and the End of History*, 121–22. Balthasar also quotes this passage in *GL*, 3:350.

60. For Bulgakov on Antichrist, see *Bride of the Lamb*, 328–30; and *Lamb of God*, xiv, 156, 419, 434. Also see O'Regan, *Theology and the Spaces of Apocalyptic*: "Bulgakov's conviction that vision is the issue of modernity helps to explain his distinctive interpretation of the Antichrist. Bulgakov thinks that Revelation (17.8) has advantages over other biblical texts such as Daniel and 2 Thessalonians (2.2–10) in thinking of the Antichrist as plural rather than singular (*BL*, 30, 329–30), and in specifying as one of the characteristic behaviors of the Antichrist that of 'false teaching' or the 'lie' (*BL*, 330)" (59).

61. Soloviev, *War, Progress, and the End of History*, 120. Also see Vladimir Soloviev, "On Counterfeits," *Freedom, Faith, and Dogma: Essays by V. S. Soloviev on Christianity and Judaism* (Albany: State University of New York Press, 2008), 147–58.

62. Balthasar, *TD*, 4:57. Cf. *TD*, 4:437, 446, 451, 468; *TD*, 5:50, 207, 271; and *GL*, 7:503. See also O'Regan, *Theology and the Spaces of Apocalyptic*, 49 and 145n48.

63. Balthasar, *GL*, 3:296–97. Balthasar links Soloviev and Dostoevsky in *GL*, 3:294–96. Also see O'Regan, *Theology and the Spaces of Apocalyptic*, 49. On the point of the ontological status of evil, Balthasar thus sides with Schelling against Hegel.

64. For secondary sources that treat Soloviev's narrative of the Antichrist, see Bernard McGinn, *Antichrist: Two Thousand Years of the Human Fascination with Evil* (New York: Columbia University Press, 1999); David Bethea, *The Shape of Apocalypse in Modern Russian Fiction* (Princeton, NJ: Princeton University Press, 1989), 110–16; Milosz, "Science Fiction and the Coming of Antichrist," *Emperor of the Earth*, 15–31; Judith Deutsch Korn-

blatt, "Soloviev on Salvation: The Story of the 'Short Story of the Antichrist,'" in *Russian Religious Thought*, ed. Judith Deutsch Kornblatt and Richard F. Gustafson (Madison: University of Wisconsin Press, 1996), 68–90.

65. Soloviev, *War, Progress, and the End of History*, 167. It hardly needs to be noted here that Nietzschean hubris (*Zarathustra* and *Ecce Homo* come immediately to mind) is at the forefront of Soloviev's consideration with this Antichrist figure, a "superman" tormented by a jealous, parodic rivalry of Christ. Cf. Balthasar, *Theological Anthropology*, 51.

66. Soloviev, *War, Progress, and the End of History*, 165.

67. Ibid., 167.

68. Ibid., 168.

69. Ibid., 184.

70. See O'Regan, *Theology and the Spaces of Apocalyptic*: "These Russian thinkers pose a question that will have to be asked again and again, and which is taken up into Catholic thought by the French poet Paul Claudel: can justice become the banner of the Antichrist?" (53).

71. Milosz, "Science Fiction and the Coming of Antichrist," *Emperor of the Earth*, 24.

72. Balthasar, *GL*, 3:296.

73. Balthasar, *TD*, 4:449–50.

74. Ibid., 446.

75. Balthasar, *GL*, 7:501.

76. Ibid., 520. Cf. "Improvisation on Spirit and Future," *Explorations in Theology*, 3:160.

77. Balthasar, *TD*, 4:447.

78. Ibid., 450.

79. For instance, Lucy Gardner and David Moss assert in "Something Like Time; Something Like the Sexes: An Essay in Reception," in *Balthasar at the End of Modernity*, ed. Gardner et al., that "if one were to speak of the 'systematic impulse' in Balthasar's work, we should recognize that this does not reside in any riveting of 'parts' on to an empty frame, nor in any correlation of God to his creature, but rather in the 'ever more deeply plumbed repetition' yielding a formidable density of the same mystery: the *kenosis* of the Son prefigured in the *Urkenosis* of the Father" (72).

80. Schelling has a brief excursus on Wisdom/Sophia in *Ages of the World*, construed as "a playful pleasure at the beginning of the life of God . . . an unblemished mirror of divine force" (163). See 163–66. Cf. Thomas Kliben-gajtis, "Sophia in Schelling's Work: From Divine Wisdom to Human Science," *Transcultural Studies* 4 (2008): 13–26. The lines of influence on this point from Schelling to the Russians (Soloviev and Bulgakov in particular) warrant further exploration. Böhme likewise has much to say about Wisdom. See O'Regan, *Gnostic Apocalypse*, esp. 67, 149, 152, 237–38n11, 245n25, 264n10. Robert F.

Brown's "Schelling and Dorner on Divine Immutability," *Journal of the American Academy of Religion* 53, no. 2 (June 1985): 237–49, draws out the influence of Schelling's philosophy on Isaak August Dorner (1809–1884), one of the most important critics of the kenoticists. Brown emphasizes the relation with Schelling especially with respect to Dorner's reflections on modifying the ancient understanding of divine immutability by introducing "livingness" (*Lebendigkeit*) to a new notion of "ethical immutability." Dorner recalls German Idealism in his understanding of infinity as "intensive," that is, inclusive of otherness (Hegel); the primacy of the ethical over the ontological (Schleiermacher), and finally, in the rearticulation of the Fichtean "not-I" as originary to God's being (Schelling). See Brown, "Schelling and Dorner on Divine Immutability," 239–40. For Dorner, see Claude Welch, *God and Incarnation in Mid-Nineteenth Century German Theology: Thomasius, Dorner, Biedermann* (New York: Oxford University Press, 1965), esp. 115–80; and Claude Welch, *Protestant Thought in the Nineteenth Century*, vol. 1, *1799–1870* (New Haven, CT: Yale University Press, 1972). For Bulgakov on the nineteenth-century German kenoticists, see *Lamb of God*, 220n12.

81. See Schelling, *Ages of the World*, 176ff.

82. For instance, see Jakob Böhme, *Reflection on Divine Revelation*, Question 3, Responses 2 and 3, in *Great Dialecticians of Christian Thought*, trans. Ernest Benjamin Koenker (Minneapolis, MN: Augsburg, 1971), 61–62. See also Jacob Boehme, *Six Theosophic Points*, trans. John Earle (Ann Arbor: University of Michigan Press, 1958). O'Regan's *Gnostic Apocalypse*, while complex, is incredibly helpful, not least because it admits the opacity of Böhme's style but nevertheless demonstrates deep familiarity with the texts themselves in its careful tracking of the Böhmian narrative of the self-manifestation of the divine.

83. Schelling, *Ages of the World*, 126–35; 171.

84. Ibid., 172.

85. Ibid., 131–33.

86. Ibid., 154. This does not invalidate Schelling's concept, inherited from Böhme and discussed here in chapter 3, of the sense world as the product of a "Fall."

87. Ibid.,145. Schelling's designator "play" recalls Hegel's dismissive comments about a God that does not suffer and thus is not "serious."

88. See Balthasar, *TD*, 4:326–27.

89. Berdyaev, *Destiny of Man*, 25. Also see Berdyaev, *The Beginning and the End*, 18ff. Also consider passages such as the following: "*Primary life . . . is not pre-eminently intellectual in character . . . it is passion, which precedes the very distinction between good and evil*" (*The Beginning and the End*, 69; italics original). This "primary life" is prior to the immanent Trinity and certainly prior to the economic. As discussed in chapter 3, Böhme's *Ungrund* is

prior to the generation of nature, or the triadic powers, out of which arises determinate freedom. Though he is massively dependent on Böhme, Berdyaev does tend to conflate two senses of "nothing," though both are considered meonic: the *Ungrund* so called, which is pure, undifferentiated potentially, and the Eternal Nature as the ground of eternal freedom. For Böhme on this point, see O'Regan, *Gnostic Apocalypse*, especially 37–42. O'Regan notes the distinction in this way: "If both the Unground and Eternal Nature can be regarded as species of *me on*, the non-Parmenidean nothing of the Unground is that of possible, even potential being, whereas that of Eternal Nature represents the refusal of the relationality and spiritual completeness of being. . . . Eternal Nature is an anti-aesthetic chaos, a chaos that is aggressively formless" (*Gnostic Apocalypse*, 37–38). Eternal Nature is thus not the most originary reality in Böhme. Further, it is Eternal Nature that introduces the possibility of (and perhaps even the reality of) evil into the divine.

90. Bulgakov, *Lamb of God*, 96.

91. Ibid.

92. Ibid., 128.

93. Ibid. Also cf. 223.

94. See, for instance, Balthasar, *GL*, 1:49, 195.

95. Cf. Balthasar, *GL*, 7:208, 226, 511. See also, for instance, Bulgakov, *Lamb of God*, 177, 344.

96. Balthasar, *TD*, 4:52; *TD*, 5:151, 246.

97. Balthasar, *TD*, 4:451.

98. Balthasar, *TD*, 5:151. See also *Mysterium Paschale*, 206–8.

99. Balthasar, *TD*, 4:58. Cf. *GL*, 7:510.

100. Balthasar, *TD*, 5:120; cf. 121.

101. Balthasar, *Mysterium Paschale*, 203; *TL*, 2:35, 323; *Theology of History*, 69. For more on Holy Saturday as a Trinitaritan event, see his "Going to the Dead: Holy Saturday," *Mysterium Paschale*, 148–88.

102. See, for instance, Balthasar, *TD*, 5:223–24; *Mysterium Paschale*, 31–32, 45–46n60, 178; and Bulgakov, *Lamb of God*, 220.

103. See Brown, "Schelling and Dorner on Divine Immutability."

104. For passages specifically on kenosis, see Thomasius, *Christ's Person and Work*, 50ff, 71, 93–100, in Welch, *God and Incarnation*. For secondary treatment of Thomasius and the other nineteenth-century kenoticists, see A. B. Bruce, *The Humiliation of Christ in Its Physical, Ethical, and Official Aspects* (Grand Rapids, MI: Eerdmans, 1955), 138–144; Welch, *Protestant Thought*, 1:3, 218–19, 225–27, 235–40, 265; and Thomas R. Thompson, "Nineteenth-Century Kenotic Christology: The Waxing, Waning, and Weighing of a Quest for a Coherent Orthodoxy," in *Exploring Kenotic Christology: The Self-Emptying of God*, ed. C. Stephen Evans (Oxford: Oxford University Press, 2006), 74–111.

105. Balthasar, *Mysterium Paschale*, 32.

106. A. E. Biedermann, *Christian Dogmatics*, in Welch, *God and Incarnation*, 306.

107. Bulgakov, *Lamb of God*, 226n13.

108. Balthasar, *Mysterium Paschale*, 33.

109. Balthasar sets out the problem of navigating this theological Scylla and Charybdis succinctly in his preface to the second edition of *Mysterium Paschale*, vii–ix.

110. See especially Hegel's preface to G. W. F. Hegel, *The Phenomenology of Spirit*, trans. A.V. Miller (Oxford: Oxford University Press, 1977). See also Cyril O'Regan, *The Heterodox Hegel* (Albany: State University of New York Press, 1994), especially chapter 4, "Epochal Overlap: Incarnation and the Passion Narrative," 189–234; William Desmond, *Hegel's God: A Counterfeit Double?* (Burlington, VT: Ashgate Publishing, 2003); and Hans Küng, *The Incarnation of God: An Introduction to Hegel's Theological Thought as Prolegomena to a Future Christology*, trans. J. R. Stephenson (New York: Crossroad, 1987). Schelling is not innocent here, either. For his claim that history requires the suffering and development of the divine, see Schelling, *Philosophical Inquiries*, 84.

111. Balthasar, *Cosmic Liturgy*, 130. For one example of Berdyaev's stipulation of the necessity of tragedy in the inner life of God, see *Destiny of Man*, 28–30. Also see Nicolas Berdyaev, *Studies in Boehme*, *Put* 20 [in Russian], referenced in *Destiny of Man*, 29n1.

112. Hans Urs von Balthasar, *Mysterium Paschale*, 62. Cf. *GL*, 5:569.

113. Hegel, *Werke II*, 1832, #19, quoted by Balthasar in *TD*, 5:225. See also Hegel, *Phenomenology of Spirit*, 10. Also see the preface to *Phenomenology of Spirit*, no. 32:

> The life of the Spirit is not the life that shrinks from death and keeps itself untouched by devastation, but rather the life that endures it and maintains itself in it. It wins its truth only when, in utter dismemberment, it finds itself. It is this power, not as something positive, which closes its eyes to the negative, as when we say of something that it is nothing or is false, and then, having done with it, turn away and pass on to something else; on the contrary, Spirit is this power only by looking the negative in the face, and tarrying with it. This tarrying with the negative is the magical power that converts it into being. (19)

114. Balthasar, "Eschatology in Outline," *Explorations in Theology*, 4:434.

115. Balthasar, *TL*, 3:41. Cf. *TD*, 4:327.

116. Balthasar, *TD*, 4:321–22.

117. Ibid., 318.

118. Balthasar does suggest that the patristic understanding of immutability was a bit more nuanced than not, and that the strong claims to divine

immutability involved the resistance to the Greek notion of pathos as (1) being subject to some external force or (2) having to do with sin, notions that are obviously to be resisted with respect to claims about the divine. See *TD*, 5:218–19.

119. Balthasar, *TD*, 4:319–28; also see *TD*, 3:506–9. I present a very similar argument in Martin, "The 'Whence' and the 'Whither' of Balthasar's Gendered Theology."

120. Balthasar, *Mysterium Paschale*, 34.

121. Bulgakov, *Lamb of God*, 232. Berdyaev would not be terribly anxious about this formulation.

122. Balthasar, *Mysterium Paschale*, 46n69.

123. In *Mysterium Paschale*, Balthasar finds fault with Bulgakov's positing of Sophia "as both uncreated and created reality, a 'condition of possibility' for the union of the two natures in Christ, and thus, so to speak, a suprachristological scheme for Christology" (46n69). A more sympathetic reading might recall Bulgakov's own intention that Sophia be understood as no more than a way of naming divine substance, or *ousia*, in a manner that prescinds from the understanding of *ousia* as a deposit antecedent to personhood, an abstracted category which metaphysically funds the persons. Though it is theoretically possible to discuss Bulgakov's kenotic theory apart from reference to sophiology as we are doing in this chapter, bear in mind that for him Sophia is the very substrate of the kenotic activity, and the reason the created order bears a "sophianic" character.

124. Balthasar, *GL*, 7:213–14. For a similar passage, see *Mysterium Paschale*, 35. Also see *TD*, 4:323, as well as *TL*, 2:177–78.

125. Balthasar, *Mysterium Paschale*, viii–ix; and *TD*, 4:323–23. See also Bulgakov, *Lamb of God*, 226. Gorodetzky's section on Bulgakov in *The Humiliated Christ in Modern Russian Thought* is a concise and articulate summary of his highly original perspective.

126. Bulgakov, *Lamb of God*, 114.

127. Bulgakov, *Comforter*, 68ff.

128. Cf. Balthasar, *TD*, 3:34,183–91; *TD*, 5:123; *TL*, 3:34; and "Spirit and Institution," and "Improvisation on Spirit and Future," *Explorations in Theology*, 4:231–35.

129. Bulgakov, *Lamb of God*, 176.

130. See Bulgakov, *Comforter*, 359–94.

131. Balthasar, *Mysterium Paschale*, 28. Aquinas and others are also in the background with respect to creation originating in the Trinitarian processions. Balthasar acknowledges both Thomas and Bonaventure on this point. See *TD*, 5:61–64).

132. Balthasar, *TD*, 4:331.

133. Balthasar, *TD*, 5:84.

134. Balthasar, *TD*, 4:323.

135. Ibid., 324.

136. Ibid., 326. Also see *Mysterium Paschale*, 34; *Theological Anthropology*, 210–11; and *Explorations in Theology*, 4:435.

137. Balthasar, *TD*, 4:327. See also *TD*, 5:245–46.

138. Balthasar, *TD*, 5:75; cf. *TD*, 5:66, 73–74. See also *TD*, 2:209ff, 238. The "power" thus takes the form of surrender: God "wishes to be almighty not solely by creating: by begetting and breathing forth, and allowing himself to be begotten and breathed forth, he hands over his power to the Other— whoever that Other may be—without ever seeking to take it back" (*TD*, 5:66).

139. Hans Urs von Balthasar, *The Von Balthasar Reader*, ed. Medard Kehl and Werner Löser, trans. Robert J. Daly, S.J., and Fred Lawrence (New York: Crossroad, 1997), 65.

140. Aristotle Papanikolaou, "Person, Kenosis and Abuse: Hans Urs von Balthasar and Feminist Theologies in Conversation," *Modern Theology* 19, no. 1 (January 2003): 42; cf. 52.

141. Balthasar, *TD*, 5:245.

142. Bulgakov, *Lamb of God*, 98; italics original. See also 128–29.

143. Ibid., 99.

144. Ibid., 225.

145. Ibid.

146. Ibid., 100–1.

147. Ibid., 313–16, 353–54, 370–72.

148. Balthasar, *TD*, 4:323–28. Others think differently. Celia Deane-Drummond, in "The Breadth of Glory: A Trinitarian Eschatology for the Earth through Critical Engagement with Hans Urs Von Balthasar," *International Journal of Systematic Theology* 12, no. 1 (January 2010): 46–64, believes that while Balthasar and Bulgakov do share demerits (both having patriarchal and monarchical portraits of God), Balthasar's Trinitarian theology—which, according to her interpretation, veers dangerously toward tritheism—far exceeds Bulgakov's in terms of positing a separation between the hypostases, so their views are not actually coincident. Deane-Drummond writes that, contrary to Balthasar, Bulgakov "always insisted that kenosis did not equate with complete separation of the three persons" (51n27) because he stipulates that at death the Father receives the spirit of the Son, who has "abandoned His body" (*Lamb of God*, 314). Yet Bulgakov does speak in terms of the Holy Spirit's abandonment of the Son insofar as the Spirit is the "palpable proximity of the Father" (*Lamb of God*, 314). It is difficult also to attenuate such statements from Bulgakov as "the Son is orphaned, and the Father is alone . . . the Son no longer lives in union with the Father, just as the Father no longer lives in union with the Son" (*Lamb of God*, 353). Also see Rowan Williams, "Balthasar and the Trinity," in *The Cambridge Companion to Hans Urs von Balthasar*, ed. Edward T. Oakes and David Moss (Cambridge: Cambridge University Press, 2004), 37–50.

149. Bulgakov, *Lamb of God*, 345.

150. Balthasar, *Theological Anthropology*, 69.

151. For a lovely article on Balthasar's theology of the descent into hell that connects the descent to the universality of hope, and to the poetry of Charles Péguy, see Juan M. Sara, *"Descensus ad inferos*, Dawn of Hope: Aspects of the Theology of Holy Saturday in the Trilogy of Hans Urs von Balthasar," in *Love Alone is Credible*, ed. David L. Schindler (Grand Rapids, MI: Eerdmans, 2008), 209–40. Also see Peter Casarella, "The Descent, Divine Self-Enrichment, and the Universality of Salvation" (lecture given at a conference honoring the work of Hans Urs von Balthasar on the 100th anniversary of his birth, April 14–17, 2005, Lansdowne Resort and Conference Center, Lansdowne, VA). For a quite severe account that calls the orthodoxy of Balthasar's view into question, see Pitstick, *Light in Darkness*.

152. Bulgakov, *Lamb of God*, 315–16. It is rather surprising that Pitstick does not acknowledge Bulgakov as a source in this respect.

153. Ibid., 316.

154. Ibid., 372–79.

155. Balthasar, *TD*, 5:517, 123.

156. Balthasar, *TD*, 4:319.

157. Balthasar, "Eschatology in Outline," *Explorations in Theology*, 4:411. Cf. *GL*, 7:209–55, 389–415. See also "Hell and Trinity," *TL*, 2:345–61, especially for Balthasar's affirmation of von Speyr's theology of hell.

158. Deane-Drummond finds the claim that the spirit provides the bond of unity during the abandonment on the cross to be "strained beyond measure," calling the Spirit in this context "a macabre figure in the form of an executioner" ("Breadth of Glory," 50). Matthew Levering also critiques Balthasar on this point in his *Scripture and Metaphysics: Aquinas and the Renewal of Trinitarian Theology* (Oxford: Blackwell, 2004), 132.

159. Balthasar, *Mysterium Paschale*, 174.

160. As I suggest elsewhere, however, the idea of this "absolute, infinite (analogical but non-ontological) distance or 'hiatus' between the hypostases, a 'separation' of God from God in the consubstantial generation of the Son from the Father . . . ought not be taken over-literally in a manner that would compromise the unity of the divine nature" (Martin, "'Whence' and 'Whither,'" 218). See Balthasar, "Eschatology in Outline," *Explorations in Theology*, 4:411–12. Cf. also *GL*, 7:231.

161. Balthasar, *TD*, 4:323. See also *Theological Anthropology*, 71.

162. Sarah Coakley, "Kenosis: Theological Meanings and Gender Connotations" in *The Work of Love: Creation as Kenosis*, ed. John Polkinghorne (Grand Rapids, MI: Eerdmans, 2001), 208; cf. Ward, "Kenosis: Death, Discourse and Resurrection," in *Balthasar at the End of Modernity*, ed. Gardner et al., 44.

163. See Balthasar, *Mysterium Paschale*, 35; *TD*, 4:319; and *GL*, 7:208.

164. Balthasar, "Some Points of Eschatology," *Explorations in Theology*, 1:262.

165. Balthasar, "Eschatology in Outlines," *Explorations in Theology*, 4:430–31. Also see "Positivity of the 'Other,'" *TD*, 5:81–85.

166. Balthasar, *Mysterium Paschale*, ix.

167. For instance, see Balthasar, *TD* 3: "In the Trinity as revealed by Christ, the two things are proclaimed simultaneously: it is as Father, Son and Spirit that God is involved with the world, for its salvation—for the doctrine of the Trinity has a profoundly soteriological significance; but it as *God* that he is thus involved. He does not *become* 'love' by having the world as his 'thou' and 'partner' . . . he 'is love' already" (509).

168. Balthasar, *Mysterium Paschale*, viii–ix; *TD*, 3:228.

169. For Balthasar's articulation of Moltmann as Hegelian on this point, see *TD*, 5:227. Also see Balthasar, *TD*, 5:245.

170. Balthasar, *TD*, 4:328.

171. Balthasar, *GL*, 7:214; cf. 221 of the same volume.

172. Bulgakov, *Lamb of God*, 213.

173. Ibid., 215.

174. Balthasar, "Eschatology in Outline," *Explorations in Theology*, 4:423.

175. Ibid.

176. Ibid., 457. Also see *TD*, 5:66–85.

177. Balthasar, "Eschatology in Outline," *Explorations in Theology*, 4:442.

178. Balthasar, *GL*, 7:516. Cf. *TD*, 5:112.

179. Balthasar, "Some Points of Eschatology," *Explorations in Theology*, 1:260–61.

180. Balthasar, *TD*, 5:57. Also cf. *GL*, 1:158; *TL*, 3:35ff, 438.

181. Balthasar, *TD*, 4:44.

182. Ibid., 46.

183. Balthasar, *TD*, 2:280.

184. Balthasar, *GL*, 2:28.

Conclusion

1. Balthasar, *GL*, 5:478.

2. Balthasar, *TD*, 2:56.

3. Ibid., 58.

4. Bulgakov, *Unfading Light*, 159.

5. See also Balthasar, *Truth Is Symphonic: Aspects of Christian Pluralism*, trans. Graham Harrison (San Francisco: Ignatius Press, 1987).

6. Balthasar, *GL*, 1:17.

7. Balthasar, *GL*, 2:23–24.

8. Ibid.

9. Balthasar, "The Word, Scripture, and Tradition," *Explorations in Theology*, 1:23; italics added.

10. Balthasar, *GL*, 5:418.

11. Ibid.

12. Ibid., 418–19.

13. Balthasar, *GL*, 2:27. See also *GL*, 1: "Christ's particular kind of unity requires a glance that traces a course back into the very mystery of God, who manifests his 'mystery, more dazzling than the light,' by this stroke of 'christological genius': he is both himself and yet also another; he is both triune and hypostatic. This is a mystery of the divine freedom, which, as in the work of art, coincides with supreme necessity" (488).

14. Balthasar, "The Word, Scripture and Tradition," *Explorations in Theology*, 1:21; italics added.

15. Balthasar, *TL*, 3:31.

16. Balthasar, *Theology of History*, 107–8.

17. Balthasar, *TD*, 2:58–59.

18. Balthasar, "Some Points of Eschatology," *Explorations in Theology*, 1:257.

19. Balthasar puts it well: "The Spirit who breathes where he will is not the mild, diffused, timeless beacon of the Enlightenment always present in the same fashion. Rather he is the Spirit of missions and special functions within the mystical body, the Spirit who, in fulfilling the Old Testament, continues its historical course, in which ever new, unforeseeable tasks sent by God erupt." "The Place of Theology," *Explorations in Theology*, 1:157–58.

20. Bulgakov, *Comforter*, 313. Bulgakov's contemporary Pavel Florensky makes a similar point in *The Pillar and Ground of the Truth*, aligning the Word with rational principles and the Spirit with freedom, creativity, and interruption; see Pavel Florensky, "On the Holy Spirit," in *Ultimate Questions*, ed. Alexander Schmemann, 137–72; and V. Ivanov, "The Aesthetic Views of Fr. Pavel Florensky," *Journal of the Moscow Patriarchate* 9 (1982): 75–78.

21. Balthasar, *Theological Anthropology*, 122.

22. Bulgakov, "The Church as Tradition," *Orthodox Church*, 9–35; here 26.

23. Ibid., 30; cf. 32.

24. Balthasar, *Theological Anthropology*, 123; cf. 121, 125, 173, 198–99 of the same volume. See also Sergei Bulgakov, "Dogmat i dogmatika,' *Zhivoe predanie: pravoslavie v sovremennosti* (Paris: YMCA, 1937), 20.

25. Bulgakov, *Unfading Light*, 77. Cf. 68.

26. Balthasar, *Cosmic Liturgy*, 236.

27. Bulgakov, *Unfading Light*, 74.

28. Balthasar, *TD*, 2:363.

SELECTED BIBLIOGRAPHY

PRIMARY LITERATURE

Balthasar, Hans Urs von. *Apokalypse der deutschen Seele: Studien zu einer Lehre von letzten Haltungen.* Vol. 1, *Der deutsche Idealismus.* Einsiedeln: Johannes Verlag, 1937.

———. *Apokalypse der deutschen Seele: Studien zu einer Lehre von letzten Haltungen.* Vol. 2, *Im Zeichen Nietzsches.* Einsiedeln: Johannes Verlag, 1939.

———. *Apokalypse der deutschen Seele: Studien zu einer Lehre von letzten Haltungen.* Vol. 3, *Vergöttlichung des Todes.* Einsiedeln: Johannes Verlag, 1939.

———. *Bernanos: An Ecclesial Existence.* Translated by Erasmo Leiva-Merikakis. San Francisco: Ignatius Press, 1996.

———. *Cosmic Liturgy: The Universe According to Maximus the Confessor.* Translated by Brian E. Daley, S.J. San Francisco: Ignatius Press, 2003.

———. *Dare We Hope "That All Men Be Saved"? with a Short Discourse on Hell.* Translated by David Kipp and Lothar Krauth. San Francisco: Ignatius Press, 1988.

———. *Epilogue.* Translated by Edward T. Oakes, S.J. San Francisco: Ignatius Press, 2004.

———. *Explorations in Theology.* Vol. 1, *The Word Made Flesh.* Translated by A. V. Littledale and Alexandre Dru. San Francisco: Ignatius Press, 1989.

———. *Explorations in Theology.* Vol. 2, *Spouse of the Word.* Translated by A. V. Littledale, Alexandre Dru, and John Saward. San Francisco: Ignatius Press, 1991.

———. *Explorations in Theology.* Vol. 3, *Creator Spirit.* Translated by Brian McNeil, C.R.V. San Francisco: Ignatius Press, 1993.

————. *Explorations in Theology*. Vol. 4, *Spirit and Institution*. Translated by Edward T. Oakes, S.J. San Francisco: Ignatius Press, 1995.

————. "The Fathers, the Scholastics, and Ourselves." *Communio* 24 (1997): 347–96.

————. *The Glory of the Lord: A Theological Aesthetics*. Vol. 1, *Seeing the Form*. Edited by Joseph Fessio, S.J., and John Riches. San Francisco: Ignatius Press, 1982.

————. *The Glory of the Lord: A Theological Aesthetics*. Vol. 2, *Studies in Theological Style: Clerical Styles*. Edited by John Riches. Translated by Andrew Louth, Francis McDonagh, and Brian McNeil, C.R.V. San Francisco: Ignatius Press, 1984.

————. *The Glory of the Lord: A Theological Aesthetics*. Vol. 3, *Studies in Theological Style: Lay Styles*. Edited by John Riches. Translated by Andrew Louth, John Saward, Martin Simon, and Rowan Williams. San Francisco: Ignatius Press, 1986.

————. *The Glory of the Lord: A Theological Aesthetics*. Vol. 4, *The Realm of Metaphysics in Antiquity*. Edited by John Riches. Translated by Brian McNeil, C.R.V., Andrew Louth, John Saward, Rowan Williams, and Oliver Davies. San Francisco: Ignatius Press, 1989.

————. *The Glory of the Lord: A Theological Aesthetics*. Vol. 5, *The Realm of Metaphysics in the Modern Age*. Edited by Brian McNeil C.R.V. and John Riches. Translated by Oliver Davies, Andrew Louth, Brian McNeil C.R.V., John Saward, and Rowan Williams. San Francisco: Ignatius Press, 1990.

————. *The Glory of the Lord: A Theological Aesthetics*. Vol. 6, *Theology: The Old Covenant*. Edited by John Riches. Translated by Brian McNeil C.R.V. and Erasmo Leiva-Merikakis. San Francisco: Ignatius Press, 1991.

————. *The Glory of the Lord: A Theological Aesthetics*. Vol. 7, *Theology: The New Covenant*. Translated by Brian McNeil, C.R.V. Edited by John Riches. San Francisco: Ignatius Press, 1989.

————. "Katholische Religion und Kunst." *Schweizeriche Rundschau* 27 (1927): 44–54.

————. *Love Alone Is Credible*. Translated by D. C. Schindler. San Francisco: Ignatius Press, 1994.

————. *The Moment of Christian Witness*. Translated by Richard Beckley. San Francisco: Ignatius Press, 1994.

————. *Mysterium Paschale: The Mystery of Easter*, 2d ed. Translated by Aidan Nichols, O.P. San Francisco: Ignatius Press, 1990.

————. *My Work: In Retrospect*. Translated by Brian McNeil. San Francisco: Ignatius Press, 1993.

————, ed. *Origen: Spirit & Fire. A Thematic Anthology of His Writings*. Translated by Robert J. Daly, S.J. Washington, DC: Catholic University of America Press, 1984.

——. *Presence and Thought: Essay on the Religious Philosophy of Gregory of Nyssa.* Translated by Mark Sebanc. San Francisco: Ignatius Press, 1995.

——. *Theo-Drama: Theological Dramatic Theory.* Vol. 1, *Prolegomena.* Translated by Graham Harrison. San Francisco: Ignatius Press, 1988.

——. *Theo-Drama: Theological Dramatic Theory.* Vol. 2, *The Dramatis Personae: Man in God.* Translated by Graham Harrison. San Francisco: Ignatius Press, 1990.

——. *Theo-Drama: Theological Dramatic Theory.* Vol. 3, *The Dramatis Personae: Persons in Christ.* Translated by Graham Harrison. San Francisco: Ignatius Press, 1992.

——. *Theo-Drama: Theological Dramatic Theory* Vol. 4, *The Action.* Translated by Graham Harrison. San Francisco: Ignatius Press, 1994.

——. *Theo-Drama: Theological Dramatic Theory.* Vol. 5, *The Last Act.* Translated by Graham Harrison. San Francisco: Ignatius Press, 1998.

——. *Theo-Logic: Theological Logical Theory.* Vol. 1, *The Truth of the World.* Translated by Adrian J. Walker. San Francisco: Ignatius Press, 2000.

——. *Theo-Logic: Theological Logical Theory.* Vol. 2, *Truth of God.* Translated by Adrian J. Walker. San Francisco: Ignatius Press, 2004.

——. *Theo-Logic: Theological Logical Theory.* Vol. 3, *The Spirit of Truth.* Translated by Graham Harrison. San Francisco: Ignatius Press, 2005.

——. *A Theological Anthropology.* Eugene, OR: Wipf & Stock, 2010.

——. *A Theology of History.* 2d ed. San Francisco: Ignatius Press, 1963.

——. *Truth Is Symphonic: Aspects of Christian Pluralism.* Translated by Graham Harrison. San Francisco: Ignatius Press, 1987.

——. "Why I Am Still a Christian." In *Two Say Why,* by Hans Urs von Balthasar and Joseph Ratzinger. Translated by John Griffiths. London: Search Press, 1973.

Berdyaev, Nicolas. *The Beginning and the End: Essay on Eschatological Metaphysics.* London: Geoffrey Bles, 1952.

——. *The Destiny of Man.* Translated by N. Duddington. New York: Harper & Row, 1960.

——. *Dostoievsky.* Translated by Donald Attwater. New York: Sheed & Ward, 1934.

——. *Dream and Reality: An Essay in Autobiography.* Translated by Katherine Lampert. London: G. Bles, 1950.

——. *The Fate of Man in the Modern World.* Translated by Donald A. Lowrie. San Rafael, CA: Semantron Press, 2009.

——. *Freedom and the Spirit.* Translated by Oliver F. Clarke. London: G. Bles, 1935.

——. *The Meaning of History.* Translated by George Reavey. London: G. Bles, 1936.

——. *The Meaning of the Creative Act.* Translated by Donald A. Lowrie. London: Gollancz, 1955.

———. *The Russian Idea.* Translated by R. M. French. New York: Lindisfarne Press, 1992.

———. *Slavery and Freedom.* Translated by R. M. French. London: G. Bles, 1947.

———. "Unground and Freedom." Introduction to Jacob Boehme, *Six Theosophic Points and Other Writings.* Translated by John Earle. Ann Arbor: University of Michigan Press, 1958.

Böhme, Jakob. *The Aurora.* Translated by John Sparrow. London, 1656.

———. *The Second Booke Concerning the Three Principles of the Divine Essence of the Eternal Dark, Light, and Temporary World.* Translated by John Sparrow. London, 1648.

———. *Signatura Rerum: Or the Signature of All Things.* Translated by J. Ellistone. London, 1651.

Bulgakov, Sergei. *The Bride of the Lamb.* Translated by Boris Jakim. Grand Rapids, MI: Eerdmans, 2002.

———. *The Comforter.* Translated by Boris Jakim. Grand Rapids, MI: Eerdmans, 2004.

———. *The Holy Grail and the Eucharist.* Translated by Boris Jakim. Hudson, NY: Lindisfarne Books, 1997.

———. "Ivan Karamazov as a Philosophical Type." In *A Bulgakov Anthology,* edited by James Pain and Nicolas Zernov, 36–41. Philadelphia: Westminster Press, 1976.

———. *The Lamb of God.* Translated by Boris Jakim. Grand Rapids, MI: Eerdmans, 2008.

———. *The Orthodox Church.* Crestwood, NY: St. Vladimir's Seminary Press, 1988.

———. *Philosophy of Economy: The World as Household.* Edited and translated by Catherine Evtuhov. New Haven, CT: Yale University Press, 2000.

———. *Sophia, the Wisdom of God: An Outline of Sophiology.* Hudson, NY: Lindisfarne Press, 1993.

———. *The Unfading Light: Contemplations and Speculations.* Translated by Thomas Allen Smith. Grand Rapids, MI: Eerdmans, 2012.

Hegel, G. W. F. *Aesthetics: Lectures on Fine Art.* Translated by T. M. Knox. 2 vols. Oxford: Clarendon, 1975.

———. *Phenomenology of Spirit.* Translated by A. V. Miller. Oxford: Oxford University Press, 1977.

Schelling, F. W. J. *The Abyss of Freedom/Ages of the World.* Translated by Judith Norman, with an essay by Slavoj Žižek. Ann Arbor: University of Michigan Press, 1997.

———. *The Ages of the World (Fragment), from the Handwritten Remains (c. 1815).* Translated by Jason M. Wirth. Albany: State University of New York Press, 2000.

———. *Bruno, or, On the Natural and the Divine Principle of Things.* Translated by Michael G. Vater. Albany, NY: State University of New York Press, 1984.

———. *Clara, or, On Nature's Connection to the Spirit World.* Translated by Fiona Steinkamp. Albany: State University of New York Press, 2002.

———. *The Grounding of Positive Philosophy: The Berlin Lectures.* Translated by Bruce Matthews. New York: State University of New York Press, 2008.

———. *Historical-Critical Introduction to the Philosophy of Mythology.* Translated by Mason Richey and Markus Zisselsberger. New York: State University of New York Press, 2007.

———. *Philosophical Inquiries into the Nature of Human Freedom.* Translated by James Gutmann. La Salle, IL: Open Court, 1992.

———. *Philosophie der Offenbarung: 1841/42.* Paulus Nachschrift. Edited by Manfred Frank. Frankfurt am Main: Suhrkamp, 1977.

———. *Philosophy and Religion.* Translated by Klaus Ottmann. Putnam, CN: Spring Publications, 2010.

———. *The Philosophy of Art.* Translated by Douglas W. Stott. Minneapolis: University of Minnesota Press, 2008.

———. *Schellings Sämmtliche Werke.* Edited by Karl Friedrich August Schelling. 10 Volumes. Stuttgart & Augsburg: J. G. Cotta, 1856–1861.

———. *System of Transcendental Idealism.* Translated by Peter Heath. Charlottesville: University of Virginia Press, 1978.

Soloviev, Vladimir. *Divine Sophia: The Wisdom Writings of Vladimir Solovyov.* Edited by Judith Deutsch Kornblatt. Translated by Boris Jakim, Judith Deutsch Kornblatt, and Laury Magnus. Ithaca: Cornell University Press, 2009.

———. *The Heart of Reality: Essays on Beauty, Love, and Ethics.* Edited and translated by Vladimir Wozniuk. Notre Dame, IN: University of Notre Dame Press, 2003.

———. *Lectures on Divine Humanity.* Edited by Boris Jakim. Hudson, NY: Lindisfarne Press, 1995.

———. "Vladimir Solovyov's Letter to L. Tolstoy on the Resurrection of Christ." *Sobornost* 1 (March 1935): 8–12.

———. *War, Progress, and the End of History: Three Conversations, Including a Short Story of the Anti-Christ.* Hudson, NY: Lindisfarne Books, 1990.

SECONDARY LITERATURE

Allen, Paul M. *Vladimir Soloviev: Russian Mystic.* Blauvelt, NY: Steinerbooks, 1978.

Beach, Edward Allen. *The Potencies of God(s): Schelling's Philosophy of Mythology*. Albany: State University of New York Press, 1994.

Beiser, Frederick C. *German Idealism: The Struggle against Subjectivism, 1781–1801*. Cambridge, MA: Harvard University Press, 2002.

Betz, John R. "Beyond the Sublime: The Aesthetics of the Analogy of Being (Part One)." *Modern Theology* 21 (2005): 367–405.

———. "Beyond the Sublime: The Aesthetics of the Analogy of Being (Part Two)." *Modern Theology* 22 (2006): 1–50.

Block, Ed, Jr., ed. *Glory, Grace, and Culture: The Work of Hans Urs von Balthasar*. Mahwah, NJ: Paulist Press, 2005.

Brown, Robert F. *The Later Philosophy of Schelling: The Influence of Boehme on the Works of 1809–1815*. Lewisburg, PA: Bucknell University Press, 1977.

———. "Schelling and Dorner on Divine Immutability." *Journal of the American Academy of Religion* 53, no. 2 (June 1985): 237–49.

Bychkov, Oleg. *Aesthetic Revelation: Reading Ancient and Medieval Texts after Hans Urs von Balthasar*. Washington, DC: Catholic University of America Press, 2010.

Clowes, Edith. "The Limits of Discourse: Solov'ev's Language of *Syzygy* and the Project of Thinking Total Unity." *Slavic Review* 55, no. 3 (Fall 1996): 552–67.

Copleston, Frederick C. *A History of Philosophy*. Vol. 7, *Fichte to Hegel*. Garden City, NY: Image Books, 1965.

———. *Philosophy in Russia: From Herzen to Lenin and Berdyaev*. Notre Dame, IN: University of Notre Dame Press, 1986.

———. *Russian Religious Philosophy: Selected Aspects*. Notre Dame, IN: University of Notre Dame Press, 1988.

Dalzell, Thomas. *The Dramatic Encounter of Divine and Human Freedom in the Theology of Hans Urs von Balthasar*. Bern: Peter Lang, 2000.

David, Zdenek V. "The Influence of Jacob Boehme on Russian Religious Thought." *Slavic Review* 21, no. 1 (March 1962): 43–64.

Deane-Drummond, Celia. "The Breadth of Glory: A Trinitarian Eschatology for the Earth through Critical Engagement with Hans Urs von Balthasar." *International Journal of Systematic Theology* 12, no. 1 (January 2010): 46–64.

De Lubac, Henri. *The Drama of Atheist Humanism*. Translated by Edith M. Riley. Cleveland, OH: Meridian Books, 1963.

Dickens, W. T. *Hans Urs von Balthasar's Theological Aesthetics: A Model for Post-Critical Biblical Interpretation*. Notre Dame, IN: University of Notre Dame Press, 2003.

Drey, Johann Sebastian. *Brief Introduction to the Study of Theology with Reference to the Scientific Standpoint and the Catholic System*. Translated by

Michael J. Himes. Notre Dame, IN: University of Notre Dame Press, 1994.

Eco, Umberto. *The Aesthetics of Thomas Aquinas.* Translated by Hugh Bredin. Cambridge, MA: Harvard University Press, 1988.

Fackenheim, Emil L. *The God Within: Kant, Schelling, and Historicity.* Edited by John Burbidge. Toronto: University of Toronto Press, 1996.

Friesenhahn, Jacob H. *The Trinity and Theodicy: The Trinitarian Theology of von Balthasar and the Problem of Evil.* Burlington, VT: Ashgate, 2011.

Gallaher, Brandon. "The Christological Focus of Vladimir Solov'ev's Sophiology." *Modern Theology* 25, no. 4 (2009): 617–46.

———. "Graced Creatureliness: Ontological Tension in the Uncreated/Created Distinction in the Sophiologies of Solov'ev, Bulgakov and Milbank." *Logos: A Journal of Eastern Christian Studies* 47, no. 1–2 (2006): 163–90.

Gardner, Lucy, David Moss, Ben Quash, and Graham Ward, eds. *Balthasar at the End of Modernity.* Edinburgh: T & T Clark, 1999.

Gavrilyuk, Paul L. *Georges Florovsky and the Russian Religious Renaissance.* Oxford: Oxford University Press, 2014.

———. "The Kenotic Theology of Sergius Bulgakov." *Scottish Journal of Theology* 58, no. 3 (2005): 251–69.

———. "Universal Salvation in the Eschatology of Sergius Bulgakov." *Journal of Theological Studies* 57, no. 1 (2006): 110–32.

Gorodetzky, Nadejda. *The Humiliated Christ in Modern Russian Thought.* New York: Macmillan, 1938.

Hammermeister, Kai. *The German Aesthetic Tradition.* Cambridge: Cambridge University Press, 2002.

Healy, Nicholas J. *The Eschatology of Hans Urs von Balthasar: Being as Communion.* Oxford: Oxford University Press, 2005.

Hendrix, John Shannon. *Aesthetics and the Philosophy of Spirit: From Plotinus to Schelling and Hegel.* New York: Peter Lang, 2005.

Horn, Friedemann. *Schelling and Swedenborg: Mysticism and German Idealism.* Translated by George F. Dole. West Chester, PA: Swedenborg Foundation, 1997.

Houlgate, Stephen, ed. *Hegel and the Arts.* Evanston, IL: Northwestern University Press, 2007.

Howsare, Rodney A., and Larry S. Chapp, eds. *How Balthasar Changed My Mind: Fifteen Scholars Reflect on the Meaning of Balthasar for Their Own Work.* New York: Crossroads, 2008.

Hunt, Anne. *The Trinity and the Paschal Mystery: A Development in Recent Catholic Theology.* Collegeville, MN: Liturgical Press, 1997.

Kilby, Karen. *Balthasar: A (Very) Critical Introduction.* Grand Rapids, MI: Eerdmans, 2012.

Kornblatt, Judith Deutsch, and Richard F. Gustafson, eds. *Russian Religious Thought.* Madison: University of Wisconsin Press, 1996.

Kostalevsky, Marina. *Dostoevsky and Soloviev: The Art of Integral Vision.* New Haven, CT: Yale University Press, 1997.

Kuzniar, Alice A. *Delayed Endings: Nonclosure in Novalis and Hölderlin.* Athens: University of Georgia Press, 2008.

Laughland, John. *Schelling versus Hegel: From German Idealism to Christian Metaphysics.* Burlington, VT: Ashgate, 2007.

Martin, Jennifer Newsome. "The 'Whence' and the 'Whither' of Balthasar's Gendered Theology: Rehabilitating Kenosis for Feminist Theology." *Modern Theology* 31, no. 2 (2015): 211–34.

Martin, Michael. *The Submerged Reality: Sophiology and the Turn to a Poetic Metaphysics.* Kettering, OH: Angelico Press, 2015.

Meerson, Michael Aksionov. *The Trinity of Love in Modern Russian Theology: The Love Paradigm and the Retrieval of Western Medieval Love Mysticism in Modern Russian Trinitarian Thought (from Solovyov to Bulgakov).* Quincy, IL: Franciscan Press, 1998.

Mayer, Paola. *Jena Romanticism and Its Appropriation of Jakob Böhme: Theosophy, Hagiography, Literature.* Montreal: McGill-Queen's University Press, 1999.

Milbank, John. "Sophiology and Theurgy: The New Theological Horizon." In *An Encounter between Eastern Orthodoxy and Radical Orthodoxy: Transfiguring the World through the Word*, edited by Adrian Pabst and Christoph Schneider, 45–85. Aldershot: Ashgate, 2009.

Milosz, Czeslaw. *Emperor of the Earth: Modes of Eccentric Vision.* Berkeley: University of California Press, 1977.

Mongrain, Kevin. *The Systematic Thought of Hans Urs von Balthasar: An Irenaean Retrieval.* New York: Crossroad, 2002.

Nichols, Aidan. "Bulgakov and Sophiology." *Sobornost* 13, no. 2 (1991): 17–31.

———. *Divine Fruitfulness. A Guide through Balthasar's Theology beyond the Trilogy.* New York: T & T Clark, 2007.

———. "Hans Urs von Balthasar and Sergii Bulgakov on Holy Images." In *Aesthetics as a Religious Factor in Eastern and Western Christianity*, edited by Wil van den Bercken and Jonathan Sutton, 1–25. Leuven: Peeters Press, 2005.

———. *No Bloodless Myth: A Guide through Balthasar's Dramatics.* Washington, DC: Catholic University of America Press, 2000.

———. *Say It Is Pentecost: A Guide through Balthasar's Logic.* Edinburgh: T & T Clark Ltd, 2001.

———. *Scattering the Seed: A Guide through Balthasar's Early Writings on Philosophy and the Arts.* Washington, DC: Catholic University of America Press, 2006.

———. "Von Balthasar's Aims in his Theological Aesthetics." *Heythrop Journal* 15 (1999): 409–23.

————. *Wisdom from Above: A Primer in the Theology of Father Sergei Bulgakov*. Leominster: Gracewing, 2005.

————. *The Word Has Been Abroad: A Guide through Balthasar's Aesthetics.* Washington, DC: Catholic University of America Press, 1998 T & T Clark Ltd: Edinburgh, 1998.

Oakes, Edward T. *Pattern of Redemption: The Theology of Hans Urs von Balthasar.* New York: Continuum, 1994.

————, and David Moss, eds. *The Cambridge Companion to Hans Urs von Balthasar.* Cambridge: Cambridge University Press, 2004.

O'Hanlon, Gerard F. *The Immutability of God in the Theology of Hans Urs von Balthasar.* Cambridge: Cambridge University Press, 1990.

O'Meara, Thomas F. *Romantic Idealism and Roman Catholicism: Schelling and the Theologians.* Notre Dame, IN: University of Notre Dame Press, 1986.

————. "Schelling's Religious Aesthetics." In *Reform and Counterreform: Dialectics of the Word in Western Christianity since Luther,* edited by John C. Hawley, 119–38. Berlin: Mouton de Gruyter, 1994.

O'Regan, Cyril. *"The Anatomy of Misremembering: Von Balthasar's Response to Philosophical Modernity.* Vol. 1, *Hegel.* New York: Crossroads, 2014.

————. "Balthasar: Between Tübingen and Postmodernity." *Modern Theology* 14, no. 3 (July 1998): 325–53.

————. *Gnostic Apocalypse: Jacob Boehme's Haunted Narrative.* Albany: State University of New York Press, 2002.

————. *Gnostic Return in Modernity.* New York: State University of New York Press, 2001.

————. *The Heterodox Hegel.* New York: State University of New York Press, 1994.

————. *Theology and the Spaces of Apocalyptic.* Milwaukee, WI: Marquette University Press, 2009.

————. "Von Balthasar and Thick Retrieval: Post Chalcedonian Symphonic Theology." *Gregorianum* 77, no. 2 (1996): 227–60.

Pitstick, Alyssa Lyra. *Light in Darkness: Hans Urs von Balthasar and the Catholic Doctrine of Christ's Descent into Hell.* Grand Rapids, MI: Eerdmans, 2007.

Przywara, Erich. *Analogia Entis: Metaphysics: Original Structure and Universal Rhythm.* Translated by John R. Betz and David Bentley Hart. Grand Rapids, MI: Eerdmans, 2014.

Quash, Ben. "'Between the Brutely Given and the Brutally, Banally Free': Von Balthasar's Theology of Drama in Dialogue with Hegel." *Modern Theology,* 13, no. 3 (1997): 293–318.

————. *Theology and the Drama of History.* Cambridge: Cambridge University Press, 2005.

Riches, John, ed. *The Analogy of Beauty: The Theology of Hans Urs von Balthasar*. Edinburgh: T & T Clark, 1986.

Rilke, Rainer Maria. *New Poems*. Translated by Edward Snow. New York: North Point Press, 2001.

Roberts, Louis. *The Theological Aesthetics of Hans Urs von Balthasar*. Washington, DC: Catholic University of America Press, 1987.

Schindler, David C. *Hans Urs von Balthasar and the Dramatic Structure of Truth: A Philosophical Investigation*. New York: Fordham University Press, 2004.

Schindler, David L., ed. *Hans Urs von Balthasar: His Life and Work*. San Francisco: Ignatius Press, 1991.

Sciglitano, Anthony C. *Marcion and Prometheus: Balthasar against the Expulsion of Jewish Origins from Modern Religious Dialogue*. New York: Crossroad, 2014.

Scola, Angelo. *Hans Urs von Balthasar: A Theological Style*. Grand Rapids, MI: Eerdmans, 1995.

Schmemann, Alexander, ed. *Ultimate Questions: An Anthology of Modern Russian Religious Thought*. New York: Holt, Rinehart and Winston, 1965.

———. "Russian Theology: 1920–1972, An Introductory Survey," *St. Vladimir's Theological Quarterly* 16 (1972): 172–94.

Snow, Dale E. *Schelling and the End of Idealism*. Albany: State University of New York Press, 1996.

Stammler, Heinrich. "Dostoevsky's Aesthetics and Schelling's Philosophy of Art." *Comparative Literature* 7, no. 4 (Winter 1955): 313–23.

Steinkamp, Fiona. "Eternity and Time: Levinas Returns to Schelling." In *Schelling Now*, edited by Jason M. Wirth, 207–22. Bloomington: Indiana University Press, 2005.

Thiel, John. *Imagination and Authority: Theological Authorship in the Modern Tradition*. Minneapolis: Fortress Press, 1991.

———. *Senses of Tradition: Continuity and Development in Catholic Faith*. Oxford: Oxford University Press, 2000.

Valliere, Paul. *Modern Russian Theology: Bukharev, Soloviev, Bulgakov: Orthodox Theology in a New Key*. Grand Rapids, MI: Eerdmans, 2000.

———. "Solov'ev and Schelling's Philosophy of Revelation." In *Vladimir Solov'ev: Reconciler and Polemicist*. Edited by Will van den Bercken, Manon de Courten, and Evert van der Zweerde, 119–29. Leuven: Peeters, 2000.

Van Erp, Stephan. *The Art of Theology: Hans Urs von Balthasar's Theological Aesthetics and the Foundations of Faith*. Leuven: Peeters Press, 2004.

Welch, Claude. *God and Incarnation in Mid-Nineteenth Century German Theology: Thomasius, Dorner, Biedermann*. New York: Oxford University Press, 1965.

———. *Protestant Thought in the Nineteenth Century.* Vol. 1, *1799–1870.* New Haven, CT: Yale University Press, 1972.

Williams, Rowan. "Origen: Between Orthodoxy and Heresy." In *Origeniana Septima: Origenes in den Auseinandersetzungen des 4. Jahrhunderts.* Edited by Wolfgang A. Bienert and Uwe Kühneweg, 3–14. Louvain: Leuven University Press, 1999.

Ziolkowski, Theodore. *German Romanticism and Its Institutions.* Princeton, NJ: Princeton University Press, 1990.

Žižek, Slavoj. "Everything You Always Wanted to Know about Schelling (But Were Afraid to Ask Hitchcock)." In *The New Schelling*, edited by Judith Norman and Alistair Welchman, 30–42. London: Continuum, 2004.

———. "Selfhood as Such Is Spirit: F. W. J. Schelling on the Origins of Evil." In *Radical Evil*, edited by Joan Copjec, 1–29. London: Verso, 1996.

INDEX

Aeneas, 134
Aeschylus, 106
aesthetics, 36, 39–78
  ambiguity of beauty, 41, 57–58
  of Berdyaev, 36, 43, 49–50, 60, 75, 76, 77
  of Bulgakov, 36, 40, 57, 72–75, 76, 77, 231n107, 239n199
  circumscribing and defining, 41–42, 223n7, 230n89
  Classicism and Romanticism, Balthasar's use of, 68–71, 229n83
  dialectical pairs
  —in Berdyaev's aesthetics, 49–50
  —in Schelling's aesthetics, 43–49
  —in Soloviev's aesthetics, 51–55
  eroticism and, 228n69
  eschatology and, 41, 50, 53–54, 77
  finite and infinite in, 44–45, 56–57, 63, 67–68, 77, 232n113
  freedom and, 78
  glory as theological analogue of beauty, 55, 56, 58–59, 62–65, 71, 77

"holy fool" phenomenon and, 71–73
influences on Balthasar's conception of, 42–43
intellectual intuition, appeal to, 45, 225n18
reception of Soloviev's and Schelling's aesthetics by Balthasar, 65–68
of Schelling, 36, 40, 42–49, 58, 61, 63–64, 65–68, 69, 72, 75, 225n15, 230n89, 232n113
as science, 233n120
of Soloviev, 36, 40, 43, 51–55, 57, 61, 65–68, 74, 75–76, 77, 223n3, 227n60
spirit and beauty, in Bulgakov's aesthetics, 72–75
theological aesthetics of Balthasar, 55–65
theurgic impulse of, 41, 75–78
Alan de Lille, 229n81
Alexander de Hales, 229n81
Alexandrian Christianity, 31–32, 37, 115, 144

Berdyaev, Nikolai (*cont.*)
  Böhme and, 79, 88–91, 97, 103,
    137, 213n51, 241n15, 244n43,
    244n45, 245n47, 248n103,
    249n133
  on Classicism and Romanticism,
    69, 235n162
  on death, 124–25, 130
  on the Fall, 89–91, 243n33
  on freedom, myth, ontology, and
    the problem of evil, 36, 79, 84,
    88–91, 97, 103, 105, 108, 114,
    115–16, 244n41
  gnostic tone of, 201, 268n32
  on hell and final judgment, 137,
    141, 143, 144, 145, 148–49
  Joachimite influence on, 166–67,
    201
  Kant critiqued by, 244n45
  methodological issues, 37
  Schelling and, 16–17, 19, 50, 79,
    88–91, 97, 110, 201, 213n51,
    241n15
  on Soloviev, 216n66
  sophiology of, 79, 165, 214n60
  source material for, 201
  theocentric eschatology of, 160,
    166–67, 178, 184, 192–93,
    272n89
  theopaschism of, 184
  on Trinity, 178, 184, 192–93,
    272n89
  wholeness or totality, interest in, 9
  works
  —*The Beginning and the End*, 49,
    97, 121, 216n66, 244n43, 245n48
  —*The Destiny of Man*, 121
  —*The Meaning of History*, 88,
    110
  —*The Russian Idea*, 117
  —"Unground and Freedom,"
    244n45

Bernanos, Georges, 5, 13, 260n106,
    260n110
Bernard of Clairvaux, 229n83
Bérulle, Pierre de, 234n146
Betz, John, 232n116
Bloy, Léon, 13
bodily resurrection, 68, 149–57
Boethius, 229n81
bogochelovechestvo, 18, 66, 206
Böhme, Jakob
  anthropocentric eschatology and,
    37
  Berdyaev and, 79, 88–91, 97, 103,
    137, 213n51, 241n15, 244n43,
    244n45, 245n47, 248n103,
    249n133
  criticism of Balthasar and, 7
  as Idealist, 230n85
  rationalism critiqued, 30–31
  Schelling and, 13, 15, 19, 79–80,
    82–83, 85–87, 93, 94, 163, 176,
    177, 241n15
  Soloviev and, 13, 15, 19, 79–80,
    82–83, 85–87, 93, 94, 114,
    213n51, 223n3
  sophiology of, 214n60, 271n80
  as source for Russian school,
    201
  theocentric eschatology and
    Trinity, 176, 177, 178, 272n89
  theogonic speculative ontology
    of, 36, 79–80, 82, 84, 85–87, 93,
    94, 103, 105, 115–16, 178,
    242n16
  works
  —*Aurora*, 85
  —*De Signatura Rerum*, 85
  —*Mysterium Magnum*, 85
Bonaventure, 5, 60, 67, 201, 229n81,
    231n103, 275n131
Bonhoeffer, Dietrich, 145
Bouyer, Louis, 209n8, 237n184

JENNIFER NEWSOME MARTIN

is an assistant professor in the Program of Liberal Studies

with a concurrent appointment in the Department of Theology,

University of Notre Dame.